FIFTH EDITION

MARKETING

MANAGEMENT

DAWN IACOBUCCI
Vanderbilt University

CENGAGE
Learning·

Australia · Brazil · Japan · Korea · Mexico · Singapore · Spain · United Kingdom · United States

Marketing Management, Fifth Edition
Dawn Iacobucci

Senior Vice President, General Manager,
Social Sciences, Humanities & Business:
Erin Joyner

Product Director: Jason Fremder

Product Manager: Heather Mooney

Content Developer: John Sarantakis

Marketing Director: Kristen Hurd

Marketing Manager: Katie Jergens

Marketing Coordinator: Casey Binder

Product Assistant: Allie Janneck

Art and Cover Direction, Production
Management, and Composition: Cenveo
Publisher Services

Intellectual Property

    Analyst: Diane Garrity

    Project Manager: Sarah Shainwald

Manufacturing Planner: Ron Montgomery

Cover Image(s): Santiago Cornejo/
Shutterstock, Mukhina Viktoriia/Shutterstock,
Nomad_Soul/Shutterstock, Redchanka/
Shutterstock, Bespaliy/
Shutterstock, hxdbzxy/Shutterstock,
Quayside/Shutterstock, Cyrustr/
Shutterstock, Subbotina Anna/
Shutterstock, elen_studio/Shutterstock

Library of Congress Control Number: 2016943749

ISBN-13: 978-1-337-27112-7

Except where otherwise noted, all content is © Cengage Learning.

Cengage Learning
20 Channel Center Street
Boston, MA 02210
USA

Cengage Learning is a leading provider of customized learning solutions with employees residing in nearly 40 different countries and sales in more than 125 countries around the world. Find your local representative at: **www.cengage.com**

Cengage Learning products are represented in Canada by Nelson Education, Ltd.

To learn more about Cengage Learning Solutions, visit **www.cengage.com**

Purchase any of our products at your local college store or at our preferred online store **www.cengagebrain.com**

Printed at CLDPC, USA, 03-19

BRIEF CONTENTS

CONTENTS

Part 4 **Capstone**

PREFACE

There are several really good marketing management texts, yet this text was created because the Cengage sales force recognized an opportunity. Existing texts present numerous lists of factors to consider in a marketing decision but offer little guidance on how the factors, lists and multiple decisions all fit together.

In this book, an overarching Marketing Framework, used in every chapter, shows how all the pieces fit together. So, for example, when facing a decision about pricing, readers must consider how pricing will impact a strategic element like positioning or a customer reaction like loyalty and word of mouth. This book is practical, no-nonsense, and relatively short, to further heighten its utility. Everyone is busy these days, so it's refreshing when a writer gets to the point. After this relatively quick read, MBAs and EMBAs should be able to speak sensibly about marketing issues and contribute to their organizations.

Chapter Organization

The form of each chapter is very straightforward: The chapter's concept is introduced by describing what it is and why marketers do it, and the rest of the chapter shows how to do it well. This what-why-and-how structure is intended to be extremely useful to MBA and EMBA students, who will quickly understand the basic concepts, e.g., what is segmentation and why is it useful in marketing and business? The details are in the execution, so the how is the focus of the body of the chapter.

Key Features

Each chapter opens with a managerial checklist of questions that MBA and EMBA students will be able to answer after reading the chapter. Throughout each chapter, boxes present brief illustrations of concepts in action in the real world or elaborations on concepts raised in the text, also drawing examples from the real business world. Chapters close with a Managerial Recap that highlights the main points of the chapter and reviews the opening checklist of questions. Chapters are also summarized in outline form, including the key terms introduced throughout the chapter. There are discussion questions to ponder, as well as video resources to serve as points for still further discussion. Each chapter contains a Mini-Case that succinctly illustrates key concepts.

MindTap

The 5th edition of Marketing Management offers two exciting alternative teaching formats. Instructors can choose between either a hybrid print and digital offering or a version that provides completely integrated online delivery through a platform called MindTap. MindTap is a fully online, highly personalized learning experience built upon authoritative content. By combining readings, multimedia, activities, and assessments into a singular Learning Path, MindTap guides students through their course with ease while promoting engagement. Instructors personalize the Learning Path by customizing Cengage Learning resources and adding their own content via apps that integrate into the MindTap framework seamlessly. Instructors are also able to incorporate the online component of Consumer Behavior into a traditional Learning Management System (e.g. Blackboard, Canvas, D2L, etc.) providing a way to manage assignments, quizzes and tests throughout the semester

Instructor Resources

Web resources for the book at www.cengagebrain.com provide the latest information in marketing management. The Instructor's Manual, Test Bank authored in Cognero, and PowerPoint slides can be found there.

Acknowledgments

Cengage Learning's people are the best! Special thanks to John Sarantakis (Content Developer), Mike Roche (Senior Product Manager), Heather Mooney (Product Manager) Jenny Ziegler (Senior Content Project Manager), Diane Garrity (Intellectual Property Analyst), Sarah Shainwald (Intellectual Property Project Manager) Laura Cheu (Copyeditor), Ezhilsolai Periasamy (Project Manager), Manjula Devi Subramanian (Text Researcher), Abdul Khader (Image Reasearcher), and Pushpa V. Giri (Proofreader).

As always, special thanks to the Cengage sales force. I will forever be grateful for your notes of encouragement as we began this project. I hope you like *Marketing Management 5*.

ABOUT THE AUTHOR

DAWN IACOBUCCI is the Ingram Professor of Marketing at the Owen Graduate School of Management, Vanderbilt University (since 2007). She has been Senior Associate Dean at Vanderbilt (2008-2010), and a professor of marketing at Kellogg (Northwestern University, 1987-2004), Arizona (2001-2002), and Wharton (Pennsylvania, 2004 to 2007). She received her M.S. in Statistics, and M.A. and Ph.D. in Quantitative Psychology from the University of Illinois at Urbana-Champaign. Her research focuses on modeling social networks and geeky high-dimensional analyses. She has published in *Journal of Marketing, Journal of Marketing Research, Harvard Business Review, Journal of Consumer Psychology, International Journal of Research in Marketing, Marketing Science, Journal of Service Research, Psychometrika, Psychological Bulletin,* and *Social Networks.* Iacobucci teaches Marketing Management and Marketing Models to Executives, MBA and undergraduate students and multivariate statistics and methodological topics to Ph.D. students. She has been editor of both *Journal of Consumer Research* and *Journal of Consumer Psychology.* She edited *Kellogg on Marketing,* she is author of *Mediation Analysis,* and co-author on Gilbert Churchill's leading text, *Marketing Research.*

WHY IS MARKETING MANAGEMENT IMPORTANT?

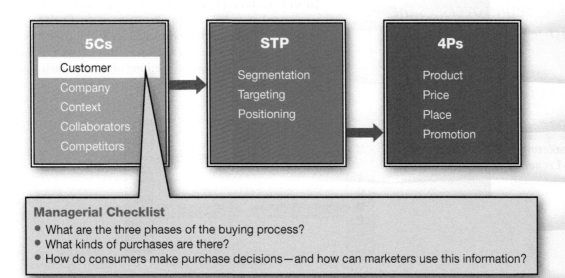

5Cs	STP	4Ps
Customer Company Context Collaborators Competitors	Segmentation Targeting Positioning	Product Price Place Promotion

Managerial Checklist
- What are the three phases of the buying process?
- What kinds of purchases are there?
- How do consumers make purchase decisions—and how can marketers use this information?

1-1 DEFINING MARKETING

Ask the average person, "What is marketing?" and they might say:

- "Marketing is sales and advertising."
- "Marketers make people buy stuff they don't need and can't afford."
- "Marketers are the people who call you while you're trying to eat dinner."

Unfortunately those comments are probably all deserved. The marketing profession, like any other, has its issues. But in this book we'll take a more enlightened view.

This chapter begins with an overview of marketing concepts and terms. We'll see the importance of marketing in today's corporation. We'll then present the Marketing Framework that structures the book and gives you a systematic way to think about marketing, and we'll define all the terms in the framework: 5Cs, STP, and 4Ps.

1-2 MARKETING IS AN EXCHANGE RELATIONSHIP

Marketing is defined as an exchange between a firm and its customers.[1] Figure 1.1 shows the customer wants something from the firm, and the firm wants something from the customer. Marketers try to figure out what customers want and how to provide it profitably.

Ideally, this can be a nice, symbiotic relationship. Customers don't mind paying for their purchases—and sometimes they pay a lot—if they really want what they're about to buy. Companies like taking in profits, of course, but great companies really do care about their customers. If we're lucky, the exchange depicted in Figure 1.1 is an ongoing exchange between the customer and the company, strengthening the tie between them.

> *Marketing oversees the customer-brand exchange.*

As a lifelong customer, you are already somewhat familiar with marketing from the consumer side. But on the job, you'll need to understand marketing from the firm's point of view. Throughout this book, you'll see both perspectives. In particular, you'll see all the issues that marketers deal with as they try to deliver something of value to their customers, while trying to derive value from them.

Figure 1.1
Marketing is an Exchange

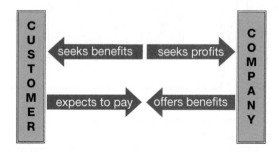

1-2a Marketing is Everywhere

Figure 1.2 illustrates that you can market just about anything. Marketing managers sell simple, tangible goods such as soap or shampoo, as well as high-end luxury goods such as Chanel handbags. Other marketing managers work in services, such as haircuts, airlines, hotels, or department stores. Marketers oversee experiences like theme parks or events like theater and concerts. Marketers help entertainers, athletes, politicians, and other celebrities with their images in their respective "marketplaces" (fans, agents, intelligentsia, opinion). Tourist bureaus have marketers who advertise the selling points of their city's or country's unique features. Information providers use marketing because they want customers to think they're the best (and thereby maximize their ad revenue). Marketers at nonprofits and government agencies work on "causes" (e.g., encouraging organ donation or drinking responsibly). Industries market themselves (think of the beef or milk ads). Naturally, companies use marketing for their brands and themselves. And you can market yourself, e.g., to a job interviewer or potential amour. These goals may look different, but marketing can be used beneficially in all these situations.

1-3 WHY IS MARKETING MANAGEMENT IMPORTANT?

Marketers have evolved beyond being merely product or production focused, where the company mind-set is, "Let's build a better mouse trap." We know that approach doesn't work. There's no point in just cranking out better gadgets unless the customers want them

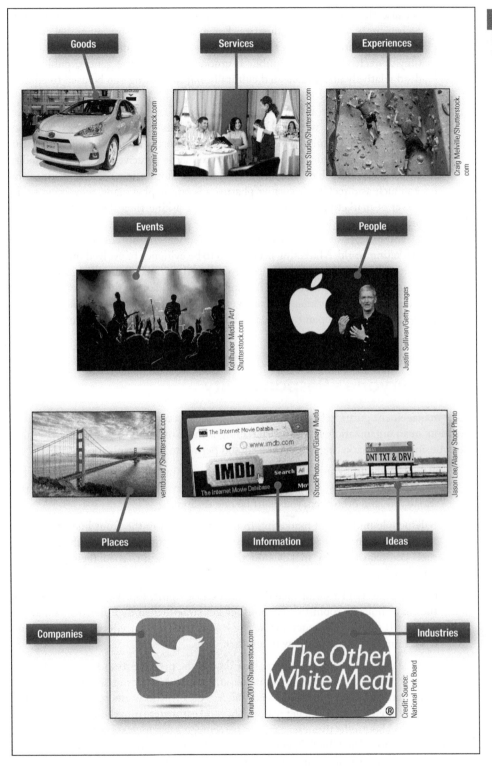

Figure 1.2

What Can We "Market"?

because the gadgets won't sell. However, there are still pockets of marketing naïveté in a number of industries. For example, some museums believe they don't need marketing. They think people should appreciate their exhibits, and, if they don't, it's because the public is ignorant. Perhaps the general public is indeed relatively unsophisticated culturally, but marketing can be used to educate the public.

We're also more advanced than the old sales-oriented days when the action in the marketplace was, "Let's make a deal." This mentality still exists in places like drug companies, which push their sales forces to impress physicians. But usually sales dynamics occur where the product is perceived to be a commodity. In contrast, marketers should be good at communicating product distinctions. As much as direct-to-consumer pharma ads annoy physicians, they attest to the power of marketing. The ads result in patients asking their doctors for particular brand names.

These days we live in a truly customer-oriented and customer-empowered marketing world. Marketing is even said to be evidence of evolved markets—that an industry or country has moved beyond production and sales and seeks true relationships with its customers. Marketers seek to identify their customers' needs and wants, and they try to formulate attractive solutions. Marketing can make customers happier, thereby making companies more profitable. Throughout the book, you'll see how.

1-3a Marketing and Customer Satisfaction is Everyone's Responsibility

Many management gurus believe that marketing has succeeded so well that it isn't just a "function" in an organization anymore. Marketing is more of a philosophy—a way to think about business. The marketing orientation should permeate the organization.

- Accounting and finance need to acknowledge the importance of marketing. Why? Because their CEOs do. Thinking about customers is unimportant only if you're a monopoly, and even then, you won't be one for long.

- Salespeople understand marketing immediately. They're the front line, interfacing with the customer. They want to push their firm's stuff, but they're thrilled when their company actually makes stuff that customers want. Then their jobs are so much easier.

- R&D people tend to understand the marketing spirit, too. They're hired because they're technically sophisticated, but they get jazzed when their inventions become popular. It doesn't take much marketing research to test concepts or prototypes and to veer an R&D path one way or another.

One of the factors stressing marketers these days is the pressure to show results. It's fair to hold any part of the corporation accountable, and results may be measured for a number of marketing activities. The Chief Financial Officer (CFO) who wants to see that a recent coupon promotion lifted sales can get reasonably good estimates from the Chief Marketing Officer (CMO) about effectiveness, e.g., the percentage sales increase attributable to the coupon introduction. The Chief Operating Officer (COO) can also get good estimates of whether a recent direct mail campaign to target customers has been effective in encouraging frequent buyers to go directly to the Web for purchasing.

However, it's important not to go overboard in the effort to quantify. For example, how does one assess the value of a good segmentation study? If segments are poorly defined, any

Marketing speaks to customers wherever they are.

TENGKU BAHAR/Staff/AFP/Getty Images

subsequent marketing efforts would be completely off, so a good segmentation scheme is invaluable. Advertising is also a little tricky. Non-marketers have the misconception that advertising is supposed to bump up sales. It can, and that bump is easily measured. But really great advertising isn't intended for a short-term effect on sales. Great advertising is intended to enhance brand image, a goal that is relatively longer term and thus more difficult to measure.

In addition to quantifying the effectiveness of marketing programs, marketers are motivated to translate their efforts into dollars for another reason: to have a "seat at the table." Marketers want to make sure that the CMO carries as much weight in the firm as the CEO or CFO or COO. They all speak finance, so the marketer is frequently motivated to translate progress into financial terms. Fortunately, technology and data are increasingly enabling more opportunities for the marketer to make such assessments. For example, a good customer relationship management (CRM) program allows marketers to run a field study to assess the impact of a new promotion, and tracking Web data allows marketers to determine the product combinations that are most attractive to customers.

1-4 THE "MARKETING FRAMEWORK": 5CS, STP, AND THE 4PS

Figure 1.3 provides the marketing management framework. Marketing is captured by the 5Cs, STP, and the 4Ps. The 5Cs are customer, company, context, collaborators, and competitors. The 5Cs force a businessperson to systematically frame the general analysis of the entire business situation. Figure 1.1 shows that the *customer* and *company* are the central players in the marketing exchange. The *context* includes the backdrop of macro-environmental factors: How is our economy and that of our suppliers doing? What legal constraints do we face, and are these changing? What cultural differences do our global segments manifest? The *collaborators* and *competitors* are the companies and people we work with vs. those we compete against (though drawing the line is sometimes difficult in today's interconnected world).

Figure 1.3

Marketing Management Framework: 5Cs, STP, 4Ps

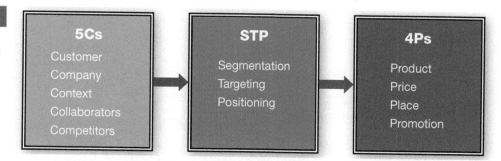

Figure 1.3

Marketing Management Framework: 5Cs, STP, 4Ps

STP stands for segmentation, targeting, and positioning. A company or a brand may want to be all things to all people, but most are not. It's best to identify groups, or *segments*, of customers who share similar needs and wants. Once we understand the different segments' preferences, we're in a position to identify the segment we should *target* with our marketing efforts. We then begin to develop a relationship with that target segment by *positioning* our product to them in the marketplace, via the 4Ps.

The 4Ps are product, price, promotion, and place. A marketer is responsible for creating a *product* (goods or services) that customers need or want, for setting the appropriate *price* for the product, for *promoting* the product via advertising and sales promotions to help customers understand the product's benefits and value, and finally for making the product available for purchase in easily accessed *places*.[2]

Marketing management oversees the 5Cs, STP, and 4Ps with the goal of enhancing the marketing exchange (of goods, services, payment, ideas and information, etc.) between a customer base and a firm. It all sounds easy! Group your customers, and figure out which group to target. Then create a position in the marketplace by means of the features of the product, its price, communications and promotions, and distribution choices. Ah, but don't dismiss marketing as only common sense; after all, consider how few companies do it well!

If marketing is an exchange, then, just like an interaction between two people, a company has its best chance at keeping its customers happy if it is in close communication with them. The company that does its marketing research and really listens to its customers will be able to deliver goods and services that delight those customers. The best marketers put themselves in the place of their customers: What are they like? What do they want? How can we play a role in their lives? In this book, we'll elaborate on these themes. If you get overloaded while reading this book, you can step back and remember this: You'll always be a step ahead of your competition if you simply think about your customers! All marketing strategy derives from that.

To elaborate on marketing strategy and develop a particular marketing plan, start with a situation analysis, and sketch answers to the following questions:

- *Customers:* Who are they? What are they like? Do we want to draw different customers?

- *Company:* What are our strengths and weaknesses? What customer benefits can we provide?

- *Context:* What is happening in our industry that might reshape our future business?

- *Collaborators:* Can we address our customers' needs while strengthening our business-to-business (B2B) partnerships?

- *Competitors:* Who are the competitors we must consider? What are their likely actions and reactions?

With that background analysis, proceed to strategic marketing planning via STP:

- *Segmentation:* Customers aren't all the same; find out their various preferences, needs, and resources.
- *Targeting:* Pursue the group of customers that makes the most sense for our company.
- *Positioning:* Communicate our product's benefits clearly to the intended target customers.

Similarly, marketing tactics to execute the intended positioning derive from a customer focus:

- *Product:* Will customers want what our company is prepared to produce?
- *Price:* Will customers pay what we'd like to charge?
- *Place:* Where and how will customers purchase our market offering?
- *Promotion:* What can we tell our customers or do for them to entice them to purchase?

That doesn't sound too difficult, right? But customers' preferences change. And the competition is also dynamic; who they are changes as well as what they offer your customers. Factors that are out of your control change as well. For example, as marketing manager or CMO, you won't have control over whether your company is merged with another whose image seems inconsistent with your brand, but you'll have to deal with it. Further, the legal environment in this country is different from that in another's, and each is always in flux. Many such contingencies call for modifying marketing plans. So the inputs keep changing. (But if marketing weren't challenging, it wouldn't be as fun!)

Good marketing makes any company better!

As Figure 1.3 indicates, if we keep an ongoing read on the 5Cs, it will make us better informed as we approach the STP task. These background indicators will apprise us of which qualities of a customer base are likely to be relevant as we identify segments. The P of positioning in STP is done via all 4Ps. Thus the 5Cs, STP, and 4Ps operate interdependently. Optimal business solutions (in real life or in class case discussions) should reflect a working knowledge of all of these elements, and their connections; as a contextual factor changes, what is the predicted impact on distribution channels? As a collaborator shifts its demands, what will that do to our pricing structure? As our company sells off a nonperforming function, what impact might that have on our positioning and customer satisfaction? The plot thickens!

1-4a Book Layout

Marketing is involved in designing products that customers will enjoy, pricing them appropriately, making them available for purchase at easy points of access in the marketplace, and advertising the products' benefits to customers. Throughout this book, we'll assume that we're talking about customers all over the world. This internationalism is already true for most big firms, and it will be true even for small entrepreneurs via the Internet or once they succeed and grow. We'll also assume the omnipresence of the Internet and always consider it a factor in data intake or in customer channels of interactions with the company. In addition to aiming for global citizenship and recognizing the Internet as essential as air, we will offer fresh, fun examples throughout the book, such as Vegas and Ferrari, instead of laundry detergent.

ethics

Ethics: Have a Heart

It is a good thought exercise to consider any dilemma from 2 perspectives:

1) Outcomes
   a) An outcome orientation is called consequentialism or teleological ethics (fancy words to impress an interviewer).
   b) This perspective believes that "the end justifies the means."
   c) As a manager, you'd ask, "What should I do to produce the most good (or the least harm)?"

2) Processes
   a) An orientation toward fair process is called deontological ethics.
   b) The idea is that the process must be fair, regardless of the outcome that might results.
   c) Managers suggest an action as the right one to take according to a principle, such as human rights (e.g., fair pay) or environmental sustenance (e.g., green packaging).

Throughout the book, we'll encounter several classes of ethical issues: don't price discriminate, don't target uninformed groups, don't advertise deceptively, etc.

   If you want an additional challenge, assess a scenario from multiple viewpoints. For example, deontologically, we might say, "We never price discriminate!" Teleologically, we might say, "To maximize value to our shareholders, we should charge different prices to different customer segments." See? The plot thickens!

This book will train you to think like a marketer. You'll see that great marketing is not a soft discipline, it's not an art, nor is it simply intuitive. Great marketing is based on sound, logical—economic and psychological—laws of human and organizational behavior. You will learn the scientific and rigorous way to think about marketing issues, so that, in the future, when your situation looks nothing like the ones you've talked about in school, you'll know how to proceed in finding your optimal solution. (*Hint:* Keep the framework close at hand!)

1-4b Learning from the Marketing Framework

There are two key features to how the material is organized in this book. First, MBA and executive students learning marketing management typically want to see a framework depicting how all the marketing pieces come together to form the whole picture. To give you the big picture as well as to provide you with the in-depth details, Figure 1.3 kicks off every chapter with a Managerial Checklist of questions and issues that the reader can expect to understand better at the close of the chapter. Those questions are revisited at the end of the chapter in a list format called Managerial Recap. The chapters are mapped onto the framework as depicted in Figure 1.4.

   You'll become very familiar with this marketing management framework. You will see the 5Cs, STP, and 4Ps over and over again, so you'll pick them up nearly by osmosis.

   We want to make great marketing part of your DNA. You'll know that any marketing strategy and planning must begin with the 5Cs assessment and then a strategic look at STP, before turning to the strategies and tactics of the 4Ps.

   When you're . . .

- Working on a case for class,

- Or trying to answer an interviewer intelligently,

- Or trying to impress your boss at work,

- Or trying to launch your own business.

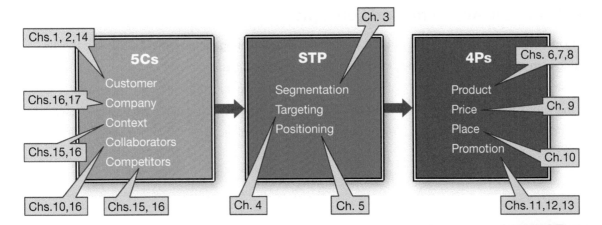

Figure 1.4

Chapters Mapped to Marketing Framework

You'll see the framework in your head. It will remind you of everything that needs to be addressed and how all the pieces fit together. The framework will make you process these marketing questions very thoughtfully and systematically.

1-4c The Flow in Each Chapter: What? Why? How?

The presentation scheme we've adopted in this book is that each chapter covers the What, Why, and How. Specifically,

- What is the topic in this chapter?
- Why does it matter?
- How do I do this? Show me what to do so that I can be successful!

Between the marketing framework and the practical flow of the chapters, you'll gain a strong, clear knowledge of marketing both at the strategic, conceptual level and at the tactical, hands-on level. Both levels of insight will help ensure your success throughout your career, whether you're a marketer, a brand manager, an advertising exec, a CMO, or a well-informed financial analyst, CEO, or world guru.

MANAGERIAL RECAP

Marketing can make customers happier and therefore companies more profitable. Marketing will enhance your career, and marketing can make the world a better place. Honest!

- Marketing is about trying to find out what customers would like, providing it to them, and doing so profitably.
- Ideally, marketing facilitates a relationship between customers and a company.
- Just about anything can be marketed.
- The overarching marketing management framework—5Cs, STP, 4Ps—will structure the book and help you to think methodically about the big picture of marketing.
- Don't forget! Stay focused on your customer! If you can remain customer-centric, you'll be five steps ahead of the competition.

Chapter Outline in Key Terms and Concepts

1. Defining marketing
2. Marketing is an exchange relationship
   a. Marketing is everywhere
3. Why is marketing management important?
   a. Marketing and customer satisfaction is everyone's responsibility
4. The marketing framework: 5Cs, STP, and the 4Ps
   a. Book layout
   b. Learning from the marketing framework
   c. The flow in each chapter: What? Why? How?
5. Managerial recap

Chapter Discussion Questions

1. Before reading this chapter or beginning class, what did you expect marketing to be? Ask a family member, classmate, or coworker what they think marketing is. See whether you can persuade them that marketing enhances a mutually beneficial exchange between a customer and a company.

2. What are examples of brands and companies you like? Why do you think you like them? What is a brand you can't stand? Why not?

3. Think about a recent time when you bought something or tried to do so and you were treated poorly as a customer. What was the essential problem? If you ran the company, what would you do to ensure happier and more loyal customers?

4. List three brands you're loyal to. List three things you tend to buy on sale. How are the product categories represented on these two lists different for you?

5. What social problem do you think is the world's biggest? Wars? Global warming? Resource imbalances? How could you start to solve a big social problem through marketing?

▶ Video Exercise: Southwest Airlines (13:55)

The Southwest Airlines brand is that of a low-fare carrier with the highest level of customer service—and with fun added into the flying experience. Southwest Airlines strives to provide its customers with a total product experience that includes check-in, boarding, flying, and baggage claim experiences. In providing this total product experience, the airline strives to fully meet the needs, wants, and desires of its customers. Southwest regularly surveys its customers regarding all components of the product experience in order to foster continuous improvement. Southwest also conducts extensive quantitative and qualitative research to better understand customers' needs, as well as to explore possible product experiences that the company might offer in the future. Southwest operates on the premise that having new products is what makes a company successful over time. Thus, while maintaining its commitment to low fares, excellent customer service, and fun, Southwest seeks to identify product experiences that different market segments would like to have. The company then builds those experiences into the ticket price structure rather than charging customers with numerous add-ons. Taking this approach enables Southwest Airlines to better tailor its total product experience to the wants, needs, and desires of its different market segments.

Video Discussion Questions

1. Describe the marketing exchange relationship between Southwest Airlines and its customers.

2. Describe the 5Cs of the marketing framework as they pertain to Southwest Airlines.

3. How does Southwest Airlines' approach to providing a total product experience capture the marketing framework elements of STP (segmentation, targeting, and positioning) and the 4Ps (product, price, place, and promotion)?

MINI-CASE

How to Design an Attractive Wearable

A large electronics manufacturer wishes to issue a new "wearable." The company wants to design it such that it will make money with the purchase of the unit, of course, but that it will also make money as its customers use it. In addition, the company would like to capture data about the customers' profiles, in terms of their activities, spending patterns, etc.

Wearables vary in many ways, and initially, the brand management team proposed to issue a design that looked like a small smartphone, to be worn on the user's wrist. Given the still relative novelty of such units, they thought they'd charge on the high end, about $100, maybe even instituting a small annual fee. To get supplementary data, they thought they'd issue periodic surveys, about once a quarter, via the unit or via e-mail.

The youngest marketer, newest to the team asked, "Well, that's good for us, but how is it attractive to our customers? Why would they want this unit—when there are plenty of others out there?" One old manager shot out a withering look. Well, that'll teach the young person to speak up in the meeting. But the senior-most manager spoke up and said, "Well, you're right, we're only looking at it from our point of view. What would this wearable look like that our customers would want—and that can be profitable to us?"

What would help these marketers? What steps could they take to design a wearable that would be both optimally appealing to its customers (and perhaps attract new customers), as well as optimally profitable?

A wearable could vary on many parameters, such as whether it would be worn on the wrist like a watch, or as an earbud like music headphones or smartphone speakers, or as an add-on unit to glasses. Early prototypes suggested that while earbuds or eyeglass designs were good at capturing GPS, they weren't as versatile in supporting multiple apps, and they weren't as precise as exercise (step) counters (for example, the head didn't move as distinctly as the user's wrist while walking). That is what led the brand managers to ask the designers to create a wrist-wearable.

Even so, there were many possibilities: Should the unit look like a small smartphone or like a nice classic wristwatch in design? Should the apps be accessed by touch only or should the apps also be voice-activated? Should there be an annual licensing fee? Should they allow co-branding with affiliations (e.g., a professional sports team or one's college alma mater)? Which features should be recommended as the unit is designed?

This electronics firm has little experience in marketing research as well, so the older managers were uncertain as to how to proceed. One mentioned a focus group, another suggested an ethnography, and a third mentioned surveys. The information that is sought, as well as the method by which the information would be obtained, are both to be determined. Naturally, the company wants to roll out the new wearable as soon as possible, so while the research project could be well-funded, they would face time pressure and would have to be judicious in their choice of research avenues.

Case Discussion Questions

1. Are the old managers right? A lot of other wearables focus on counting steps or enabling apps. Is that what this group should design, so as to be seen as a legitimate competitor and not confuse customers, or should they design something different to be seen as innovative?

2. Are the people in the room a good proxy for their customers? Are the young managers a better proxy than the older managers?

3. What additional information would be helpful to strengthen a recommendation?

4. How would that information best be obtained?

CUSTOMER BEHAVIOR 2

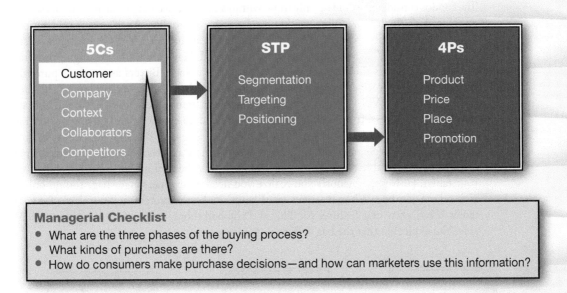

5Cs	STP	4Ps
Customer	Segmentation	Product
Company	Targeting	Price
Context	Positioning	Place
Collaborators		Promotion
Competitors		

Managerial Checklist
- What are the three phases of the buying process?
- What kinds of purchases are there?
- How do consumers make purchase decisions—and how can marketers use this information?

There is some subjectivity in marketing (and in business generally), but there are also many known, reliable patterns that comprise the science of consumer behavior. Most of this chapter talks about these effects and how managers can use this knowledge wisely. To prepare, we first consider the three major phases that consumers go through when making any purchase. Next, we'll see the different kinds of purchases that consumers make. Then we'll drill down and see what makes consumers tick.

2-1 THREE PHASES OF THE PURCHASE PROCESS

Customers go through predictable stages in making a purchase. In the pre-purchase phase, the customer identifies that something is lacking—there is a need or a desire to be satisfied. Critics sometimes say that marketers create desires in people that they didn't already have. There is some truth in that (e.g., "Is your breath fresh?" "Do you own the coolest running shoes?"), but even without marketers, people really do need and want all kinds of things. Then the hunt begins. Buyers search for information about products and brands that may be suitable.

For example, a newly minted MBA student has multiple wants: new clothes, a car, a condo and furnishings, a list of restaurants in a new city to take clients or visiting friends, a new dentist, a drycleaner, etc. Such consumers might search for alternative solutions by going online or asking friends. They might evaluate alternatives by reading *Consumer Reports* or going to BizRate.com. By comparison, a newly promoted business executive might want a corporate jet. Possible vendors would need to be investigated, and alternatives could be evaluated by soliciting and entertaining bids. While the objects and details of these two purchases may look different, they both entail a variety of pre-purchase activities.

During the purchase phase itself, the consumer is creating a consideration set that includes all the brands that are deemed potential candidates for purchase and that excludes the brands that have been rejected.[1] The MBA student may limit the car search to include only hybrids. The condos considered would be only those within a certain price range. The restaurants selected might be only those with menus that can be previewed online. Analogous considerations factor into the executive's jet quandary: What attributes are important? What attributes must I have or not have? What attributes don't I care about and therefore will not pay high prices for?

The final stage is the customer evaluation post-purchase. Buyers assess their purchase and the purchase process, posing such questions as: Am I satisfied as a customer? Will I buy this brand again? Will I tell my friends what a great brand I've found? Figure 2.1 shows the complete process, from seeing that there is a need, to choosing and buying something expected to be a solution to the need, and finally, to assessing one's satisfaction with that purchase. For example, imagine running to an interview and the strap on your messenger bag breaks. You're able to grasp the bag before it hits the ground and possibly shakes up your tablet. However, obviously you realize you need a new messenger bag. You go online and order a new bag. When it arrives, you like the looks, the protective inner sleeve for your tablet, it has a few new features you like, and you had thought the price was pretty reasonable. You're pleased that the bag achieved its mission.

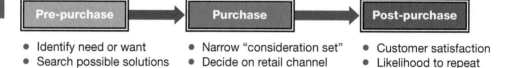

Figure 2.1

The Purchase Process

Pre-purchase	Purchase	Post-purchase
• Identify need or want	• Narrow "consideration set"	• Customer satisfaction
• Search possible solutions	• Decide on retail channel	• Likelihood to repeat
• Build consideration set		• Generate word of mouth

B2B Buying Center Roles

In B2B, big, expensive, purchases can be complicated because it's not just one person making the decision. Each purchase involves a half dozen or so roles in a buying center:

- *The Initiator:* An administrative assistant who notices that one of the printers in the office is frequently breaking down.
- *The User:* Every staff member who tries to use that printer.
- *The Influencer:* The IT guy who says, "Well, Brand X is cheaper, but Brand Y is cooler."
- *The Buyer:* The head administrative person whose responsibilities are to facilitate supplies but also to answer to . . .
- *The Gatekeeper:* A conservative accountant type whose job it is to tighten purse strings.

A decision to buy a new printer is complicated by the fact that each of these roles seeks slightly different attributes. Some care only about price, others want great features, and still others may appreciate wiggle room in negotiating delivery dates or follow-up customer service.

The buying process is consistent whether the buyer is a consumer or a business. Consumer buying is easy to relate to. It involves people buying something for themselves or their households, and we are those people. A business customer is an agent buying something on behalf of an organization. The agent can be an administrative assistant deciding to use UPS or FedEx, or the agent can be a group of people, representing different aspects of the organization (accounting, operations, etc.), comprising a collective buying center. All purchases, business-to-consumer (B2C) or business-to-business (B2B), go through the three stages, but the amount of time spent in any stage depends in part on what is being bought. For example, sometimes the pre-purchase phase is extensive, and sometimes it is very quick. So let's consider some classes of purchases.[2]

2-2 DIFFERENT KINDS OF PURCHASES

Marketers distinguish between types of purchases. For consumers, a convenience item is a fairly mindless purchase of "staples" (standard, frequently-consumed goods, such as bread or gas) or an impulse purchase (such as candy or magazines that are available near grocery checkouts). There are also shopping purchases, which require some thought or planning, as when using OpenTable to find a restaurant before heading out of town. Finally, there are specialty purchases such as a car or new laptop. These purchases are occasional, they are often more expensive than other types of purchases, and as a result they require more thought.

For B2B customers, the terms are different from consumer buying, but the ideas are analogous. A purchase can be a straight rebuy, such as when the office copier needs toner and the office manager buys the usual brand. Another purchase may be a modified rebuy, such as when the copier lease comes up and there is a desire to consider a different vendor. Last, there is the new buy. For example, perhaps the company is considering buying teleconferencing equipment for the first time, and it is not yet well-understood what attributes to consider.

As Figure 2.2 indicates, what differentiates these purchases is not the product itself. The distinction is more in the minds of the customers and in their involvement with the brand and product category. For example, the purchase of the same product—an energy drink—can be convenience when shoppers mindlessly put their usual brand in their grocery cart; it can be a shopping purchase when customers see a new offering that they consider trying; and it can be a specialty purchase when customers see an expensive brand that promises antioxidants, which they choose to read up on before making a purchase.

	← Customer Involvement →		
	Low	Medium	High
B2C	Convenience	Shopping	Specialty
B2B	Straight rebuy	Modified rebuy	New buy
Action	"Add to Cart" or "Click to buy"	Needs some thought	Needs research and serious thought

Figure 2.2

Types of Purchases in B2C & B2B Is a Matter of Customer Involvement

Consumers purchase convenience items—or business customers a straight rebuy—in a fairly mindless manner. It's the proverbial no-brainer. Buyers won't spend much time thinking about brands or attributes because they just don't care enough to do so. The challenge for marketers is to break that thought pattern (not that it's very thoughtful!)—to shake up the consumer with news of their brand and break through that white noise clutter.

For items that customers care more about, they'll expend some time and effort prior to the purchase, seeking out more information to be a smart shopper and to obtain good value. For even higher customer involvement, as in specialty purchases or new buys, the customers are more engaged. A great deal of effort is put into researching the best brands, quality, and price. The marketer's challenge is to convince the buyer that their brand is the best choice.

Types of B2B Customers

B2B customers are often classified according to what they sell:

- Installations (e.g., equipment for new factories)
- Accessories (e.g., computers to help run the office)
- Raw materials (e.g., lumber, plastics)
- Components (processed items that are components in a later finished product)
- Business services (e.g., insurance, legal, consulting)

Ultimately, the most important classification is how much the buying business cares about the purchase. Then we'll know whether they care primarily about quality or price.

The category that a brand and target segment is in will suggest the appropriate marketing activities that we'll select from in the chapters that follow. For example, for lower-involvement purchases, we can expect customers to be somewhat more price sensitive. They'll pay more when they buy things they really like or want (e.g., a cool laptop) or that they expect to be of high quality (e.g., a great restaurant) or that is important to them (e.g., health care for their parents).

Consider the implications for loyalty programs. The marketer can create such programs regardless of the level of customer engagement, but they'd take different forms, e.g., price discounts for low-involvement purchases vs. brand communities and events for high-involvement products and brands. Customer satisfaction can be fine for low-involvement purchases, but customers won't generate word of mouth; they don't care enough. In contrast, for high-involvement purchases, strong followers and satisfied customers can be zealots and brand ambassadors.

Consider the implications for channels of distribution. Low-involvement products need to be widely available so that the customer can pick them up without thinking. High-involvement products will be sought out by more customer activity.

Finally, consider the implications for promotions. For low-involvement products, the marketer just hopes to cut through the noise and clutter—getting customers' attention only long enough to register the brand name in the mind of the customer for sheer familiarity. With high-involvement purchases, customers are hungry for information, and marketers can provide much more.

Marketing satisfies (and creates) consumers' needs and wants.

Anatomy of a Grocery Store

In the produce section similar items are close together (for example, fruits and vegetables).

The dairy section contains milk, which is the most commonly purchased item. Because of this, it is located in an area of the store that requires the customer to travel through the store, increasing the likelihood of impulse purchases.

In grocery stores, consumers form consideration sets (and then choose brands) as a function of brand recognition (brand recall helps when searching online). Retailers also place specific brands where they can be seen by specific customers, such as brands aimed at children shelved at eye level to toddlers seated in shopping carts.

Complementary items are close (chips and dip).

Checkout counters provide the store the opportunity to capture customer information through the use of loyalty cards, and bar codes can provide a wealth of data that can be mined to provide insights into customer purchasing decisions.

Layout is designed to facilitate the shopper. Upon entering, the shopper has a choice of selecting a traditional shopping cart, a smaller basket, or shopping carts designed for shoppers with children. For physically challenged shoppers, motorized shopping carts are often provided.

The end of each aisle and the area at the checkout lanes are likely to hold high-profit items or grouped items (such as marshmallows, chocolate bars, and graham crackers for s'mores) designed to inspire impulse buys. Sometimes those aisle-ends are used to promote sale items. "People are 30% more likely to buy items on the end of the aisle versus in the middle of the aisle—often because we think what's at the end is a better deal," says Brian Wansink of Cornell University and author of *Mindless Eating*.

© Cengage Learning 2013

So how do customers learn about brands and make choices? In the rest of the chapter, we'll look at how customers think and how marketing can have an impact on their decisions and choices.

2-3 THE MARKETING SCIENCE OF CUSTOMER BEHAVIOR

Consumers are human beings and, as such, are sometimes simple and predictable, but often rather complex. In this section, we'll delve into consumer psychology, examining sensation and perception, learning and memory, motivation, attitudes, and decision making.

2-3a Sensation and Perception

When marketers formulate positioning statements or produce perceptual maps, they presuppose a complicated system through which consumers sense and perceive their environment. An enormous wave of sensory stimulation washes over and through us every day. We are selective in our attention, choosing to consider certain stimuli and effectively screening out others. For example, if we are in the market for a car, we'll watch TV ads for cars. If we're not in the market for a car, we barely "see" the TV ads for cars. We know that consumer involvement creates a state of heightened motivation to learn more about a purchase or to pay attention to advertisement. The human organism is very efficient at adapting to the multitude of stimuli, helping us focus and block out what we deem to be irrelevant.

Let's consider how marketers can use information through each of the senses. Visual stimuli are obviously important to marketers. Ads show products, product design, print information, imagery visualization to facilitate desirable lifestyles, etc. Even simple colors imbue brand associations and can be integral to some brand identities:

- Toothpaste packaging is dominated by whites and blues, implying freshness, cleanliness, water, etc.
- Tiffany's aqua blue boxes have saved many a marriage.
- Dell's blue is deeper and darker than Tiffany's, and also trademarked.

Marketers frequently use color to convey information. There are color wheels to guide the brand manager considering a new logo or packaging. For example, blue seems to connote dependability and is used widely (American Express, Ford, Intel). Red tends to imply passion, as in the excitement of breaking news (CNN) or sporting events (ESPN). Green often implies environmental sustainability (although judge for yourself whether that applies to the green in BP, or whether it's relevant to H&R Block).

The symbolism of colors also varies across cultures, so it is important for a brand manager responsible for a global multinational brand to test the color's meaning in its major markets. In the U.S., brides wear white because it symbolizes purity (like newly fallen snow). In India, red conveys purity. In the U.S., red conveys danger and passion; a bride in red would be . . . unusual. In Western civilizations, purple has traditionally denoted royalty; but in Thailand, it's the color of mourning. Mourners in Egypt wear yellow, yet yellow implies courage in Japan and the opposite, cowardice, in the U.S. There are a zillion colors and many cultures. Imagine the challenge for a brand manager in selecting packaging or logo designs for global multinational brands.

Brand Colors

- White   Apple, Wikipedia, Honda
- Yellow   Hertz, Shell, National Geographic
- Orange   Crush, Fanta, Harley-Davidson
- Red   Coca-Cola, CNN, Kellogg's, Target
- Purple   Hallmark, Yahoo
- Blue   AT&T, Dell, HP, IBM, Tiffany's
- Green   BP, John Deere, Starbucks
- Brown   M&M's, UPS
- Black   Channel, Gucci, Prada

Hearing is also important to marketers. Research shows that when retailers play background music that is energetic, with a quick tempo, customers spend more. There are other aural brand associations:

- iPhone vs. Samsung vs. T-Mobile vs. AT&T ringtones
- United Airlines' frequent use of Gershwin's *Rhapsody in Blue* in their ads
- Fancy Feast television commercials feature a high-pitched "ding, ding" (a fork clinking against fine crystal) implying that the food is special, and therefore worth its higher price.

Car and motorcycle enthusiasts know that manufacturers are meticulous in delivering distinctive sounds, and, as a result, consumers have come to learn the sounds, expect them, and pay for them. A high-end Honda motorcycle runs about mid-$20k, whereas a Harley-Davidson runs in the high $30k. Obviously, the sound is not the only difference between the two bikes, but if the Harley didn't sound like a Harley, a biker won't fork over the extra $15k. Similarly, a Porsche 911 turbo at $150k is no clunker, but Ferrari's engineers create a symphony of car sounds and charge $250k. Again, even acknowledging other differences, sound is nevertheless a part of the purchase decision.

A third sense is smell. Think of how many times you've walked through a shopping mall and felt carried away on the wafting scent of a Cinnabon store or an Auntie Anne's pretzel store in the food court. Strong perfume scents are a large part of the Bath & Body Works or The Body Shop stores' ambience. Scent can also be alluded to, drawing on the consumer's memory, as when Folger's coffee commercials depict a person being awakened by the aroma of brewing coffee.

A fourth sense is taste. A classic marketing exercise is to run blind taste tests in order to declare that one's own product is superior to the market leader, or that a "me-too" brand is liked as well as a market leader. These tests can be dramatic and compelling. They are also interesting to marketers because they clearly distinguish the power of the brand from the product itself. For example, most people swear they can identify a Pepsi vs. a Coke, and yet many people actually cannot. Try it on your friends.

A fifth sense is touch. The predominant means of conveying brand imagery through touch is when marketers create well designed products, compared to products intended to be positioned for value. For example, design can mean good ergonomics, as in good kitchen knives, wrist-friendly mice or keyboards, good office chairs, etc. Design can also mean clean lines, simplicity, and beauty, such as the products that Apple creates. Finally, design can also certainly mean a sensual experience, like leather interior options in cars, compared to their less expensive, less touchable alternatives.

Finally, a discussion about sensation and perception wouldn't be complete without mention of so-called subliminal advertising. The idea is that an ad can be shown very quickly, on TV, online, or in the movies, so that it doesn't quite meet the threshold of liminal recognition and consciousness, and therefore it is said to be subliminal. Yet somehow the vision is captured subconsciously, and marketers hope the message will compel action (e.g., buy more popcorn). Print ads depend not on brief time exposure but on ambiguity. If you think companies don't do this anymore, take a look at the logo for the Chicago White Sox baseball team (at whitesox.com) in Figure 2.3. What does it spell?

While marketers have debunked the notion that subliminal advertising works, they nevertheless conduct a great deal of research in areas called "mere exposure" and "perceptual fluency." Neither of these effects is subliminal, per se, but they share a certain subtlety. For example, mere exposure, as its name suggests, says that, though you might not think the billboard you drive past every day is having a persuasive effect on you, it is. Marketers know that repeated exposures to a brand name brings familiarity, and with familiarity comes a comfortable, positive feeling. Thus, brands advertised on billboards or that keep appearing in sidebar ads online are familiar and would probably rate fairly positively.

Perceptual fluency is also a subtle phenomenon. When consumers thumb through a magazine or click through websites, they are probably paying most of their attention to the content of the message. However, other information is being expressed. Colors and fonts can make a message seem more professional, more emotional, more contemporary, more gothic. Those cues make an impression as well. The cues are liminal but subtle, and they are part of the brand.

Figure 2.3

Subliminal Ad

Staff/MCT/Newscom

2-3b Learning, Memory, and Emotions

All those sensory and perceptual impressions can become brand associations. To say that consumers have brand associations means that, in their memory, they have stored certain attributes attached to the brand. When the brand is mentioned, those associations are brought to mind. Learning is the process by which associations get past the sensory and perception stages into short-term memory and then, with repetition and elaboration, into long-term memory. There are several theories about learning, but two are so fundamental and pervasive that every marketer should know them.

The first way that people learn is through classical conditioning. This type of learning is so well known and integrated into our culture that most people have heard of the demonstrations by Ivan Pavlov of his salivating dogs. The learning goes through stages:

- *Stage 1:* A food bowl placed in front of a dog naturally elicits its drool.
- *Stage 2:* A bell rung in front of the dog initially elicits no response.
- *Stage 3:* A bell rung while a food bowl is simultaneously placed in front of the dog elicits drool.
- *Stage 4:* With time, bell rung in front of the dog elicits drool. The dog has come to learn that the bell is associated with food.

Perhaps you're thinking, "But that's just a dog." Indeed. However, consider Figure 2.4. It's common to hear that "sex sells," but why or how does it work? The process is this:

- *Stage 1:* A babe (male or female) elicits drool.
- *Stage 2:* Some brand or product initially elicits no response.
- *Stage 3:* That brand or product in a picture with aforementioned babe elicits drool.
- *Stage 4:* With time, the brand itself elicits drool.

That might sound a little far-fetched, but that's the learning process. Consider more neutral stimuli, such as the logos in Figure 2.5. At their introduction, these abstract symbols convey no information and function much like the bell in Pavlov's lab. With time, while logos might not elicit drool, consumers come to learn and associate these fairly similar looking symbols with their unique brands.

It's also worth noting, in this ever changing world, that sometimes companies want to shed negative associations, and they change their names and logos to do so. For example, in recent years, Blackwater became Xe, Philip Morris became Altria, ValuJet became AirTran, and Andersen Consulting became Accenture. The hope is that the slate has been wiped clean, so that fresh associations might become attached to the new company names and logos.

Source: SKYY Vodka

Figure 2.4

Sex Sells Due to Classical Conditioning

Michael Dechev/ Shutterstock.com

36b/Shutterstock. com

©Leonard Zhukovsky/ Shutterstock.com

Figure 2.5

Logos Gain Meaning Through Classical Conditioning

A fun use of classical conditioning is jingles. It takes only a few exposures before people learn the catchy lyrics. Consider these jingles; it's hard to resist finishing them, and it's hard to stop thinking about them:

- M'mm m'mm good . . .
- Gimme a break, gimme a break, break me off a piece of that . . .
- Plop, plop, fizz, fizz . . .
- Oh, I wish I were an Oscar . . .
- I'd like to buy the world a . . .
- Sometimes you feel like a nut; . . .

And the master of all jingles:

- Two all-beef patties . . .

The second way that people learn is through operant conditioning. This type of learning is also so well known that most people have heard of Skinner boxes. B. F. Skinner studied pigeons pecking at a target, or rats pressing a bar, to receive food pellets. The pigeon learns the desired behavior by being rewarded. The behavior is said to be positively reinforced.

Skinner boxes are programmed to reward the pigeon every time it pecks, or only after every fourth peck, or only at 20 after the hour, etc. When the bird is rewarded every time or every fourth time, the reinforcement schedule is said to be on a fixed ratio reinforcement schedule. When the bird is rewarded on average every fourth time (so perhaps after two pecks, then after six pecks, then after four, etc.), the reinforcement schedule is said to be on a variable ratio. This difference matters because the unpredictability of the variability drives the birds (and humans) a little nuts. In the same amount of time, say 30 minutes, the bird will peck a lot more on the variable, rather than on the fixed, ratio schedule.

So what? Well, consider loyalty programs. Marketers reward consumers who carry their loyalty cards by giving them every 10th coffee free, for example. If marketers want their consumers to purchase even more frequently and ring up more sales, they would design a variable ratio reinforcement program. Each coffee card could have a scratch-off number indicating that the customer would receive a free coffee after, say, seven coffees. The next card might say five or 15, etc.

With current programs, the customer's behavior is very predictable. With a variable program, the customer would be excited about the seven because it means a free coffee is coming much faster than after 10. Even when they scratch off and get a higher number, like 15, they'll still recall that they have had smaller numbers in the past. So the sooner they get to 15 and redeem this card, the sooner they'll get another card, perhaps with a smaller number.

There are also reinforcement schedules based on duration lapses, but these are not implemented in marketing as frequently. One famous exception, however, is the policy by Southwest Airlines that allows passengers to obtain their boarding pass classification 24 hours prior to the flight, but no sooner. Passengers who wait too long get less desirable status, so many fliers find themselves poised over their keyboard to press the right letters at just the right time. Keyboard pressing is not that different from pigeons pecking.

As any student knows, a big factor in learning and memory is motivation. Thus, we consider it next.

2-3c Motivation

Figure 2.6 depicts psychologist Abraham Maslow's hierarchy of needs. We have to meet basic needs—have food on the table and a roof overhead—before we think about buying

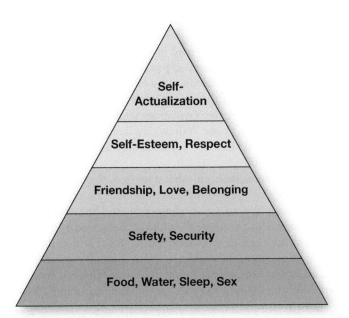

Figure 2.6

Maslow's Hierarchy of Needs

nice clothes. Once we have met our basic needs, we are driven by more abstract motivations, such as love and esteem, qualities that begin to define humanity. At the peak of this pyramid is the phrase, self-actualization, an achievement of our ideal self, with no needs, no excessive wants, no jealousies, etc.

One way that marketers use this hierarchy is by identifying their product with a certain level of needs. They use imagery to appeal to those motivations. For example, the VW crash ads appeal to our need for safety. Similarly, the entire Volvo brand is positioned for safety. Beyond cars, other examples involve different kinds of security. For example, in B2B, they used to say, "You won't get fired for buying IBM." Even though IBM was often the most expensive choice, buyers knew that the quality would be good, so any risk-averse buyer would feel security in having chosen a good brand.

Many of us are fortunate enough that our simpler needs are met, so a great number of brands are positioned to heighten a consumer's sense of belonging or, at the next level, social acceptance and respect. Belonging can be signaled by explicitly affiliative products, such as team logos, or by conspicuously branded products, as in certain men's athletic shoes or women's handbags. Belonging can also be more subtle; many ads appeal to a person's concern with fitting in with the norm. For example, when you start a new job, are you wearing the right clothing? If all your friends drive a hybrid, will they accept you and your SUV? And so on.

At the higher level, the acceptance, by self (esteem) and others (respect) is often signaled by marketers by pointing a consumer to an aspiration group. You might be a business school student right now, but ads will show you the clothes, restaurants, and cars that the most successful CEOs wear, dine in, and drive. The implication is that you should begin to shape your preferences accordingly so that, when you achieve that CEO status, your purchases will exhibit good taste.

Another way that marketers have used this hierarchy is to offer an extended brand line that encourages a customer to reach ever higher in the pyramid. For example, Mercedes makes their entry-level C-Class for the driver who wants the brand but cannot afford much. Mercedes hopes that drivers will like the C-Class and, when they're ready, trade it in for an E-, then S-, then CL-Class. This product range is a simple manifestation of customer relationship management.

Yet another way that the hierarchy is used is when brand managers think about positioning their brands as high in the pyramid as possible. Walmart makes basic sneakers that satisfy simple needs at the bottom of the hierarchy. However, stronger brands like New Balance can charge more, not just because the product may be somewhat better but because the consumer wants to believe that the shoes will make them better—better athletes, more fit, more attractive, better people. The basic Walmart sneaker probably can't be positioned too high in the pyramid, but it would behoove any other sneaker maker to strive for imagery as high in the hierarchy as possible.

Beyond the Maslow pyramid, there are other ways to distinguish needs and motivations. Many consumer psychologists speak of utilitarian vs. hedonic products in fulfilling needs and wants. A consumer might need a new interviewing suit but want the Armani threads.

Consumer psychologists also point to the motives that co-exist in all of us, for conformity vs. individuality. One need may be more salient than another throughout a person's life, or over an array of situations. If conformity is winning, the consumer buys a popular brand; if individuality is more important, then the consumer finds an atypical, quirky brand. Luckily, in most product categories, there are large brand assortments; hence, either need may usually be satisfied.

A final means of distinguishing consumer motivations is whether they are risk seeking or risk averse. In some product categories, consumers may be very knowledgeable, opinion leaders, and ready to try the newest that the market has to offer (the latest music, fashion, etc.). In other product categories, those same persons may be more risk averse for a variety of reasons, including caring less about the category or not having the expertise to make choices confidently. For these purchases, the consumers would be more conservative, trying to prevent a bad purchase, rather than striving for a good purchase.

Predicting the Weather and Brand Choice

We can't even predict the weather very well, so why would we expect to be able to predict consumer purchasing?

Weather is simple compared to human decision making and purchasing. It's comprised of very few components: wind, water, dirt particles, gravity, and temperature. Yet the best we tend to say is, "Tomorrow's weather will look something like today's." Similarly, we make the fewest marketing forecast mistakes if we say, "You'll buy the same brand of toothpaste this time as you did last time."

Consider the factors that enter into a toothpaste purchase: What did mom buy? What's on sale? What flavor do I like? Do I need a small tube for travel or a big tube for home? Do I want a whitener? Are my teeth sensitive? Do I want to try something new? Do I have a coupon? Am I buying this for myself or someone else? Do I need floss because that brand is bundled with a container of floss? It's complicated!

Yet marketers have sophisticated research techniques to enhance predictions and answers to questions such as whether this customer is likely to be a brand switcher, sensitive to a price discount, affected by recent advertising, etc. Methods to gather information from customers are discussed throughout this book and in particular are concentrated in Ch. 15 on marketing research.

Eenie, Meanie, Jelly Beanie

In their article, "Active Choice: A Method to Motivate Behavior Change," Professors Punam Keller and Bari Harlam studied different kinds of so-called opting behaviors:

1. Opt-in: Check this box if you wish a reminder to . . .

2. Opt-out: Check this box if you do not wish a reminder to . . .

Options 1 and 2 did okay, but the setup that was much more effective was:

3. Check one: I will remind myself to . . . vs.
                  Yes, please send me a reminder to . . .

Getting reminders is very important to engaging in a variety of behaviors, such as getting flu shots, signing an organ donation card, or enrolling in a company's 401k program.

2-3d Attitudes and Decision Making

Marketers want to understand how consumers think and what motivates them so that they might persuade the consumers to have positive regard for a particular brand and see it as superior to all others, at least for their needs. Attitudes and decision making affect the extent to which consumers will buy a brand, repeatedly purchase it, become loyal, and recommend it to others. If we're really lucky, our brand fans will prefer our brand so much that they'd even be price insensitive if we had to, or wished to, raise prices. So if we seek to enhance attitudes about brands and encourage particular brand choices, let's begin with two questions: What are attitudes? What does the decision making process look like?

Attitudes are conceptualized as a mix of beliefs and importance weights. Beliefs are opinions, such as BMWs are fast, they're nice to look at, they're expensive, etc. Importance weights are things like, "I don't care much about whether my car is fast, but I would like it to be attractive" or "I care about the cost." People can differ on both their beliefs and importance weights. Some people might say that BMWs aren't that attractive or expensive relative to other cars. Some people might not care how much a car costs but care very much about speed.

Importance weights are like the concept of customer involvement. It is an important truism in marketing, with its natural implications, that, in any purchase category, customers can be classified according to how much they care about the given purchase. For the things consumers care about, they spend more time learning about the options and brands, and they're usually willing to pay more for excellence. For the things consumers care less about, they spend less time investigating, and it's likely that they won't want to pay much.

The job of marketers is to play with both components of attitudes—beliefs and importance weights. Marketers seek to make the beliefs in an attribute or benefit more positive and to make the attributes on which the brand dominates other brands seem even more important. The beliefs and importance weights are modified or strengthened through learning and memory and by appealing to consumer motivations that the brand purportedly satisfies.

Attitudes contribute to decision making and brand choice. In some product categories, there aren't that many choices, so brands can be compared fairly readily. In categories with a lot of choices, consumers usually proceed through two stages. In the first, quick stage, they decide which brands should be considered in more detail vs. those that don't make the cut to be in the consideration set. The second stage is relatively prolonged, during which consumers compare the brands in the set to make a purchase choice.

The first stage is thought to be conducted quickly by non-compensatory mechanisms. "Non-compensatory" means that some attributes are very important. If the brand has them, then it may be considered further; otherwise, the brand is precluded. Even if the brand excels at something else, that other excellent attribute does not compensate for the lack of the first, important quality. For example, if a consumer is set on buying a hybrid car, then that's the first attribute that reduces the set—cars that are not hybrids are cut from further consideration. Whichever brands make the cut on this first dimension continue to be considered. The consumer proceeds lexicographically, selecting the attribute or dimension that is next most important, etc. That subset of brands is compared on the next most important attribute and so on until the set is reduced to only a few brands.

Once the consideration set has been reduced to a manageable number, consumers switch gears and use a compensatory model. This model uses a costs and benefits logic, whereby excellence on one attribute can make up for the fact that the brand is not so great in some other ways. One such model is that of averages, e.g., if a brand is strong on attribute A and only so-so on B, it may dominate a brand that is average on both attributes A and B.

A lot of online sites allow consumers to select from a number of brands or models to enable side-by-side comparisons. This information sorting helps consumers see which brands are best on the attributes they care most about. The algorithms request that consumers first select the brands to be compared. This stage mimics the non-compensatory stage in reducing the number of possible brands to a more manageable number for further consideration. The online comparators facilitate the second, compensatory stage, in that the attributes are lined up for easy viewing. A brand choice is made, and the decision process is completed.

Cross-Cultural Consumer Behavior

When multi-national companies launch brands internationally, they face the global-local decision. Should the brand be a unitary, global entity, the same in every market, or should it be tailored for the tastes and preferences for local customers. Those who argue for a single global brand say that there needs to be brand consistency across markets to keep a brand strong and its image clear, and to allow some financial and operational efficiencies. Those who argue for tailored offerings say that customers will be more favorably inclined to build a connection to a product that is more meaningful to them. The essence of this strategic decision will be revisited throughout the book, but in this chapter, the main concern is an understanding of consumers.

There may be ways to leverage some similarities across some countries and cultures so that a company can enjoy some efficiencies and not have to reinvent a truly unique brand for every marketplace. Many researchers have studied the similarities and differences among many countries, but perhaps the best-known framework is that of Geert Hofstede. He uses 5 dimensions to differentiate countries:

1. "Power distance": clear delineation between those who have power and those who do not. High power distance cultures are typically very hierarchical, such as Brazil, England, Japan, Portugal, and many Latin, Asian, and African countries. Low power distance cultures are more egalitarian, such as Israel, New Zealand, Norway, and the U.S.

2. Cultures also vary along the continuum from "individualism," in which people mostly look out for themselves, to "collectivism," in which people's identities and esteem are rooted in the groups to which they belong—their families, their companies, their country, etc. Does a person tend to think in terms of "I" or "we"? Individualistic countries include the U.S. and Canada, Australia and New Zealand, England, France, and Germany. Collectivistic cultures dominate Asia, Latin America, and Africa.

3. Countries and cultures differ on whether they are characterized as "masculine," focused on achievement, success, and assertiveness or "feminine," and more focused on modesty, caring for others, and enhancing the quality of life. Masculine countries include China, Hungary, Italy, Mexico, the U.K., and the U.S. Feminine countries include Chile, Denmark, Finland, the Netherlands, Portugal, and Sweden.

4. "Uncertainty avoidance" is the extent to which people are uncomfortable by ambiguity and therefore try to resolve such situations, usually by imposing rules and structure. Countries with high uncertainty avoidance are: Belgium, France, Germany, Greece, Italy, Portugal, and Spain. Countries with relatively more tolerance for ambiguity are: Denmark, Ireland, Poland, Sweden, the U.K., and the U.S.

5. "Long-term orientation" is the extent to which people of the culture look to long-term traditions and look to and save for the future compared to short-term orientation which is a focus on achieving quick results. Countries that are longer-term oriented are China, Hong Kong, Japan, compared to shorter-term oriented U.K., U.S., and Latin American countries.

These differences have clear marketing implications. For example:

- The marketer can expect more conspicuous consumption, in masculine countries, in which achievement is celebrated, thus helping Cartier, Rolex, and Philippe Patek be judicious in the marketing dollars they allocate across countries.

- Similarly, in high power distance countries, such as Brazil or Japan, people tend to dress up, a bit formally, to show respect and to reflect their own position. By comparison, people in low power distance countries will dress more casually. It's no accident that "casual Friday" was invented in the U.S.

2-3e How Do Cultural Differences Affect Consumers' Behavior?

In addition to individual differences in how consumers respond to ads and brands, there are also predictable sociocultural effects. We'll consider two examples: social class and age.

Some societies have clearer class distinctions than others, but gradations in socioeconomic standing are discernible even in relatively classless societies. People tend to be more comfortable with others in comparable standing.

Social class is a construct that is more complicated than just economic access to resources. Income is important, but so is family background (e.g., old money vs. nouveau riche) and career paths (e.g., some allowance for social mobility). Old-monied people seek exclusivity in their brands, to affirm their special standing in society. They are alarmed by the mass-class movement, in which designers of high-end luxury goods produce far less expensive lines (albeit not of the same quality) to allow access by us peasants.

In contrast, nouveaus try to make purchases to attain their status, the purchases being the so-called status symbols. They indulge in conspicuous consumption, e.g., buying goods with garish, loud branding that shows the world they've made it. Obviously, designing products, brands, and marketing communications for these two different groups calls for different approaches.

Age cohorts also produce reliable, predictable shopping patterns. Some patterns are obvious, following the household composition and income availability. Young people first buy furniture and kitchenware, entertainment and travel, and large screen TVs. They proceed to the stage of buying diapers and toys and minivans. Soon there is college to pay for, then maybe travel, and, soon, health care. All highly predictable.

Age groups are particularly important when they are large in size. The infamous baby boomer group is beginning to retire. Older people are traditionally ignored by advertisers who like to feature youth, but the deep wallets of baby boomers will soon force companies to pay attention. Cruises will sell, whereas sophomoric movie comedies might decline.

The baby boomer generation was always societal minded, so we might expect to see large-scale altruism and record levels of infusions of resources into nonprofits. In an odd contradiction, this generation was also dubbed "the me generation," and indeed sales of Viagra and cosmetic surgeries have also begun inching upward.

Social class and age cohort are among the various sociocultural factors that impinge on how buyers form impressions and preferences, collect information, form opinions, and make brand choices. Gender matters: Men and women are socialized differently, they think about products differently, and they shop differently.

Finally, ethnicity and country culture provide different perspectives, and they can be very interesting (and complicated). We'll see examples throughout the book. Be forewarned: It is difficult to provide generalizations without devolving into stereotypes, so note there are always exceptions. To foreshadow a few observations now:

- Wealthy Chinese like their consumption conspicuous. Due to their purchases, Louis Vuitton has found its busy season has moved to late-January and early-February, just before Chinese New Year (from traditional 4th quarter peaks, attributable to Christmas shopping).

- Danes are fond of luxury goods, and their society is so egalitarian that they believe luxury goods should be accessible to all.

- European brands tend to dominate the high end, due not just to a perception or cultural heritage but also to structural industry differences, such as:

  - Fine craftsmanship in watches built in Switzerland,
  - Fashion or exotic cars designed in Italy, or
  - Supply chains such as extensive fields of flowers or vineyards for perfumeries or vintners in France.

MANAGERIAL RECAP

Keep the buyer in mind, whether you deal with consumers or business customers. Marketing managers can be nimble and adaptive to industry changes if they have a basic understanding of consumer behavior:[3]

- There are three major phases of consumption: pre-purchase, purchase, and post-purchase.

- There are three major classes of purchases: For B2C, these are called convenience, shopping, specialty; for B2B, these are called straight rebuy, modified rebuy, and new buy. The difference among the three has to do with customer involvement.

- How do consumers think?

  ○ They begin with sensing and perceiving information, which may be learned and stored in memory.

  ○ Motivations help marketers understand what consumers are seeking to satisfy with their purchases.

  ○ Attitudes and decision making are subject to influence by good information as well as biases.

  ○ Finally, social norms, such as generational preferences or choices based on wealth, define us as well.

Chapter Outline in Key Terms and Concepts

1. The three phases of the purchase process
2. There are different kinds of purchases
3. The psychological science of customer behavior
   a. Sensation and perception
   b. Learning, memory, and emotions
   c. Motivation
   d. Attitudes and decision making
4. Managerial recap

Chapter Discussion Questions

1. If consumers are being deluged by sensory overstimulation, what can a marketer do to cut through the clutter?

2. Using the principles of classical conditioning or operant conditioning, design a marketing program for a nonprofit or for a political candidate.

3. What should ads say to help brands make the first (non-compensatory) cut in decision making and be included in a consumer's consideration set? What should ads say to help a brand be chosen, once in the set?

4. Run a taste test. Compare Pepsi vs. Coke, or bottled water vs. tap, or an expensive bottle of wine vs. the boxed stuff. Note participants' level of knowledge and surprise.

5. New businesses are frequently launched as a means to address a current glitch in the industry. Pick an industry and identify a typical customer problem. What changes could you make to enter that industry and enhance customer satisfaction (and be profitable)?

6. Go online and find the average length of a "lifetime" for purchases in the categories of: houses, cars, gym memberships, baby diapers, birth control pills, and Viagra prescriptions.

Video Exercise: Scholfield Honda (5:48)

The video features Roger Scholfield, owner and general manager of Scholfield Honda in Wichita, Kansas, and several of his employees describing the characteristics and profiles of the dealership's customers. With respect to purchases of both new and used vehicles, customers tend to be very interested in vehicles that are fuel-efficient and environmentally friendly. The video focuses on describing the key characteristics of customers who are interested in and knowledgeable about hybrid or alternative fuel vehicles. Factors such as the customer's age, level of education, attitudes, and needs are explored. Scholfield acknowledges that prospective customers often comparison-shop at other dealerships—and he says that he welcomes such buyer behavior. He believes that his dealership has a competitive advantage over other dealerships because of the friendly atmosphere and exceptional service people receiveat Scholfield Honda. Appealing to customer's needs, desires, attitudes, and beliefs enables Scholfield Honda to attract and retain customers.

Video Discussion Questions

1. Using the purchase process (i.e., pre-purchase, purchase, and post-purchase), analyze the customer information provided by the owner and employees of Scholfield Honda.

2. Chapter 2 identifies three types of purchase decisions for consumers. Describe the type of purchase decision that characterizes the buying behavior of the customers of Scholfield Honda.

3. What attitudes and needs seem to be influential in people deciding to patronize Scholfield Honda?

MINI-CASE

Insight into Consumer Decision Making for 3-D TV

Various media equip consumers to make side-by-side comparisons of brands' relative strengths (e.g., *Consumer Reports*, bizrate.com, etc.). These comparisons are not acclaimed from the manufacturer, but a third party, so they're perceived as objective and neutral. The table below (based on reviews at cnet.com) compares 3-D televisions on a number of criteria. The attribute of "crosstalk" (in the table) is not a good thing—it's the ghost-like double images that shadow some 3-D objects, depending on the technology; hence, less is better. All the TVs are about 65" currently. The 3-D glasses must be purchased with each TV (the technology is proprietary within firm and TV, so the Panasonic glasses won't work with the LG TV, for example). The glasses run about $150 a pair.

Sometimes customers know just what they want: a particular brand, or a particular feature. Sometimes their thought processes are little more meandering. Some consumers are rather systematic decision makers, such as when they follow a procedure that will eliminate some alternatives by some criteria. Use the table below to simulate the thought processes of a consumer.

Brand	Panasonic	LG	Sony	Samsung
Model	TC-PVT25	PX950	XBR-HX909	UNC8000
Technology	Plasma	Plasma	LCD	LCD
Price	$2,479	$1,850	$2,497	$2,999
Least crosstalk	☺☺☺☺	☺☺☺☺	☺☺	😐
Clear color	☺☺	☺☺☺	😐	😐
Clear, deep black	☺☺☺	☺☺	😐	😐
3-D from angle	😐	😐	☹☹	😐
Flicker	😐	😐	☹☹	😐
3-D glasses	Ugly and uncomfortable	Rechargeable via USB	Comfortable, good peripheral	Light to wear

Case Discussion Questions

Imagine you were a consumer thinking about buying a 3-D TV.

1. First, quickly at a glance, what TV do you think you would buy?

2. On what criteria do you think you based that decision?

   Try these decision making processes, see what brand results for each, and see how confident you feel about the resulting brand suggested from each approach:

3. What attribute do you find least informative? Eliminate that row. Continue to do so until a clear brand winner emerges.

4. Which brand of TV would seem to be riskiest to buy? Eliminate it. Continue until an obvious choice results.

5. If you made a price-based decision, would you be happy?

6. How would your final brand choice define you?

   Which of these criteria wouldn't have concerned you? How similar was this thought process to your natural analysis? How can you find out if your consumers think along these lines?

3 SEGMENTATION

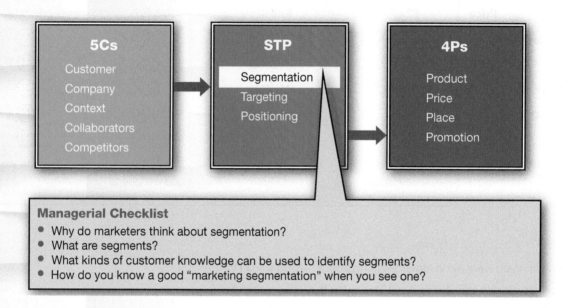

5Cs	STP	4Ps
Customer	**Segmentation**	Product
Company	Targeting	Price
Context	Positioning	Place
Collaborators		Promotion
Competitors		

Managerial Checklist
- Why do marketers think about segmentation?
- What are segments?
- What kinds of customer knowledge can be used to identify segments?
- How do you know a good "marketing segmentation" when you see one?

3-1 WHY SEGMENT?

Think about the last time you went to a movie with a couple of your friends.[1] Afterward, when you talked about the movie, how did people respond? Was everyone in complete agreement about whether they liked the movie? Did everyone agree on the acting or special effects or music? Probably not. Even among our friends, who tend to be similar to us, tastes and opinions vary. No one is right or wrong (well, okay, you were right, and your friends were wrong); it's just a matter of differences in preferences and attitudes.

Psychologists would say that people have different motivations. Recall from Chapter 2 Maslow's hierarchy from biological needs to more abstract ones. Consumers purchase products to fulfill their needs. For example, consumers who are price conscious make purchase decisions using value as a primary attribute, whereas consumers with high needs for social approval purchase brands with much less of a concern for price.

> *A company can't be all things to all customers. It must choose a segment to serve.*

Economists talk about this differently. They call it "imperfect competition"; that is, consumers have unique needs and desires, so collectively a marketplace of consumers is heterogeneous. Differences in perceptions and preferences require that different products be provided to satisfy the different segments' needs. When a large, heterogeneous market is segmented into smaller, homogeneous markets, a company can focus on meeting the demands of one or two of these groups and create something that is closer to what the customers want.

In marketing, we deal with all these customer differences through segmentation. An entrepreneur might create a new gadget, or a brand manager a new line extension, or a consultant a new piece of software, and each might hope that the whole world will like and buy their market offerings. But it won't happen. And it's not smart marketing to go after the whole market. Why not?

- How could you provide a product that has high enough quality to satisfy premium customers and yet is priced low enough for price-sensitive customers?

- How could you afford to place your advertisement in the disparate media that different customers enjoy, (e.g., online, in teen or car or cooking magazines, on network television, etc.)? How many versions of the ad could you afford to create to communicate effectively to those different audiences?

- How could you develop a brand image that appeals to the masses seeking comfort in conformity and simultaneously appeal to fashion setters mavericks or other customers who seek to express their individualism? The goals are incompatible.

Instead of trying to appeal to the entire marketplace, the smart marketer and smart company will try to find out what different kinds of customers might like, and decide which groups they can serve best. That strategy begins with market segmentation.

3-2 WHAT ARE MARKET SEGMENTS?

A market segment is a group of customers who share similar inclinations toward a brand. On a continuum from mass marketing to one-to-one marketing, market segmentation is in the middle (see Figure 3.1).

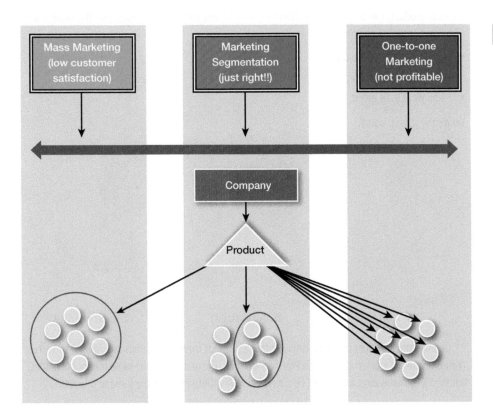

Figure 3.1

Marketing Segmentation: Groups of Customers

Mass marketing means that all customers are treated the same. This approach might sound attractive because it simplifies the business (i.e., only one product needs to be offered), but it is usually unrealistic (because customers differ). Think of a simple commodity product like flour. We should be able to mass market flour; flour's flour, right? *Au contraire, Pierre.* There is all purpose flour, unbleached flour, wheat flour, brown rice flour, buckwheat flour, organic soy flour, whole grain oat flour, self-rising flour, flower power, etc. Different types of flour are available to meet the distinct needs of the flour-using segments.

At the other extreme, *one-to-one marketing* means that each customer serves as his or her own segment. This approach sounds appealing from the customer's point of view because the product would be tailored specially for each person's idiosyncratic desires. Some manufacturers of computers and cars are experimenting with letting customers design their own models. Are these companies truly offering one-to-one tailored products? Not really. Dell's website may seem to do so, but users are allowed to choose only from short lists of features. Nevertheless, even those variations result in a large number of combinations, such that one person's computer seems rather different from another's. The result approaches one-to-one marketing.

Some companies tried mass customization but rolled it back because it was not cost-effective or because it was difficult to exert quality control. Yet increasingly technology offers the benefits of scales of economy. Financial services don't need to have set rates; instead, they can vary depending on a customer's portfolio. Coupons that are printed at grocery checkouts are a function of items the customer just purchased. Ads that pop up on many websites are eerily responsive to what the surfer has been typing.

Potayto, Potahto

Identical products can be positioned differently to different segments. For example, the same baby diaper can appeal to parents:

- thinking about their baby's comfort.
- who want to avoid messes.
- who want to be green.

Yet it's the same product.

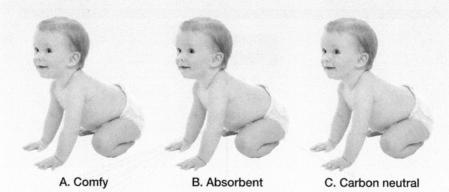

A. Comfy   B. Absorbent   C. Carbon neutral

Or, in another product category, consider the razors that men and women use. Gillette produces "Venus Divine" for women and "Fusion ProGlide" for men. The razors have the same number of blades, but the XX version is pink, and the XY version is black. Are these products the same or different?

Between these two extremes is the typical concept of *segmentation*. The marketplace is thought of as being comprised of several segments, each of which is more (or less) favorable to your brand. The segments that like your brand might not be the customers you want, but that is a marketing issue of targeting and (re)positioning, topics to be addressed in subsequent chapters.

As the contrasts of mass and one-to-one marketing illustrate, segments become more heterogeneous as they increase in size. As a result, they are more difficult to satisfy with the same product (the problem with mass). The goal of homogeneity in customers' likes or dislikes is more likely to be achieved as the segment size gets smaller, but if the segment is too small, it might not be profitable (the problem with one-to-one).[2] So we need to understand how to find optimal, serviceable segmentation schemes.

Niche marketing is a type of segmentation in which the company strategically focuses, targeting a smaller market, with particular needs that the company can serve well. In Figure 3.1, niches would fall between the one-to-one and segment strategies. Niches might be small segments, but they can be very profitable.

3-3 WHAT INFORMATION SERVES AS BASES FOR SEGMENTATION?

3-3a Demographic

All kinds of information about customers have been used in segmenting markets (see Figure 3.2). Some customer attributes are easily identified. For example, in many product categories, a company produces two varieties, one for men and one for women,

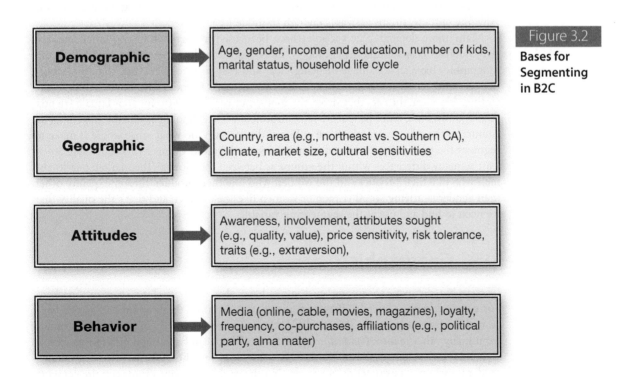

Demographic → Age, gender, income and education, number of kids, marital status, household life cycle

Geographic → Country, area (e.g., northeast vs. Southern CA), climate, market size, cultural sensitivities

Attitudes → Awareness, involvement, attributes sought (e.g., quality, value), price sensitivity, risk tolerance, traits (e.g., extraversion),

Behavior → Media (online, cable, movies, magazines), loyalty, frequency, co-purchases, affiliations (e.g., political party, alma mater)

Figure 3.2

Bases for Segmenting in B2C

such as razors, vitamins, running shoes, and television channels. Sometimes the products are constructed differently, e.g., four blades on razors for shaving those he-man whiskers vs. a razor shaped to fit in the palm of a woman's hand to facilitate shaving sensitive areas. Sometimes the product formulations are identical, but the perceptual factors differ in the marketing appeals. Alternatively, a company might focus on serving only the men's or the women's market.

Other easily identified demographic qualities of customers include their *age, household composition*, and *stage in the life cycle*. Spending is quite predictable:

- Young adults are interested in music and entertainment technologies.

- Young couples buy furniture and vacations together.

- Families start financial planning to support their kids' college educations.

- Older couples that are empty nesters start dreaming of spending their greater discretionary income on travel and hobbies.

- Still older people investigate health care options and charitable giving.

We constantly hear so much about the baby boomers (in the U.S. and worldwide) because this group of customers is so huge that it affects the sales of nearly every product category. A note to the budding entrepreneur: Make something that older people like or need because boomers are heading in that direction.

Two additional demographic characteristics frequently used in segmentation studies are *education*, which helps shape consumer preferences (e.g., opera vs. opry), and *income*, which facilitates certain consumer choices (e.g., Four Seasons vs. Motel 6). You've heard it said that time is money, but, in fact, time seems to be negatively correlated with money. Families with higher household incomes hire more service workers (e.g., lawn care, nannies) to help with their daily needs because of their time drought.

Ethnicity is clearly important. In the U.S., the African-American and Hispanic-American populations each number more than 40 million, and Asian-Americans are at about 12 million. Any one of these groups is sizable enough to influence a market.

Many more demographic variables have been used in segmenting consumer markets. Any variable has potential depending on its relevance to the product category. While demographics have an advantage of being clear and easy to recognize, they sometimes border on being simplistic stereotypes. Think of your male friends: Are they all alike in the clothes they wear, the cars they drive, the foods they eat? No. Ditto for your female friends. Analogously, some older people are uncomfortable with technologies like the Internet, but, counter to the stereotype, others are online and very savvy. So what sense would it make to segment the market into men and women or into older and younger people if there are at least as many differences within the groups as between the groups? The marketer seeks the men who like their product and the women who like their product. So some quality other than gender is driving whether men or women like the product, and that's the quality that we need to find and use as the segmenting variable.

3-3b Geographic

Geographic distinctions among customers have also been used to segment markets. For example, given societal differences, international tourist destinations can wreak havoc with logistics, e.g., while Brits and Germans tend to be orderly in queuing, customers from many other *countries and cultures* are less so. There can be cultural differences within a country, e.g., a spicy salsa in the U.S. Southwest is very hot, whereas it is formulated milder for wimpier customer palates in the Northeast. *Urban* living affords certain elements

Figure 3.3

Prizm Segment Samples

	25–44 years old	45–64 years old
Affluent	**"Kids & Cul-de-sacs"** • Kids • Suburban • Upper middle income • Home owners • College grads	**"Money & Brains"** • Maybe kids • Urban • Upper income • Home owners • Graduate plus
Less so	**"Family Thrifts"** • Kids • Urban, small city • Lower middle income • Renters • Some college	**"Mobility Blues"** • No kids • Urban, small city • Lower income • Renters • Some college

of entertainment, and smaller town living is different. *Climate* offers still another consideration; snow-blowers tend to sell better in the North than in the South, whereas the reverse is true for chlorine.

When geographic and demographic information are combined, the segmentation schemes can be even smarter. A service called Prizm posits that MBAs who live in New York have a lot more in common with their counterparts in London, São Paulo, and Tokyo, for example, than they do with their neighbors in New York who are relatively less educated or wealthy. Figure 3.3 shows several segments, with their distinctive labels and profiles.

3-3c **Psychological**

It would be ideal to get inside the heads and hearts of our customers: What do they want? Do they know? Could they be persuaded to like our brand? Could we change our brand to match their interests better?

Psychological traits vary in terms of how much insight they lend to issues of marketing and brands:

- For example, while men and women show many consumption differences, they can be quite similar in consuming certain product categories, such as cereals or cell phones.

- Or, for example, do extraverts and introverts differ in their purchases? Perhaps some purchases may vary, e.g., vibrant colors of clothing or tendencies to throw dinner parties vs. attend book club readings. But do they differ in the pets they own, in the restaurants they frequent, or in the investments they buy?

It would be more useful to the marketer to understand the psychological and lifestyle choices that are relevant to the brands the marketer is pitching. For example, if we know consumers are avid readers, sports nuts, or wine aficionados, we know something more about what they enjoy, their social orientation, and the categories of purchases they'd be easily enticed to make. We can cross-sell Kindles or iPads to the reader, season ticket packages and large-screen TVs to the athlete, and expensive refrigerators and trips to Argentina to the wine connoisseur.

A popular tool for segmenting using psychographic data is called VALS. The idea is that the attitudes people hold and their value systems determine their orientations toward certain product categories and brands. For example, so-called strivers are people who are trendy and fashionable in order to impress others, and they are often impulsive buyers. Marketing managers would study their customers to understand what they value, and then the managers would be able to communicate more persuasively to those customers. For example, VALS has been used to identify potential customers for cosmetic surgery: Who would be interested? Who could afford it? Why would they want it? All of this shapes the advertising.

Naturally, customers vary in their marketing-oriented attitudes. Hobbies are examples of purchase categories in which customers vary in their level of expertise (some newbies, others experienced and sophisticated). Customers vary in their levels of involvement with the purchase category (how near and dear it is to their hearts). If customers are known for their expertise and involvement in a category, and if they've demonstrated a willingness to share information and give advice, they will be perceived by others as opinion leaders, innovators, or market mavens and would be ideal persons for the marketer to identify as people likely to generate word of mouth. Some customers are early adopters, caring about new developments in their category, seeking out new products. Other customers either care less about that category, or they are more risk averse, and they wait for someone else to try the new gadget or get the kinks out of the beta testing before they purchase the item for themselves.

All the qualities that marketers care about may be mapped onto segments in any product category. For any purchase, a segment of customers will seek premium purchases, another will be brand conscious, and another will be price sensitive. And, of course, just to provide us with a challenge, a customer who seeks quality benefits in one category (e.g., clothing) might be price sensitive in another (e.g., travel).

In addition to understanding who customers are and what kinds of activities they enjoy, it is also important to gauge who customers wish to become. These aspirations help us predict the new categories they will enter. For example, when a person picks up a how-to book (e.g., remodeling), they will likely buy more such books before moving on to learn a new skill. Someone enrolling in beginner's tennis lessons will start noticing brands and attributes of tennis equipment and start gearing up. One reason celebrity spokespeople are thought to be effective is that ordinary people aspire to be like the celebrity, in whatever

VALS

VALS segments people based on three motivations: ideals, achievement, and self-expression (www.strategicbusinessinsights.com/vals):

- *Ideals* people are guided by knowledge and principles. These consumers buy the newest laptop technology, were first to adopt e-readers, do extensive information searches comparing all the brands before they buy just about anything.

- *Achievement* consumers buy products and services that demonstrate success to others. They drive sexy, expensive cars, and they carry, wear, and drink high-end brands.

- *Self-expression* people desire social or physical activity, variety, and risk. These consumers are the first to go bungee jumping, heli-skiing, or any other extreme sport (and accompanying gear), and they can be brand-fickle.

manner that is achievable—if not in the celebrity's full lifestyle, then perhaps in the hairstyle or brand of sunglasses.

3-3d Behavioral

Beyond attitudes, psychographics, and lifestyles, marketers would like to know what customers purchase, not just what they report they intend to purchase. Grocery scanner data are an example of compiled behaviors. A customer might report to be eating healthy foods, but evidence of their M&M purchases would belie their good intentions.

Behaviors are important in and of themselves (e.g., to help us make predictions regarding future purchasing). In addition, watching what consumers do tells us something about who they are. Attitudes are not directly observable, but we can use behaviors to infer attitudes and psychological states. For example, people have preferences for movie genres, and marketers know it. Thus, when we go to an action movie, we'll see previews for other action movies, and when we go to a romantic comedy, the previews are a different batch.

One behavioral segment of great importance to the marketer is the current user of the focal brand. It is relatively easy to communicate to this group, as messages on soup packaging or direct marketing on a favorite website. The type depends on the level of relationship the company has with its customers. Current users have already shown an affinity for the brand. Some current users may be high maintenance, but most will be worth trying to keep satisfied.

In contrast, it is more challenging to identify, obtain information on, and woo customers who are currently using a competitor's brand or who aren't even purchasers in the category altogether. The first group asks: Why should I switch, why is your brand better than what I'm familiar with and relatively happy with? The second groups asks: Why do I want to buy this at all? In addition, when given the choice, customers vary in their preferred means of contact and access—shopping online or through catalogs or at the malls.

Within the current or competitor's user groups, there also exist variations on the extent of loyalty or of the ease with which customers may be lost and gained, as well as frequency of usage, which can have impact not only on revenues but also on logistics costs. You've heard of 80:20, meaning 80% (or so) of your sales come from 20% (or so) of your customers. You've also heard the rules of thumb about how "It costs six times more to

Social Media Segments

Forrester has found 7 segments of social media users:

1. Creators produce lots of media for everyone to see—posting blogs, or uploading videos, sharing lots of online content.
2. Conversationalists update their status on social networking sites and are heavy users of Twitter.
3. Critics respond to others' postings, write product reviews, may contribute to wikis.
4. Collectors gather and organize info for themselves and ship it out to others, e.g., via RSS feeds.
5. Joiners are active members of multiple social networking websites.
6. Spectators read blogs, watch others' videos, read others' product reviews and ratings.
7. Inactives are just not into it.

acquire a new customer, compared with retaining a loyal customer." Thus, these behavioral tendencies—frequency, loyalty, etc.—are worth knowing, so we'd like to be able to identify frequent users.

Marketers also study patterns of co-purchasing; skis, for example, are purchased or rented with boots, snowsuits, lift tickets, hotel rooms, and spiked cocoa. An increasingly popular means of using co-purchasing patterns to generate cross-selling suggestions are Internet recommendation agents. Providers like Amazon examine what you've bought (and clicked on to view), and they make suggestions by comparing your data with what other customers have bought. For example, given that many customers buy mysteries by two writers, Whodunnit and Thebutler, then, when you buy a book by one, you'll be recommended a book by the other.

3-3e B2B

While we have been focusing on categories of segmentation data that are particularly useful for consumers, marketers segmenting their business clients most frequently use size. Size can be defined in a number of ways: company sales, market share, number of employees, client's share of provider's business, etc. Businesses plan for, and interact differently with, their larger clients than with their smaller ones. They assign more client service personnel and extend more relationship management efforts because the big customers are worth it; larger clients tend to be profitable ones.

Segments can be formed from any kind of data, from age to Zip code.

However, size does not always correlate with future growth potential or with costs associated with high-maintenance clients, who might not be worth retaining regardless of the size of their orders. So, as shown in Figure 3.4, there are other bases for segmenting business customers. Note the close analogies with the consumer concepts.

The primary distinction between segmenting businesses and consumers is that the data sources tend to be different. There aren't scanner data prevalent for businesses, for example. On the other hand, the number of businesses who comprise one's customer base will be far fewer than the potentially millions of consumers. In addition, there tends to be good corporate knowledge about business customers, in part because such transactions typically rely on a sales force, so there is a knowledgeable front-line interacting with the business customer.

Figure 3.4	Segmenting Consumers	Segmenting Businesses
Segmenting Consumers & Business	• *Demographic* (e.g., age, gender, income and education, household life cycle, #kids, marital status)	• *Demographic* (e.g., company size, NAICS industry, account size)
	• *Geographic bases* (e.g., country, area (e.g., northeast, vs. Southern CA) climate, market size)	• *Geographic bases* (e.g., country, sales force coverage)
	• *Behavior* (e.g., *media (magazines,* cable, online, movies), loyalty programs, purchase frequency)	• *Type of firm* (e.g., architects bidding for government (conservative projects, slow to pay, but big), retailer (aesthetics important, manufacturers (efficiency is important), etc.
	• *Attitudes* (e.g., awareness, involvement, price sensitivity, risk tolerance, convenience, prestige)	• *Attitudes* (e.g., price sensitivity, risk tolerance, corporate culture, profitability, high vs. low "maintenance" accounts)

Of course, companies could do a better job of systematizing the sales force knowledge, which would provide a clearer database for segmentation studies and other purposes.

3-3f Concept in Action: Segmentation Variables

Chapter 15 describes cluster analysis, the technique used to form segments once the marketer has these demographic, geographic, psychographic or behavioral variables. Here is an example from the automobile insurance industry. The industry is huge and competitive, so it's not surprising that companies turn to segmentation to get an edge.

This particular company began with survey data on its customers. The first analytical question is to find survey questions that can detect variability in how respondents think about an issue. If there is none, that would say that the customers are homogeneous in their perceptions, which in turn would indicate that that variable would not be useful in the segmentation. Remember, splitting customers into segments requires some differences across groups.

For example, Figure 3.5 shows simple results on two survey items. The question at the left indicates that most customers like the convenience of consolidating with a single company as their source of insurance for their home and car. While that information is interesting, it is not useful for segmenting because most of the customers are in agreement.

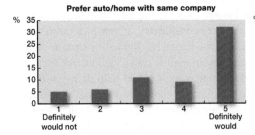
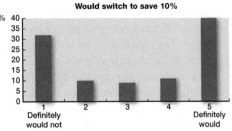

Figure 3.5

Insurance: Looking for Segmentation Variables

Geek Alert! Cluster Analysis

How do I find segments? Marketers and consultants use cluster analysis. Clustering models identify groups of customers who are similar to each other, and customers in one cluster are different from those in another cluster, or segment.

- B2B customers are usually segmented by volume, price sensitivity, and geography.
- B2C customers are segmented using data on demographics, attitudes, and transactions.
    - E.g., Pepsi offers Pepsi, Diet Pepsi, Caffeine Free Pepsi, Mountain Dew, and Aquafina, all for different consumer needs.
    - E.g., cruise ship operators offer different trips to satisfy different customer segments looking for uniqueness, low price, or a lot of programming for children.

Marketers label their segments (e.g., "green" or "price sensitive") to help personify the segments, to facilitate the choice of whom to target, and to develop ad content.

Marketers also verify that clusters that appear to be different on attributes such as age, income, price sensitivity, etc. truly (statistically) are different; if not, the groups are combined.

In contrast, the survey question about the discount (on the right) shows much greater promise as a variable that would help distinguish segments. These data indicate that there are two groups: one who would switch to save a mere 10% (the price sensitives) and one who would not (the brand loyals or the inertias). This variable would be included in the company's segmentation analysis.

3-4 HOW DO MARKETERS SEGMENT THE MARKET?

Marketers identify segments best when iterating between two approaches—a managerial, top-down ideation and a customer-based, bottom-up customer needs assessment. Marketers begin with some knowledge base about the marketplace: the customers, competitors, and the company's own strengths. Then they can gather information to understand the customer perspective.

Knowledge of the marketplace will clearly also enter into the decision as to which of the segments the company should eventually target. A market segment may look desirable in terms of its size and even future growth potential, but it may already be saturated with offerings by other competitors. There may be richer potential opportunities in other segments. The managerial perspective is also clearly important in terms of assessing the extent to which the servicing of a segment is consistent with corporate goals.

As an example of the required integration between the managerial and customer perspectives in formulating segments, consider the service industry of personal investment advisors. These professionals know that their client base may be divided by certain demographic variables such as income level, as well as psychological traits such as risk aversion. They can obtain geographic data as a proxy for income, which would help them conduct a cost-effective direct mailing to ZIP Codes that are known to be proportionally wealthier. Upon identifying sales prospects, the financial advisor can send the potential client surveys to measure their comfort level with risk. The advisor is using extant knowledge and data (e.g., about income and ZIP Codes) in a manner to prime more favorable responses, also complementing this knowledge with personal evaluations (e.g., comfort with risk) to know which financial products might seem most appealing to the client.

The iteration between the managerial and customer perspectives is also important because sometimes a marketing manager might hold beliefs that are not consistent with the customer data. For example, say a marketer for a London theater production company believes that some customer behavior such as income is predictive of the behavior of interest, i.e., the purchase of theater subscriptions. That belief might be based on years of anecdotal data (listening to friends, overhearing transit conversations, etc.). But those anecdotes are not systematically gathered data and probably do not represent an unbiased selection of customers. Thus, the marketer's beliefs would need to be reconsidered when confronted with real, better data that in fact the correlation between income and theatergoing isn't that strong. Empirically, arts-related behaviors (such as the frequency of museum attendance) are better predictors of who belongs to the theatergoer segment.

3-4a How to Evaluate the Segmentation Scheme

The iteration between marketing managers' good sense and the customer-based data continues when evaluating potential segmentation scenarios. A set of segments may be very clear from a statistical perspective, but they need to be useful from the managerial point of view. So the question is: How do you know a good marketing segmentation when you see one?

Data to Identify Segments. If one element of an iterative segmentation is a smart marketer, the other element is good customer data. Are data available of the sort you'd like to identify the customer segments? For example, census data are always available, but they might not be stored in refined categories, and so they prove too rough to be useful. Commercial data, such as Prizm or VALS data, are available, at a cost, and if you have a large budget, you're fine. But if you're an entrepreneur, you might need to approximate their results on your shoestring budget. If you're seeking surveys of very specific topics, such as consumer reactions to electronics, the data may be trickier to locate.

Databases to Access Segments. A related question is whether databases are available that identify potential customers because, after you identify segments, you'll want to access the customers in the target segments. For example, if you want to communicate to people who own homes in New York and Palm Beach, how will you do so? Are there listings of such people? Will you have access? Could you find indirect access, by advertising in the in-flight magazines for airliners carrying passengers between those cities or by sponsoring promotions with the two cities' rental car, limo, and taxi agencies?

Profitability Matters. Most marketers are curious about the relative sizes of the identified segments, but it's not size that matters so much as how profitable the segment is or is likely to be. Segment size is just numbers of customers, but profitability is smarter information: How frequently do the customers purchase? How large (in terms of money) is their purchase? How price (in)sensitive are they? How stable is the segment? What is its growth potential? Together, the numbers and profits information can be used to project the value of approaching any of the segments. Sometimes small segments can be highly profitable if the marketer pays attention and satisfies those customers' needs—the essence of niche marketing.

Sometimes segments appear small only because the clustering was done too finely. If you're working with too many segments, you'll know it because, when you try to describe

Wholefoods, grocery shopping for the upscale, discerning segment.

akatz/Shutterstock.com

Anatomy of a Market Segment

Starting point: U.S. population is 320 million

Cut #1: Of the U.S. driving-age population (16 years old & up), 210 million have a driver's license (i.e., 66%).

Cut #2: To date, there is still little interest in EVs (electric vehicles), due to price, concerns of range, reliability, performance and power. Only about 5% of consumers are interested. Now, down to 10.5 million (still could make a buck!)

Cut #3: Most EVs are priced around 26-32k. Teslas's at 125. %population with incomes > $100k is 20%, thus now at 2.1 million (again, still could make a buck!)

Tesla might want to advertise to all U.S. consumers, but it would be wiser (and result in better ROI) to focus on the segment of customers who would be interested in an EV and who could afford to buy one of theirs.

each segment, their descriptions are blurred. For example, suppose Segment A is a young guy, who cares about video games and cars but not about fashion. Say Segment B is all that but he cares marginally more about clothes. Are you working with distinct segments or with minor variants on a theme? If you're Saks Fifth Avenue, you'd keep the groups distinct; if you're Nintendo, you'd assume the groups were similar for your purposes and you'd combine the segments into one.

Fit with Corporate Goals. An upscale customer segment always seems attractive, but if your marketplace image is that of a store with EDLP (everyday low prices), you'd confuse existing customers if you tried to appeal to a them with new high-end products. Further, new high-end customers might not pay attention to your ads because, to date, your offerings hadn't been relevant to them.

Another strategic question regarding segment selection has to do with the strength of competition devoted to that same segment. The ideal goal for the marketer is to find an untapped (or underserved) group of customers whose needs can be met easily and profitably. But if other companies have beaten you to that group, or if they could easily redirect their efforts after watching your success, the market share for that segment gets divided, effectively reducing its size and profitability.

Actionable. Lots of segmentation schemes fail because marketers focus on the wrong criteria. Specifically, the statistics and clusters might be crystal clear (e.g., four clear clusters of customers), and even the interpretation and managerial meaning might be clear (e.g., one segment in particular seems to be a great fit). However, the segmentation is useless if the marketer is at a loss as to how to put it into action.

For example, customers' psychological profiles are extremely important to understanding their basic needs, wants, and motives in order to shape an appealing market offering. While attitudes help the marketer understand the why of the customer, the marketer needs demographic information also to understand the "who" and "where" of the customer. The "who" information helps advertising creatives depict the target in ads (e.g., matching gender, age, income level), and the "where" helps inform the design of the channel structure (e.g., where the customers live and shop and where we can advertise). A good segmentation scheme should come alive—you should be able to imagine a customer in your target segment, know what they look like, and know what they'd like to talk about.

It's not unusual to see a segmentation study comprised of some usage variable (e.g., heavy vs. light users) or some attitudinal variable (e.g., positively inclined toward our brand vs. being loyal to a competitor) in a cross-tab with some demographic variable (e.g., gender or age in some breakdowns like the census: 18–25, 26–45, 46–65, etc.). While the behavior usage or attitude information is the most relevant information, the demographics help marketers take action (e.g., select media for ads). The hope is to find relationships among these variables—that men tend to like our brand, or the middle-agers tend to be loyal to a competitor, etc. Then the variables of gender or age become our workable proxies for the attitudinal variables that we really want.

We'll close with a preview of what marketers do with segments. Figure 3.6 depicts several segments identified in a marketplace. Figure 3.7 illustrates a company that is trying to reach more than one segment with its product. Figure 3.8 illustrates a strategy whereby a company has decided they want to be everything to a particular segment, serving those customers very well. Figure 3.9 depicts a strategy of customizing the market offerings, creating different products for different segments. Any of these strategies can be smart and sustainable, depending on the company's strengths and the marketplace environment (e.g., competitors).

Finally, consider the topic of business expansion (see Figure 3.10). If you currently market primarily to women between roughly 25 and 55 years of age by placing ads in women's magazines, but sales are flat, in which direction would you expand your business? Would you advertise via multiple media outlets to the same segment of women? Would you try to shape the product and imagery to be compatible with men's goals? Would you try to extend your market base by age, appealing to consumers who are younger or older than your current purchasers? Clearly, profitability analyses and questions of corporate fit must be addressed, and these issues are clarified by a good, basic understanding of the segmentation structure of the marketplace.

Figure 3.6

Segments in the Marketplace

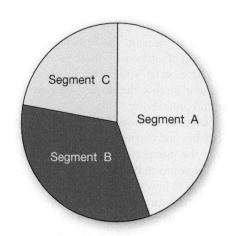

Figure 3.7

Breadth Strategy: Reaching Multiple Segments

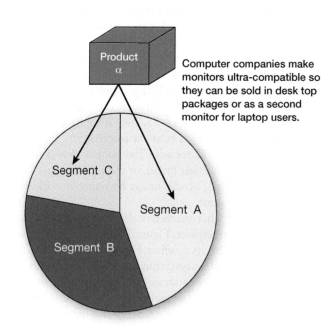

Computer companies make monitors ultra-compatible so they can be sold in desk top packages or as a second monitor for laptop users.

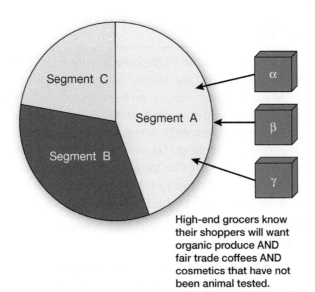

Figure 3.8

Depth Strategy: Serving One Segment Well

High-end grocers know their shoppers will want organic produce AND fair trade coffees AND cosmetics that have not been animal tested.

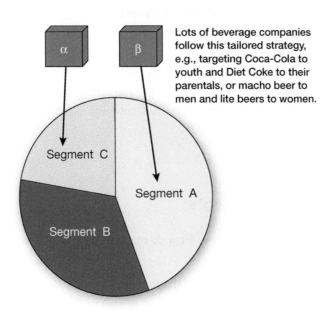

Lots of beverage companies follow this tailored strategy, e.g., targeting Coca-Cola to youth and Diet Coke to their parentals, or macho beer to men and lite beers to women.

Figure 3.9

Tailored Strategy: Customizing for Segments

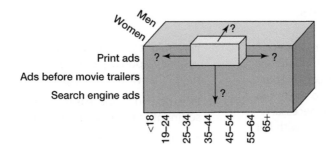

Figure 3.10

Serving a Segment and Branching Out

MANAGERIAL RECAP

Unlike the claim by Gordon Gecko, the Michael Douglas character in the movie *Wall Street*, greed is not good. It's not just a value judgment; it's not good business.[3] Rather than trying to capture the entire market, the smart marketer—the smart company—will segment the market and selectively target groups.

Segments don't have to be huge, but they must be profitable. Otherwise, we would just fold the group in with another segment and offer the same product to both groups. The marketer must be able to identify the segment; hence the reliance on demographic and behavioral data in addition to data on attitudes and purchase intentions. Segments must also be accessible, that is, there must be some media that will reach them, hopefully in a cost-efficient manner. Last but not least, the segments selected for targeting must match the soul of the company—its position in the marketplace and its marketing and production capabilities.

- Marketers create segments because customers vary in their preferences, and it is usually impossible to please all customers with one product.

- Market segments are groups of customers with similar reactions to the company's brand.

- Segments can be formed on nearly any kind of differentiating information, e.g., demographics, geographics, psychological attitudes, and marketplace behaviors.

- Segments are best created iterating between the managerial understanding of the marketplace and good data that may be processed (e.g., via cluster analysis) to identify similarities in purchasing propensities.

- The resulting segmentation scheme should be one based on data, sustained by a database to help access the customers, profitable enough to serve, sensible with respect to the larger corporate goals and planning, and finally implementable.

Chapter Outline in Key Terms and Concepts

1. Why segment?
2. What are market segments?
3. What information serves as bases for segmentation?
4. How do marketers segment the market?
   a. How to evaluate the segmentation scheme
5. Managerial recap

Chapter Discussion Questions

1. Say you've got a friend who is an entrepreneur. She's making the best software, wine, or whatever, that the world has ever seen. She is certain that everyone will like her new product, so she thinks your idea about segmentation is not necessary. How can you convince her and help her with her business?

2. What variables would be useful to segment visitors to your city's public aquarium?

3. How might you obtain data to segment visitors to your city's public parks, by day of week and time of day? What would you expect to find?

4. Who do you suppose is the ideal customer segment to target for donations to:
   a. American Cancer Society?
   b. Your university?
   c. World Relief Fund?

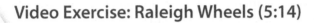

Video Exercise: Raleigh Wheels (5:14)

Founded in 1887 in Nottingham, England, Raleigh Wheels became known as the original all-steel bicycle manufacturer. Eventually, ownership of a Raleigh bike became a status symbol. Raleigh's product development has been significantly influenced by trends in the European market where biking had long been a lifestyle choice. Then, in the past 10 to 15 years, technological advances have fueled bikers' desires for equipment that is lighter, faster, and better. All companies in the industry, including Raleigh, began incorporating these technological advances into their products. Sensing that it was getting lost as a company, Raleigh returned to what customers really expected. It returned to its roots as a steel bike producer for customers who are committed to bikes and biking as a lifestyle choice. Part of this impetus for returning to the all-steel bike came from the desire for messenger-style bikes by customers of Raleigh America. Customers who pursue biking as a lifestyle choice want durable equipment and a quality ride, both of which are provided by the all-steel bike. To ensure that Raleigh continues to satisfy its customers' wants and needs, Raleigh America's marketing manager constantly uses various venues to gather input from bike enthusiasts.

Video Discussion Questions

1. How can market segmentation be useful for producers of bicycles?
2. On what factors does Raleigh Wheels base its market segmentation?
3. How can Raleigh Wheels benefit from the market segment that it pursues?

MINI-CASE

Health Care Tourism

In the face of ever-rising health care costs, more people than ever before are looking for the best medical treatment at the best price, and they're willing to go anywhere in the world. Most of the businesses in this space are the health care providers themselves—hospitals, globally connected networks of specialty centers, etc. However, increasingly the hospitality industry is waking up to the opportunities that this type of travel may afford them. Several large hotel chains that already have an international presence are seeking medical business partners and airline partners to create packages that offer seamless service for health care tourists. The airline partnerships are nearly in place—these classes of entities have been cooperating together for decades. The medical alliances are trickier, because ultimately the medical service providers still care most about health care provision, and concerns regarding business are still relatively novel; e.g., they find it somewhat distasteful to be approached by a hotel chain to talk business.

Secondary data shed a clear light on the segments of customer-patients in this burgeoning world. There are essentially three groups of customers (not necessarily exclusive or exhaustive).

First, some people seek primarily relaxation and stress reduction. They travel to health spas, enjoy aromatherapy massages, and herbal and homeopathic treatments. They engage in yoga classes and they expect the resort's menu to be detoxifying.

A second group of health care travelers are getting elective surgery done and they want to recover away from their friends and family. These people are having face lifts, liposuction, breasts implants, etc.

The final class of traveler has relatively serious medical conditions that are fairly essential to their health. The procedures these folks are looking for range from joint replacements to cancer treatments to heart surgeries. The operations will require more extended hospitalization, and the primary motive of this segment of traveler is price reduction compared to home, even for those patient-customers with insurance.

Most of the hotel chains have access to this segmentation information. Some have not sought it out. Others have seen it but are not considering it, because they figure that their service, beginning with the hotel room itself, would be welcome by any of these travelers.

There's a hotelier based out of London that is considering using this segmentation information. Their competitors think they're nuts, and will be depriving themselves, by definition, of access to the other segments' business. The London firm, however, thinks the segmentation-based approach may be a good way to begin. The information would allow them to be more selective in their appeals, both to the end users (the patient-customers), but also in these still early stages of finding medical partners. They reason that as they gain access, experience, and credibility, the doors to other medical partners may open later.

Case Discussion Questions

1. Which kind of hotel manager do you agree with—the ones that do not wish to limit themselves given their business is good for all three segments of travelers, or the London firm and its approach? Why?

2. If you wish to follow the first strategy (all customers could benefit), what would your marketing communications be to the end-user patient-customer? If you followed the second strategy, what would your marketing communications look like?

3. If you were based in London, which countries would be the first you would approach to develop such relationships? If you were based in Paris, which countries would you approach for your network inclusion? If you were in Houston? Rio? Why?

TARGETING 4

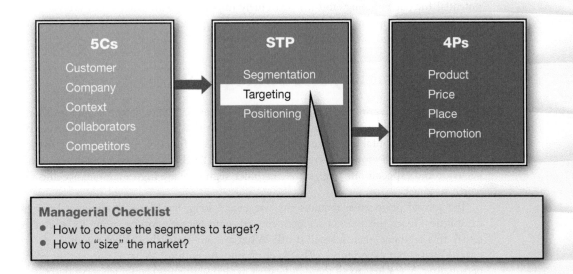

5Cs	STP	4Ps
Customer	Segmentation	Product
Company	**Targeting**	Price
Context	Positioning	Place
Collaborators		Promotion
Competitors		

Managerial Checklist
- How to choose the segments to target?
- How to "size" the market?

4-1 WHAT IS TARGETING AND WHY DO MARKETERS DO IT?

At this point, the segmentation scheme is based on customer variables that are both important (e.g., they're tied to psychological profiles of attitudes and brand preferences) and useful (e.g., demographics or media choices). We now proceed to targeting.[1]

The term "target" is drawn from a shooting or archery range metaphor, and it says, "We've got our customers in our sights. Now let's get them!" For readers who don't care for that metaphor, imagine instead that we have a set of binoculars, and when we get our target segment in our sights, we use a slingshot to softly lob cool products and great deals at the target.

The idea of targeting is selection. We have analyzed the marketplace, our competitors, and our internal strengths, and we can see that they align better with some segments than with others. So we will try to serve the segments whose needs match our abilities to deliver, and, in doing so, we hope to make very happy, very loyal customers who will be very profitable for us.

We target for the same reasons that we segment: It's foolhardy to try to be all things to all people. Most markets are not comprised of customers with identical tastes, thereby facilitating the identification of segments. The targeting question is this: Which of those segments do we want to be our customers?

> *Targeting: the selection of ideal customer segment(s).*

4-2 HOW DO WE CHOOSE A SEGMENT TO TARGET?

There are two perspectives in assessing the attractiveness of each segment in terms of its potential for our targeting, and it is extremely important to consider both. We will iterate between our top-down vision of corporate strategy and a bottom-up, data-informed approach on segment size and profitability.

4-2a Profitability and Strategic Fit

The first perspective in assessing segments to target is a view of the segments themselves, and the primary question is: How likely is it that the segment will be profitable (and just how profitable)? Potential profitability is a function of the current market size, its anticipated growth, current and anticipated levels of competition, and customer behavior and expectations (e.g., some customer segments are high maintenance and not worth serving).

The second perspective requires that we take a long, hard look at our own business capabilities: Does this market segment fit with who we are? Are we going to be able to satisfy this segment—can we pull it off? What are our strengths? What resources do we have? What is our experience? What is our corporate culture? What is our current brand personality? According to all these indicators, which segment(s) could we serve best?

Figure 4.1 captures the possibilities. In the upper left, if a market segment looks attractive and if serving that segment fits our corporate abilities, the pronouncement is a simple, "Go for it!" For example, suppose we manufacture athletic clothing. We learn that corporate volleyball teams are growing in popularity, and they need team shirts with their logos. We can do that and likely be successful.

Figure 4.1

Strategic Criteria for Targeting Segments

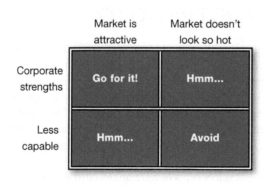

In the lower right, if a segment doesn't look promising and it doesn't fit naturally with us anyway, we let the "opportunity" go. For example, e-books are taking off, but with varied platforms. There are still uncertainties ahead. Furthermore, even if our company manufactures PCs, we may not have any particular advantage with e-book technology or distribution. So let's not bother.

Those two cells in the matrix are the no-brainer choices (go/no-go). Now things get more complicated.

In the lower left quadrant, the scenario is that the market looks sweet, but we're not particularly capable (e.g., video games are profitable and growing like crazy, but we produce thumb drives). A key question would be whether we can develop sufficient capabilities (e.g., hire teenage boys to do programming and pay them in thumb drives). Depending on how far the newly-required capabilities are from our current in-house expertise, taking this path could mean a huge investment of time and money. Maybe that's an investment we wish to make. If we're private or have patient shareholders, we may have the time to develop new skills (e.g., hire new people, create new channels, do whatever it takes). Or maybe it's an investment we'll have to make if some trend suggests that the segment is growing.

Finally, in the upper right quadrant, there is another dilemma scenario: What if the market doesn't look so great, but we are awesome at creating products of this sort? The key question in this case is whether we can develop a market. Can we get a segment to understand the benefits of what we provide? This strategy would also require investing, but in different things: in marketing research to understand the customer's level of knowledge and points of resistance, in possible product modifications to make it more appealing, and in advertising to educate the customer about our stupendous products.

We will have more to say about corporate fit in Chapter 16 on marketing strategy. For the moment, a simple, popular framework for trying to objectively assess one's own corporate strengths is the SWOT analysis, depicted in Figure 4.2. SWOT stands for strengths, weaknesses, opportunities, and threats. With the S and W, we're characterizing the company: What are our strengths and weaknesses? With the O and T, we're characterizing the broader environment (e.g., industry, suppliers, government, etc.): What are the opportunities and threats? S and W are considerations internal to the organization; O and T are external.

	Favorable	Unfavorable
Internal (corporate)	Strengths	Weaknesses
External (environment)	Opportunities	Threats

Figure 4.2
SWOT: Strengths, Weaknesses, Opportunities, and Threats

SWOTs are useful in clarifying just about any marketing question. In such an analysis, we can declare our strengths and weaknesses relative to our competitors, but our opinion doesn't matter as much as that of the customer base. Hence, we'd obtain some marketing research data, such as the perceptual maps described in the following section. If our brands, product lines, and company have perceived weaknesses in areas that customers care about, we should be motivated to make changes to address those shortcomings. If our brands and products have perceived strengths, we will consider what we can do to ensure that these will be sustainable competitive advantages, and we'll advertise them like crazy.

Opportunities and threats are usually driven by changes in one of the 5Cs: The economic or environmental context might be changing, a supplier might be morphing into a competitor, a competitor might be offering extended services that are desired by our customers, etc. Whether any of these shifts is perceived as a threat or opportunity depends a bit on corporate philosophy: Is the glass half empty or half full? Are we nimble enough to respond and react, thus seeing the changes on the horizon as opportunities? Or are we bureaucratic or not very creative, reacting pessimistically to the changes as threats?

" **S**trengths
Weaknesses
Opportunities
Threats "

We will return to SWOTs, particularly when considering marketing strategy. In the following section, we begin to see how the relative strengths and weaknesses may be determined, as seen through the customer lens.

4-2b Competitive Comparisons

A company can try to assess its corporate strengths in terms of absolute measures. However, relative comparisons to its competitors may be more relevant. After all, customers make purchase choices based on comparing brands.

Figure 4.3 is an example of such a comparative analysis, called a "perceptual map." This map shows customers' perceptions of our strengths (and weaknesses) vis-à-vis our competitors'. The two dimensions of quality and price might look generic or abstract, but indeed most attributes and benefits in many product categories can be whittled down to these two. Price is self-explanatory. The important thing to remember about quality is that the defining dimensions vary with the industry: For sporting goods stores, quality might mean huge variety at big box stores, or it could mean depth of category at stores that specialize in, say, camping equipment. For campus restaurants and bars, quality might be not only the food and drink but also the ambience—whether they draw the right crowds (i.e., others like oneself). For a suit for interviewing, quality could mean whether one feels like "a million bucks" wearing it. And so forth.

Figure 4.3

Competitive Analysis

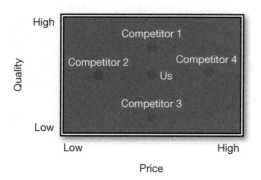

The market depicted in Figure 4.3 has good news and bad news. Our firm isn't seen as the worst provider or the most expensive. But neither are we seen as terrific in either aspect. Indeed, we are seen as relatively average on quality and on price. We dominate competitor 3 on quality and 4 on price. However, we too are dominated by competitor 1 on quality and by 2 on price.

What does this information gain us, with respect to targeting? If a segment we are considering as a target is price sensitive, we have to be especially wary that competitor 2 will react. They will be attuned to such a move in the marketplace because they own that price point identity. Given that price is their strength, they could and probably would react swiftly, and in all likelihood they would kick our, er, win that fight. Similarly, if we are considering targeting a segment that values quality, we would be more concerned with competitor 1 than with any other.

Figure 4.4 offers a different perspective to consider when selecting a segment to target. It compares segment profiles along various business parameters. These simple profiles enable us to assess the likely attractiveness of each segment. Segment 1 is not the largest existing market; segments 2 and 4 are bigger. But segment 1 growing the fastest, which makes the market exciting. Of course, growth can be a double-edged sword. Although few competitors exist at the moment, should the market grow big enough, it will attract more. Yet the fit

Characteristics:

	Size	Growth	Competitors	Fit	Priority?
Segment 1	$1 mm	5%	Few	Yes	★
Segment 2	$2 mm	3%	1 big	OK	?
Segment 3	$1 mm	3%	Few, weak	OK	?
Segment 4	$2 mm	1%	Few, weak	No	

Figure 4.4

Strategic Segment Comparison

Have a Heart

Unfortunately, there's a rotten form of targeting that unethical marketers have used … The accusations are that marketers have pitched:

- sugary cereals and junk food to kids,
- cigarettes and alcohol to ethnic minorities,
- confusing and exploitative financial instruments to the elderly, and
- marked-up goods and services to socioeconomically disadvantaged groups,
- while not marketing certain services (e.g., in health care) to segments that would likely be unprofitable (e.g., the elderly, people with certain chronic conditions).

Ethical marketers are supposed to consider whether any harm is likely to a particular at-risk or vulnerable segment, and if so, the segment should not be targeted. The good news is that while some people and companies are indeed icky, most are pretty amazing.

is the best with who we are. So even if more competitors enter the marketplace, we should be able to take them on because we know we can serve this segment well.

Segment 2 has possibilities. It looks attractive because it is a big market, and it's growing reasonably quickly. Yet two issues give us pause: The one dominant competitor may be daunting, and it's not our best corporate fit.

Segment 3 has its strengths. It has few competitors, and those that exist, we could likely dominate. But it has its weaknesses too: It's not a huge market, it's not growing the fastest, and ultimately it's also not a great fit with our corporate abilities.

Segment 4 is one we can pass on with few regrets. It's the smallest and slowest growing. Regardless of competition, we wouldn't know what to do in that market anyway.

In sum, segment 1 should be our priority. If segment 1 is sufficient in size for our goals, we're good. But if segment 1 is too small, we might consider expanding our targeting of segment 1 to include either or both of segments 2 and 3 down the road. We could roll out and target the segments sequentially, after we've spent the resources to reach and penetrate segment 1 and if we can produce a consistent market offering and communication to additional segments without putting off customers in segment 1.

We began this section by saying that the choice of a target segment involves information about both the size of the market and the fit with corporate goals. In many ways, the second is the more challenging; i.e., it's easy to get swept away by a big segment, making us think we should serve it, when in fact we may have no particular strengths to guarantee we can serve it well. So we need to say no. Ultimately that assessment is conceptual: Who are we as a firm? Who do we want to be? The other piece of information, however—the size of a market segment—is something we can estimate, as we'll do next.

4-3   SIZING MARKETS

In Figure 4.4, segments were described in terms of market size and likely growth rate. The inquiring marketer is no doubt wondering how to derive such characterizations. We turn now to consider sizing markets, and then we'll discuss projecting growth rates.

We'll walk through a couple of scenarios of creating estimates so that you get the logic. You'll see that some of the inputs into these estimates will be numbers you're confident about. For the numbers you're less confident about, you'll want to have a rough interval and probably do some what-if scenarios, varying those numbers, seeing how sensitive the ultimate projections are, and what are the likely upper and lower bounds on your predictions. A lot of estimates go into the final calculation, so each component needs to be as precise as possible. Otherwise, the errors in the estimation just get compounded. One helpful factor to consider is that the more precisely defined the target market is, the easier the numbers are to estimate.

We'll look at an example of estimating the size of a market in the context of selling *Personal Brander* services to busy professionals. These people offer a variety of consultative skills, depending on the professional careerist's needs, from help with public speaking, to crafting a self-brand statement, overseeing social media for tasteful self-promotion, even use as sounding boards to reflect on various actions and comments observed and received in the workplace. After this example, we'll consider more generally the kinds of factors that you'd include for estimating your particular product-segment market size.

Targeting Yogis

A cataloger known for its environmentally friendly goods and body-soul philosophy was considering adding yoga clothes to its line. Data on the fitness lines in the apparel industry suggest customers may be segmented into the following categories. The relative size of the segments follows:

- 30% college students
- 20% stay-at-home moms
- 20% introverts
- 15% post-cardiac men
- 10% women 20-30
- 5% men 20-30

A consultant told them to "follow the money," meaning, go after the three biggest segments to capture the majority of the market: college students, stay-at-home moms, and introverts. The cataloger's CMO agreed in spirit with "follow the money," but supplemented information on segment size with profitability estimates and likely segment growth rates. They went after the post-cardiac men: small in number but easy to find, devoted in following, and plenty of cash. The cataloger hasn't looked back. Cha-ching!

Anatomy of a Market Segment

American male

~60% married

Growing and peak earning years (35–55 years old)

US population is 309,000,000, men 35–55 is approximately 43,000,000 (~13.9% pop.)

Subscriptions to *Sports Illustrated;* picks up *Esquire, GQ, Men's Health* at the airport or online

DVRs and relaxes with *Mythbusters, Handyman, Dexter, The Simpsons, Deadliest Catch,* and *Stuff my Dad Says*

Watch by TAG Heuer, Citizen, or Omega

Infiniti sedan (parked in lot), has a Chevy Silverado or Ford F-350 at home, wants a Corvette

Shoes (below) by Hugo Boss, Kenneth Cole, or Nike

Suit by Ralph Lauren, Diesel, Calvin Klein, or Gucci

We know our target customer:
- What he's like
- What he likes
- And media we can use to reach him

4-3a Concept in Action: How Much of My Consultative Advice Can I Sell?

Consider the market of B-school grads making, and hoping to make, zillions. You have a friend who has served both as an eminently successful and respected CEO and who, subsequent to his early retirement, has been serving as a mentor to many others still active in the marketplace. His name is Boone, and he believes there's a mint to be made by selling such consultative services, especially as they help to promote and launch a young person's professional career, i.e., services of a "Personal Brander." So you are trying to help him determine, "What's a mint?" You're going to help him *size* this market by estimating potential demand. Here's how.

A terrific online source of U.S. demographic data is Census.gov; there we can find the numbers or percentages of people (or businesses) in a variety of categories (e.g., by age, by income, by residence, etc.; see Factfinder.census.gov). Figure 4.5 captures the basic statistics; the U.S. census is currently estimated at about 309 mm, and the age brackets that your friend Boone believes to be most relevant (25 to 44 years old). The segment size by age is 26.6% of the population. The census data contain a number of further descriptors, some information might be relevant, some might not be (e.g., percentages by gender, marital status, home ownership, etc.).

Figure 4.5

Market Sizing

U.S. population = 309,000,000
By age:

- 25-29: 6.8%
- 30-34: 6.5%
- 35-39: 6.5%
- 40-44: 6.8%
Sum: 26.6%

So, market potential is:
309,000,000 people
$\times$ 26.6% age relevant
= 82,194,000
$\times$ 18% professionals
= 14,794,920

Vegas focus = 580,000 $\times$ 26.6% $\times$ 18% = 27,770
~ 28k potential customers

An initial cut on the data is to construe a chain of probabilities: 309 million citizens, 26.6% of whom begin to define the target market. That result is 82,194,000 people, but that number still includes people who don't have the education or likely career trajectories to find a Personal Brander useful (and of course, pay for the services). Together you and Boone decide to target the 18% of those age brackets whose employment is classified (at Census.gov) as "professional," high-end and potential managers and such. So, take the 82.2 mm figure, condition it on 18% professional career status, and call that the potential market. Crunch, crunch, crunch, and Boone's eyes pop—a market of almost 15 million Personal Brander buyers.

At first this obviously appears to be a huge cha-ching opportunity, but you take a deep breath and explain that the 15 mm figure is obviously a ceiling estimate (as if everyone would buy the services). Furthermore, as yet, nothing has been determined regarding costs, prices, or margins of such service provision. For example, presumably a menu of services would be offered from basic and minimal to deeper and more extensive, thus varying the service along quality and price dimensions to the customers, affecting profitability estimates.

As a next step, Boone considers that it might be best to start the service locally, in his hometown of Las Vegas. Given the attractiveness of Vegas as a destination, he is confident that he'll be able to draw people to him, once the program gets established. For now, he expects to draw on his network to find leads of potential customers as well as other mentors who can help fulfill the role of a Personal Brander. The last adjustment in Figure 4.5 is to focus on the Vegas market which yields a smaller local target estimate of almost 28 thousand potential customers.

Is this market potential big enough to be attractive? That's a subjective call, but the estimation process demonstrated the basic steps: Get all the data you can, make your assumptions clear, and think hard about segment differences. Some of the data inputs will seem like pretty good estimates (e.g., population size from Census.gov). For other data inputs, we may have less confidence in the numbers. If that's the case, it is worth doing some sensitivity analyses; take each numeric input, drive it up and redo the analysis, then drive it down and do the same. Doing these thought experiments provides two great results: First, it will help to identify the elements in the estimation that are important (because the outcomes change a lot when the elements are changed). As a result, these pieces should be estimated the most precisely. It may be worth it to pay for additional data to obtain greater accuracy on these values. Second, it will illuminate the upper and lower bounds of the overall market sizing, thus helping with planning.

Additional Factors We began this chapter by discussing a number of criteria that together make a market more or less attractive. This analysis is so far only about market size. We should also consider growth, and we could easily lift more data from Census.gov regarding the size of additional age cohorts, or job classifications, and obviously geographic expansion.

It's always a little risky to extrapolate and predict growth, but a smart technique would be to obtain sales data in this industry for the past three or four or 10 years and extrapolate through a moving average. A three-year moving average would take the data from years one, two, and three and compute a mean, take the data from years two, three, and four and compute a mean, take the data from years three, four, and five and compute a mean, etc. Then you'd fit a curve to these data (e.g., via regression). The idea is that including data on the surrounding years helps stabilize the estimates. If there's a weird year in the series somewhere, it doesn't unduly influence the prediction of the future.

A second issue is that we don't yet know the likely profitability of this market. We haven't addressed issues of pricing (we'll do so in Chapter 9), so we can put this discussion off for now. We can probably assume that the profitability, per customer, depends on their segment membership, but we don't know yet how to translate the numbers into $.

A factor that will enter into those profitability estimates derives from the quality of people hired to offer the consultation. Services are usually associated with more variable costs than goods. Fixed costs for selling goods as varied as cereals and laptops include a plant, some machines, a few employees, and so forth; the variable costs would include things like our suppliers' raw materials. In services such as retail, a fixed cost would be the shop, some equipment, and so forth, but many materials and the employees themselves would be variable costs because, as the retail service takes off, it would need a bigger staff.

A third issue that we'd be naïve not to consider is that, as yet, we have no information regarding competitors. One quick "analysis" would be to take a look at Yellowpages.com for Vegas or any other cities under consideration. If there are many comparable service

Get That Perpetual Surprised Look Now!

A U.S. medical group with a specialty in plastic surgery made the decision to focus on facelifts, reasoning that this particular service would be increasingly desired as baby-boomers aged. The professionals were excellent in their medical service, but not surprisingly less informed about business and marketing. They also didn't want to spend much money on any kind of advertising.

Looking at the medical group's records covering their last two years of service, these are the number of patients in each gender and age group.

	Men	Women
21-40:	1	15
41-60:	9	31
61-80:	1	3

The center avoids patients over 80, for health reasons (any surgery is riskier), and those under 21, for what they consider to be moral and ethical reasons.

The center chose to target the men, 41-60, arguing their profitability (greatest discretionary funds) and women, 61-80, arguing theirs was the growing boomer segment. Do you agree with their strategic choice of target segments?

providers, in a sense that's good news since obviously others think there's gold to be had; at that point, the question is whether a new business could break into such a mature market.

Back to market sizing. B2B sellers sometimes have it a little easier. The Census.gov site cross-classifies businesses by sector (e.g., NAICS codes) and by size (e.g., by sales or number of employees). If, say, you produced vans or small recreational vehicles, the industries to which you could sell would be limited only by your imagination: not just retirees or rental agencies, but mobile blood collections, mobile pet services, mobile haircuts, dentistry, piano lessons, whatever.

In any event, regardless of whether you're working B2B or B2C, the logic in market sizing estimation is always the same. We start with the total population and break it down into the proportions that are relevant.

A very general way marketers have approached this analysis is by estimating the purchase decision-making process: the elements of awareness, trial, repeat, etc. For example, the first cut would be to take the total population, multiply it by the percentage of the customers who are aware of our brand, and compute:

$$\text{Population} \times \%\text{aware}$$

Next, ask what proportion of customers have tried our brand? Then ask how are we doing with regard to repeat purchasers? So far, this logic looks like the following string of proportions:

$$\text{Population} \times \%\text{aware} \times \%\text{trial} \times \%\text{repeat}$$

We could drill down further by asking: How much does each customer tend to buy and when do they buy? Then our analysis resembles the following equation:

$$(\text{population} \times \%\text{aware} \times \%\text{trial} \times \%\text{repeat}) \times \text{Per annum purchase}$$

Translating this per customer annual consumption into dollars is easy; just multiply the number by the average retail price paid.

Market sizing isn't difficult. Good demographic data exist for consumers and businesses, for the U.S. and increasingly for international markets. The final probability estimates in these examples indeed require additional information, e.g., industry knowledge or data that may be obtained from surveying customers for their opinions.

Determining which segments to target depends on an interplay of two factors: (1) quantitative issues, such as size of segment, profitability, and growth, and (2) strategic issues, primarily having to do with the fit of the segment's needs to corporate philosophy and intended positioning. We have focused on target sizing in this chapter. Profitability is a topic covered in Chapter 14 (on customer satisfaction and loyalty).

Source: Molson Canada

Who is the target market?

MANAGERIAL RECAP

Targeting is important but not difficult.

- Choosing the market segment(s) to serve involves iterating between understanding corporate fit and having information about segment size and likely profitability.

  - To help clarify corporate fit, marketers find SWOT analyses helpful. Ask of your company: What are our strengths and weaknesses? Ask of of the industry in general: What are the opportunities and threats?

  - Segment sizing is relatively straightforward. Many secondary data help get the probabilities started (e.g., demographics at the B2B or B2C levels). Customer survey data on attitudes and preferences and behavioral data (past purchasing) can smooth out the remainder of the estimation.

Chapter Outline in Key Terms and Concepts

1. What is targeting, and why do marketers do it?
2. How do we choose a segment to target?
   a. Profitability and strategic fit
   b. Competitive comparisons

3. Sizing markets
   a. Concept in action: How many can I sell?
4. Managerial recap

Chapter Discussion Questions

1. This question gives you more market sizing practice (it's a skill you'll need). Using the logic from the chapter, try to estimate the possible market for the number of pairs of football pants a manufacturer could sell in your city. Hints:

   a. Go online and find the number of high schools in your city's school districts. If you live in a large city, focus on only the largest school district.

   b. Assume that 90% of those high schools have both a varsity football team (with 40 players) and a junior varsity team (35).

   c. Assume also that each player gets 2 pairs of game pants (one in the dark school colors, and one in the light), and on average, 1.5 pairs of white pants for practice.

2. Go to your b-school's home page. In the general information somewhere will be basic descriptive statistics on your student body demographics. Use that data to size the market for vending machines that dispense thumb drives, flavored coffees, and packets of no-doze. What other data would be helpful to increase the accuracy of your estimate?

MINI-CASE

GoodBite

GoodBite is interested in selling a new form of teeth-whitening strips. They dissolve in your mouth, and leave less of a gunky residue feeling than current competitors.

Whitening strips seem to appeal to people 20-29 years old. Competitors' data on existing strips suggest they appeal to women slightly more than men, but for the moment, GoodBite is not planning on differentiating on gender in the advertising. So, let's ignore gender and just consider that 20-29 year old age category.

Say the U.S. population is 301,000,000, with 41.1 million in the target age bracket. About 7.5 million people have tried competitors' whitening strips (GoodBite's aren't on the market yet), and roughly 3 million of them are semi-serious, frequent users.

GoodBite is trying to guesstimate the size of its target market, and its likely profitability. The GoodBite product is sold in packages of 14 sets of strips (each set is an upper and lower pair) in each box.

GoodBite isn't sure of the frequency with which a typical purchaser will buy a set yet, as the product category is still relatively new. However, they reason that an upper bound would be about 26 boxes bought by a consumer a year (52 weeks in the year, divided by the 2 weeks supply that is sold in each box). A more conservative estimate would halve that (13 boxes; roughly 1 bought each month). A more conservative estimate still would be that a customer buys "a few" (2 or 3) boxes a year.

GoodBite expects to charge $25 per box.

Case Discussion Questions

1. Should they launch GoodBites?

2. What assumptions were made that might be revisited?

POSITIONING 5

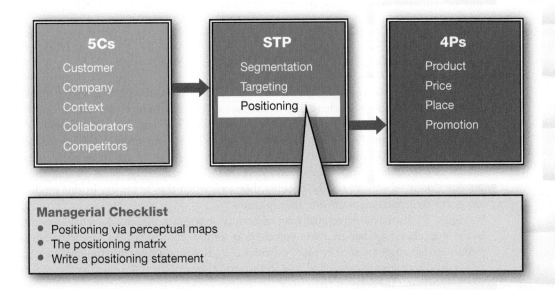

5Cs
Customer
Company
Context
Collaborators
Competitors

STP
Segmentation
Targeting
Positioning

4Ps
Product
Price
Place
Promotion

Managerial Checklist
- Positioning via perceptual maps
- The positioning matrix
- Write a positioning statement

5-1 WHAT IS POSITIONING AND WHY IS IT PROBABLY THE MOST IMPORTANT ASPECT OF MARKETING?

We know how important it is to segment the market and decide on a target; we've seen the S and T in STP.[1] In this chapter, we turn to positioning.

Positioning has many physical elements, but even more perceptual ones. It's about identity: who your brand or company is in the marketplace vis-à-vis the competition and in the eyes of the customer. Once you see who you are, you can determine who you want to be.

Positioning comprises much of a marketer's responsibilities. It requires:

- Designing a product with benefits that the target segment will value. How do you want your customers to think about your brand?

- Pricing your product so it's profitable, yet seen as valuable. How high a price can you command for your brand?

- Building distributor relationships to make the market offering available. Where do customers go to find your brand?

- Communicating all of this to the customer through an array of promotional activities—what do you say about your brand?

In other words, positioning involves all the marketing mix variables. This chapter kicks off the rest of the book. We'll discuss the concept of positioning in this chapter, and we'll see the details of the marketing mix activities in the chapters that follow.

We begin by discussing the concept of positioning via perceptual maps. We then see the positioning matrix, which will give us a framework in which to understand the marketing mix 4Ps (covered in subsequent chapters). We close with guidelines for writing a positioning statement.

5-1a Positioning via Perceptual Maps

They say a picture is worth a gigabyte of words. Marketers and senior managers like to see graphical depictions of where their brands are and where their competitors are, in the minds of their customers. These pictures help us envision how customers think about our brand and give us initial answers to many questions: What are our strengths and weaknesses? What are those of our competitors? Even though we think of certain companies and brands as our competitors, do customers view things the same way? Who do they think are our closest substitutes for the benefits they seek when they're buying in this product category? Perceptual maps provide these pictures.[2]

Figure 5.1 depicts a perceptual map of brands of watches. Brands depicted as points in the map close together are those perceived as similar (e.g., Seiko and Timex), whereas brands farther apart are seen as more different (e.g., Rolex and Swatch). The north-south, east-west directions are perceptual, and in this map they may be interpreted as the quality of the watch and the relative expense.

Figure 5.1 **Competition in Perceptual Maps**	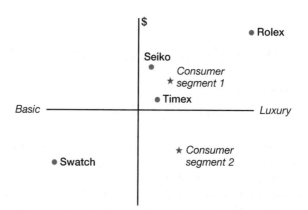

The brand managers and corporate headquarters of all of these firms would probably not be surprised by these results, in that they indicate that customers view a Seiko and a Timex as the most interchangeable, at least among this set of brands. In comparison, the Rolex and Swatch watches are not competing with each other. We also see information on customer segments. Segment 1 is situated near the Seiko-Timex group of brands, and these models would predict that one of these two brands would be the segment's first choice. The segment might not be loyal to one or the other, but either is preferred over the Rolex or Swatch.

Customer segment 2 is at the lower right, where there are few brands. Holes in perceptual maps offer intriguing possibilities for new market opportunities. In this case, we might not wish to pursue the opportunity: These customers seek luxury at inexpensive prices. Many companies would not find this position profitable or the image desirable. (It's hard to be convincing that one provides luxury at base prices.)

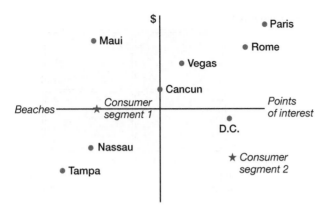

Figure 5.2

Positioning via Perceptual Maps

Figure 5.2 is a perceptual map of cities in which a large, global hotel company has resorts.[3] The company wants to know more about its customers' travel needs because they're trying to redesign some of their vacation packages. The dimensions equivalent to north-south/east-west are perceptions of whether the city is a relatively expensive or inexpensive place to visit, and whether the destinations allow investigations of cultural tourism and related activities, or serve primarily as a place to soak up sun and decompress.

This perceptual map tells us about the positioning of these cities vis-à-vis the dimensions of expense and activity. Paris and Rome are seen as places that have lots to see and do, but they're relatively expensive. Nassau and Tampa are perceived as beach trips that are relatively affordable.

Given that these maps capture perceptions, one question in the mind of a marketer is always: Is my brand optimally positioned? Or, is my intended position the one that customers perceive? For example, this hotel company had spent a lot of money on an advertising campaign trying to make potential travelers aware of the many cultural offerings of Nassau. That is, the company was trying to move the Nassau position farther to the right. It doesn't look like they were too persuasive.

The map also identifies two customer segments. This survey was conducted on the company's typical traveler, and the sample was obtained from visitors to all its hotels. That is, the perceptions are those of their current customers, not of their potential customers, who might belong to a different segment. The hotel is known for being "reasonable" in its rates, and so it tends to attract younger crowds who don't have quite the deep pockets of older travelers. As you might imagine, the hotel likes having a youthful appeal (or position!) but realizes that it's somewhat unfortunate that it's also drawing people with less money. Probably older, wealthier travelers would agree that Paris is more expensive than Tampa, but they could afford it and would travel there nevertheless. The hotel's repositioning might also consider an ad campaign that emphasized its reasonable rates even in destinations known to be more expensive.

The customer segments on the perceptual map offer another diagnostic to the company about what's going on in the marketplace. The first customer segment is very well served: They are looking for beaches and cheap trips, and the company has hotels in both Nassau and Tampa to cater to those tourists. The second customer segment, however, is seeking more to do on their holiday, yet still hoping for reasonable rates. The company has less to offer them, although perhaps they can play up Washington, D.C.

Figure 5.3 offers a different kind of perceptual map. It contains descriptors for a single service provider, a yoga studio. Patrons have rated the studio on a number of qualities: the convenience of the location, the variety of the morning classes it offers, and whether the staff is helpful, friendly, and trained to give helpful instructions. Customers have also

Figure 5.3

Perceptual
Map: Strengths
and Weak-
nesses of a
Yoga Studio

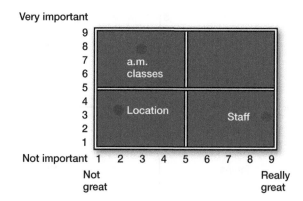

given their judgments on the importance of each of the qualities when choosing a yoga studio.

The figure tells us that the studio is not very conveniently located, but people don't seem to care about that attribute (so we won't get hurt too much for that). The staff is seen as a strength, but here, too, people don't seem to care (so we won't get bonus points for that). More problematic is that the number and variety of morning classes isn't huge (time and space are constrained of course), and that's rather important to the yogis.

This type of perceptual map may be modified for a competitive analysis, as in Figure 5.4. This figure allows us to determine the perceived strengths and weaknesses of our yoga studio (studio 1) compared with our competition (studios 2 and 3). This map is not great news. Studio 1 (that's us) is seen as relatively expensive or at least no better than studio 3, where studio 2 provides better value. Then, on the attribute of morning classes, both our competitors dominate us. Something's got to give, unless customers value some other attribute at which we excel and that's not represented in this plot. Part of the problem with the plot in Figure 5.4 is that we can only look at two attributes at a time, so we'd have to look at many plots.

Figure 5.4

Perceptual
Map:
Competition

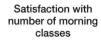
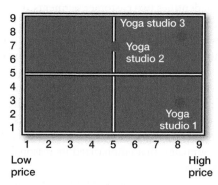

Figure 5.5 doesn't look like a map per se, but it's definitely still expressing the competitors' profiles of perceptual data. Here, more attributes may be presented with these three (or more) studios for comparative purposes.

5-1b The Positioning Matrix

Just as consumers are quite demanding, wanting the very best of everything (fast car, good mileage, great looks, and—oh by the way—low prices), companies can be equally irrational.

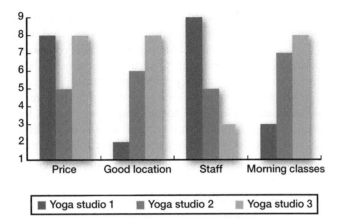

Figure 5.5

Competitor Analysis

When you read their propaganda—er—mission statements on their websites or in their annual reports, most companies say that they are the very best at everything, that their customers are their sole reason for existence, that their employees are the very best in the workforce, and all that. Well, customers can't have it all, and companies can't be great at everything.

So the question is: What do you want your position in the marketplace to be? The coolest brand? The brand that offers the best value? Either of these goals is achievable. But, at the same time, both are probably not. Let's look at the marketing 4Ps and see what makes sense.

In Figure 5.6, we see the juxtaposition of two marketing Ps: product and price. As a warning, we're going to make some simplifying assumptions for a while. First, let's say that we could choose a low vs. high pricing strategy. That's already a simplification, allowing no shades of gradation in between. Let's also say that the product may be characterized as having low vs. high quality, again with no compromise intermediate brand and no specific attributes of the product represented, just general quality levels.

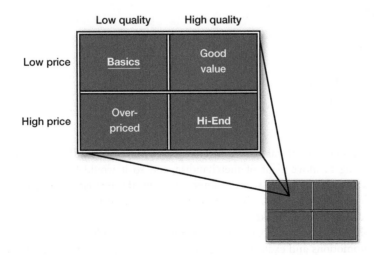

Figure 5.6

Marketing Management Framework Product Quality by Price

In the basic 2×2 matrix in Figure 5.6, we can see already that a match of low-low and high-high—that is, low or modest quality stuff but cheap vs. high-quality stuff at a higher price—makes sense.[4] Occasionally brands come along that offer high quality at low prices, and we would refer to these as good values. But with time, it's hard for a company to resist raising prices or letting quality settle a little lower due to cost-cutting measures. Conversely, occasionally brands come along that are priced high but are kind of junky. However, customers are no fools, and these kinds of brands don't last. The company needs to either adjust the price downward to be more competitive, improve the quality to be in sync with the price charged, or, even more frequently, just leave the marketplace.[5]

In Figure 5.7, we see an analogous 2×2 matrix for the other two marketing Ps: promotion and place (i.e., distribution). Here too, to keep things simple, let's say the most important decision on promotion is whether to spend a lot or only a little (i.e., heavy vs. light promotion), and the decision on channels is whether to distribute widely or more selectively. (We'll talk about all these Ps in detail in the chapters to come.)

Figure 5.7

Marketing Management Framework Promotion by Distribution

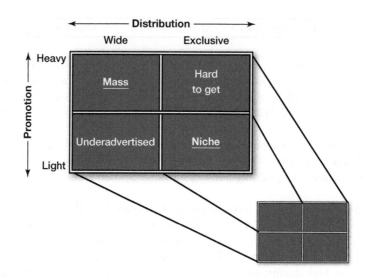

Position 1 of 2

- High price
- High quality
- Exclusive availability
- Light promotions

Figure 5.7 also has a natural match. If a company promotes broadly and heavily, they're probably looking to move a lot of merchandise, and so it would be smart to make the goods widely available. It would seem counterproductive if they made their goods available only through selective channels. Similarly, if a brand has a relatively exclusive image and distribution chain, it would make better sense not to overly promote it as if it were common, available to the masses. So, the heavy promotions and wide distribution pairing and the lighter promotions and exclusive distribution pairing make more sense than the other options.[6]

In Figure 5.8, we have all 16 combinations of our 4Ps. At this point, we can acknowledge that, sure, theoretically any combination is possible. You could provide high quality in exclusive channels and promote lightly and still charge cheap rates, but why would you? So let's see whether some other combinations are more or less sensible.

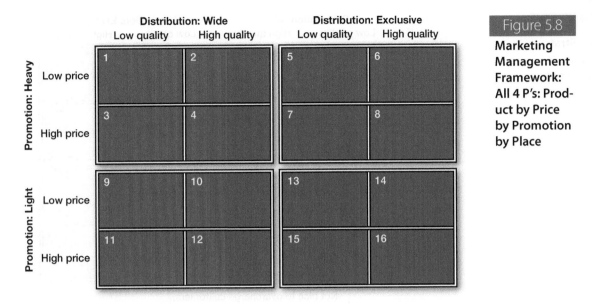

Figure 5.8

Marketing Management Framework: All 4 P's: Product by Price by Promotion by Place

Figure 5.9 suggests eliminating the low price and exclusive distribution combinations. Presumably, if a brand is priced low, the company needs to sell a lot of volume to make money. This characterization is an assumption, of course, because the company really needs to look at the profitability or margins. However, low prices indeed frequently go with low profitability; after all, you can eke out more profits from higher prices. There are exceptions, of course, but, as the old expression goes, the exceptions just prove the rule.

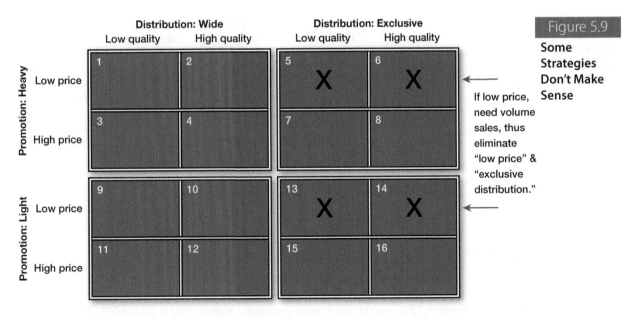

Figure 5.9

Some Strategies Don't Make Sense

Figure 5.10 indicates the elimination of the combinations that involve the high price and low quality strategies. It's disrespectful to your customers to overcharge them. For example, when *Consumer Reports* says of laptops that they're "stylish but expensive" with "undistinguished tech support and reliability," won't customers veer to other brands until that company feels the pressure to get its prices more in line?

Figure 5.10

Some Strategies Don't Make Sense

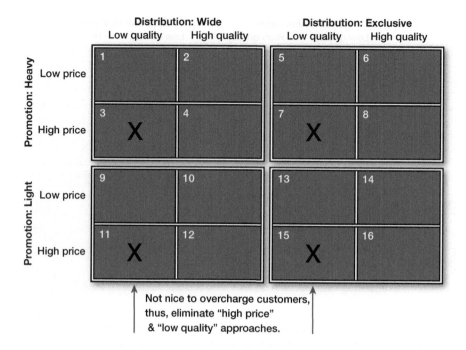

Figure 5.11 suggests that we eliminate the heavy-promotions and exclusive-distribution combinations. It would be exceedingly frustrating for customers to be tantalized constantly with messages to "Go buy our stuff!" and then not be able to find that stuff.

Figure 5.11

Some Strategies Don't Make Sense

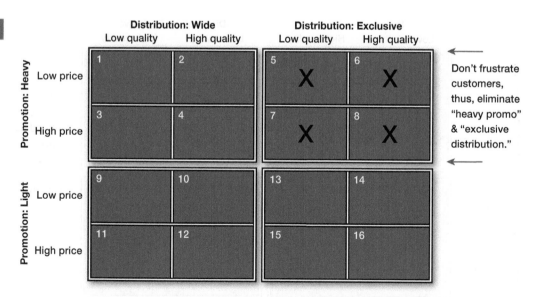

Figure 5.12 shows the good-value purchases: high quality at relatively low prices, a position that is hard to sustain. A company will be tempted to raise prices or let quality slip, settling back into an equilibrium on quality and price.

Similarly, Figure 5.13, shows wide distribution and light promotion, combinations that are rather inactive strategies. The brand is available, but, with light promotion, the company is paying the brand little attention. This strategy can be characteristic of mature brands that customers buy habitually—a cash cow being milked for money. However, with no attention

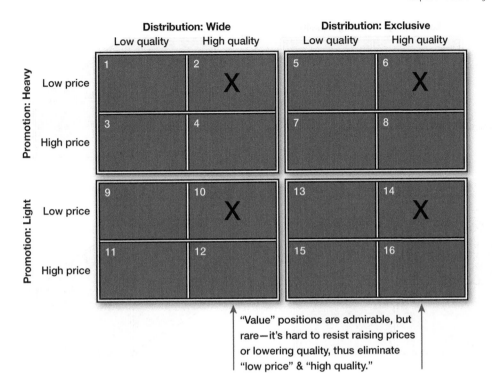

Figure 5.12

Some Strategies Are Hard to Sustain

"Value" positions are admirable, but rare—it's hard to resist raising prices or lowering quality, thus eliminate "low price" & "high quality."

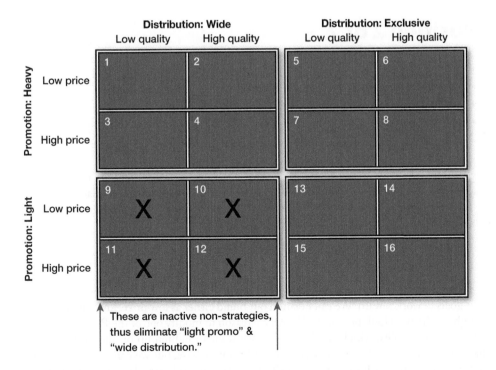

Figure 5.13

Some Strategies Are Hard to Sustain

These are inactive non-strategies, thus eliminate "light promo" & "wide distribution."

by the marketer and no investment to assure the brand's future existence, the brand will probably collapse eventually.

Figures 5.14 and 5.15 show how we can represent some of what we've learned so far. We don't often see overpriced or good value products. We more often see basics (low price,

Figure 5.14

Quality and Price Tend to Re-Align

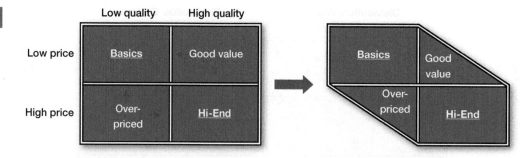

Figure 5.15

Promotion and Distribution Tend to Re-Align

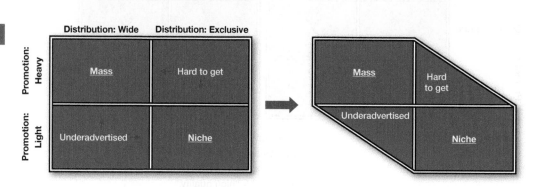

Position 2 of 2

- Low price
- Low quality
- Widely available
- Heavy promotions

low quality) or high-end products (high price, high quality). Similarly, we usually see a match of the heaviness of promotion with greater availability in the marketplace.

At this point, even though we began with 16 combinations, we've simplified this positioning matrix to essentially the two strategies depicted in Figure 5.16:

- Low price, low quality, widely available, heavy promotions
- And high price, high quality, exclusive availability, light promotions

The advantage of these simplifying assumptions is that these two extremes give us very clear goals to work toward. We can position our brand either as low price, low quality, etc. or as high quality with high prices, etc. If we have reason to modify one of the Ps—say, go with low price, low quality, widely available—but we want to lighten up on promotions, then that is our strategic and tactical choice. It might not be wise, but we can try it. These two extremes clarify the goals of a brand's position in the marketplace and can help us align the many decisions that need to be made, all the way from product design to choice of channel for delivery to the marketplace.

In Figure 5.17, we see that many brands may be classified in those extreme upper-left and lower-right cells; the combinations that we're claiming are optimal and the

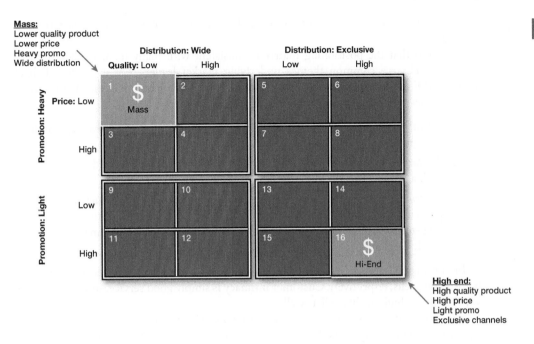

Figure 5.16

Two Strategies Make Perfect Sense

Mass:
Lower quality product
Lower price
Heavy promo
Wide distribution

High end:
High quality product
High price
Light promo
Exclusive channels

Figure 5.17

Example Brands in the Framework

		Distribution: Wide		Distribution: Exclusive	
		Quality: Basic	High	Basic	High
Promotion: Heavy	Price: Low	Visa	Google	OnStar	Gold's Gym
	High	Absolut	Lexus	Curves gyms	Viagra
Promotion: Light	Low	Costco	Sharpie pens	IKEA	MoMA
	High	Microsoft	Starbucks	Six Flags Parks	Four Seasons

most common. Nevertheless, let's back up and briefly acknowledge that while we've been making simplifying generalizations (ones that hold up frequently in the real world), there can be exceptions. That is, some brands appear in all the other suboptimal combinations. We might question how long a company or brand can be sustained in a suboptimal position, but, at any given point in time, there could be market offerings spanning the matrix.

Note also that the positioning matrix is consistent with many management strategy gurus who observe common themes underlying market leaders. For example, Michael Treacy and Fred Wiersema, in *The Discipline of Market Leaders*, describe three basic corporate strategies to creating value and achieving market stature:

1. *Operational excellence*: These companies are good at production, delivery, price, and convenience, such as FedEx, McDonald's, Southwest Airlines.
2. *Product leadership*: These companies pride themselves on quality and innovation, such as Apple, BMW, Mont Blanc.
3. *Customer intimacy*: These companies are willing to tailor their products to their particular customer needs, which can be expensive but is expected to pay off in long-term loyalty and enhanced customer lifetime value, such as Amazon, IBM, Verizon.

In the matrix, operations and products would map roughly onto the low-cost and high-quality cells, respectively. Customer intimacy is simply good service, so we could classify that in the high quality cell as well.

Similarly, Michael Porter, in his books on *Competitive Strategy*, discusses generic strategies driven by keeping costs down and prices competitive, by leading by differentiation (e.g., excellence in quality or innovation), or, when appropriate, by niche positioning. The latter is merely a matter of exclusivity and size, and the first two can be mapped onto our basic combinations of low price vs. high quality. (We'll see more of Porter and Treacy and Wiersema in Chapter 16 on strategy.)

Thus, the assumptions we made in the positioning matrix may not be unduly restrictive. In particular, the positioning matrix is useful. The focus helps us make decisions in many marketing scenarios: Very simply, do we go basic (low price, low quality, wide availability, and heavy promotion), or do we go upscale (higher price, high quality, exclusive availability, and lighter promotion)? You can move off these two extreme positions in the matrix, but you better have a reason. Is that what your customers want? Can you make money there?

5-2 WRITING A POSITIONING STATEMENT

Once a company has decided on its positioning, either for the corporation as a whole or for one of its brands, it must be able to communicate succinctly the parameters of that position to a number of different audiences (to customers, employees, shareholders, general public, etc.). A positioning statement is that communication, and it takes a pretty standard form.

Just as marketing itself begins with the segmentation part of STP (segmentation, targeting, and positioning), a positioning statement also includes the specification of the target segment(s). As we have tried to illustrate in the chapter on segmentation, you don't want to strive to be all things to all people. So your positioning statement should address your target segment. Anything else you say in the positioning statement will have no meaning to customers who are not in that segment. For example, take the positioning statement, "We at Alphatronics are the gym for the serious body builder." The target segment is the "serious body builder," implying that the weekend weight lifter or the soccer mom need not apply. Indeed, customers not in the target segment will probably be intimidated because the positioning statement implies a collection of steroid-pumped dudes; you wouldn't want to compete with or hang out with them.

The next element of a positioning statement is what has been called the *unique selling proposition* (*USP*). The idea is to express your brand's competitive advantage clearly and succinctly. The USP concept captures two things: First, what is the product category (the SP)? Second, how does your market offering dominate these other providers (the U)? Why should a customer buy from you and not one of your competitors? How are you better?

If you cannot answer this question—much less put it into a positioning statement— either your position is not clear, or your product has little differentiation. There is no excuse for this situation, given that your position can be based on real attribute differences or on perceived differences based on images you've built. If you don't have real differences and cannot see a way to create them, then create an image-based difference.

It's also important that these statements be succinct. A simple statement facilitates communication and an understanding of the marketplace. Thus, while you might think your brand rocks on a zillion attributes, try to think of a word that captures the essence of those words and use that. Or make a list of your brand's benefits and prioritize them. Then take the most important, most compelling difference, and insert that difference into the positioning statement. You can cycle through some of the other qualities in some of your communications, but they should all be consistent with the basic message in the positioning statement itself. This goal is more easily achieved if you can abstract from the level of the brand's attributes to the more general intangible benefits to the customer. All you have to do is ask why a customer would care?

Positioning Red Lobster as fresh—a fisherman near the source.

The Alphatronics positioning statement compares itself directly to other gyms, so gyms comprise the product category or the competitive frame. However, its point of differentiation is implied more than stated explicitly. For example, the "tronics" part of the gym's name suggests the presence of high-tech gym equipment.

So a positioning statement captures the qualities of how you wish to be perceived. To compose a positioning statement, answer the following questions:

1. Who are you trying to persuade? Who is your target segment?

2. Who are you competing with? What is your major product category? What frame of reference will customers use in making choices?

3. How are you better? What is your uniqueness, your competitive advantage, your point of difference? Do you have any attribute or benefit that dominates competitors?

Put these elements together, and the result is your positioning statement:

For customers who want [segment], *our brand* is the best at [unique selling proposition—competitors and competitive advantage].

Some positioning statements are a bit surprising. For example, Volvo is known for safety, yet at Volvo.com you'll see: "*We offer transport solutions to demanding customers around the world.*" Perhaps Volvo's dominance on safety is so well known that the benefit doesn't need stating.

Some positioning statements are straightforward, such as Sam's Club's "Savings Made Simple" or Walmart's "Save money. Live better." Others are more abstract and inspiring, such as Lowe's "Let's Build Something Together," Porsche's "Engineered for magic. Every day," or American Cancer Society's "The Official Sponsor of Birthdays."

The positioning statement can serve as an internal memorandum, keeping all managers aligned as a basic guiding principle in all their collective decisions, so as to enhance the likelihood of consistencies in the results of those decisions. Positioning statements can also serve as the foundation of the communications offered to external audiences, including customers, shareholders, and others as advertising taglines or as more extensive messages. Given these audiences, positioning statements should be succinct in order to communicate efficiently and positive and passionate in order to be noteworthy and to spur attention and affection.

MANAGERIAL RECAP

As you can see, positioning is central to the marketing manager's activities:

- Seen through the eyes of the customer, perceptual maps facilitate an understanding of a company's or brand's position in the marketplace.

- Positioning is achieved via a manipulation of the marketing mix 4Ps, and the positioning matrix demonstrates that certain combinations make more sense than others.

- Positioning statements help guide marketing strategies and tactical actions. They include an indication of the target segment, a competitive frame of reference, and a competitive advantage or the brand's unique selling proposition.

Chapter Outline in Key Terms and Concepts

1. What is positioning, and why is it probably the most important aspect of marketing?

   a. Positioning via perceptual maps

   b. The positioning matrix

2. Writing a positioning statement

3. Managerial recap

Chapter Discussion Questions

1. If you were to create a perceptual map for the product category of watches, what attributes should you include to illustrate both the similarities and differences among the brands?

2. Find a company that is struggling. Where is it in the positioning matrix? Could the company be more successful if it changed any of its Ps (e.g., to head to the lo-lo-lo-lo or hi-hi-hi-hi cells)?

3. Write a position statement for yourself to convince your favorite company to hire you.

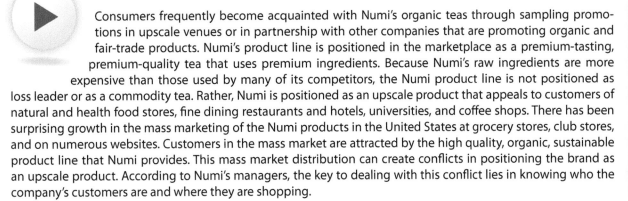

Video Exercise: Numi Organic Tea (6:50)

Consumers frequently become acquainted with Numi's organic teas through sampling promotions in upscale venues or in partnership with other companies that are promoting organic and fair-trade products. Numi's product line is positioned in the marketplace as a premium-tasting, premium-quality tea that uses premium ingredients. Because Numi's raw ingredients are more expensive than those used by many of its competitors, the Numi product line is not positioned as loss leader or as a commodity tea. Rather, Numi is positioned as an upscale product that appeals to customers of natural and health food stores, fine dining restaurants and hotels, universities, and coffee shops. There has been surprising growth in the mass marketing of the Numi products in the United States at grocery stores, club stores, and on numerous websites. Customers in the mass market are attracted by the high quality, organic, sustainable product line that Numi provides. This mass market distribution can create conflicts in positioning the brand as an upscale product. According to Numi's managers, the key to dealing with this conflict lies in knowing who the company's customers are and where they are shopping.

Video Discussion Questions

1. Describe Numi's product line in terms of the four Ps of marketing: product, price, place, and promotion.

2. Incorporating product, price, place, and promotion into the strategic marketing management framework, describe the strategic positioning of Numi's product line.

3. Does this strategic positioning make good marketing management sense or not? Explain your answer.

MINI-CASE

Positioning Fast Food

Compare two fast food restaurant chains—Chipotle and McDonald's (who no longer owns Chipotle). Chipotle has locations throughout the U.S., but that presence is obviously dominated by McDonald's vast network. Chipotle is positioned as offering fresh food, made to the customer's requests, that is relatively healthy. The company rarely advertises. In contrast, McDonald's brand associations revolve more around convenience, inexpensive food, and given their advertising, family outings.

These brands appeal to their customers with very different philosophies. Indeed, on the surface, they appear to have little in common, other than their sector.

Case Discussion Questions

1. Characterize these companies' positions in the marketplace from your best estimates as to the customers' perceptions. In which cell does each exist in the positioning matrix?

2. Would the two chains see each other as competitive threats?

3. What could either do to make its business (profitability) even stronger?

PRODUCTS: GOODS AND SERVICES 6

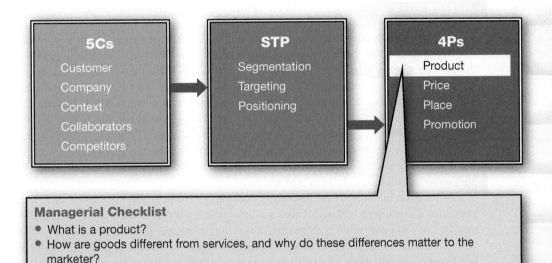

5Cs	STP	4Ps
Customer	Segmentation	**Product**
Company	Targeting	Price
Context	Positioning	Place
Collaborators		Promotion
Competitors		

Managerial Checklist
- What is a product?
- How are goods different from services, and why do these differences matter to the marketer?
- What are the core elements of the firm's market offering, and how does the product definition help us identify competition?

6-1 WHAT DO WE MEAN BY PRODUCT?

"Product" is the general term we'll use for both goods (e.g., skis) and services (e.g., ski lessons).[1] We'll talk about how these classes of purchases differ and build on the differences when necessary, but remember that, in either case, the fundamental objectives of marketing are the same. Marketing managers want to understand and please their customers whether they're the brand manager for Body Solid's weight machines or for the health clubs they're in, like Gold's Gyms.

Sometimes the term "product" is also used as a more general term, referring to the full product profile, that is, the entire market offering, including the product along with its price, the image of the brand, etc. We discuss product, price, place, and promotion separately because there are so many details to consider for each element. But the execution of the 4Ps is integral. Each piece needs to send a consistent message for the overall "product" to be attractive to the customer.

The product is the most central of the 4Ps, the ultimate customer purchase. Drivers who purchase Volvos are buying safety, yes, but they're buying a safe car. Safety is a

> *Marketing is useful for goods, services, experiences, . . . anything!*

modifier; the essential product is a car. Volvo worked to create good product features to distinguish the product into a brand that's become *sine qua non* for safety.

In this chapter, we'll distinguish the qualities of goods and services, and we'll acknowledge that most purchases are a combination of the two. In the next two chapters, we'll continue with the P of product, but focus on brands and new products.

6-1a The Product in the Marketing Exchange

The product is something that the company believes will benefit its customers. We think of marketing as an exchange, so the company offers something (e.g., a hotel room), and the customer offers something in return (e.g., payment). Each party—the customer and company—seeks something of value, and each offers a trade. The company can make the package more attractive (e.g., concierge service, tickets to local events), and the customer can, too (e.g., by being more loyal, purchasing more often, generating positive buzz online). Of course, the company can also make the package less attractive, intentionally or not (e.g., downsizing employees so that customer service suffers), and so can customers (e.g., by being "high maintenance" and demanding customized attention from a system designed for high-volume, quick, and standardized service).

Several questions arise in the marketing exchange. First, what do customers want? Some segments of customers will seek value and low prices, whereas others will seek premium quality. But what do "value" and "quality" mean for a particular product and industry? Still other customers seek specific attributes, sometimes quite idiosyncratic features and benefits. These questions about insights into customers' needs and wants are addressed through the techniques of marketing research (see Chapter 15).

The question from the other side of the exchange is: What is it that the company is well suited to offer to its customers? What will the company's value proposition be? Given the company's position in the marketplace (who they are) and the vision of what the company would like to evolve toward (who they'd like to be), is there an optimal, profitable intersection of what the company can do for the customer and what certain segments of customers would like? It would be most desirable if the market provision had a clear point of differentiation because commodities cannot be sustained as competitively advantageous. These issues are questions of corporate and marketing strategy (see Chapter 16).

Marketers have long realized the benefits of morphing short-term-oriented purchase-transaction exchanges into longer-term relationship marketing. This notion is reflected in such sayings as, "It costs six times more to get a new customer compared to retaining

The Word "Product" Is:

- A broad term that refers to goods: "C'mon down to our dealership, where we sell only the best product!"
- A general term that includes services: "We sell only safe financial investment products!"
- A term that can be used to refer to the entire portfolio of 4Ps, such as when "product" implies a car purchased along with its price and financing, dealership service, and promotion and image.
- Part of the customer-company exchange.
- A mathematical term for multiplication.
- Yes, all of the above!

a current customer." The repeated nature of a relational exchange begins with customer satisfaction and loyalty. Such interactions strengthen and come to fruition in customer relationship management (CRM) and in database marketing systems (discussed in Chapter 14). Marketers put together combinations of goods and services to try to strengthen those customer relationships.

6-2 HOW ARE GOODS DIFFERENT FROM SERVICES?

Some marketers make a big deal of the differences between goods and services. Others say marketing is marketing—that it's the same whether you're marketing pretzels or medical checkups. We're going to play it both ways. We'll emphasize the similarities to facilitate your learning, but there are many tactical differences in the marketing of goods and services, as well as some conceptual and strategic differences. So throughout the book, if there are marketing implications, we'll consider how goods differ from services, and why those differences matter to marketers.

6-2a Intangibility

Marketers have always talked about goods and services being on a continuum. As depicted in Figure 6.1, some products seem like pure goods (e.g., a bike, or shoes), and some services seem like pure services (e.g., consulting, realtors). Other purchases seem like a mix of both a good and a service (e.g., car leasing). The key seems to be the extent to which the purchase is *tangible*. When you purchase clothing, you have something concrete to take home from the store. When you go to a concert, it's a fun time, and you might come out a changed person, but the changes aren't necessarily visible to someone else. Or with consulting, you're getting advice, and maybe a white paper to show for it, but mostly with consulting you've paid to have someone talk at you. It's intangible.

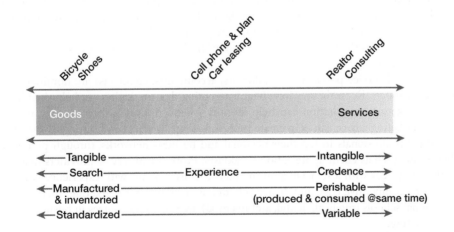

Figure 6.1

Goods to Services Continuum of Products

The concert is an example of "experience marketing," where the experience is the main part of the service. For example, themed retail outlets, such as Crayola Café, Build-a-Bear, ESPN Zone, and Lego stores are as much about providing a shopping and playing experience as they are about moving merchandise. Cirque du Soleil promises a circus and acrobatic performance and a one-of-a-kind experience. MotorTrend.com offers car enthusiasts an opportunity to try out their favorite cars through virtual road tests and simulations. The user gets to see the performance of the car in action.

Intangibility Index

The Intangibility Index (II) is defined as the ratio of R&D to capital spending. It's high for software and pharmaceuticals companies; it's low for oil companies, consumer packaged goods, and computer hardware manufacturers. It rises when more companies emphasize the intangibles and invest in R&D, and it falls with expansive capital expenditure.

6-2b Search, Experience, Credence

The goods-to-services continuum is related to the concepts of search, experience, and credence. *Search* qualities are the attributes that may be evaluated prior to purchase, as the customer learns about the competitive offerings. For example, when you go to a department store to purchase socks, you can just look at a pair and know before buying them whether you'll like them. You can see the color, the price, the material they're made of, and you can imagine immediately what they'll feel like on your toes.

Experience attributes are those that need some trial or consumption before evaluation. If friends recommend a new restaurant, you might trust your friends, and you might expect to like the restaurant. But it's not until you personally go there, experience the ambience and service, try the food, pay the bill, etc., that you can judge the purchase as satisfactory or not for you.

Finally, *credence* qualities are those that are difficult to judge even post-consumption, hence the term "credence." You just have to trust or believe that the quality is good. When you leave your psychotherapist's office, did the therapy improve you? That vasectomy, did it work? Sometimes credence means we go beyond trust to sheer hope, e.g., we hope the mechanic fixed our car and didn't cause any new problems. This sentiment is captured perfectly when Charles Revlon says of his company: "In the factory we make cosmetics; in the store we sell hope."

Professional service providers (e.g., doctors, accountants, architects) are dominated by credence elements. Recently they have begun accepting that marketing can help their businesses. Marketing consultation can help identify where to locate offices or how to find clients. Marketing advice can help create professional appearances and settings. Marketers have urged professionals to tap their personal and business networks, through parties or other events such as client appreciation breakfasts. Professional service providers may begin their practices with a reluctance to "market" themselves, but with experience comes a desire for a competitive edge and, hence, a better appreciation for marketing. Increasingly, professional schools (medical, dental, architectural) are providing courses in business skills and marketing.

Goods are dominated by search and experience qualities, and services are mostly comprised of experience and credence qualities. These distinctions drive some marketing implications. For example, it's easier to price a pair of socks than it is to attach a numeric value to consulting advice. And given that customers can more confidently assess the socks purchase than the consulting advice, consultants will want to take marketing actions to cue the client that their advice is sound and that the quality of the service they provide is excellent.

Note that goods are not necessarily simpler purchases, and services are not necessarily more complex. A huge part of the US and global economy is related to automobiles, and cars are highly complex goods. Similarly, laptops, durables, aircraft, and hospital equipment are all complicated but tangible goods. Conversely, some services, such as restaurants, hotels, and credit card services are relatively simple, standard purchases.

6-2c Perishability

Services differ from goods in other ways: Services are *simultaneously produced and consumed*. Whereas goods can be manufactured and then inventoried in distribution warehouses, most services have to be created on the spot in the presence of the customer. For example, you have to be present to have your hair cut. This inseparability of production and consumption leads to the inevitable result that services tend to be more perishable. When an airplane leaves the ground with some seats vacant, the airliner cannot recoup those empty seats during rush traffic. Your time is inelastic in this manner too. If you're a tax consultant, the hours you spent twiddling your thumbs in August cannot be applied toward crunch time in early April. Perishability has consequences for the marketer to even out demand, a topic we'll consider in Chapter 9 on pricing.[2]

The inseparability of production and consumption also has consequences in the interaction between the service provider and the customer. For example, a cast rehearsing a Broadway play is offering roughly the same service during the rehearsal as when they perform during show times. But when the audience is present and able to respond with laughter or applause, the cast is more energized, and the adrenaline and pheromones in the theater make for a different experience. The nature of interactions varies with setting and societal norms, of course. An orchestra playing in the same auditorium would generally expect no laughter, and applause at only appropriate breaks in the music—premature applause would be censured by the frowns of other patrons at the offending novice.[3]

6-2d Variability

The final major difference between goods and services is that services are said to be more *variable*. Manufacturers of goods can set quality standards like Motorola's 6σ (only three or four errors per million pieces produced) because a machine is producing their products. For a service provider, say a hairstylist, experiences vary across customers or even with one customer across time. Your friend might swear by this stylist, but you prefer classic styles and your friend's hair is always a little . . . edgy. Even with your own stylist, someone you ordinarily like, some days you're in one mood or the other, or the stylist is. The heterogeneity across experiences is due in large part to the 'people' component of services. The service marketing exchange happens between a customer and a service provider representing the company. The frontline rep and you have different and changing, needs, abilities, etc., and the customer service interaction can be fruitful or frustrating.

Self-service is advancing in many industries, such as banking, airport check-in, prescription renewals, grocers, and so forth.[4] When customers interact with technology and machines, the variability of the service encounter is reduced by the standardization of the equipment. It should be noted that, like cholesterol, there is good and bad variability. Bad variability involves errors in the system (e.g., poor customer service), and managers of logistics, human resources, and marketing are concerned with its reduction. In contrast, good variability involves the customization and tailoring of the service delivery for the customer's unique needs, and, not surprisingly, it often enhances customer satisfaction. Automated services are usually introduced to reduce the errorful (bad) variability. With time, as menus become more sophisticated and offer more options, it is conceivable that good variability may also be enhanced (at least for customers who can deal with the technology).

Perhaps the most pervasive and successful example of self-service is online shopping. Shopping at home in one's jammies at 3 A.M. is the ultimate in convenience. In addition, comparing information on prices and product attributes is easier online than IRL, and made even easier with the AI of shopping bots. Furthermore, the advantages of the technology and standardization are clear: A website may occasionally crash, but it's seldom cranky. The online purchase is a mix of goods and services and of tangible and intangible.

Continuum

Remember, goods and services lie along a continuum, and the distinction can be a little fuzzy. Some simpler services may resemble goods. For example, we call a variety of things "financial services," and yet . . .

- a service is intangible, but you can hold your credit card,
- a service is inseparable production and consumption, but you don't need to be at your bank to access your checking account,
- a service is perishable, but you can use your credit card whenever you want
- a service is variable, but there is standard, mass production of insurance policies, savings accounts, data systems for bond traders, etc.
- (see fsmhandbook.com).

6-2e To Infinity and Beyond Goods and Services

Intangibility, the search/experience/credence qualities, inseparability of production and consumption, and variability comprise the fundamental differences between goods and services. We'll bring in each concept, where appropriate, when discussing marketing issues throughout the book. There will be issues regarding advertising (e.g., portraying a realistic service encounter to set clear expectations), branding (e.g., communicating a consistent image in the face of the variability of the service encounter), pricing (e.g., for yield management), logistics (e.g., creating a clear flow process for the customer service), human resources (e.g., empowering the frontline employees to facilitate service recovery), etc.

It is helpful to think of goods and services along a continuum because many purchases have both elements, and the distinctions can be blurry. For example, Canon sells copiers and also customer service packages. Customers buy toothpaste and also hope it will make them more attractive.

6-3 WHAT IS THE FIRM'S CORE MARKET OFFERING?

Some marketers say that everything we buy has some element of a good and some element of a service. They maintain that perhaps only raw materials such as coal or wheat are examples of pure goods. Everything else has been processed, and that processing is a value-added service. Thus we can examine any business and consider what are its the core vs. the value-added services. Distinguishing these elements also helps us identify our competition. For example, Figure 6.2 depicts the purchase of a car, for which the provision of the automobile itself might be considered the core purchase; it's the corporate fundamentals, the reason the car maker is in business. These are the qualities that the company better get right; they're the basics of what customers expect. The value-added supplemental services are those on which the car company might distinguish itself; they might claim their financing and service plans are more generous, their people more competent and friendlier, etc.

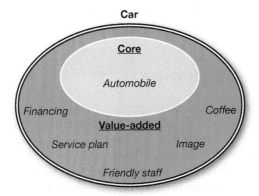

Car

Core

Automobile

Financing   *Coffee*

Value-added

Service plan   *Image*

Friendly staff

Figure 6.2

Core and Value-Added Offerings

Core: a salon service; Peripheral: relaxation and peace.

Syda Productions/Shutterstock.com

When we discuss customer satisfaction (in Chapter 14), we'll see another distinction between the core and value-addeds. The core elements have come to be expected; they're givens. So if they're good, a company doesn't earn points in the eyes of the customer, and the customer won't rave to friends about how great the brand is. But if the core elements are bad (e.g., the car is a frequently recalled model), they can definitely trigger dissatisfaction. In contrast, a marketer can affect a customer's level of satisfaction (or dissatisfaction) through good (or bad) value-addeds (e.g., better service packages). Companies often compete on the value-addeds. For example, Starbucks is known for its service and combinatorial menu selection. Want just a regular coffee? Yeah, they do that too.

While the concepts of core and value-added seem straightforward, it's not as easy as it looks. Companies can make the mistake of being myopic when they define their core business, focusing on their product offerings (e.g., "We sell laptops"), instead of recognizing that their true goal is offering benefits and value to their customers (e.g., "We sell IT solutions"). When business is good, this myopia is not a problem. But as Internet sites increasingly offer software and storage, the particular configuration of the end user's machine become less important. If the company fixates on their laptops, instead of recognizing that the laptops are morphing into dumb terminals, they may be out of business soon. If the company defines its business more broadly, it could be on the frontier of developing software platforms for their customers.

6-3a Dynamic Strategies

Core businesses change as industries change or as a firm's competencies change. For example, the business of the Victoria's Secret mega brand used to be driven 70% by apparel, but it is now 70% beauty and fragrance lines. As the production and sales proportions evolve, the questions for adaptation become: What business are we in? What benefits do we want to provide to the consumer? Who is our competition? If Victoria's Secret sees itself as primarily a lingerie provider, it would compete with department stores' lingerie departments. If it has come to see itself as a provider of beauty and fragrance goods, it would compete with the department stores' cosmetic counters.

In the huge and hugely profitable business of sports, we may identify the core service as the ball game and the value-addeds as the experience at the park, on TV, or online. The performing teams might be great (or not), and a family or friends can have a great consumer experience. It is smart to define competition broadly here also: While the team competes with others in its league, the marketer competes with other sports (e.g., for corporate skybox dollars) and with other forms of entertainment, such as movies (e.g., for families' weekend amusement dollars).

Figure 6.3
What is Our Business? Who is Our Competition?

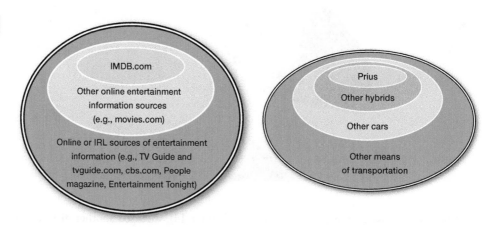

The definition of a company's core business is somewhat like asking for its mission statement. When a company says, "We're an advertising agency," is that it? What precisely are you good at? What distinguishes you from the next ad guy? A more informative (albeit a little clumsy) statement is, "We're the ad agency who can help integrate your customer Web interactions and targeted direct mailing efforts."

Figure 6.3 shows just how broadly competition can be defined in the minds of customers. It's important to brand managers not to focus on defining competition too narrowly, as when we compute market shares. The Internet Movie Database[5] isn't fighting just Fandango, but anything that provides information about the entertainment industry.

Services Flowcharts

One of the ways that services marketers try to understand, manage, and control the service encounter experience is to borrow from operations the notion of flowcharts. In services flowcharts, there is a delineation between what a customer sees (e.g., a car valet) and what the company produces to make that part of the encounter as flawless as possible (e.g., a sufficient number of valets who are well-trained to be polite and good drivers, plentiful nearby parking, etc.).

- Each part of the service encounter is described in steps that flow over time to simulate the process of the encounter, and each step is described in two portions—that which is visible to the customer, or "on stage," and that which is "behind the scenes."
- For quality assurances, flowcharts include several key performance indicators to be measured at each step to track what is working well and what needs to be streamlined in the process.

6-3b Product Lines: Breadth and Depth

All product-related issues become more complicated when we broaden our scope to include not just a particular brand of focus, but the company's larger portfolio. Managers speak of a product mix, comprised of several product lines, which can vary in both width and depth. In Figure 6.4, we see that a hair salon carries only one product line, but does so with depth to reflect their expertise in this product category. A grocery store carries more product lines, but the hair care line is no longer covered in such depth. A large discount store has even greater breadth and less depth in the product lines they sell.

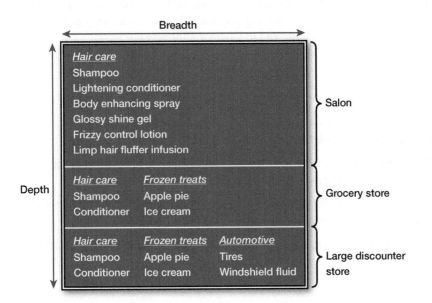

Figure 6.4

Product Lines: Breadth and Depth

While a brand manager's responsibilities are to focus, supervising product line managers must oversee these entire portfolios. Product lines can be pruned (e.g., if customers see no distinctions between brands or lines) or supplemented (e.g., if the company recognizes an opportunity for producing something that customers will value, especially if the company can make the new brands or lines easily and better than competitors).

When economic times are good and one's current market offerings and brands are financially healthy, it is tempting to leverage one's strengths and successes into more products (in either the breadth or depth direction). Doing so can absolutely be a good thing. Indeed, in many ways, it's a smart thing to diversify products in the same way that you're taught to diversify investments. After all, a brand is an investment.

Figure 6.5 shows a different way to think about expansion. The two scenarios at the left depict a company serving its particular customer base very well, by offering one or more products that suit their tastes.

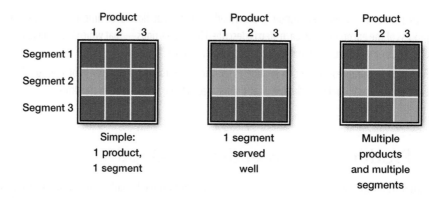

Figure 6.5

Product Lines Strategies

At the right, a company is trying to offer different products to different customers. This strategy is rather inefficient given that it doesn't leverage the company's knowledge of its customers or its products. Extensions into breadth or depth business ventures have to be done for smart, strategic reasons. Are the new launches consistent with the current positioning of the brand or company? If not, can the brands be directed to different target segments without diluting the existing position? We'll continue with questions like these in Chapter 7 for brand building and in Chapter 8 for new products.

MANAGERIAL RECAP

Products are goods and services, a central offering in the marketing exchange between a customer and a company.

- Goods and services, as well as their marketing and management, share many similarities, but there are differences too. Services are relatively more intangible, inseparable, perishable, and variable.

- A firm's market offering is comprised of the core (the central element of what is purchased), and the value-addeds. The core helps define the company to its target segments, and the value-addeds enhance customer satisfaction.

- Competition should be considered broadly, and a company's competitors can evolve over time, as product lines are further developed in length and breadth.

Chapter Outline in Key Terms and Concepts

1. What do we mean by product?

   a. The product in the marketing exchange

2. How do goods different from services?

   a. Intangibility

   b. Search, experience, credence

   c. Perishability

   d. Variability

   e. To infinity and beyond goods and services

3. What is the firm's core market offering?

   a. Dynamic strategies

   b. Product lines: breadth and depth

4. Managerial recap

Chapter Discussion Questions

1. When you get your hair cut, what's the "core" of what you buy vs. what are the "value-addeds" in the purchase? What's a consultant's core vs. value-addeds? What are the core vs. value-addeds for music?

2. Consider one of these purchases: health care, a car, a time-share condo. What elements are tangible vs. intangible? How do the tangible vs. intangible components contribute to your satisfaction or dissatisfaction with the consumption?

3. Some companies have traditionally been known for their excellence in tangibles, e.g., Xerox in copiers, IBM in computers, who now describe themselves as primarily service companies. Do you agree? What does it take for a company to declare itself as a service organization (e.g., a percentage of business, a certain strategy or mission)? What would it take for you to believe such a claim?

Video Exercise: Kodak (9:21)

Kodak's Graphics Communication Group (GCG) is one of the company's largest growing businesses. On one hand, Kodak's GCG serves customers using offset or analog printing that requires long production runs to be cost efficient. On the other hand, the company also serves customers who use digital printing to provide quick, on-demand, short production runs. The company markets four types of products—digital printing, consumables, workflow, and services—to commercial printing, corporate, and government customers. Most of the customers are commercial printers, which is one of four market segments targeted by the GCG. The other three market segments are the packaging industry, publishers, and customers engaged in transactional printing (i.e., printing of checks and documents). To more precisely target customer subsets within these different market segments, the company relies on a customer relationship management (CRM) system that contains a variety of detailed information about the needs, location, and characteristics of the customers. The company also seeks lots of feedback from its customers to better understand their needs and their perceptions of the company's operations vis-à-vis the customers. This feedback is used to foster continuous improvement.

Video Discussion Questions

1. What are the main products offered by Kodak to its customers, and how would you position these products on the goods-to-services continuum of products?

2. Describe the core elements and the value-added elements of Kodak's product line(s).

3. Describe the breadth and depth of Kodak's product line(s).

MINI-CASE

Volta Financial

Volta's core business is the financial investment instruments it wants to sell. Its value-addeds include financial advisors who provide nearly free counsel.

Like most financial advisors, Volta's people sell products that seem simple to them, but complicated to most of their customers. Financial investments are a classic credence purchase, implying that the customer won't know for a long time whether the advice to invest in certain ways was indeed optimal. Volta's clients come for advice because they figure that the advisors have knowledge and abilities that they don't.

Volta is a business, and as such, has a business manager. Some 18 months ago, the manager asked the advisors to have their clients fill out periodic customer satisfaction surveys. The survey captures customers' perceptions regarding: whether a receptionist was polite when taking a call to make an appointment with an advisor; how quickly the appointment could be made; how professional was the advisor, did the advisor's work area appear to be organized and professional, and so on.

Case Discussion Questions

1. What do you think about the survey? What measures do you believe would be good indicators of an advisor's performance?

2. How could the brand be positioned to be more tangible and experiential (and even more search) so that consumers could be more confident in Volta's quality and Volta would have more obvious bragging rights about its brand?

3. What elements of financial investment assistance would you classify as "core" and what would you list under "value added"? How could Volta distinguish itself from other financial advisor firms by modifying their core or value-added services?

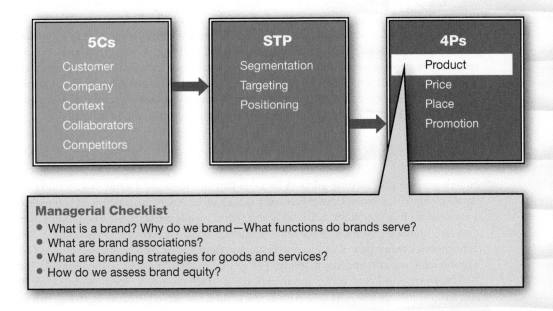

BRANDS 7

Managerial Checklist
- What is a brand? Why do we brand—What functions do brands serve?
- What are brand associations?
- What are branding strategies for goods and services?
- How do we assess brand equity?

7-1 WHAT IS A BRAND?

What do you think of when you hear these names: Apple and Microsoft, McDonald's and Burger King, Rolex and Cartier? Business magazines regularly feature them on lists of top ten global brands.[1]

Why do marketers care about brands? If branding is good or important, how do we do it? Why are the brand strategies of The Gap and Versace both strong and yet so different?

In the last chapter, we discussed goods and services. In this chapter, we won't discuss products as classes of purchases, but brands as particulars: specifically, not shoe stores but Zappos; not cars, but Fiat 500s; not printers, but HPs. Services get branded too, e.g., Turbo Tax software; St. Thomas hospitals; Canyon Ranch resorts; Google and Bing as information sources; and MoMA and the Louvre as specific museums.

Marketers believe that brands have value above and beyond the benefits of the product itself. It's not just that Coca-Cola is a well-known name; it's that the name immediately invokes certain images: the shape of the Coke bottle, the logo, the red color, some of their ads. So while a brand begins with the name that a company uses to label a specific product, a good brand goes well beyond that: It's a portfolio of qualities associated with that name.

The brand associations begin with qualities under the company's control. The product shape and its packaging can be distinctive; e.g., from that Coke bottle to a Corvette. Brand logos are shapes and symbols that may begin with little inherent meaning, but they come to be associated with the brand and become shorthand for the brand itself; e.g., Nike's swoosh and McDonald's golden arches are internationally known. Some brands are closely associated with particular colors, e.g., Pepsi's red, white, and blue vs. Dr. Pepper's burgundy, or John Deere's green, and UPS's "What can *brown* do for you?"

Beyond the name and other tangible qualities, other associative elements may also enhance the imagery and market perceptions of brands. Companies build associations via classical conditioning in consumer learning, e.g., a jingle, a slogan, a spokesperson. The hope is that the catchy tune is in your head when you're at the grocer (e.g., "Ask any mermaid you happen to see . . .), or that the slogan suggests the company has a worthy mission (e.g., "Like a good neighbor, State Farm is there"), or that the spokesperson is admired and the customer emulates the person through the purchase (e.g., Halle Berry for Revlon).

Other brand associations are not under the company's control but are every bit as real. Maybe when you were a kid, your mom substituted 7UP for root beer to make you ice cream floats, or your soccer coach had cold 7UPs waiting for the team after every game, or in college you asked for a 7UP instead of a beer at a party and someone called you a dork.[2] The company can't control all these representations, but it can make certain that every outgoing message from the company to the marketplace is excellent and positive.

7-1a Brand Name

So let's get down to the nitty gritty. A brand is first and foremost a name. Some marketers say that a brand is a symbol, but it first has to be a name. Otherwise, how would you register a dot-com for it or search for it. To the extent that all words are symbols in communication, then fine, brands are symbols. Some brand names immediately convey information, e.g., You Tube captures the essence of user-created entertainment. Other brand names originate as not a far stretch from a benefit they're implying, e.g., Bud Light, Optical4less, The Home Depot.

Many firm and brand names are merely those of the founders. These tend to have no inherent meaning, show little creativity in marketing, and serve primarily as an ego trip for the founder. Yet family names aren't entirely lame as brands. Their lack of explicit meaning allows them to translate well to other brands across the firm, e.g., Hugo Boss, Christian Dior, René Lacoste, Yves Saint Laurent, and Mario Prada have all lent their names first to their clothing lines and then branching out to shoes, jewelry, eyewear, perfume, and cell phones. And, with time, no one thinks of the people, such as Mr. Enzo Ferrari in 1898, or Professor (seriously!) Ferdinand Porsche in 1948. Rather, they think of their companies' cars. (Still, readers with entrepreneurial dreams should forgo ego and choose brand names that convey information to customers about the benefits of the brand.)

7-1b Logos and Color

Regardless of the amount of information inherent in the brand name when it is introduced to the marketplace, brand name meaning is built over time through the firm's communications to customers. The marketer educates customers about the meaning of the brand as well as its logos and symbols. Just as the brand name engages the customers verbally, the logos and packaging colors engage the customers visually and sensually. Think of how distinctive the fonts of *The New York Times* and Google look. The first is an elegant, Old-English font simply in black, cast against the white page; the latter is sans serif, bold, simple, and colorful. These simple cues are sufficient to identify the brands.[3] Figure 7.1 shows logos that combine a brand name with a symbol meant to suggest the brand's value proposition.

Figure 7.1

Brand Names and Symbols as Logos

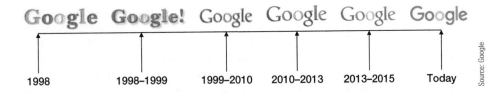

Source: Google

Figure 7.2

Logo Memes Updating and Morphing

Companies lucky enough to survive for decades need to adapt even down to their logos. Figure 7.2 shows a logo morphing over time. It began pretty fancy schmancy and then got simplified and stylized. Do you like the changes over the years? (Does it matter? Would you avoid a company because of a logo change? Probably not.) Companies use brand names and logos as a shorthand way to communicate to the customer: "This is who we are. This is what we look like."

7-2 WHY BRAND?

The U.S. Patent and Trademark Office issues more than 100,000 new brands each year. Some say that consumers are becoming less brand loyal. But let's face it, with such continued brand explosion, companies are dividing their money pies more and more finely. Together, the sheer numbers of brands and the heightened competition over them indicate that branding is more important than ever.

So why all these brands? Brands first *convey information* to customers. Brand names identify company production and ownership.[4] For example, when Honda puts its name on a car, a motorcycle, or a lawnmower, it's saying, "We're proud to offer these products. These are ours." And with time, the brand name has gained status among consumers as being high quality, "Honda is a good *brand*"; that is, anything that comes from the house of Honda will be good.

Why Brand?

For customers:

- Brands convey information
- Brands signal consistent quality
- Brands confer status
- Brands reduce customer risk
- Brands makes many purchase decisions easier

For the company:

- Brands enhance loyalty
- Brands allow charging premium prices
- Brands inoculate the company from competitive action
- Brands assist in segmentation, targeting, and positioning
- Brands encourage channel partners' support

Brand building is based fundamentally on the predictability of the item being purchased. It would be difficult for a customer to say that they value Dell's laptops if some worked well and others didn't. Brands can gain reputations for being bad, but the goal of a marketer is to create a product that is *reliable*, that is *predictable in quality*. Some brands have avid fans because their products work not just predictably but fabulously.

When the brand name is an assurance of reliable quality, the customer's *decision-making is made easier*. There is *less perceived risk* associated with the choice among the products offered in the marketplace when the customer knows which brands are good. Risk, as in financial transactions, is essentially a measure of variability. Reliability is the opposite; it implies consistency or predictability in the performance of the product. Reliability is a signal that time and again the product will perform to quality standards; thus, across time or customers, the product performs with little variability but high quality. The brand is a known entity. Customers can count on it to perform as they've come to expect it to.

Legal Stuff

A trademark is the legal ownership of identity. A trademark can include just the brand name, just the logo, or, more inclusively, the name, logo, phrases, symbols, design, colors, sounds, etc.

Claims of trademark infringement occur when a me-too competitor makes part of their brand identity similar enough to an extant trademark that it could lead to confusion among customers of the me-too with the original brand.

The trademark symbol (™) essentially means, "Hands off, these are our ideas" (i.e., trademark rights are claimed). When the trademark symbol graduates, it becomes a register mark (®), a more serious designation that means, "Hands off, or our lawyers will get you" (the trademark has been registered).

There are different types of trademarks:

1. Fanciful: using a word as a brand name, which, prior to your use had no particular inherent meaning, e.g., Geico
2. Arbitrary: when you appropriate a word with common meaning, e.g., Amazon
3. Suggestive: brand name that suggests the customer benefit, e.g., Jiffy Lube

With time, what had been company property can change, especially perversely if the brand becomes "too" successful. For example, "Aspirin" had been a trademark of Bayer, but the name is now deemed generic so other pain relievers can also call themselves "aspirin."

Trademark issues arise online in the form of domain names and ownership. Generic names cannot be defended as registered.

Laws in different countries are wildly different, but services are available that search for prior brand elements (brand names, slogans, etc.) to see whether they're free of ™ or ®. In the states, this can be done via the US Patent and Trademark Office (uspto.gov).

It is also clear that many brands serve as *status symbols*. The reason for knockoff designer handbags or watches is that it's thought to be cool to own one, yet the prices of the genuine articles are out of reach for many consumers. BMW, Lexus, and Mercedes have entry-level cars so that young successful people can show the world they've made it (yet pay as little as possible to own a piece of the brand). The prestige of such brands bolsters the consumer's self-image.

If those are the benefits of branding for customers, let's consider the rewards of brands for their companies as well.

Good brands can *induce loyalty*. Repeat purchasing might be unthinking due to inertia, whereby the customer just reaches for the familiar (brand name, package, logo, color). If the brand is known to be high quality and reliable (not risky), then the brand choice is easy to justify. Customers don't have to think about the purchase or brand choice anymore. Repeat purchasing and true brand loyalty can also be a more mindful process, whereby customers return to the brand because, quite simply, they like it. With that brand, the customer obtains the particular attributes and features they seek, further supporting their perceptions of high quality.

To a company's delight, most customers are willing to *pay premium prices* for brands they value. Customers so appreciate the reliability, high quality, and status of their favorite brands that they're less price sensitive, knowing that they're getting something good even if they're paying somewhat more.

Companies can also use brands or variants of their brands to provide different offerings to satisfy different *market segments*. For example, Porsche's 911 sells predominately to men (90%), who are over 50 with a household income over $300k. Their Boxster customer profiles are slightly younger and oriented more to women (30%). These different car lines allow the macho 911 driver not to be offended by the infiltrating women buying the sister model.

Services Brands

A brand implies consistency, making brand building a challenge for services marketing. Some services are rather standardized, so creating a service brand for a hotel chain, an airline, or even a restaurant is much like doing so for tangible products. But many services are more heterogeneous due to the interpersonal exchange between the customer and the front-line service provider.

- To enhance reliability and branding, service providers seek high quality when selecting employees and take longer to train them to ensure their uniform interactions with customers.

- Consistency across customer-employee interactions is enhanced if the training includes tight specifications on the service delivery processes and, on the flip side, clear strategies for service recovery, should the encounter proceed less than optimally.

- Drawing a customer experience flowchart and noting various metrics at each point in the process (e.g., time elapsed, customer satisfaction, etc.) can help diagnose problematic components that might be redesigned and streamlined.

How does a brand name come to convey meaning, imply quality and consistency, reduce the riskiness and ease decision making, induce loyalty, achieve prestigious status, and command higher prices? The mechanism that gives brands meaning is the set of associations that are linked to the brand in the customer's mind. These associations are created through a number of sources: They're built from the company's advertisements and communications in the marketplace, the customer's own experiences with the brand and company and competitors' brands, and the stories related about the brand by other customers. So we need to understand brand associations.

7-3 WHAT ARE BRAND ASSOCIATIONS?

Branding may begin with simple physical qualities (a name, logo, color, packaging, etc.). But the far more interesting and flexible aspects of a brand are the intangible cognitive and emotional associations that the company helps the customer connect to its brand. Marketers talk about a hierarchy of brand associations. At the bottom of a brand value hierarchy are the concrete product attributes, such as color, size, shape, flavor. As we travel up the hierarchy, these brand attributes extend to product benefits; e.g., this blue sweater will be flattering; this messenger bag has a protective sleeve for my tablet; that new restaurant should be friendly and informal enough for meeting a friend. Benefits are more intangible than attributes.

Emotional benefits are the next level, and they're even more intangible; e.g., a flattering sweater is a means to the goal of being attractive; a good bag is a means to being productive, etc.

Strategically, the concrete features are easiest to deliver and explain to customers, but competitors also match them relatively easily. The more abstract benefits are values that are more meaningful to customers, as well as easier for a company to claim as a competitive advantage, but they're also more difficult to create.

The key brand association is the extent to which the customer likes or even relates to the brand. For example, think of Mac users who use their Apples for anything a PC can do, with an edge of cool. Or think of young executives who drive BMW 3-series cars as a reward and symbol that they are on the road to great achievements. Brands aren't just extensions of the customer; they are expressions of customers' *ideal* selves or the selves to which they aspire. A brand carries a promise that it can help customers achieve their desired persona. This aspirational function of brands begins in childhood, when kids believe that their popularity and acceptance are partly a function of wearing the right sneakers or listening to the right music on the right device. Adults may deny that they use brands in the same manner, but watch their behaviors: They attend "certain" schools, drive "certain" cars, and wear "certain" designer clothing and shoes.

Brands can also serve other social functions. Brands can become the focal point of bonding, as in so-called brand communities, such as for Mini Coopers or Subarus, and exemplified by the Harley treks, or communities around Lego and Barbie, Being Girl, H&R Block, or even traditional fan sites (e.g., thousands for Taylor Swift), etc. To non-marketers, it can seem surprising that fan dedication can be rabid—that people can talk about loving (some) brands.

All these connections can be depicted, as in Figure 7.3, in a brand association network. The nodes in the network include elements such as the brand name (and perhaps competitors), along with attributes and abstract benefits about the brand. The links between the nodes indicate some connection (unlinked nodes have either no connections or weak ones), and strong links are depicted with bolder lines.

Figure 7.3

Brand Association Network

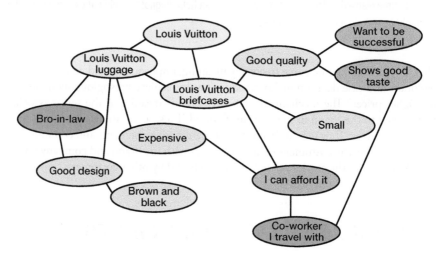

This mapping is not meant to be a literal representation of what customers have in their heads, and yet it's not a bad metaphor. This idea is that we have stored in memory quite a lot of information about a brand, and when the brand name is activated (e.g., through advertising), the brand associations are subsequently (even instantaneously) triggered (like brand information jumping across neurons). Links that are further from the brand may take milliseconds longer to retrieve and activate than those most closely and directly associated with the brand. That is, while the brand's associations include even the indirect links, those attributes are not likely to be the very first qualities that come to mind when the brand name is mentioned. In addition to memory implications, there are attitudinal ones. For example, measures of customer satisfaction with the brand are most heavily affected by the positivity or negativity of the nearest links.

When company advertising emphasizes one benefit, the cognitive maps may be simple, for example, the mental link between Volvo and safety dominates everything else; ditto Tesla and technical innovation. If those solitary links are strong and positive, the focused message has been delivered, and the position of the brand in the marketplace will be clear and positive. Networks can be more complex, either due to a consumer's fuller knowledge of the brand (e.g., McDonald's fries, quick and inexpensive meals, the two-all-beef-patties jingle, road trips, fatty food concerns, etc.) or due to inconsistent advertising messages or customer experiences.

In addition to classic studies of brand associations to understand customers' memories and attitudes, recent research has examined two special classes of brand associations: brand personalities and brand communities. We'll look at both.

7-3a Brand Personalities

One way that marketers get customers to relate to their brands is by creating a brand personality. A brand doesn't have to be personified or anthropomorphized, such as the Jolly Green Giant or the Keebler elves. Any brand can be said to have a distinct personality.

In Figure 7.4 we see a conceptualization of five different kinds of brands: sincere, competent, exciting, sophisticated, and rugged.[5] The personalities capture information specific

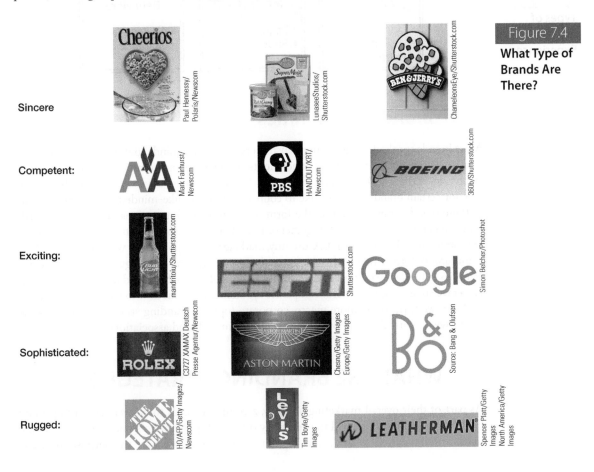

Figure 7.4

What Type of Brands Are There?

Sincere

Competent:

Exciting:

Sophisticated:

Rugged:

to the brand, as well as holistic perceptions about the brand and company position in the marketplace. For example, when customers say Campbell's is sincere, they mean partly the soups (e.g., they use only quality ingredients) and partly the company (e.g., those ingredients come from fair trade sources).

Competence often characterizes technical firms, exciting brands are those that are innovative or cool, sophisticated brands are often leaders in tasteful design and fashion, and rugged brands bring to mind their toughness. None of the personality profiles are better than the others; they're just different. If the brand strategy had been to attain a certain personality, and customer perceptions concur that the brand achieved that characterization, then the branding and marketing efforts succeeded. If the brand manager doesn't like the brand's current profile, then new marketing initiatives may be undertaken to reposition the brand. For example, a marketing manager of a "competent" brand might be envious of an "exciting" or "sophisticated" brand, but competent is good, just different. There's a lot of space and reward in the marketplace for competent. A brand would begin to lose its identity (and risk its current customers) if it aimed to be otherwise.

Consistent with their personalities, different brand experiences highlight different elements. Figure 7.5 illustrates that Disney appeals more to customers' hearts, inducing feelings and sentiments. Lego building blocks stimulate one's curiosity and problem-solving, engaging the customers' head, and Gillette is action-oriented, results in a bodily experience, affecting customers in a behavioral manner.[6]

Figure 7.5

Types of Brand Experiences

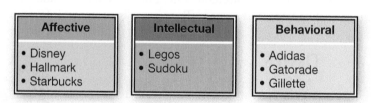

7-3b Brand Communities

Most brands speak of engaging their customers' hearts and minds, and increasingly marketers are seeing even more extreme attachments. There are brand communities around Apple, Nintendo, and even Duck brand duct tape.[7] Some customers are so passionate about their love for certain brands that they like to connect with other like-minded customers. Whether these brand communities take the form of social media interactions or interactions IRL (like the Harley posses who ride together or Lego fans who build projects together), customers are coming together over brands. Currently, marketers don't quite know what to do with these communities (other than trying to engage them to spark viral campaigns). Will brand communities enhance the bottom line? Probably. How could it not be a good thing if people gather to rave about your brand? But companies are still figuring out how to monetize the groups.

Next, we turn to the more macro, corporate topic of branding strategies. That is, what might we do with all our knowledge of our customers' brand associations?

7-4 WHAT ARE BRANDING STRATEGIES?

As part of their overall marketing strategy, a company needs to answer several important branding questions. First, will the company offer multiple products under the same brand name or roll them out with distinct brand names? Second, what are the purposes of brand extensions, line extensions, and co-branding? How is brand equity determined and valuated? How are brands best rolled out globally? What is the role of a store brand? We'll examine the factors that affect the answers to each question.

7-4a Umbrella Brands vs. House of Brands

Most companies start by offering a single product in the marketplace. The brand name might be the company name. As the company adds products, they have to decide: Should they put the corporate name on every new product? Or should new brand names be chosen for the subsequent products?

A company that attaches the same brand name to all of its products is using an *umbrella branding* approach.[8] There are lots of examples, such as The Virgin Group, which sells cruises, balloon flights, mobile services, radio, etc., and calls them all Virgin. Nike makes athletic shoes, sports jerseys, gym bags, and other products, all of which bear the same company brand name and swish logo. Canon's cameras and photocopiers say Canon. GE puts its corporate brand on its diverse lines of appliances, lighting, financial services, and engines.

In contrast, with a *house of brands* approach, the company introduces a new brand name for every major line of product it brings to the marketplace. Procter & Gamble (P&G) is a famous house of brands. It produces some 80 major brands, including Charmin, Crest, Downy, Gillette, Hugo Boss, Ivory, Pringles, Swiffer, Tide, and on and on. There are no connections among these brands that are apparent to the customer. Unilever does the same (Axe, Dove, Hellmann's, Knorr, Lipton, etc.). In B2B land, DuPont had similarly introduced a portfolio of great brands: Kevlar, Kalrez, Lycra, Teflon, Thinsulate, and Stainmaster.[9]

Each approach has strengths and liabilities. With an umbrella branding approach, once the company has established the key brand name in the marketplace, subsequent product introductions sharing the same brand name are easier for the customer to understand and accept. The new product line will begin with higher than usual levels of awareness. In addition, given that the two products share a brand name, there will be some overlap between two different products' associations. Thus, it is critical that the majority of the existing brand's associations are positive, or new products will be introduced to the market with a perceived handicap.

In contrast, given the nature of the multiple brands' autonomy in the house of brands approach, the independence between brands assures that any problems with one brand shouldn't negatively affect any of the others. Even if a brand isn't in the spotlight for being a problem (e.g., tires that blow out, beverage bottling problems, weight control OTCs that cause heart problems), a company with multiple brands almost surely is watching those brands from different points in their life cycles. A brand whose image is waning is less a liability in a house of brands where the names aren't shared across the product lines. A more positive way to interpret this brand independence is that the brand images need not be consistent, allowing the company to reach multiple segments. For example, Marriott's portfolio has Courtyard and Fairfield to serve one part of the market, with The Ritz-Carlton (without the Marriott name) at the high end; none of the segments of customers would be confused or would expect an experience that the other hotels offer.

Evidence suggests that the umbrella branding strategy provides stronger financial outcomes to the company than the house of brands. One reason is that certain costs are cut; e.g., the house of brands approach requires more advertising to build the multiple brands' equity, whereas advertising for the umbrella brands builds the shared brand name synergistically across the products. In addition, psychologically, customers seem to build stronger connections to the specific, concrete product; thus, the customer thinks positively about Ivory without necessarily considering anything about its manufacturer, P&G. For umbrella brands (e.g., Sony), the product-level associations replicate the same name across multiple products (Sony memory sticks, Sony theater systems), and thus the attitude is reinforced (Sony, Sony, Sony), thereby enhancing brand loyalty.

7-4b Brand-Extensions and Co-Branding

Brand extensions are a strategic use of a brand's equity, in which the marketer leverages the brand's good name to get customers to buy something new. Recall the breadth and depth dimensions of product lines from Chapter 6. Here, too, the brand name may be applied within a product line to go for depth; these are called line extensions. Or the brand name may be applied across different kinds of products; these are called product category extensions.

Figure 7.6 illustrates brand extensions in the direction of breadth (product category) and depth (line) in a familiar context. The vertical line extensions provide varieties of the core product, and the horizontal product category extensions are the company's ventures into other product categories. Some companies focus on deepening brand extensions:

- Oscar Meyer has different length hotdogs for different length buns, and makes Lunchables and bacon, all with the Oscar Meyer name.

- SAS (the statistical computing company, not the airline) has versions of its software for marketers, big data visualization, students, etc. They're all called SAS.

- Cheerios rolls out different flavors: apple cinnamon, honey nut, frosted, all called Cheerios.

- Häagen-Dazs has different flavors of ice cream: apricot and cream, cappuccino truffle, dark chocolate orange, green tea, rum and raisin, strawberry cheesecake.

Other brand extensions aim for breadth:

- Dove soaps took their wholesome value proposition and brand name to offer deodorant, body lotions, and hair care products, all called Dove.

- Amazon has famously extended from books and CDs to drugstore goods, computers, furniture, jewelry, services (e.g., registries), just about everything.

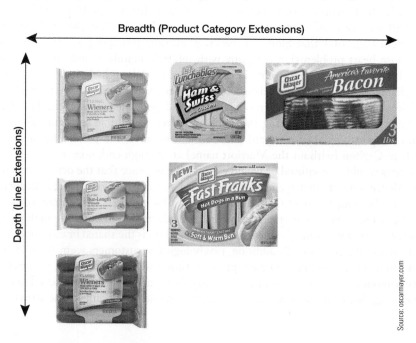

Figure 7.6

Brand Extensions

Source: oscarmayer.com

Anatomy of a Brand Extension

First movie, *Frozen*

Joe Seer/Shutterstock.com

Success begets success . . .

and excess . . .?

Plans for second movie, *Frozen 2*

Source: cinemablend.com

Keith Homan/Shutterstock.com

Source: marandarussell.com

dean bertoncelj/Shutterstock.com

LET IT GO

FROZEN

Toys   and   **Music**   and   **Children's books**

. . . but wait, there's more!

Disney/*Frozen* Partners

Disney forges partnership with many manufacturers—temporary co-branding arrangements, where synergistic sales are boosted by both brands. Frozen's LA premiere was cosponsored by Kellogg's, and Frozen character pictures are found on packaging for Band-Aids and Popsicles.

Joe Seer/Shutterstock

Source: Walmart

Source: popsicle.com

Sometimes the distinction between a brand and line extension isn't crystal clear. For example, Hyundai has long been positioned as offering relatively inexpensive, small cars (e.g., Elantra, Accent), and these might be considered brand extensions which extend the line (depth). But with the introduction of the Equus model, Hyundai is dipping its corporate toe into the luxury car pool, an altogether different business venture, targeting a segment with different needs. So it would probably be better considered a brand extension that crosses product categories (breadth).

The difference is a matter of degree: A slight new model twist may be going for depth; a vastly different model/product extends the breadth. Per the logic of brand extensions, Hyundai might have launched the Equus without reference to the umbrella Hyundai brand name, allowing it to achieve greater independence as a new brand in the house of Hyundai. However, by keeping the Hyundai imprint on the Equus, Hyundai's challenge will be to impress upon potential luxury car buyers—previous owners of Infinities, Lexuses (Lexi?), BMWs, etc.—that Hyundai, a brand known for good but admittedly more basic cars, can pull off the luxury positioning.

Co-branding is when two companies collaborate in a joint venture to create a good or service for the customer: "Brought to you by …" both companies. Tevlar fabric is used and touted when selling protective body gear (vests, helmets), bicycle tires, racing sails, and so forth. *Ingredient branding* is the primary form of cobranding in which one of the companies and its product is the primary host, and the other company and its product add value to the host product. For example, Intel is inside many PCs, and Brembo brakes are in Aston Martins, Lamborghinis, Maseratis, and Paganis. The Intel and Brembo brands are known on their own merit, but obviously the customer buys the PC or car, of which the processor or brakes are a component. The distinction between co-branding and ingredient branding is one of degree: Co-branding implies symmetry between the two providers, whereas, in ingredient branding, one brand dominates the other.

Dawn and Olay Co-Branding.

Terri Miller/E-Visual Communications, Inc.

Marketers might go further and begin to brand one of their own ingredients to make it seem like a particularly high-quality point of distinction from competitors. When a company is launching a relatively minor change, such as tweaking a current attribute (e.g., a new scent for an existing laundry detergent), then cobranding (specifically ingredient branding) might be fine for the short term, but in the long term, a self-brand is better, such as Tide's EverFresh scent. When the new product innovation is greater, e.g., involving an altogether new attribute, such as adding cough relief medicine to candy, cobranding is better, providing strategic benefits in the short and long term.

7-4c How are Brands Best Rolled Out Globally?

First, what is a global brand? To be defined as global, at least 30% of the brand's revenues should come from other countries (no more than 70% from the brand's home country).

Second, how do we roll out global brands? Analogously to the house of brands vs. umbrella branding decision, some companies go global with different brand names in different countries with the motto, "Manufacturer globally, brand locally." This is the so-called philosophy of glocalization. Other companies maintain the same brand name in every country they enter.

Just as it was said to be typically more advantageous to choose the umbrella path vs. the house of brands path, here, too, there appear to be greater advantages to maintaining a single brand name worldwide, if possible.

A true global brand (and perhaps neither surprisingly nor coincidentally, the biggest brands), carries one brand name and logo anywhere it is offered, and it is available in most markets in the world. Amazon.com looks just like Amazon.co.uk, for example, and Google.com looks like Google.fr. There are corporate efficiencies to using the same brand information, communications, and strategies everywhere. Strictly speaking, true global brands are those that seek, achieve, and maintain similar positioning in all their markets.

If a company wishes to serve different kinds of customer segments in different markets, they would opt to use different brand names in those markets. For example, one of the functions of a brand name is quality assurance, but quality per se might be of varying importance, depending on the culture, segment, or product. And, of course, we've all heard the examples of brand names that simply do not translate well. Finally, legal restrictions may curtail certain marketing activities and even brand names (e.g., Diet Coke vs. Coke Lite) that vary among countries. Still, these (admittedly big) caveats aside, the best marketing guru thinking seems to be to use the same name globally if you can.

7-4d Store Brands

What's the role of store brands? Don't laugh! While the name sounds like an oxymoron, store brands are big business. The traditional idea behind private labels is that they're less expensive and more of a me-too product offering than an innovative brand. Most of us are price sensitive in some product categories that are usually (by definition) those we don't care much about. In product categories we care more about, we're less price sensitive. Some customers seem to be price sensitive across the board. These are customers with sort of a cheap gene, a broader trait or propensity to go for store brands, across numerous categories (or, of course, they're simply working with limited resources).

Cost savings for customers aren't the only motive for store brands. Retailers are also offering premium private labels. While traditionally, generic (non)brands were packaged unattractively and thought to be of lower quality, these days the packaging and quality are usually on par with the big national brands, and many customers don't recognize the store brand as such. Walmart's brand of "Sam's Choice" might be an obvious name, but consider Target's "Archer Farms" or Kroger's "Private Selection." These are high-end or specialty products made available at so-called value prices.

The retailer can offer decent quality for lower prices because certain costs are reduced. They can advertise very inexpensively in local newspaper weekend flyers and radio spots, and clearly and easily, they can promote the brands in the store. Thus, to the customer, it looks like a brand, and it smells like a brand, so it must be a brand. And if it's a brand, it might be high quality. As is always the case, the advertising helps ensure trial, and the quality of the product determines satisfaction and repeat purchasing.

A lot of private label and pricing games go on in retailing. Retailers naturally want their shoppers to buy their brands, and, given their tremendous growth in power, they have been demanding better package deals from other source manufacturers. Between the added competition (including the store brands) and the aggressive deal demands, the manufacturers aren't going to sit still, of course. Premium (i.e., real) brands are launching their own second label, priced near the store label, to provide an alternative to price-sensitive customers, rather than losing them to the store brand (or to other competitors). What do the premium brand manufacturers do next? They raise the price of their original premium brand. Yeesh.

Also note that if brands represent culture, then non-branded goods are embraced by various countercultures. Such free spirits eschew big national brands due to the commercialism they represent.

7-5 HOW IS BRAND EQUITY DETERMINED?

In recent years, the popularity of branding, coupled with factors that have required marketers to be more accountable for their marketing expenditures and programs (e.g., slow economy, intense competition), have resulted in efforts to measure the worth of a brand.[10] Figure 7.7 lists the top 20 US and non-US brands as reported annually by *Business Week*. Do any of the brands on the list surprise you? Are these companies or brands not so great by any parameters? If Coca-Cola were to slip to tenth or eleventh in next year's poll, would you really consider it a lesser brand?

What is a brand's value?

How are the rankings in Figure 7.7 determined (see Interbrand.com for details)? When Rolls-Royce sold its brand to BMW for $60 million, where did that number come from? Let's see what goes into the consideration of a brand's value.

Figure 7.7

Top Brands

U.S.	Non-U.S.
• Apple	• Toyota
• Google	• Samsung
• Coca-Cola	• BMW
• Microsoft	• Mercedes-Benz
• IBM	• Honda
• GE	• Louis Vuitton
• McDonald's	• H&M
• Amazon	• SAP
• Disney	• Ikea
• Intel	• Zara

Branding Places

Branding cities and countries is becoming increasingly popular, as destinations seek more tourism or business investment (see Morgan, Pritchard, and Pride's book on *Destination Brands*). A unique positioning can be claimed on the basis of historical, social, or cultural values:

- Singapore highlights its blend of modernity, boasting a strong economy and a luxurious hospitality industry, with a setting that is perceived as an exotic destination for many tourists.

- Macau, barely a dot on the map 20 years ago, is one of the world's richest economies due to its gambling revenues, which surpass those of Las Vegas. It is now seeking to make a name for itself in medical tourism, differentiating itself from China, for example, as a safer alternative.

- Some cities, like some brands, are well-known but desire a shift in perception via re-positioning. Milan is currently seen as a business destination but it seeks to enhance potential travelers' awareness of its cultural and entertainment offerings.

- The national profile of the Australian brand is characterized by high awareness and relatively positive brand associations. Much of these branding successes may be attributed to movies (e.g., *Crocodile Dundee, Mad Max, Thorn Birds*). Tourism leaders seek to extend this strong position by enhancing awareness about specific cities, nature trips, and food and wine.

The basic idea in brand valuation is to derive measures that translate as best as possible into a financial vocabulary. The reasoning seems fair and sound: If marketers argue that their brands are assets, then they should be able to attach a monetary figure to that worth.

Some of the numbers that enter into these calculations are available in annual reports for public firms. Other numbers are obtained from customer survey data. Still other numbers are proprietary to the firms, such as Interbrand, doing the calculations.

One approach is to find out just what sort of price premium the brand can demand. A conjoint study can be run in which one attribute is brand (e.g., Shell Oil vs. unbranded fuel). Price can be one of the other attributes, or it can be what is measured (e.g., How much are you willing to pay for gas at a Shell station? vs. How much are you willing to pay for gas at a local gas station?). (We'll say more about conjoint in Chapter 8 on new products and in Chapter 15 on marketing research.)

A related approach focuses less on the price per se but compares the brand to an unbranded form of the product that is otherwise matched, feature-by-feature. Preferences and customer choices are measured (e.g., How much do you like this Sony flat screen, costing $499, with screen-within-a-screen, and holograph projection? vs. How much do you like this unknown brand flat screen, costing $499, with screen-within-a-screen and holograph projection?).

The Interbrand method is essentially to assess the value of a firm, subtract its physical and financial assets, and call the rest the value of the brand. That's a little simplistic because, while this calculation exposes a firm's intangibles, there are other intangible assets beyond the firm's brand (e.g., real investments in human resources or R&D's patents). So they still have to tease out the effect of the brand. These days, some 50% of a typical firm's value is estimated by determining its intangible assets, including its brand names. It may be challenging to estimate the value of those intangibles, but it is certainly done, therefore it is important to do it well.

So, how to actually do it? Figure 7.8 tracks the following computations. First, open up this year's annual report for your favorite brand, and find the operating earnings generated by that brand (e.g., a corporate earnings number for an umbrella brand or a brand number for a brand in a house of brands). Say you find that the net sales figure is $25,000,000, and the operating earnings figure for that brand is $7,000,000. Those earnings are taxed (say 25%), so subtract the taxes ($1,750,000). Suppose the tangible capital figure is $12,500,000, and multiply it by a rate of return of, say, 6% (a little conservative) and subtract this $750,000. The result is the figure for the earnings based on intangibles.

Figure 7.8

Brand Valuation

	Work sheet		Numbers Needed
a. Net sales (revenue for the brand)	$25,000,000		
b. Operating earnings			$7,000,000
c. Tax on earnings	25% × b	→	−1,750,000
d. Tangible capital	$12,500,000		
e. Rate of return	6% × d	→	− 750,000
f. Intangible earnings			$4,500,000
g. Brand contribution index (bci)	40%*		
h. Brand earnings	g × f		$1,800,000
*Depends on product category			

The next step is the magic of teasing out the brand effect. Interbrand estimates that brands are very important for perfumes, e.g., 90% of a firm's intangibles may be attributable to its brand, less important for cars (40%), and still less for retailers (20%). When this so-called brand contribution index is used as a multiplier against the intangibles, we derive the proportion of those intangible earnings that we may claim are due to the brand. We have an estimate of the brand value.

The method's not perfect, and the proprietary nature of the indices is annoying. But work in the area of brand valuation is new, so look for better developments soon. Regardless of any of the methods' shortcomings, when customer judgments of numerous brands are gathered, and the data are correlated with their companies' financials, marketers find clear evidence of strong positive relationships linking brands to shareholder value.

Strong brands deliver greater returns and with less risk (the classic desired state of higher means, lower variance) than comparable benchmarks. Marketing matters. Brands make companies financially healthier. Marketing always helps!

MANAGERIAL RECAP

Brands are promises to customers. Brands are names and logos and colors and fonts. In addition:

- Brands signal information to customers about predictability in their purchases, about anticipated reliability and expected quality.

- Brands can command higher prices because the brand offsets any uncertainties or risks associated with the purchase in the mind of the customer.

- Brand associations are the cognitive and emotional elements that combine to create the larger brand story.

- Companies can employ any of a number of strategies with their brands; they can put their corporate name on everything (i.e., an umbrella brand), or they can create a portfolio of different brands (i.e., the house of brands).

- Brand valuation, e.g., per the method of Interbrand reported in the *BusinessWeek* annual polls, are all the rage, and it is likely to continue to be important to branders for the future.

Chapter Outline in Key Terms and Concepts

1. What is a brand?
   a. Brand name
   b. Logos and color
2. Why brand?
3. What are brand associations?
   a. Brand personalities
   b. Brand communities

4. What are branding strategies?
   a. Umbrella brands vs. house of brands
   b. Brand extensions and co-branding
   c. How are brands best rolled out globally?
   d. Store brands
5. How is brand equity determined?
6. Managerial recap

Chapter Discussion Questions

1. What is one of your favorite brands (why)? What is a brand you hate (why)?

2. Which brand personality best describes you? Your business school? What is it about these images you like? What would you change about these images to make them even more desirable (and how would you do so)?

3. Read the methodology of Interbrand.com for brand valuations. How might you improve their methods and the sorts of measures they use to assess brand equity?

▶ Video Exercise: Method (7:43)

Eric Ryan and Adam Lowery, cofounders of Method, a line of household cleaning products, discuss how the product concept came into being and subsequently was developed into a premium line. Ryan and Lowery saw an opportunity to create a premium brand from the observation that the lucrative $20-billion-a-year household cleaning products category suffered from product sameness that was uninteresting and uninspiring. Method's philosophy of branding stresses that "the brand is the promise that the consumer gets from the product you are selling and the product itself delivers on that promise." Ryan and Lowery created a line of nontoxic, high-performing cleaning products that would make a home feel fresher, more livable, and more beautiful. These products were packaged so attractively that they would market themselves on stores' shelves. They sought to extend the reach of the brand by focusing on audience segmentation rather than product segmentation, wherein Method cultivated customer loyalty to the brand across all the company's cleaning products rather than cultivating loyalty to a particular cleaning product.

Video Discussion Questions

1. What are the key product features or qualities that define the Method brand of household cleaning products?

2. What value accrues to customers who purchase the Method brand of household cleaning products? What value accrues to Method itself?

3. Is Method's line of household cleaning products a luxury brand? Explain your answer.

MINI-CASE

6MD

A biotech firm creates bone replacements that have been used successfully for about 5 years in a variety of applications—joint replacements, trauma, etc. The parts are primarily titanium, a metal that has a decent track record for such uses because it is strong yet lightweight. It is also said to be biocompatible (i.e., rarely causes rejection problems).

None of that is new. What's new to the firm's technology is that the titanium is calci-plated. Bones wear down faster than titanium, and in fact, titanium is so strong that it causes further wear on surrounding tissue. The calcium-like plating surrounding the bone pieces offers the advantage of slowing down that friction, making the pieces last longer, but also greatly slowing the onset of any returning aches and pains. A by-product of the calci-treatment is that it does not set off security systems at airports.

The firm is obviously happy about their products' successes, but they are regretting their status as a component piece. They wish to begin branding their pieces. Much like the success of the "Intel Inside" advertising campaign for their micro-processing chip, the biotech firm draws an analogy and wants people to understand that they are offering an excellent "ingredient" brand.

The firm is pretty set on calling the product lines by the brand name 6MD. It began as a skunkworks project nickname, representing the bio-engineers' respect for the Six Million Dollar (6 m.d.) Man. They had even hoped to get Lee Majors to be their spokesperson, but initial contact made clear that he was too expensive. He was also looking a little long in the tooth. The name also stuck because the "MD" piece of the brand name should resonate with one of the constituencies who would use the brand.

Case Discussion Questions

1. Who is/are the biotech firm's customers?

2. How should they position this brand?

3. Will the customers appreciate the brand's USP (unique selling proposition)? Why?

4. What directions might you suggest to the biotech firm for brand- or line-extensions?

NEW PRODUCTS AND INNOVATION 8

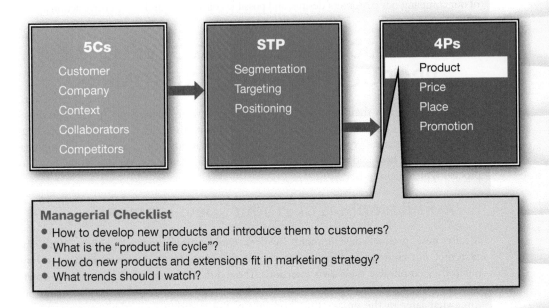

5Cs	STP	4Ps
Customer	Segmentation	**Product**
Company	Targeting	Price
Context	Positioning	Place
Collaborators		Promotion
Competitors		

Managerial Checklist
- How to develop new products and introduce them to customers?
- What is the "product life cycle"?
- How do new products and extensions fit in marketing strategy?
- What trends should I watch?

8-1 WHY ARE NEW PRODUCTS IMPORTANT?

"New and improved!"[1] You see it everywhere. Why? New products are fun for customers, they're fun for employees to work on, and they fuel the company's income.

Companies, like people, are ever evolving. The primary way that companies make changes is by offering so-called new and improved goods and services to customers. Companies seek to *improve* their current products for numerous reasons: a simple point of corporate pride, to be consistent with an image of being innovative, as an effort to better satisfy current customers or attract new customers, or to stave off competition. Having achieved some success with its existing portfolio, the company poses a question with product development: What else can we do that might appeal to customers and that is something we're likely to be able to do better than our competitors? How can we leverage our strengths and technical advantages? How can we serve new markets?

Change is inevitable. The macroenvironmental context continually shifts, and trends in demographics create predictable transformations in markets and in customer demands for new and different products (which we'll discuss later in the chapter). For example, the availability of natural resources—even simple supply-side basics such as oil, wood, and sugar—have implications for many companies.

Change is good. New products increase a company's long-term financial performance and value.

And change is fun! From the customers' point of view, if you like cars, you can't wait to see next year's models. If you like fashion, you eagerly anticipate each new season. If you like movies, you can't wait until Friday. From the marketing manager's point of view, it's fun to work on a new project, to be a part of offering something new in the marketplace, and to watch the customers respond (ideally) positively!

In this chapter, we'll look at the process of new product development and the stages of the product life cycle. We'll examine strategies to maintain strong product portfolios, and, as already implied, we'll need to keep a close eye on our classic Cs: change in the business context, strengths of our company, our customers' desires, and possible collaborator and competitive actions.

8-2 HOW DOES MARKETING DEVELOP NEW PRODUCTS FOR THEIR CUSTOMERS?

Companies differ in their approaches to designing new products. Some pride themselves on being innovative, whereas others are more conservative, launching me-too products after other companies break new ground. We'll see that one of the primary philosophical differences is in how and when companies involve their customers. We'll then see how the process typically unfolds.

8-2a Philosophies of Product Development

Ideally new product development involves conversations and interactions with the customer, but companies differ in how much they draw from customers relative to how much they emphasize their own assertions. These differences are referred to as "top-down" (when a company thinks up a new idea, develops it, and doesn't involve the customer until somewhat later in the process) or "bottom-up" (ideas spring from the customers themselves, and the company then pursues them in development). The top-down approach is often favored in companies with technical expertise (e.g., engineering and medical), but both approaches have their strengths, as we shall see.

Top-Down. The process of developing new products depends first on a company's culture. Some companies take a nearly exclusively top-down approach, beginning with idea generation, proceeding to design and development and then to commercialization. Marketing is essentially an afterthought, something to help with the final launch phase to introduce the product to customers.

A top-down approach is found frequently among companies with strong engineering orientations, pharmaceutical and biomedical firms, financial services, and many high-technology companies. The internal R&D team has expertise that the end users lack. So it creates cutting-edge products (e.g., a new computer, pill, mutual fund, TV), with such advanced technological benefits and advantages that seem so obvious to the experts that the team believes the product will sell itself.

This approach is the build-a-better-mousetrap philosophy, and it has facilitated zillions of successful new products. It's not necessarily a simple process, or a particularly quick one (e.g., drugs spend years in development). Furthermore, the process can be top-down for poor reasons, such as a CEO with a pet project who won't let it go.

Top-down is sometimes also called "inside-out" because the idea comes from within the company. Feedback from the outside (customers, suppliers, etc.) is sought

> *Change is good, and change is fun!*

later in the process. As long as any feedback is obtained from customers, this can be a perfectly fine approach. It is indeed usually the case that such companies can envision more cool new products than their customers could have articulated.

Bottom-Up. If this process is called top-down (or inside-out), its opposite should be called bottom-up (or outside-in), but these days it's referred to as "co-creation" (with the customer). The truth is, in the real world, neither extreme occurs—i.e., where the engineers or IT guys are consulted and the customers are not, or vice versa. So the difference between these styles is just a matter of when and how frequently feedback from customers and business partners is sought.

8-2b Marketing

In marketing-oriented companies, customer feedback is sought at most phases in the process. As is true of most marketing phenomena, consumer packaged goods companies (and those that provide some simple services) excel in the iteration between thinking up what the company can create and testing that with customers. Even the kinds of companies that have traditionally ignored marketing are becoming increasingly aware of its importance. Mercedes-Benz says, "Here's our new car; you're lucky if you can buy it." And they're right. Whereas Honda says, "We can configure all kinds of features and services for our cars. What would our customers want?" And they're the better marketers.

The new product development process might sound simple: Get an idea, develop it, put it out in the market. As Figure 8.1 indicates, for most products, the process is more complicated. For example, a great deal of refinement occurs throughout the entire process, including winnowing ideas and tweaking them in-house.

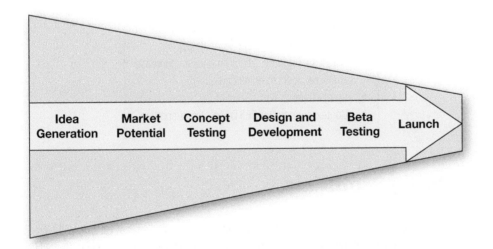

Figure 8.1

New Product Development Process

| Idea Generation | Market Potential | Concept Testing | Design and Development | Beta Testing | Launch |

The figure is also a little misleading because it looks linear and straightforward (step 1, step 2, etc.) when in fact, a lot of iterations occur. A decision may seem appropriate, and then, in subsequent stages, the earlier decision becomes untenable. It may seem obvious in the abstract that we shouldn't continue to push forward with something that is already known to be problematic. Unfortunately, that happens a lot (e.g., people tout sunk costs, want to meet preannounced launch dates for PR or investors, don't want to create political waves). Clearly it's better to revisit decisions and get things straightened out, even if it may feel disappointing to go backward temporarily or to seem to be slowing down.

Marketing management is involved throughout. In the early stage of idea generation, a knowledge of customer needs and wants interact with corporate and marketing strategies to see what potential new products makes sense for the firm. Marketing research should also be involved in all the refinement phases and in the decisions about the marketing mix that must be made as the launch approaches. Ideally, all the marketing components (e.g., pricing, packaging, channels) are treated holistically from the beginning of the process through to launch; thus, as the product concept is refined, so are decisions about retail outlets, price points, etc., in order to offer the customer a consistently positioned product. Let's look at the new product development process in greater detail.

8-2c Idea Creation and Market Potential

Ideas can come from anywhere (see Figure 8.2). If necessity is the mother of invention, one source of new products is marketers' observations of the world around them. This nonsystematic, qualitative form of marketing research helps marketers identify customer's problems that might be solved with products the firm could offer. Your kids don't like brushing their teeth? No problem; our toothbrushes light up like a game.

Figure 8.2

Where Do New Ideas Come From?

Internal

- The Boss
- R&D, In-house experts, Brainstorming
- Employees (e.g., suggestion box)
- Feedback from front-line, sales force

External

- Customers (complaints, lead-users, marketing research—focus groups, scan blogs)
- Business partners (requirements to decrease costs, requests to enhance quality),
- Competition
- Context (remember PEST); i.e., Trend-spotting

Solving Problems

- The Shanghai Automotive Industry Corporation (SAIC) has created a concept car that will have a negative carbon footprint. It creates an artificial photosynthesis process, like a plant, that will enable the car to remove more pollution than it creates. The car is called, "Yez," which is apparently Chinese for "leaf."
- To help Mother Nature, a hyperabsorbent peat moss has been invented that cleans oil spills in water. The moss is scattered on the oil spill and it absorbs the oil but not the water. The moss is then scooped up like kitty litter, and, voila, there is clean H_2O (Inhabitat.com).
- Medical tattoos insert nanosensors to monitor conditions such as diabetes, which turn colors when glucose levels change (Ideaconnection.com).

Ideas can come from observing social (or cultural or economic) trends, from listening to customers, your sales force, or your frontline service workers. Ideas are often somewhat serendipitous, but remember what Louis Pasteur said: "Chance favors the prepared mind." For example, Viagra was originally created to relieve heart pain. It wasn't particularly effective for that symptom, but users reported an interesting side effect. The rest is history.

The typical method of idea generation begins with good old-fashioned, coffee-fueled brainstorming meetings. These sessions generate discussions on the basis of the classic, "No idea's a bad idea; let's get everything up on the whiteboard." Companies that pride themselves on being innovative are increasingly putting real resources behind their claims, including supporting employees' allocating a day a month to work on their own pet projects, to be assessed later and perhaps funded for development.

After many ideas have been generated and sketched out, the next step is in-house winnowing and refinement. This is the phase during which we acknowledge, "Okay, maybe some ideas are in fact bad ideas." Ideas are screened for their plausibility in construction and provision, their compatibility with corporate and marketing goals, and their likelihood of success with customers. At this point, the expertise of the designers, engineers, chemists, etc., are being balanced with the marketers' knowledge of the target customer segment(s) and management's guidance about the firm's identity. (e.g., Rolex doesn't want to make an affordable watch, and Disney needs to stay wholesome.)

While feasibility assessments and business analyses are somewhat fuzzy at this stage, they are valuable exercises in making assumptions explicit: Who is the target segment? What is its size? What competitors already seek their dollar? What products of our own might we cannibalize? Do we have channels already in place for the distribution of this product, or should we be studying those issues as well? How does the new product initiative fit with our organizational goals and our marketing objectives? As the product development process continues, teams can be assembled to investigate answers to these component questions.

8-2d Concept Testing and Design & Development

At this stage in the new product development process, the company has a number of ideas that it thinks might work, and it's time to get customers' feedback as to which ideas sound the most promising. The form of the marketing research at this stage is usually focus groups and, increasingly, web surveys (especially for technical target audiences). The particular marketing research techniques used aren't half as important as the fact that any marketing research is conducted at all. This stage is the first of several during which marketing research can save a company from a bad idea, yield information to tweak a half-baked idea, or result in encouragement that the company is pursuing an idea with true potential. Time and again, new product success (vs. failure) is attributed to good (vs. poor or nonexistent) marketing research.

If focus groups are the vehicle of choice, then two to three groups (per segment) of eight to 10 target customers are invited to see the concepts and offer feedback. These (one-and-a-half- to two-hour) discussions can begin as broadly as asking the customers to describe their uses of products in this category (e.g., household goods, foods, their driving habits, etc.). The aim is to get background information that can inform the product development or the positioning of the product via communications materials developed subsequently. The concepts might be described verbally, but visual cues are very helpful. These visual aids can be as simple as artist's renderings, but they can be sleek photos or mockups and prototypes. Still more complex is a rendering via virtual reality. Competitors' products can be provided also, as a point of discussion, to get the customers to react to tangible, existing goods.

Descriptions and photos (of proposed and existing products) can also be shown via Web surveys.

In either a focus group or an online study, a conjoint procedure can be run. In a conjoint study, different combinations of attributes are put together and compared. The customer is simply asked which product combination sounds best, next best, and so on. From those overall evaluations, the conjoint analysis derives which attributes matter more than others. For example, the company may learn that it's important for laptops to be light and powerful and less important that they're encased in color. For the attributes that customers care most about, what are the levels sought; e.g., for qualities like a laptop being light and powerful, clearly lighter is better, and more powerful is better. But for a segment that cares about color, what do they want? High-tech gray? Neon blue? And if an important attribute is that the laptop be "preloaded with lots of software," what programs in particular do customers want to see?

Conjoint is great because it gets at customers' trade-offs. It's not unusual for customers to say they want the best of everything and—oh, by the way—at a really cheap price. Typically a company cannot offer all of that profitably. So a conjoint allows the detection of what price a customer is willing to pay for the loaded laptop, or, if the customer isn't willing to pay a high price, what features all-of-a-sudden become less important. That is, what features are they willing to trade off?

After the marketing research conducted in this concept testing stage, the marketing manager has a better sense of which products and features seem to be the most attractive to customers. Internally, the second major winnowing-and-refinement phase critically assesses the paths that no longer appear to have potential and should be discarded or tabled (e.g., those that require advances in technology or societal acceptance), and those that customers find appealing or might with further modifications.

"Marketing Research is Important," Says P&G!

Marketers point to Procter & Gamble and say that the company learned about the importance of marketing research after a slump in the 1920s and hasn't had to relearn the lesson.

Insights from customer feedback are often quite eye-opening. In-house experts assume they know what's best and are frequently surprised by customers' reactions. When customers do not like the proposed products, the experts can be dismissive, regarding the customers as stupid. Nevertheless, those unenlightened souls comprise the target purchasers; hence the difficulty lies in the product or the vision, which apparently isn't being communicated clearly. For example, it is not unusual for creators of high-tech gadgetry to overload their new products with all kinds of whiz-bang features. Yet customers' reactions can be lukewarm because the multitude of options and capabilities seems overwhelming, and the product seems difficult to use.

Another round of refined-concept testing might occur if ambiguities remain, or if sufficient changes were made that the reactions to the initial concept are likely to be no longer relevant. When the company is confident it has a handle on which product to develop, it begins to do so. Usually only a single prototype is developed, rather than multiple prototypes, in part because development can be expensive but also, more humanly, because the issue is about narrow attention spans. It's just easier for the product development team to focus on one product at a time: If one product development goes forward, great, otherwise, it's back to the drawing board to work up the next one serially, rather than process several in parallel.

8-2e Beta-Testing

At this point, a beta version of the product is made available for trial and consumption. Ideally, the product is used in the consumer's home or in as similar a setting as possible to simulate a real-world purchase decision and evaluation, for more accurate forecasting later.

While the product is being developed, so should be the marketing materials. Their early development and refinement will help make consistent the positioning information being absorbed by the customer. Thus, while products are being shown to customers for their reactions, advertising copy is also shown to them, price points are made clear, distribution and availability are explained, etc. Showing the customer the marketing information both helps clarify the image of the product and allows the company to get feedback on the marketing information itself.

The marketing manager now has evidence of customer potential, and the product has been repeatedly refined. It's time to try the product in the market on a small scale, before a more expensive full-scale commercial rollout.

Thus far, the marketing research has been comprised of fairly tightly controlled stimuli: A product and ad and price are shown to a set of customers, and their reactions are noted. Even if competitors knew of the new product development efforts, they cannot interfere with the tests being conducted. Yet, when customers are sitting in a focus group or answering questions online, they know they're doing something out of context (it feels weird); their behavior isn't likely quite the same as what it will be in the natural marketplace environment (e.g., at a grocery store, at the mall, or at Amazon). So the idea underlying test marketing is to try to simulate a real-world setting to help customers' reactions be more predictive of their subsequent actual purchasing behavior when the product is launched.

Area test markets are a neat idea. Some 40–50 small metropolitan areas throughout the United States are known to marketing research firms as having characteristics (e.g., demographics, socioeconomic status) that are representative of the country as a whole. A few (two or three) of these areas are randomly sampled to be test markets, in which the product is made available for purchase (and the remaining areas serve as control markets). Ads are run in the test markets, deals are made with the local retail chains, etc. Sales are observed through the test period (three to 12 months) and compared to sales in the control markets in order to give the company a sense of how well the product is likely to sell.

Area test markets aren't used that frequently any more, mostly because they're expensive. They require setup that, while small-scale, nevertheless requires manufacturing, machines, personnel training, etc. They also signal to competitors, who are living and observantly watching in those test markets, just what might be coming down the pike, and many a lawsuit has been filed over a product that has been scooped by a competitor. Finally, each of those areas, while chosen for being fairly representative of the broader target population, can have their own local flavors and oddities that can bias the results in unpredictable ways; i.e., if sales are high in one area but low in another, did something about the markets spuriously inflate or suppress sales?

Electronic test markets are also a cool idea. A sample of metropolitan areas is selected, and, within each market, some households are designated to be test and others to be control. All the local context is therefore equated (local TV stations, newspapers, local stores, local brands, cultural interests, etc.). So whatever differences exist between the households' purchasing is more cleanly attributable to some households having exposure to ads (e.g., via cable transmissions not sent to the control households) or having access to the product (e.g., in stores closer to their homes), etc. Given the tighter constraints, the validity of the electronic test market dominates that of the area test market.

Today, *simulated test markets* are the popular means of premarket launch tests. A customer is recruited (e.g., via email) to go to a website, where they are given a budget and have an opportunity to buy the new product, which is offered among competitors' or related products. Virtual grocery store aisles are displayed (sometimes in 3-D or virtual reality, but often just in a 2-D view) that provide the same information the customer would see on a typical trip to the grocery. There would be row after row of pictures of competitors' products, and the new product embedded, on the "shelf," as it would be when eventually launched. The marketer is looking for how often the new product is selected in this quasi-realistic context.

The advertising materials would be available with competitors' ads and offered subtly (e.g., in the context of a popular magazine), or TV ads would be inserted into natural commercial breaks of shows the customer might be asked to view. Marketers would watch the "purchases" of the new product, and the customers would be asked to fill out a litany of survey questions. All of this customer data would be used as inputs to sales forecasts.

8-2f Launch

In the final steps toward commercialization, both time and money matter. Let's consider money first.

Forecasting. Upon completion of the test marketing, the marketing manager takes the customer data and tries to predict the product's likely success. If the predictions of sales are not promising, this stage is the last opportunity for the company to abort before launching (and likely failing). If the predictions are promising, the company will proceed to commercialize. The forecasting numbers are useful throughout the organization—to accounting and finance for budgeting purposes, to the sales force for setting goals, to production and logistics for planning regarding equipment, storage, and transportation, etc.

Forecasting can be highly technical, but here's a simple formula to get a sense of the basic logic. The goal is to estimate the sales potential ($SP), which is not the same as estimated sales but more like a ceiling.

The first estimate we need is the market potential (MP); that is, how many units might possibly be sold. Recall the chaining model approach from Chapter 4 on targeting. We might start with secondary data (e.g., the size of the target potential by census demographics) or with other relevant in-house benchmarking data. For example, if the new product is somewhat like a current offering, as with a brand or line extension, then the company would know its numbers for the existing product.

The next piece is the estimate of purchase intention (PI), or the likelihood that the target segment will buy the product. This number comes from the most recent marketing research that was conducted. Let's say that, among the customers sampled from the target population, the average stated purchase intention was $p = 0.7$. It is important to know that customers predictably overstate their purchase intentions. Companies with databases of past new product launches can look to compare the PI vs. realized sales and adjust accordingly. For companies without such experience or data, research has suggested ratcheting the estimate downward by a factor of ¾. Thus, if the data said $p = 0.7$, the estimate to be used in the forecasting would be PI = ¾ (0.7) = 0.525.

Finally, the component that is under the company's control is the price the company intends to charge (Pr). (Of course, as economics would tell us, the components in the equation aren't entirely independent; PI is likely to increase a smidge as Pr drops.

That's why the marketing mixed should be tested with customers along with the product itself.) These pieces come together in this equation:

$$\$SP = MP \times PI \times Pr.$$

For example, a mid-level electronics manufacturer has developed a cell phone that allows users to be represented as holographic avatars. The holograms are not yet particularly realistic-looking, so the designers simply created avatars that resemble cartoon characters more than real people. As a result, the company thought the product would likely appeal to kids more than adults. Very young children are not likely to have their own cell phones yet, so the company has in mind as a target population kids from 13- to 15- years old.

In cooperation with a national cell phone carrier, the electronics firm is test-marketing its holographic avatars, or holotars for short, in an affluent Dallas suburb, and of course it will want to extrapolate the findings to the broader US. The population estimate of the US is a little over 300 mm (million). Of that number, the US teen population is 33 mm, and roughly one-third of them are assumed to be in the 13- to 15-year-old age bracket. From cell phone industry statistics, let's say the company learns that about 20% of eligible target customers are likely to purchase this model of phone. Based on those gross secondary statistics, an upper limit estimate for MP is some 2.2 mm (= 33 mm ÷ 3 × 0.2) young teens to whom the holotar phone is targeted. If testing suggested that PI (with the correction factor already included) is 0.525 and if the company plans on charging $99 for the phone, then the estimate is:

$$\$SP = 2,200,000 \times 0.525 \times \$99 = \$114,345,000$$

That number is not profits; it's (potential maximum) sales with no development or production or marketing costs factored in yet. Is that number good news, or is it barely enough to make the company bother? If corporate decides that's a worthy goal, then the next step is to launch the product, which means that finally, after months and sometimes years in development, the product sees the light of day. Woohoo!

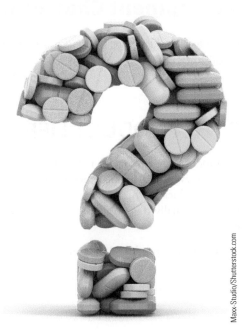

Maxx-Studio/Shutterstock.com

New products forecasting is hugely important for Pharma companies.

Timing. New product development can move along fairly speedily for straightforward brand or line extensions in the context of a mature consumer packaged goods company. In other settings, the development process can seem torturously slow. For example, pharmaceutical testing begins on animals[2] (for months to years), and then the drug is tried on 20–100 healthy patients (for months) to check basic safety (e.g., side effects). Next, the drug is tested on several hundred patients with the particular disease (from three months to two years) to continue to check safety and to add checks on efficacy. Finally, hundreds to thousands of people (healthy and sick) are observed (for one to four years) to check safety and efficacy and to tweak dosage.

Time is indeed money, and, to recoup the cost of this extended testing and investment, pharmaceuticals spend $20 billion annually on promotional efforts, e.g., providing retail samples to doctors. D2C (direct to consumers) pharma advertising is growing like crazy (doubling every two years). It is interesting to marketers and salient in business news because of its novelty, but as yet it is actually still fairly small in size (e.g., 5–10% of sales). There can also be external, regulatory delays to product launches:

- The FDA (Food and Drug Administration) is trying to reduce the length of time to market with shortcuts on clinical trials. Yet every action is met with an equal and opposite reaction, and the FDA is under investigation for pushing drugs to market too quickly (arising from problems with drugs that produced rare but serious side effects).

- Other industries voice complaints about delays by analogous approval agencies, such as patent offices. Some big companies ask for court intervention to speed things up so that they don't lose millions of dollars in opportunity costs.

- Comparable issues occur with copyright registrations for intangibles like software, movies, video games, music, and architectural plans. A current controversy concerns when a copyright takes effect. Is the material copyrighted when it's registered, or is it sufficient to have simply filed and applied for the registration?

Product Development Challenge

Businessweek.com reports a Boston Consulting Group study in which "length development times" was the #1 obstacle in innovation.

8-3 WHAT IS THE PRODUCT LIFE CYCLE?

Another reason that new products are important is that the company's product portfolio may be aging. The product life cycle is a popular metaphor in marketing to describe the evolution and duration of a product in the marketplace (see Figure 8.3). Just as people are born, grow, mature, and eventually die, products are thought to go through a similar life cycle. The stages are:

1. Market introduction (the new product development phase we've been discussing)

2. Market growth

3. Maturity

4. Decline

Sales and profits behave predictably during the different phases (indeed, usually the phase in which a product exists is determined by these indicators), and the marketing actions that are thought to be optimal during each phase are also clearly prescribed.

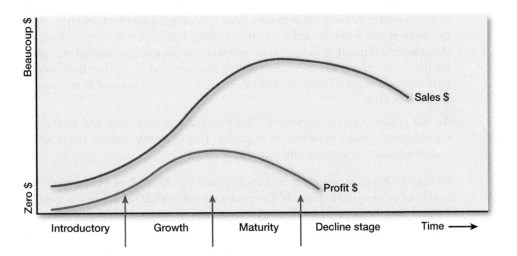

Figure 8.3

**The Product
Life Cycle
(PLC)**

During *market introduction*, a new product (good or service) is brought into the market-place with heavy marketing spending (e.g., communications to spark awareness). In addition to advertising to provide information and attempts at persuasion, promotion can include samples and coupons to spur trial. Strategically, prices might start low (penetration), but they often start high (skimming) in part to recoup development costs and in part due to the fact that early on there is little competition. Distribution is somewhat limited in these early phases, and all of these factors contribute to the typical result that sales are low and slow in the beginning.

The second phase is *market growth*. Sales accelerate and profits rise at first. Customer awareness is stronger, and there may be some buzz in the marketplace. Distribution channel coverage is greater, so access also contributes to stronger sales. The firm might be able to begin increasing prices (resulting in higher margins and greater profits). At the same time, competitors observe the pioneering company's successes and start sniffing profit potential, so they enter the game. Competitors either kill each other off, or they begin to specialize a little, identifying emergent segments to which their products can be tailored and targeted. The initial firm can sustain the competition if it had had enough foresight to have launched a product with some reasonable edge of a competitive advantage and if the product can be slightly altered to maintain distinctiveness (and supporting possible price maintenance for interested segments). At this stage, advertising is intended to persuade customers that the brand is superior to all competitors' brands.

At some later point, a product nears *market maturity*. Advertising continues to try to convince customers of a brand's relative advantages and serves as a reminder to buy in the product category. Products may proliferate to a fuller product line in order to satisfy more segments of customers. Industry sales have leveled off, so competition is intensifying; there is more competition than in any other stage in the life cycle. The stiff competition has induced higher marketing costs and likely lower prices; thus, while sales are stronger than ever, profits have declined. In addition, the pie is no longer growing in size, so strong competitors gain market share or increase their sales only by taking it away from other competitors. Hence, weaker firms begin to fall out of the marketplace. In addition, because firms are going after each other, their product offerings often begin to homogenize to the point that customers see fewer distinguishing characteristics. Instead of swirling into price drops with competition, it's smart to try to find new benefits and to either increase or at least maintain current prices.

The final phase in the product life cycle is *market decline*. Sales and profits are both dropping, and new products are replacing older generations. The firm needs to decide what to do with the old product.

- Sometimes it is divested. If this route is taken, the decision should be made as early as possible because the best sales price is obtained if it is sold off early, while the product still looks attractive to another firm. Unfortunately, early timing for divestment is difficult to judge; often companies aren't sure the product has quite hit the decline stage, and they aren't willing to give up on it. So they hold onto it until it is typically too late to be sold off, i.e., it is no longer a desirable investment for another firm.

- An old product can be "harvested." The firm reduces supportive and marketing expenditures in order to extract more profits. They're merely milking the product, and they know that demand will continue to drop.

- Perhaps the happiest prognosis for a dying product is when a firm wishes to rejuvenate it, as in "new and improved!" The product is refurbished to have new beneficial features that the target customer might desire.

While the product life cycle is an intuitively appealing metaphor, critics point out that it is just that, a metaphor. They point out that brands and products are not organic; therefore they don't have to die. They argue that the life cycle is actually a self-fulfilling prophecy; e.g., when a firm determines that a product is mature, it might lessen the advertising support, in effect causing the product's decline.

The lengths of product life cycles vary a lot. Researchers point to the short lifespan of movies (years and millions of dollars spent in development for only a few weeks in theaters). Yet movies are "born again" or "reincarnated" (to continue the life cycle metaphor) into international box office, cable, DVD rentals and sales, with each reincarnation reinvigorating the product and sales, albeit in a different guise and to a different target audience. Other products and brands, such as Coca-Cola, Tide, or Holiday Inn, seem to be in that juicy sales phase of "maturity" for an extended life.

Finally, the length of product-category life cycles tends to be longer than those of individual brands. That is, a particular movie might not live a long life, but the category of movies is 100 years old. Or the macro level category of sports is a healthy and very mature product, but one could point to NASCAR as an example of a recent, young subproduct with explosive growth.

8-3a Diffusion of Innovation

In addition to the marketing actions underlying the product life cycle, marketers have also developed a theory about what customers are doing during these phases as well. The concept is that new products are like, well, contagious diseases. If a person with a cold is in a room full of people and sneezes, think about who will get sick the soonest: the people closest to Sneezy.

A similar phenomenon is thought to occur when a new product is introduced. The friend in your circle who likes new high-tech gadgets will get a new electronics toy (business instrument) and show it to all his friends. They'll ooh and ah, and, the next thing you know, some of them have the new toy as well, and they're telling their friends. Or the friend in your circle who likes movies will naturally read more and know more about what new movies are coming out. She will be among the first to see the new show, and she will then inform all her friends about the movie and recommend that they see it or not. This word-of-mouth or "viral" marketing helps activate the process of the diffusion of innovations.

Anatomy of a Product Life Cycle

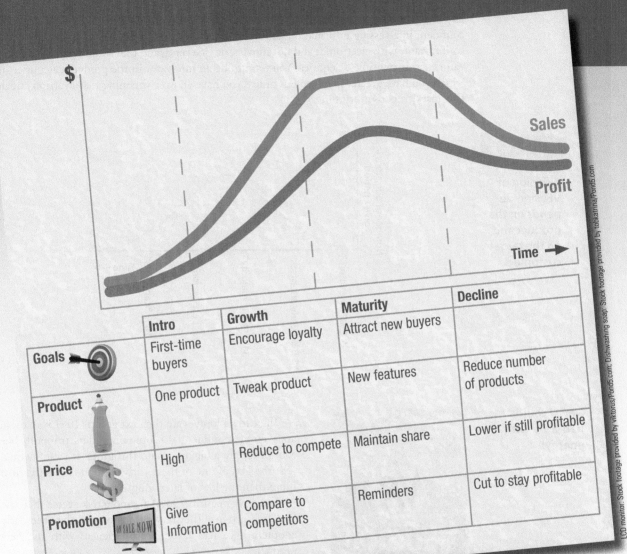

	Intro	Growth	Maturity	Decline
Goals	First-time buyers	Encourage loyalty	Attract new buyers	
Product	One product	Tweak product	New features	Reduce number of products
Price	High	Reduce to compete	Maintain share	Lower if still profitable
Promotion	Give Information	Compare to competitors	Reminders	Cut to stay profitable

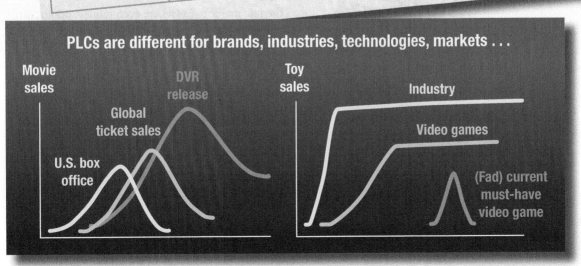

PLCs are different for brands, industries, technologies, markets . . .

Movie sales
Toy sales

DVR release
Global ticket sales
U.S. box office

Industry
Video games
(Fad) current must-have video game

The model itself is pretty simple. Marketers posit a normal curve (see Figure 8.4) and partition the customer base into groups. The so-called innovators are the first 3–5% who like to try new ideas and are willing to take risks. They tend to be relatively educated and confident in assessing information about a product on their own. (Note that you might be an innovator with electronics and not movies, or vice versa, and that some people are innovators across multiple categories. You tend to be an innovator in the product categories in which you have greater involvement unless you have an overwhelming risk-aversion streak that just dampens everything.)

Successful diffusion of VFusion depends on the product and on the target customers

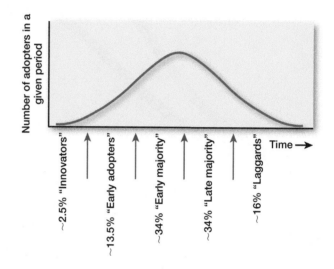

New! I coulda had-a V8, with energy!

Source: pinterest.com

The early adopters are the next group (10–15%); these are even more influential as opinion leaders, primarily because they are a bigger group. This group is so influential that the loss of one of these early adopters costs the firm more than the loss of later adopters.

The early majority (34%) are more risk averse than the first two groups. They're waiting to hear that the early adopters have had favorable experiences with the new product.

The late majority (34%) are even more cautious, often older and more conservative, and wish to buy only proven products.

The final group, the laggards or non-adopters (5–15%), are the most risk averse, skeptical of new products, and stereotypically lower in income (and so perhaps cannot afford to be risky with their purchases). Sometimes the product category has no relevance to them (e.g., your grandfather probably doesn't appreciate the features on your new phone).

The curve of new adopters at each point in time (in Figure 8.4) can be recast to show cumulative sales—the number of adopters thus far at each point in time, such as the S-curve in Figure 8.5. The point at which the sales rate increases rapidly—when sales take off—is determined via calculus as the point of inflection in the curve. In contemporary parlance, it's referred to as the "tipping point," the point at which the product or idea catches on and moves like wildfire throughout the marketplace.

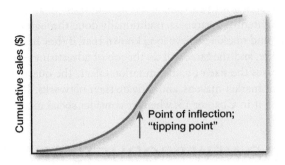

Figure 8.5

Cumulative Diffusion

Marketers have forecast sales using this logic. In the equation in Figure 8.6, we are trying to forecast n_t, the number of units we will sell during time period t. The prediction is a function of several components: N_{t-1} represents the number of units we have sold so far (cumulative sales in units). M is the max on the likely market potential. The term on the right, $(M - N_{t-1})$, means, how we are doing so far: What's the difference between what we could sell (M) and what we've sold so far (N_{t-1})?

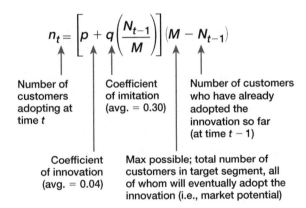

Figure 8.6

Model of Diffusion

Traditionally the pieces that interest marketers are the parameters p and q. The first, p, is called the coefficient of innovation; it's the likelihood that someone will buy or adopt the new product due to information obtained from the marketer. The second, q, is the coefficient of imitation, the likelihood that someone will buy or adopt the new product due to word-of-mouth information obtained from another consumer (e.g., an innovator).

There are two different ways the diffusion model has been used. First, we can observe early sales data, fit the model, and make predictions about the future. For example, once sales begin, we'll have numbers for n_t and N_{t-1} (t can be yearly data, quarterly, weekly, hourly, etc.). We conduct market sizing exercises (Chapter 4) to obtain an estimate for M. We then solve for estimates of p and q. Alternatively, we can use past results on products similar to ours and plug in those numbers to make predictions about the future even before launching the product.[3]

The imitation effect (q) is usually bigger ($p{:}q$ is about 1:10), and, if you consider the massive size of the majority in Figure 8.5, it's easy to see why. The percentage of innovators and early adopters (the customers who are driving p) is about 10–15% of the market, whereas the remainder of the market (the majority, etc.) is 85–90%, and they're driving q. Marketers can speed up innovators (make p bigger) by introducing price decreases early, or they can speed up imitators (make q bigger) by introducing price decreases later.

Marketers are interacting with customers throughout these phases. The first job in a new product launch is heightening awareness, traditionally done through advertising. Advertising can be expensive, and marketers have long known that, if they have a hot product, word will spread like wildfire, and the buzz will do the job of advertising—for free. In diffusion, word of mouth increases the size of q, the imitation effect. The question is how to identify the opinion leaders, or market mavens, and activate their networks. This topic is so important that we'll focus on it in Chapter 13, when we consider social media.

8-4 HOW DO NEW PRODUCTS AND BRAND EXTENSIONS FIT IN MARKETING STRATEGY?

We've been examining the new product development process, the product life cycle, and the diffusion of innovation. Let's zoom back out and check in on the marketing Cs. A company can begin its new product plan internally by identifying the corporate and marketing missions and objectives to be achieved via the new product or service. Applying SWOT analysis, the marketer asks of the company: What are our strengths and weaknesses? Of the industry, the question is: What are the opportunities and threats?

It should be clear that customers are important in the feedback they provide in the new product development process. A number of factors influence customers' acceptance of new products and the diffusion of the innovation throughout the marketplace. Customers will ask: What is the benefit of this new thing? Why should I buy it?

Consumer acceptance tends to be higher when the new product:

- Has a clear relative advantage over existing products.

- Is compatible with the customer's lifestyle.

- Is not overly complex, or the complexity is masked by a user-friendly interface.

- Is easily tried or sampled in order to facilitate initial assessment.

The customer is important from the beginning, when marketing identifies the target and conducts market analyses to begin to project sales forecasts (e.g., estimating size, growth, customers' unmet needs, trends, etc.).

Competitor analysis is integral to the mission planning in that the differentiating benefits of the new product (sustainable competitive advantages in the value proposition) must be clear. For instance, customers can ask, "How is yours better than the competition?" And competitors can ask, "Why don't we offer the same thing—even better?" Competitor analyses also take the form of identifying which industries and companies are truly competitors and guesstimating their likely reactions.

Most companies offer multiple product lines, so they're constantly balancing the strategic needs of products at different points in their life cycles. Different stages in the life cycle require different investments; e.g., periods of growth need cash, while periods of slower growth might generate cash to be reinvested to maintain share. For new service innovations, some of the R&D investment is the training of employees before the service is launched as operational.

Much like the personalities of people in the diffusion of innovation, companies vary in whether they desire to be known as cutting edge. Some companies value their reputations as innovators, and their business relies on new product market growth. Other companies are more comfortable in their roles as reactors. They might not be the innovators, but they can be quick responders, coming to market soon with slightly different attributes or with better price points, for example. Finally, later companies may be more risk averse or not aggressive marketers, and they offer a product only when it's clear that customer demand exists.

Much research has been generated investigating each of these strategies. Market pioneers have difficulty with really new products. The first to market is often the first to fail. A new concept takes awhile to sink into the minds of customers. By comparison, first movers may have advantages in launching incrementally new products because there is less risk. In either case, after the first firm, the next few early follower firms have approximately the same survival risks when launching either the really new or the incrementally new products. Next-generation products (e.g., smartphones, desktops, video games) are easier to launch because there is an existing customer base, channels of distribution, and much more predictability.

8-4a Strategic Thinking about Growth

Marketers have to be smart about where all these new products fit into their marketing and corporate portfolio. It's true that some things in life are serendipitous and that we might occasionally behave opportunistically, but, as a company gets bigger and bigger, lots of people are counting on a product's success. The top folks need to show they have vision, know where the company is going, and not react willy-nilly to whatever's going on around them.

The strategic paths to growth that marketers typically talk about may be classified by whether you stick to your current product mix and take it to new target segments or you generate altogether new products. That's all it comes down to new stuff or new peeps. Figure 8.7 shows the matrix of growth opportunities.

	Current products	New products
Current markets	Market penetration	Product development
New markets	Market development	Diversification

Figure 8.7

Growth Strategies

Market penetration means we're hunkering down and trying to sell more—the same stuff to the same customers. If the customers are not completely tapped, this is certainly the easiest of all the four strategies. We don't have to make anything new, and we know how to reach these customers. Companies strive for more sales (via this strategy) by suggesting new ways to use the product, by opening more stores, or by improving the marketing mix (more intriguing advertising, better pricing, better reward program, better in-store service, better store ambience, etc.).

First to Market is Not Always Best

A *Fortune* magazine article by Jon Birger talks about a "second mover advantage" in which Lowe's is compared to number one Home Depot. The second mover is in a good position. They watch what number one does, and then they do something different (e.g., number two Target vs. number one Walmart; PepsiCo vs. Coca-Cola). The number twos will do their best to compete on price, cost, operational efficiency. Lowe's has wider aisles, brighter stores, and friendlier salespeople. Being number one, you're a natural target.

Product development is for the company that wishes to be innovative. New or modified products are offered to the current customer base to keep them happy. These new products may be as dramatic as brand and line extensions, but often they are modest extensions (e.g., larger sizes, new flavors, different packaging, etc.).

Market development is the path we take when we're settled on our product mix and we think there are more segment opportunities to target. This path can be dramatic when we launch our brand internationally, but it is also more often subtle (e.g., trying to appeal to a slightly younger or older crowd, trying to appeal to men if the product mostly sells to women, etc.). The product may remain the same, but, to reach the new target, we might need to expand our channels and modify our promotional communications to create a new image for that new target.

Finally, *diversification* is the toughest. We're going after new customers with new products. If you think of the 2 × 2 matrix in Figure 8.7 as a game board and the company starts in the upper left corner (market penetration), moving to the right (product development) or down (market development) isn't that difficult. From either of those places, it is easier to move to diversification. But it's just too big a jump for most companies to go from "doing what we know how to do for the customers who like us" (upper left) to "doing something we don't have a clue about for customers we don't know and who don't know us" (lower right). Baby steps: Go right or down. Then go down or right.

8-5 WHAT TRENDS SHOULD I WATCH?

It's important to keep an eye on how the world is changing and the directions things are going because trends form the context in which all new product forecasting occurs. Demographic, lifestyle, and cultural trends can boost or constrain the success of a new product.

Perhaps the most stunning demographic trend in America and Western Europe is the aging of the population (e.g., more elderly, fewer kids and teens). In 20 years, 20% of Europeans will be 65 years old or older. Sheer age carries both health and wealth concerns. Aging brings greater health care needs because the populace will experience predictably more rheumatoid arthritis, osteoporosis, prostate problems, etc. Supplemental health enhancement industries will also grow. For example, in the vain attempt to delay the aging process, witness the growth of botox and health spa consumption. And to help with those creaky old bones, people in the US are retiring to the sunbelt (Southern and Western states), which will have huge real estate and retail implications.

A wealth implication of aging revolves around whether retirees have prepared to be financially independent. For example, in the US and Japan, people spend what they earn (or more), so retirees are going to be hurting. Italy's citizens are among the oldest in

Europe, but they're good savers. Germany's age demographics and savings habits are somewhere in between.

Among other large-scale demographic shifts are the facts that in the US, 1 in 7 people is Hispanic and that this subpopulation is growing faster than any others. The power of the Hispanic consumer is therefore a substantial trend: They control nearly $1 trillion in spending power, a number that cannot be ignored by any firm except the most niche or naïve of players.

Beyond simple demographics, numerous lifestyle trends should be salient when companies are considering new directions. For example, there are more wealthy Americans than ever before, accompanied by an expectation that the number is still rising. Baby boomers are in their peak earning years, and they're becoming empty nesters and hence will have more discretionary funds. Worldwide financial wealth is also tremendous; the top countries for numbers of millionaires are: the US (about 4.3 mm of them), Japan (2.5 mm), Germany (1.1 mm), China (0.9 mm), and the UK (0.5 mm). The top countries for numbers of billionaires are: the US (536), Germany (103), India (90), Russia (88), Hong Kong (55), Brazil (54), U.K. (53).

There is also a growing concern for the environment and corporate social responsibility. For example, consumers are concerned about air pollution from transportation, and, in B2B land, industrial equipment by-products are a concern. Companies are learning that green marketing can be profitable; e.g., the use of agriculture for fuel would help both pollution and farmers.

A final class of trends to watch would be cultural differences, across countries or even sometimes within them. For example, university students take their online access for granted, but consider these Internet penetration numbers: more than 80% in the US, Japan, Germany, the U.K., France, and Korea, but less than 50% in China, India, Indonesia, Vietnam, and Egypt.[4]

Clearly China's sheer numbers are going to drive a lot of near-future phenomena. They've been a strong manufacturing force for years, but their role has primarily been behind the scenes. Now they are trying to break out into their own global branding presence to demand better margins and to make a point of national pride (e.g., Beijing's cooperative with IBM to produce Lenovo). Yet, to put things into perspective, Japan's per-capita GDP is about $46,000, the US is about $48,000, and China compares at a different level at $6,000.

Techno Trends

Apps: Apps are making many market transactions smoother, and more fun. There are apps to let you try on a new haircut, voice changer apps, apps that ask questions to do a mood check, and apps that wake you with gentle sounds. Trendwatching.com highlighted several new apps:

- WordLens lets travelers aim their phones at a sign or a menu to get a translation.

- Leafsnap uses visual recognition so that while out and about, nature hikers can take pictures of a leaf and get their phone to identify the species of tree to which it belongs.

- Google's Skymap lets astronomers and dreamers aim their phones at the sky to learn details about the constellations they're viewing.

- Maybe for a class project, you can create an app to estimate market size or fit a diffusion model and become really rich!

Lastly, other countries to watch would certainly be the fast-growing economies of the BRIC (Brazil, Russia, India, China). Less prominent but perhaps even more promising (given that US and Western European companies are getting tired of the issues they have to deal with in India and China) are Egypt, Mexico, Poland, South Africa, South Korea, and Turkey.[5]

MANAGERIAL RECAP

New (and improved!) products are fun to create, and they are crucial to a company's growth. To develop new products, marketers go through a process:

- From idea generation to testing the market potential, to concept testing, design and development, then beta testing, and ultimately the launch (review Figure 8.1).

- Reinvigoration along product lines is important because products evolve through a life cycle:

  ○ From introduction, to growth, maturity, and decline;

  ○ Each stage is recognizable by its sales and profitability,

  ○ And each stage carries standard recommendations for the 4Ps.

- Models can be used to forecast sales. Most include factors that reflect word-of-mouth or buzz marketing. Information technology is facilitating viral marketing.

- A manager who wants to be seen as innovative and foresightful would do well to study trends.

Chapter Outline in Key Terms and Concepts

1. Why are new products important?

2. How does marketing develop new products for their customers?

   a. Philosophies of product development

   b. Marketing

   c. Idea creation and market potential

   d. Concept testing and design and development

   e. Beta Testing

   f. Launch

3. What is the product life cycle?

   a. Diffusion of innovation

4. How do new products and brand extensions fit in marketing strategy?

   a. Strategic thinking about growth

5. What trends should I watch?

6. Managerial recap

Chapter Discussion Questions

1. Consider the trends described in the chapter (e.g., aging, heightening environmental concern, or China). How will each affect the business you are in (or were in before coming to b-school)?

2. Make a list of 3 of your favorite brands. What would be a great brand-, or line-extension that you would like to see developed as a new product?

Video Exercise: Smart Car (12:52)

Smart USA, headquartered in Bloomfield Hills, Michigan, sells the Smart Fortwo: a two-passenger vehicle that is produced in France by the Mercedes Benz car group. Smart Fortwo is the smallest car sold in the United States, and it is the most fuel-efficient vehicle outside of the hybrid cars. Smart Fortwo offers three different vehicle models, each with a different price point and a different package of standard equipment and options. When the Smart Car entered the U.S. market in 2006, and before a full network of dealerships was established, Smart USA discovered that it needed to connect with prospective customers in a different way. The company essentially took the Smart Car to consumers by (1) using a reservation program so they could move ahead in the sales process as the dealer network was being established and (2) conducting a 50-city road tour in 2007 where the vehicles were displayed and promoted. The Smart Fortwo defies traditional target marketing, and it appeals to all socioeconomic strata and cuts across all age groups. The reasons the Smart car appeals to different customer groups are price, size, and to serve as a second or third vehicle.

Video Discussion Questions

1. What methods did Smart USA use to test market the Smart Fortwo car among prospective customers?

2. What trends are influencing the market potential of the Smart Fortwo car?

3. How does Smart USA utilize buzz marketing

MINI-CASE

Wild Foods

A huge, highly regarded consumer packaged goods firm wishes to branch into pet food. The company knows a lot about packaging, communications, and pricing. It has a great reputation in trade so the channel partners should be supportive. It figures that selling pet food can't be all that different from their current strengths.

The company is beginning with cat food. It is developing product lines currently, and plans to launch within 6 months. About a year after that, they'll follow with their dog line. The company has talked about developing foods for other pets (ferrets, snakes, and hamsters), but to date, no firmer plans have been made.

The brand is going to be called Wild Foods and the new-to-the-world feature that the brand will offer is that these canned goods will comprise wild animals. Instead of cat food being the same meats eaten by their owners (e.g., beef, turkey, chicken, tuna), the foodstuffs will be mice, rats, crows, and pigeons (the company's first recipes).

The company expects their new pet food line to be wildly received by pet owners—they expect that pet owners will say, "Finally! A company that knows what my cat wants to eat!" The company also thinks it will earn huge points from people concerned with the environment, given that they're creating a useful by-product of large populations of some unpopular animals usually regarding as vermin or pests.

Case Discussion Questions

1. In the company's projection of their product line's likely success, what assumptions do you believe they've made, and do you agree with all of them?

2. What kinds of pre-launch marketing questions, about any of the 4Ps, do you have?

3. What kinds of marketing research would you suggest for them to address your concerns?

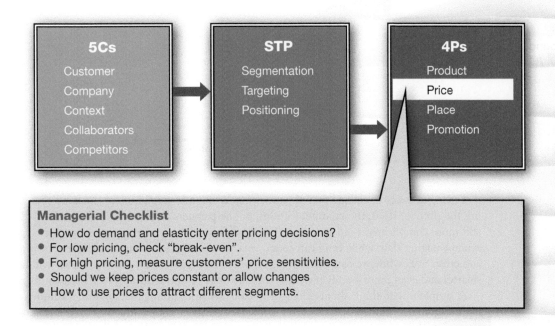

5Cs	STP	4Ps
Customer	Segmentation	Product
Company	Targeting	**Price**
Context	Positioning	Place
Collaborators		Promotion
Competitors		

Managerial Checklist
- How do demand and elasticity enter pricing decisions?
- For low pricing, check "break-even".
- For high pricing, measure customers' price sensitivities.
- Should we keep prices constant or allow changes
- How to use prices to attract different segments.

9-1 WHY IS PRICING SO IMPORTANT?

Our mantra is that marketing is the exchange of benefits and costs between a customer and a company. Yet most of the marketing 4Ps are focused outward, with the company attempting to deliver value to the customer by making a good product, making it available through accessible channels, and communicating the product's benefits clearly. It's price, though, that provides the company a mechanism for obtaining value back from customers.

Marketers need to know how to set prices. Whether the brand positioning is at the low end or high end, prices must be set accordingly. To know how prices will be received and affect demand, marketers have to understand how customers perceive prices and price changes, like promotions. Finally, we'll see how to use price as a segmentation tool.

> *How do you know if the price is right?*

9-2 BACKGROUND: SUPPLY AND DEMAND

If you know supply/demand charts like the back of your hand, you might wish to skip this section and go right to reading about "Low Prices." If you're not an economics whiz or could use a refresher, read on.

You learned in economics that demand tends to fall off as price goes up (Figure 9.1). If a firm prices its brand too low, they could probably raise prices and pull in more money (better margins and profitability). If the brand is priced too high, generally sales drop off. So if prices are adjusted downward, then the volume of sales would pick up, and, again, the company could pull in more money (better demand and greater volume in unit sales).

Figure 9.1

Demand Curve/Line

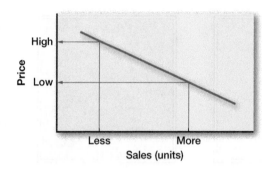

Pricing is easier to change than the other marketing mix variables (e.g., imagine changing the product itself, the communications, or the partners in the supply chain), but it is still more complicated than it sounds. We'll talk about the major approaches to pricing, acknowledging that, while it all can sound very precise, there is always an element of trial and error. Still, while we can acknowledge a need for wiggle room, pricing policies will be smarter and even more readily revised if they are built on thoughtful, systematic planning.

A simple way to think about pricing is to consider price points that are low, medium, or high. Figure 9.2 illustrates these three simple—and most frequently employed—pricing strategies. The lowest sensible price is set by covering costs and then adding some margin. The highest possible price is set by figuring out just how much a customer is willing to pay and pricing near that mark. Competitive pricing is somewhere in between, using competitors' prices as a starting point and adjusting from there.

Figure 9.2

Pricing Strategies

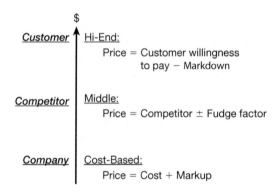

Note that the Cs of marketing directly affect pricing: The costs inherent to the *company* help determine the low price point, the *customer's* sense of the product's value help determine the high price point, and what the *competition* charges helps determine a sensible intermediate price point. Once you establish these three benchmarks for your brand, it is a strategic move to choose among them.

There are numerous other considerations in setting prices, and we will examine them as well. For example, pricing typically varies over the course of a product's life cycle. Willingness to pay varies across segments, so a firm might offer differential prices to those different segments. Prices can have multiple elements that can be tweaked.

Not only is pricing unusual among the marketing 4Ps in how easy it is to change, and thus it is frequently tempting to do so. It is also true that the impact of changing price is easier to measure than modifications of the other Ps. However, it is important to resist dropping prices to enhance a quarterly sales bump because this is short-term thinking.

Pricing is not just about making money. It's as important as any of the other Ps in terms of sending a signal to customers, competitors, and collaborators regarding the positioning and image of the brand. You're sending a message to these constituencies: We're low price (a good value or just cheap?). Or, we're expensive (exclusive or just overpriced?).

One might even argue that price is more important that the other Ps as a signal because price is so clearly assessed by the customer. For example, customers might see an advertisement for a retail shop and think, "Oh, the brand is upscale" but not be sure, whereas there is little ambiguity in a high price tag. Or a retailer partner might think, "Gee, that manufacturer doesn't seem to be supporting that brand with service much anymore," and any uncertainty would be removed when the manufacturer slashes prices.

Thus, it's worth being thoughtful about pricing. From a marketing perspective, pricing should be about the customer. Let's look at the variety of pricing strategies and figure out how to choose among them.

Clearly your price point affects your profitability. If we define profit as

$$\text{Profit} = \pi = (\text{Price} \times \text{Demand}) - (\text{Fixed costs}) - (\text{Variable costs} \times \text{demand})$$
$$= [(\text{Price} - \text{Variable costs})] \times \text{demand} - (\text{Fixed costs})$$

then profits increase as price increases. Per the demand function in Figure 9.1, however, demand typically falls off with those price increases. So we have to find a happy medium.

In another kind of marketing paradox, note that profits also increase as fixed or variable costs decrease. Yet sometimes companies do things to enhance their brands, such as by providing special services that raise costs. If instead, they were to cut those costs, it can often result in perceptions of reductions in quality in the minds of customers, thus indirectly causing a drop in demand.

As the demand line in Figure 9.1 implies, at the extremes, we could get stinking rich by either selling something like gum for a really cheap price and selling it to everyone (i.e., go for volume), or we could sell something like fine art for an exorbitant price and we'd need to sell only 1 or 2 pieces every once in a while (i.e., profit margin).

Don't cut prices! Increase customer benefits!

But what is that cheap or exorbitant price? If our gum is selling like crazy, why not raise prices and make more money? At what point would customers get annoyed and walk away, thinking, "Forget it, it's just gum, it's not worth that price"? For that matter, paintings don't fly off the walls at art galleries; so if something's not selling, how does the gallery manager know that the special buyer is still to come as opposed to deciding that the piece is overpriced?

These questions suggest that the oh-so-precise-looking line in Figure 9.1 has some wiggle room. Officially, that wiggle is known as "elasticity" or "price sensitivity." One way elasticity has been described is like this: If the company drops prices, there should be a volume increase (more units are sold). The question is whether enough additional units will be sold to "stretch" and cover the profits lost due to the price decrease.

Another popular interpretation of elasticity is from a consumer's point of view: If there is a price drop (or increase), just how much does demand (units sold) increase (or decrease)? If demand is barely affected, the demand is inelastic; if demand bounces around, it's stretchy and elastic.

More technically, in Figure 9.3 we see two demand scenarios. In the left plot, demand is relatively elastic (the slope is flatter than in the right plot). When the price is $7, the number of units sold is 10, for a total revenue of $7 × 10 = $70 (boxed areas 1 and 2). If we drop prices to $4, we'd sell 40 units (areas 1 and 3), for $4 × 40 = $160. So yes, with the price drop, we more than made up (with the $160) the original revenue of $70. We'd say that demand is elastic.

Figure 9.3

Elastic vs. Inelastic Demand

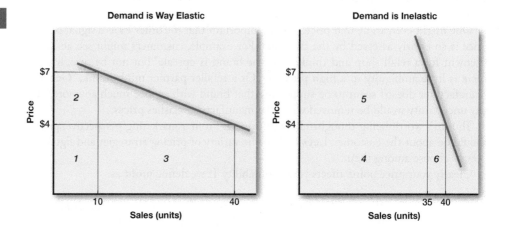

Or, conversely (to get facile with these plots), stay with the left scenario. Now imagine that we began at $4, bringing in the $160, and then we raised prices to $7 and watched sales drop off to $70. Thus again we see that consumers' demand is elastic (of course, it's the same plot).

In contrast, in the scenario to the right, demand is more inelastic. If we simulate the same scenario, we begin with a price point of $7, sell 35 units (areas 4 and 5), for $7 × 35 = $245. Dropping the price to $4 results in 40 units sold (areas 4 and 6), taking revenue down to $4 × 40 = $160. Demand is inelastic. We changed price a bit, and demand didn't change much. We lost margin (the $3 price difference), and we didn't make it up in volume (an increase of only 5 units). Thus, the margin wasn't made up by the too few additional unit sales. IRL, inelastic means that this is an item that many customers will purchase even if we raise prices (e.g., sporting events, musical concerts).

In Figure 9.3, we see that elasticity is characterized differently depending on the slope of the lines. Indeed, elasticity is defined by the slopes. Elasticity is defined as the proportion change in quantity compared to the proportion change in price. Elasticity is

$$E = \frac{\dfrac{Q_2 - Q_1}{Q_1}}{\dfrac{P_2 - P_1}{P_1}} = \frac{P_1(Q_2 - Q_1)}{Q_1(P_2 - P_1)}.$$

Thus, in Figure 9.3:

$$E_{left} = \frac{\dfrac{400 - 100}{100}}{\dfrac{5 - 8}{8}} = \frac{3}{-0.375} = -8 \text{ and } E_{right} = \frac{\dfrac{105 - 100}{100}}{\dfrac{5 - 8}{8}} = \frac{0.05}{-0.375} = -0.133$$

Elasticity is always computed to be negative, so the negative signs are just ignored (they're a given). Then E is assessed:

- If $E > 1$, as in the left plot, demand is said to be elastic. Price and revenue go in opposite directions: With a price drop, revenues shoot up; with a price increase, revenues fall off.

- If $0 \leq E < 1$, as in the right plot, demand is inelastic. Revenue follows price in the same direction: If price goes up, revenue goes up; if price goes down, so do revenues.

- If $E = 1$, demand is said to be unitary. Prices goes up or down, but revenues remain about the same.

What Is a Good "Value"?

Value pricing sometimes means low (i.e., good prices, good deals, inexpensive) and sometimes means high (i.e., it's the price customers are willing to pay because they perceive value in the product).

That was economics-speak. Now let's talk marketing. Figure 9.4 depicts typical marketing findings. For the purchase of almost everything, there are very likely to be these two segments. Brand loyal customers are inelastic, less price sensitive; they'll buy our brand no matter what the price. In contrast, the price-sensitive segment is quite elastic and deal prone, and they will run to a competitor (or even drop out of the category) when we raise prices.

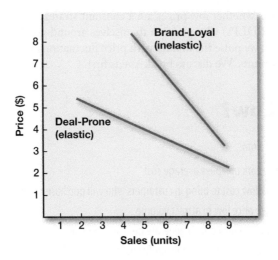

Figure 9.4

Elasticity Varies with Customer Segments

So if we can raise prices as demand goes up or as supply dries up, what factors drive demand? Demand goes up as a function of a customer's desire: the more customers there are who want the brand, or the more any customer wants the brand. Demand goes up with enhanced perceptions of the product's benefits or brand image. Demand goes up if competitors' brands aren't great, i.e., if there are few good substitutes, or they're priced even higher.

Alternatively, instead of considering demand, which is focused on the brand or product or company, consider the flip side: the factors that drive a customer's price sensitivity. Customers are more price sensitive (price is more elastic for them) when they don't care that much about the purchase, purchase category, or brand. If their preferences aren't strong, they feel no brand loyalty. Price sensitivity is greater when the item is a luxury good rather than a necessity, when many substitutes are available, when the purchase is a relatively big one (compared to a customer's household income). Finally, it's no surprise that price sensitivity is generally greater for customers with lower household incomes.

π = Profit

In marketing models, profit is often denoted as π. Market shares are often depicted in pie charts, round figures with the sizes of "slices" representing a brand's proportion of sales in the marketplace. Hence pi, like pie. Get it? Yes, well, econ humor.

Price sensitivity should increase when price information is easily available to customers to compare across competing brands. Thus the Internet is having an interesting effect on prices for many items. Price comparisons are easier online than driving from store to store, and in particular shopping bots such as Bizrate.com facilitate easy and quick comparisons.

9-3 LOW PRICES

Regarding low prices, there are two issues: First, how do we determine whether costs are covered? To address this basic question, we will compute a variety of break-evens—simple math computations that determine how many units we have to sell to make money. The second pricing issue is whether low prices are a constant strategic choice, such as everyday low price providers (EDLPs) who position themselves around good value in the minds of consumers. Or should we pulse the market with price fluctuations, offering and rolling back temporary price discounts. We discuss break-evens first.

Why Go Low?

Low price points come from:

- Cost-plus pricing: mark up above average cost
- Loss leaders: sell below cost to bring in customers who will purchase other products
- Market penetration: price low to attract volume
  - Early in the product life cycle to generate buzz and demand
  - Late in the product life cycle to milk profits before the brand dies
- Nearly predatory: price low enough to discourage competitors

To make sure you can stay in business, covering costs sets the absolute minimum floor on pricing. Cost-plus pricing is simply computed per unit, as

$$\frac{Unit\ Cost}{1 - X\%},$$

where $X\%$ is the intended return (say, 30%, so we'd compute: Unit cost/0.7).

If your fixed costs (including marketing, advertising, R&D, depreciation, etc.) are high relative to variable costs (which include labor or unit components), the strategic objective is to maximize sales volume (to spread the fixed costs over as many units as possible). If instead, variable costs are relatively high, the strategic objective is to maximize per unit margins. (We can't bring down price in hopes to build sales volume because volume drives up variable costs.)

9-3a Concept in Action: Break-Even for a Good

So what is a break-even (BE)? A break-even analysis is a means of figuring out how many units you'd have to sell before you make back your costs. Here's a thought experiment to illustrate. Say you're heading out of town to meet a client. You can take a cab from your place, or you can drive to the airport. Say a cab costs $20 + $5 ($1 airport fee and $4 as a 20% tip), and it costs $20 a day to park in your city's airport parking lot (pretend gas is free). For trips of what length is it smarter (cost-efficient) to take a cab vs. drive and park at the airport?

- If the trip is 1 day (i.e., you're flying to a nearby city and back the same day) and you take a cab, it would cost $50 (roundtrip). If you parked, it would cost $20.

- If the trip is 2 days, the cab still costs $50, and parking now costs $40.

- For 3 days, the cab is $50, and parking is $60.

- For d days, the cab is yes, still $50, and parking is $20d.

So, if the trip is 1 or 2 days, then the smart thing is to park. If the trip is three days or longer, take a cab.

Some companies (e.g., Walmart) use 'every day low prices.' Others (e.g., Kroger, Safeway) use 'high-low' variable pricing (i.e., sales).

You do break-evens intuitively like this all the time. Now we have to make your thinking official. Let's also be clear up front that we're pricing for a one-time transaction.

If marketers are long-term focused, as in relationship marketing via CRMs, they might be willing to not quite break even on the first purchase because they expect to break even shortly thereafter. The early hits on the company are investments in the customers.

A breakeven can be computed in terms of number of units sold or monetary values. We'll look at BE in terms of units sold first. As the term "break-even" suggests, we can look at how many units we need to sell before we make any money. Our profits are defined as

$$\text{Profit} = [(\text{Price} - \text{Variable costs}) \times \text{Demand}] - \text{Fixed costs}$$

If we just broke even, profits would be zero at a level of demand that we will call BE:

$$0 = [(\text{Price} - \text{Variable costs}) \times \text{BE}] - \text{Fixed costs}$$

Rearrange terms to solve for BE:

$$BE = \frac{\textit{Fixed costs}}{\textit{(Price} - \textit{Variable costs)}}$$

That's it. The last term, [(Price − Variable costs)], is also called "contribution per unit to fixed costs."

Let's turn to an example slightly more complicated than the taxi vs. parking issue. Imagine you have a friend who is thinking about launching a business targeted to business students in which leather portfolios were embossed with a subtle, elegant logo of their university. The friend would buy and stock the basic leather portfolio (in black, navy, and brown), and upon receipt of an order, emboss the lower right corner of the front panel of the portfolio with the requested university logo. For such a business proposal, Figure 9.5 breaks down the basic costs. The fixed costs include a modest income for your friend, some marketing and administrative costs, and rental space (maybe a small office in a shopping mall or on campus). The variable costs are listed as well: $75 for the portfolio and $5 for the embossing. The bottom figures show how much it would cost to set up a shop to sell 30, 60, 90, or 120 portfolios per month.

Figure 9.5

Costs for Portfolio Business

Fixed costs for 1 month:	
Your friend's salary	$1,000
Marketing, admin	350
Space rental, utilities, part-time help	650
Total	$2,000

Variable costs per portfolio:	
Leather portfolio	$75
Embossing	5
Total Unit Variable Costs	$80

Total costs for quantity portfolios sold:

30	2,000 + (30 × 80)	= $4,400
60	2,000 + (60 × 80)	= $6,800
90	2,000 + (90 × 80)	= $9,200
120	2,000 + (120 × 80)	= $11,600

Figure 9.6 begins with revenues generated, which is, as you keep hearing, a function of price and demand! So at the max (lower right of the top table), if we could sell about 4 portfolios a day (can we?) and if people would pay $140 for it (would they?), we could make $16,800. Woohoo!

Income				
	Number of portfolios sold:			
Price	30	60	90	120
100	$3,000	6,000	9,000	12,000
120	3,600	7,200	10,800	14,400
140	4,200	8,400	12,600	16,800
Recall Total Costs were:				
	4,400	6,800	9,200	11,600
Income − Total Costs:				
	30	60	90	120
$100	−1,400	−800	−200	400
$120	−800	400	1,600	2,800
$140	−200	1,600	3,400	5,200

Figure 9.6

Break-Even for Portfolio Business

But wait. Now we have to subtract our costs. In the table at the bottom, we see that there are many scenarios of price-and-demand combinations where we lose money!

In this example, we use the BE equation for each price we're considering, as follows:

$$BE = (Fixed\ costs) / [(Price - Variable\ costs)]$$
$$BE100 = 2,000 / (100 - 80) = 100$$
$$BE120 = 2,000 / (120 - 80) = 50$$
$$BE140 = 2,000 / (140 - 80) = 33.3$$

The first equation shows that if we priced at $100, we would need to sell 100 units to break even; if we priced at $140 dollars, we would need to sell only 34 units.

Now that we can compute a breakeven, let's face it, breaking even isn't a great business goal. It's simply how low can we go. Here's a better idea: Let's look at the scenarios in which we would actually make money! If we charged $100 and sold at least 120 readers or charged $120 (or $140) and sold at least 60, we'd make at least a little bit of money.

These are daunting scenarios: The prices seem high, and who knows whether we could really move 2-4 portfolios a day? Alternatively, could we cut costs and become more efficient or "productive," e.g., could we ask our friend to take less in salary? Could they find a supplier that could offer a better discount? But these are managerial questions to ponder, separate from the issue of the breakeven.

9-3b Concept in Action: Break-Even for a Service[1]

Let's look at a BE scenario that involves pricing for a service. Services are tricky because they are notoriously disproportionately high in variable costs. As a result, the cost numbers will move faster with an increase in demand.

So let's consider a slightly different scenario. Say we have another friend who is considering a business with a storefront where consumers can bring their tablets and a service is provided in which the customer's favorite software is loaded, the machine customized, new apps put on, etc. We'll keep the fixed cost constant from the previous example just for some consistency and to be able to compare across a good and a service to see the effect of the service and its inherent variable costs.

Figure 9.7 shows the variable costs. (In the previous example of the portfolios, there were variable costs as well but they were smaller than for this tablets example.) It costs the store's staff time to load the software (given their salaries and their time, say that averages out to about $30 a tablet), and the store must maintain legal licensing fees on a variety of software packages (say this is roughly $3 a tablet).

Figure 9.7

Costs for Tablet Customization Business

Fixed costs		2000	2000	2000	2000
Variable costs	Number of sold: 15		30	45	60
Labor ($30)		450	900	1,350	1,800
Licensing ($3)		45	90	135	180
Total monthly variable costs		495	990	1,485	1,980
Total costs (fixed and variable)		2,495	2,990	3,485	3,980

The question remains: How much should or could be charged for the service? How many customers would be needed before the store makes money?

In Figure 9.7, the first row reminds us of the fixed costs, and the next rows capture the variable costs, with the totals at the bottom. Figure 9.8 shows possible income, depending on price and demand. Figure 9.9 contains the differences, or profits. This analysis could be refined, using continuous numbers rather than our rougher numbers (15, 30, etc.). Similarly, the prices charged could be assessed in a more refined manner, with a continuous scale ($0 to 500 a unit), but again the discrete price points gives us a sense of the breakeven problem.

Figure 9.8

Break-Even for Tablet Customization Service Business

Number of served:		15	30	45	60
Cash inflow	$30	450	900	1,350	1,800
Revenue	$50	750	1,500	2,250	3,000
Sales	$100	1,500	3,000	4,500	6,000

In Figure 9.9, let's take a look at the money we'd make (or not). First, note that $30 is just a totally ridiculous baseline. We'd lose money fast, and, as we service more machines,

we'd lose even more money. If we charged $50, we're still not doing well. Increase the charge a little more to $100, and we can make money if we customize 30 e-book readers or more.

Number of served		15	30	45	60
Sales –	$30	−2,045	−2,090	−2,135	−2,180
Total	$50	−1,745	−1,490	−1,235	−980
costs	$100	−995	10	1,015	2,020

Figure 9.9

Break-Even for Tablet Customization Service Business

So how do we decide on pricing? We will compute this in a more refined manner in a moment, but just looking at this table, to breakeven, we'd have to charge at least $100 (and service at least 30 tablet customers). Later, when we talk about the value to customers or their willingness to pay, we can figure out whether we could charge just $100 or even more. Depending on the ZIP code of the mall, $200 may be quite tolerable. If that's the case, why would we charge the mere $100?

Once more, return to the BE equation. Fixed costs are $2,000, and variable costs are $33 (the $30 labor and $3 licensing per e-book reader). For a price of $100 for the service

$$BE = \text{Fixed costs} / (\text{Price} - \text{Variable costs})$$
$$= 2,000 / (100 - 33)$$
$$= 29.85$$

Round that up to 30 since table customers are integers. That's the number of units we'd need to sell to break even.

BEs are usually computed in terms of the quantity we need to sell. If we wanted to see the revenue required for the break-even point (from which costs will be recovered), we merely translate our figures by multiplying the BE quantity by the price point under consideration. Specifically, 29.85 times $100 for $2985.

Finally, we can, of course, have a profit target, not just the break-even point where profit = 0. To incorporate that goal, we would say

$$\text{Target profit} = [(\text{Price} - \text{Variable costs}) \times \text{Demand}] - (\text{Fixed costs}),$$

so

$$BE = (\text{Fixed costs} + \text{Target profit}) / (\text{Price} - \text{Variable costs}).$$

Figure 9.10 shows the break-even goal in terms of linear functions from which we may interpolate. The number of units sold forms the horizontal axis, and money (both costs and revenue) form the vertical axis. The first horizontal line in the graph itself shows the fixed costs, steady across all number of units (of course, it's fixed). The line labeled "Total costs" includes these fixed costs and have an increasing slope because they also reflect the variable costs, which increase with numbers of units produced and sold. The "Revenue" line is our income, and the point at which this line intersects the "Total costs" line is our breakeven point, as we just computed, right at 30.

BE analyses should be performed for every price decision to understand the lower bounds. Let's turn now to the upper bounds.

Figure 9.10
**Break-Even,
if Service
Fee = $100**

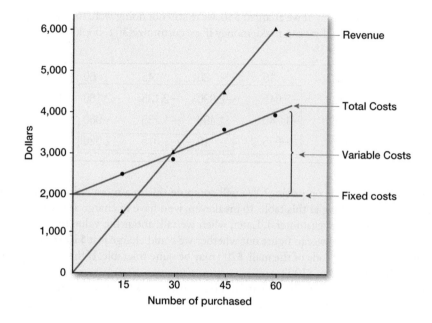

Figure 9.10
**Break-Even,
if Service
Fee = $100**

9-4 HIGH PRICES

The MasterCard commercials that end with "…priceless" are great fun, but most of us have an upper limit on what we'd pay for many items. The trick for marketers is to discover that upper bound and price just below it.

We've discussed the concept of price elasticity and can compute it (for any brand or segment) to answer the question: How much would sales drop off in the face of a price increase? In markets that are fairly stable (e.g., mature products with few technological introductions), marketing managers might see that their price sensitivity estimates are also fairly stable. If that's the case, we can turn the elasticity or price sensitivity (*PS*) equation inside out. The price changes are under our control. If *PS* is largely stable, we can plug that estimate in and solve for a decent forecast as to what the sales change might be.[2]

$$\% \ change \ in \ sales = \frac{PS \times (P_2 - P_1)}{P_1}.$$

This estimate would be very useful in budgeting. If we have no good estimate for price sensitivity, or if the recent historical data move around a lot, we should get current estimates. There are several means of obtaining the data require to make good guesses of price sensitivity. Let's take a look at a few.

9-4a Using Scanner Data

Any marketing manager working on consumer packages goods has the luxury of working with scanner data, which can yield very precise estimates of demand and price sensitivities at numerous price points. Scanner data include indicators of which brands are bought, the quantities bought, the shelf price of the objects, the paid price (e.g., whether a coupon was used), the price of competitors' brands that week, a flag for whether any of the brands were

featured in local weekend newspaper flyers or in end-of-aisle displays in the store, advertising exposures to panel households, etc.

If all of these variables remain constant, a firm can run an experiment by randomly selecting some outlets as a test market and dropping prices, say by 20% in some stores, 33% in others, and allowing still other outlets to serve as a control group, a benchmark for comparison (in case anything like the displays or competitor prices change). For example, the effect of a 20% decrease would be estimated to be

$$PS = \frac{\left(S_{@\,20\%\,off} - S_{benchmark}\right) / S_{benchmark}}{\left(P_{@\,20\%\,off} - P_{benchmark}\right) / P_{benchmark}},$$

where the benchmark might be initial sales or the sales averaged over the control group outlets.

If this *PS* is large, then the 20% discount was effective in stimulating sales. If it is small, then either the discount wasn't big enough or these customers just aren't price sensitive.

Price appeals are relevant for high-end services.

Image Courtesy of The Advertising Archives

Even firms not interested in conducting experiments, per se, can use the scanner data and run straightforward regressions to forecast expected changes in sales. For example, we can forecast sales as a function of price and include any other marketing or market information we might have as control variables, to see the effect of price:

$$Sales\ estimate = b_0 + b_1 Price + b_2 Ad + \ldots + b_k Factor_k.$$

9-4b   Using Survey Data

Even without scanner data, several marketing research tools can be used to assess a customer's willingness to pay (WTP). For one, we can simply ask our customers: What are you willing to pay? (Radical!) Imagine a survey in which some annual online banking service was described, and consumers are asked:

Q1	At $25.00, I definitely would not buy	1 2 3 4 5 6 7	definitely would buy
Q2	At $35.00, I definitely would not buy	1 2 3 4 5 6 7	definitely would buy

Even if we're not price-sensitive types, most of us prefer to pay as little as possible. So it wouldn't be surprising if the average score for question 2 was lower than that for question 1.

Still, the items can convey information. Some people simply aren't interested in the banking service no matter what the price, so their scores would look something like Q1 = 2 or 3, and Q2 = 1 or 2. At the other extreme, some people might be really keen for the service, so their scores would be Q1 = 6 or 7 and Q2 = 5 or 6. A final segment might be sort of interested in the banking service, if the price was right; their scores would be something like Q1 = 4 or 5 and Q2 = 3 or 4.

Price studies can also be tested using different samples. Some customers would be randomly assigned to fill out survey form A, and others would fill out form B. The surveys would be identical except the price in A would be higher than that in B. More versions than two could also be used to obtain a finer estimate of demand sensitivity to prices.

Price as High as You Can

High price points come from:

- Determine customers' willingness-to-pay, then price right below that sensitivity point
- Price high for margins, not worrying about volume (the 'market skimming' strategy often used early in the life cycle of a high-end brand to heighten its sense of exclusivity)
- Prestige or status pricing: price high for image appeal
- Price high due to real quality differences or true rarity

9-4c   Conjoint Analysis

More than surveys, marketing managers' favorite tool to study pricing is conjoint. In a conjoint study, customers are shown products with various combinations of features and attributes, price being one of them. The customers are asked: Which combination do you prefer most? Then: Next most? And so on.

For example, in Figure 9.11, a Red Bull class energy drink is offered in a 4-pack for $2.99 or $3.99, and a store brand drink of the same variety is offered at the same price points. Two different kinds of segment preferences are represented in the figure.

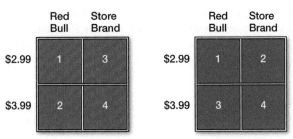

Figure 9.11

A Conjoint Experiment

1 = Most preferred, . . ., 4 = Least preferred

Both segments say their most preferred choice would be the Red Bull at the cheaper price, and both would least prefer the store brand at the higher price. What distinguishes these segments is whether they value the brand or price more. On the left is a consumer who wants the brand and who is willing to pay more. On the right is a consumer who appreciates a good deal, and gives up the brand to retain the lower price.

Pricing in the Middle

Mid-point prices come from seeing what competitors price at, and adjusting according to corporate and brand strategy:

- Price higher if you offer more benefits or brand equity, wish to enhance image
- Price a little lower if you wish to be perceived as good value

What's neat about the conjoint approach is that customers aren't ever directly asked about price, so the method obviates the customer's natural inclination to say, "I want to pay less." We also know that customers are indeed willing to pay more for what they want, and the conjoint technique helps detect what those attributes are. Customers are asked for a simple judgment: Which one of these do you like most, next most, etc.? And they can do this easily and quickly. We derive from the conjoint analyses the attributes that customers seek, including what price they're willing to pay. (We'll do a conjoint in Chapter 15.) The analysis allows us to infer their price sensitivities.

Part of the point of developing a brand is to charge a premium price. If brand associations go beyond the basic features, customers will pay higher prices accordingly. Some marketers define a good brand by whether the customer is price insensitive, i.e., the customer is determined to buy the brand regardless of its cost.

9-5 UNITS OR REVENUE; VOLUME OR PROFITS

There is, of course, a difference between maximizing the number of units sold to produce volume vs. maximizing revenue and profits. Figure 9.12 illustrates the comparison among cellphone calling plans. For a similar package of minutes and data, AT&T, T-Mobile, and

Sprint are fighting over a particular city. AT&T leads on numbers of customers (45%), and T-Mobile and Sprint have similar shares. AT&T charges $99 monthly, T-Mobile charges $49, and Sprint charges $79. Thus for revenue, the picture is that AT&T still leads, but Sprint does better than T-Mobile because it charges more.

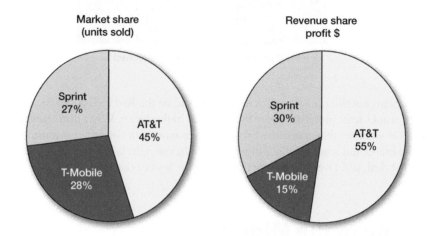

If Profit = Revenue − Expense and Revenue = Price × Quantity sold, then to maximize profits we need to find a price where any further increase in price would lead to a large falloff in demand. Specifically, profit maximization (P_{max}) occurs when marginal revenue (MR, the extra money brought in by selling one more unit) equals marginal cost (MC, the extra cost by selling one more unit); that is

$$P_{max}: MR = MC$$

In Figure 9.13, we see where this matching occurs. Prices are listed from $1 to $2 for, say, a soft drink from a vending machine. Naturally, as price goes up, fewer customers partake (as the price in column 1 goes down, quantity sold in column 2 goes up). The third column represents the variable (or marginal) cost of $1 a unit, and the fourth column shows revenue (price × quantity).

Figure 9.13

**Profit
Maximization**

Price	Quantity	MC $1/unit	Revenue	Marginal revenue
$2.00	100	$100.00	$200.00	
1.75	200	200.00	350.00	$1.50
1.50	300	300.00	450.00	1.00
1.25	400	400.00	500.00	0.50
1.00	500	500.00	500.00	0.00

The final column presents marginal revenue. These numbers are computed as follows: the $1.50 is [($350 − $200)/(200 − 100)], the $1.00 is [($450 − $350)/(300 − 200)], and so on. Marginal cost was stated to be $1, and marginal revenue achieves $1 when we price at $1.50, thus covering costs nicely.[3]

9-6 CUSTOMERS AND THE PSYCHOLOGY OF PRICING

Our pricing discussion thus far has involved some strategic thinking and a lot of number crunching. Yet any model you'll ever see (marketing, statistical, economic, etc.) will be of the form

$$\text{Our prediction} = \text{Our model} + \varepsilon$$

where ε (epsilon) is the error term, also referred to as noise, variability, heterogeneity, a fudge factor, or "beats me." The idea is that, no matter how well we think we know a system (e.g., the factors that influence a consumer's decision to purchase something), we are still dealing with human beings. And even if the purchase seems simple, seemingly endless factors contribute to the decisions. We typically don't have good data on all the factors, and actually we typically don't even know all the factors. So we acknowledge that the model is a simplification of the world, and that we'll make some errors in prediction, but we'll do as good a job as we can (until we can get better data on more factors).

Sometimes we use models and they're consistently off, always predicting too high or too low. When we identify such systematic biases, then we know that something else is going on in ε land. In particular, much of pricing has been derived from economics, and it sort of makes economists nuts that human beings introduce systematic variation into ε. There are eight kinds of so-called biases that are actually quite rational.

First, price often serves as a *cue to quality*. Counter to the anticipated economic effect of higher prices causing a decrease in demand, for some products and services, higher prices can make a purchase seem more appealing. For some purchases, customers use price as a cue to quality, implicitly reasoning that the brand can command a high price because its quality is so good. That argument assumes a belief in the efficiency of the marketplace, yet many studies have demonstrated that there is no correlation between price and quality for most product categories. But our beliefs persist.

A price's role as a cue is so strong that prices are known to contribute to the formation of expectations prior to a purchase. A price is a clear, tangible cue, and higher prices set higher expectations.

B2B Pricing

B2B pricing tools are the same, even if they're called different things:

- Trade discounts and price discrimination: discounts for cash, quantity, bulk, seasonality
- Trade allowances: cut prices to intermediaries based on the functions they perform, such as participation in advertising or sales support programs
- Differential prices based on geography: based on distance and transportation costs
- Transfer prices: pricing passed along through the channel network
- Forms of barter: payments in goods, services, or buying agreements rather than in cash

Price differentials can reflect different product functionality, but different prices can also reflect mere cosmetic differences. To say the product differences are superficial is not to say they are not relevant or rational if they contribute to brand image differences. Further, if an ad claims that a brand is superior due to the presence (or absence) of some feature, customers frequently trust that somehow that feature is therefore important. A high price point almost becomes the sought feature, as when basic Visa cards can be obtained with no annual fee, but American Express charges $2,500 for their elite Black card.

Second, *consumers process absolute numbers and relative numbers differently.* Say you receive some email coupons for Office Max. Your Office Depot is much closer. Would you drive to the Office Max for $15 off a box of printer toner (that costs $49)? What about if the coupon was for $15 off a new tablet (that costs $199)?

In both cases, the coupon offers the same face value, a $15 discount, but for the toner, $15 off is a larger proportion ($49 vs. $199), so it seems like a better deal. Rationally, we'd assess the absolute value; but there's a logic to assessing the relative value as well.

Third, the *contextual frame* in which information is expressed matters—the spin, if you will. Imagine you're planning a spring break trip with a friend, and you've narrowed your choices down to two vacation packages: One is priced at $499, the other at $599 with a $100 discount when you book. Which choice seems more appealing? In either case, your credit card is going to be charged $499. But the second choice starts at a higher price, so it's not unusual to assume that maybe the trip package is of better quality (e.g., nicer hotel, more activities). You'll feel like a smart shopper by getting more value, a $599 trip for just $499. $499 is $499, but it's not irrational when we have a rationale.

Fourth, price discounts serve as *mood inductions.* Temporary price discounts are not only an economic lever. Customers think they're smart shoppers when they get a good deal. People feel good when they get something for a price that's better than usual. The experience is about feelings of happiness, pride, appreciation, confidence, etc., not about money per se.

Fifth, there's a reason the prices of many things—groceries, books, clothing, cars—*end in 9*, such as $4.99 or $49.99 or $4,999.99. Wouldn't you think that their whole number counterparts ($5, $50, $5,000) would be easier to understand and advertise? Well, it's reliably known that $4.99 is far more attractive than $5, much more than the penny difference. Why? Apparently, because we read from left to right, we process and internalize the "4" before we hit the ".99." So we're thinking, "Oh, the price is $4-ish," not, "Wow, the price is $5!"

Sixth, consumers keep track of their spending; it's called *mental accounting.* They also rationalize compensatory or future purchasing. Just as we speak in financial terms of discounting future sales for the time value of money, we do this mentally also. If we buy a case of wine for an upcoming party, the current purchase is seen as an investment, not spending. And the later consumption of that wine at the party is seen as "free" because it's not tied closely in time to when it was purchased. This concept of an immediate vs. future cost-benefit analysis has also been used to explain why we don't do things in the short term that are good for us (as individuals or collectively as a society) in the long term (e.g., engage in healthy behaviors, or sound environmental ones). We simply pay less attention to future consequences.

Cupcakes

If you normally sell 5 cupcakes for $10 and you wish to have a promo, you're better off announcing "5 cupcakes for $8" than "5 cupcakes and 1 bonus cupcake free for $10." For "vice" purchases, consumers have an easier time justifying a price discount than a quantity bonus. If you sell celery stalks, do the opposite. For more, see research by Professor Mishra (University of Utah).

Another form of mental accounting is how we think of categories of money. You might think that money is money. It's fungible: Money spent on one household item comes from the same budget as a competing item. However, we often classify money as if it were non-fungible, meaning that we categorize our purchases and budget within the categories. For example, just because we splurged at a great restaurant last weekend doesn't mean we will cut corners on spending as we plan next month's vacation.

A relatively new phenomenon is the customer processing of alternative currencies—no, not the euro vs. the yuan. Rather, all the zillions of companies' loyalty programs are generating additional currencies, which usually have fairly transparent monetary values (and can be traded or given away). The airline mileage programs are the most mature, and it is not infrequent to see customers behave in seemingly inconsistent manners, e.g., refusing to pay for business class seats but having no problem redeeming points for upgrades.

Seven, marketers frequently observe the *compromise effect* in consumers. To illustrate, consider the following: One group of consumers was given the choice of buying two professional basketball tickets for $250 or two tickets several rows up for $200. On an order of 2:1, most (67%) went with the cheaper seats ($200).

Next, an entirely fresh sample of consumers was offered two tickets for $200, two slightly better seats for $250, or two even better seats for $300. About 10% went for $300. Of the remaining 90%, the preference for the $200 and $250 reverses from the first scenario: 2:1 with 60% of the sample asking for the $250 seats and 30% for the cheap $200 seats.

This effect is called a "compromise" because the middle choice in the second choice set is an attractive compromise between the two extremes. The seats are probably better than the $200 seats, but the tickets are not as expensive as the $300 ones. It's thought that this effect occurs because ultimately, whether we can articulate it explicitly or not, we apparently believe in an efficient market. That is, if a company charges more, we assume that they must be providing something better or more of something. If they were not, eventually consumers would figure it out and the company would have to drop prices. Note that the company doesn't really care how many $300 tickets it sells; it introduces the $300 tickets to make the former high price of $250 seem more enticing.

Eight, and lastly, consumers work with *referent pricing*. When we evaluate a product's price to determine whether we think the price being charged is fair, we compare the price to some reference, either an externally available price or an internally (mentally) stored price. Sometimes a product's price tag will offer this comparison to encourage the consumer to believe that the current price is a good deal, such as, "MSRP is $49.99, now available for $35.99!" Other external reference forms are popular during sales; e.g., "Now $14.99, regularly priced at $35.00!" Or some companies position themselves as having an EDLP (everyday low price) when they state, "Our price $34.99, compare at $45.00!" Whenever we refer to someone experiencing sticker shock, the idea is that the price on the sticker is much higher than the referent.

The reference price point can also be internal. The expectation regarding how much the product costs comes from a variety of sources, including the buyer's experience. For example, if the product being purchased is one that consumers buy a lot, they would be familiar with the product's typical price. Internal references can, of course, be faulty or not very relevant; e.g., how much you paid for your last car (even though that was 5 years ago, and it was an economy car vs. the luxury model you're now buying). Internal references can also be based on inferences, e.g., is the store an upscale one, leading us to believe that perhaps the prices of the store's service are a bit inflated? Or do the high prices imply high-quality brands?

We know that customers vary, and that's why we consider segmentation. They also vary in these psychological profiles of reactions to prices, and we can use that information to price smartly.

9-6a Price Discrimination, a.k.a. Segmentation Pricing

Price Discrimination, with a capital P and D, is not legal. We're not allowed to charge different prices to different people for the same goods or services. However, marketers frequently speak of price discrimination, with a small p and d. Let's instead call it segmentation pricing.

Legal Stuff Related to Pricing

- No "price fixing" (two or more firms agree on what price to charge, to reduce the effect of competition that drives prices (and profits) down; Sherman Antitrust Act 1890 and Federal Trade Commission Act 1914).

- No "vertical price fixing" (manufacturers cannot force a retailer to charge a certain price, hence we see "MSRP" or Manufacturer Suggested Retail Price). Retailers need to charge the manufacturer's minimum price, to ensure the manufacturer gets some profits, not just the retailers; Fair-Trade Laws.

- No "predatory pricing" (cannot price "unreasonably" low to drive out competition; Unfair-Trade Laws). Yet grocery stores routinely sell certain products cheaply, e.g., below costs, call them "loss leaders," count on their attracting traffic to the store. Also, huge companies routinely drop prices to discourage new competitors (then lawyers define "unreasonable").

- No "price discrimination" to consumers or channel partners (cannot charge different prices to different customers for the same product; Robinson-Patman Act 1936). Different prices must reflect a difference in costs, e.g., the loyal segment gets a deal because it costs less to process them, or they're charged more because they require more services.

- No "deceptive pricing," a.k.a. "bait and switch" (cannot mislead customers by advertising one product, but only making another, usually more expensive, product available for purchase, or by posting one price, but scanning and ringing up another).

Good marketers will do their homework and inevitably find customer segments who value different things. Then it is perfectly acceptable to charge different customers different prices for different goods and services. In most markets, there are almost always a price-sensitive segment and another that seeks quality. (Remember Figure 9.4.) There is nothing wrong with a company offering a stripped-down product at lower prices to the former and a souped-up version at a higher price to the latter.

For example, periodic deals are offered on soft drinks, oil changes, dinners at local restaurants, and so forth. Some customers will buy their favorite brands and hardly pay attention to the deals. How can a marketer price when there are different segments?

In Figure 9.14, we see that as price goes up (in column 1), demand falls off for both the deal-prone and brand-loyal segments (columns 2 and 3). The difference is that there is high volume of buyers in the deal segment at the low prices, whereas the brand-loyal segment is willing to pay more. Column 4 sums these purchases in units and revenues. Column 5 shows that, if we offer just one price, contribution is maximized at a price of $4.

Price ($)	"Deals" Segment	"Brand" Segment	Total Units ($)	Contribution (−1$ per unit)	Just Deal Segment	Just Brand Segment
2	9	0	9 ($18)	$1 × 9 = 9 = $18 − $9	1 × 9 = 9	1 × 0 = 0
3	7	9	16 ($48)	2 × 16 = 32 = 48 − 16	2 × 7 = 14	2 × 9 = 18
4	5	8	13 ($52)	3 × 13 = 39 = 52 − 13	3 × 5 = 15	3 × 8 = 24
5	2	7	9 ($45)	4 × 9 = 36 = 45 − 9	4 × 2 = 8	4 × 7 = 28
6	0	6	6 ($36)	5 × 6 = 30 = 36 − 6	5 × 0 = 0	5 × 6 = 30
7	0	5	5 ($35)	6 × 5 = 30 = 35 − 5	6 × 0 = 0	6 × 5 = 30
8	0	4	4 ($32)	7 × 4 = 28 = 32 − 4	7 × 0 = 0	7 × 4 = 28

Figure 9.14

Pricing and Brand and Deal Segments

The final two columns break out the segments. For the deal-prone customers, $4 remains the optimal price. For the brand-loyals, we maximize at a higher price, $6 or $7, and as long as they don't seem price sensitive, we might as well charge the higher of these two choices, $7. Now, what do we do with this information? Either we can determine that a high-end image is our strategy, price at $7, and let the deal-prone group fall off. Or we can price $7 during a regular season and get the purchases of the brand-loyal segment, and then we price around $4 for the deal-prone segments during promotion times.

It is important to keep these distinct segments separate. Customers can get irritated if they learn that they've paid more than another. Web designers need to be sensitive to this issue also: When a checkout process prompts customers to "enter promotional codes" (a digital coupon), some customers may be a little annoyed to realize they don't have one. A suggestion is to offer the customers a back door part of the website to obtain the deal.

Trade-off Ethics?

Say you're in a crunch. You need to withdraw $20, and you draw it from another bank's machine. The ATM is clearly labeled as saying that it will charge $1.50 for transactions for users who are not its customers. In this case, since the withdrawal value is so low, that fee is 7.5%. Is the fee unethical? A rip-off, highway robbery, usury? Yes. Kinda stupid of you? Um, yes. But unethical? No. You're paying for convenience, and you had full knowledge. (For more, see D. Kirk Davidson's *Moral Dimension of Marketing*.)

9-6b Quantity Discounts

Another completely legitimate and accepted form of segmentation pricing is to offer quantity discounts—the more you buy, the more you save! Figure 9.15 works through the numbers on an Internet offer. We begin with sales or survey data, determining how many customers want 1 month of Internet access for $15, or 2 months for $25, or 3 months for $30. Customers are used to seeing these offers, they can compute the average price per unit, and demand falls off with higher prices. None of that surprises us. In the column labeled $, it looks like we should go for the "3 for $30" because $960 is the biggest number. However, the per unit sales registered in the last column shows us that we would do best to use the "2 for $25" deal.

Figure 9.15

**Pricing with
a Quantity
Discount**

				Consumers, interested in buying:				
				1 month for $15?	25 said yes			
				2 months for $25?	35			
				3 months for $30?	40			
Number of Buy	for$	Avg Price	Net (-2 cost)	Net Profit	Demand	$	Per Unit
1	15	15.0	13.0	13.0	25	325	325.0
2	25	12.5	10.5	21.0	35	735	367.5
3	30	10.0	8.0	24.0	40	960	320.0
a	b	$c = b/a$	$d = c - 2$	$e = d \times a$	f (above)	$g = e \times f$	$h = d \times f$

9-6c Yield or Demand Management

You know the expression, "Time is money." Just as customers can be divided into segments that are more or less price sensitive, customers can also be more or less time sensitive.

In particular, services are said to be perishable, meaning that there is no such thing as storing inventory or excess capacity. All the customers rush a system when they want to be served, and, if they overload capacity, it can be a problem for the service provider, and the quality of service can deteriorate. So another example of segmentation pricing is to vary prices during peak and nonpeak seasons.

For example, if you're willing to go to the movies during the day, when most people are working and the theater owners would like encourage better attendance, you get a price break. You can also frequently get price breaks by making airline or hotel reservations far in advance of your needs, which these service providers appreciate so that they can plan better. (You can also, if your plans are flexible—that is, if you're not in the time-crunch segment—get price breaks at the very last minute because they wish to operate at full capacity.) Some restaurants recognize different segments by pricing differently during the weekdays vs. weekends.

Whether a customer experiences a price or time shift, it's important that the company manage perceptions of fairness. With regard to time, FIFO (first-in/first-out) seems universally fair in queuing, but customers also tend to be understanding when there are exceptions (e.g., larger parties wait longer to be seated at restaurants).

These practices of yield management are popular in services, many of which are characterized by high fixed costs and lower variable costs (e.g., airlines, hotels, rental cars) to enhance revenue and capacity utilization. The systems have also gotten very complex, but an advantage of this approach to pricing is that it is based on the market, not on costs per se.

9-7 NON-LINEAR PRICING

If it's not complicated enough to set a single price, marketers further complicate things by trying to coordinate the pricing of multiple pieces of their product offerings. Some prices are set using a so-called two-part tariff: A customer pays some amount for one part of the service (usually a fixed fee, such as an entry fee at a night club or a ticket to enter a theme park) and another amount for another part of the service (usually a charge per unit of usage, such as drinks at the club, or food, T-shirts, and memorabilia at the theme park).

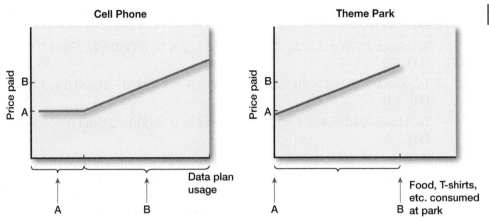

Figure 9.16

Two-Part Tariffs

For example, in Figure 9.16, we see an illustration that cell phones charge a monthly fee with some basic coverage, but calls beyond that are charged extra. The plot to the right illustrates the theme park, with an initial charge (the admissions ticket) and additional fees for whatever consumption is enjoyed in the park (e.g., beverages, T-shirts). Part A of each graph shows the base fee, and part B shows the extra fees, so the total amount charged per customer depends on how much the customer wishes to buy.

Figure 9.17 depicts data sampled from patrons of local upscale restaurants responding to survey questions about the fees proposed for a newly opening wine bar. The wine bar plans to offer wine classes during which customers would sample triplets of wine as the sommelier describes them. For access to this instruction, the wine bar hopes to charge a cover fee (like a bar charging a cover for live music). The entrance fee is the first tariff, and the glasses of wine that the consumer drinks comprise the second part of the price structure. The graph (or table) tells us that 35 respondents said they'd go to the wine bar once (in a month) if the cover charge was $5, and slightly fewer (20) said they'd go twice if the entrance was priced at $5. Ten said they'd go once (in a month) if the cover charge was as high as $15, and no one said they'd go four times (once a week) if the price was that steep.

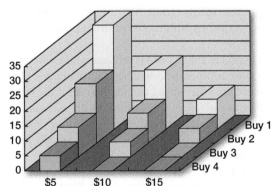

	Number of visits sold				Total
Price	1	2	3	4	
$5	35	20	10	5	
$10	20	10	5	0	
$15	10	5	0	0	
@$5	$105	$120	$90	$60	$375
@$10	$160	$160	$120	$0	$440
@$15	$130	$130	$0	$0	$260

Figure 9.17

Using Self-Reported Demand Data to Set Prices

Let's weight the number of sales by the profitability. Say we take $2 as a variable unit cost. The values in the lower part of the table are computed as follows:

- In column 1: $105 = 35 \times (\$5 - 2)$, $160 = 20 \times (\$10 - 2)$, and $130 = 10 \times (\$15 - 2)$
- In column 2: $120 = 2 \times 20 \times (\$5 - 2)$, $160 = 2 \times 10 \times (\$10 - 2)$, $130 = 2 \times 5 \times (\$15 - 2)$
- In column 3: $90 = 3 \times 10 \times (\$5 - 2)$, $120 = 3 \times 5 \times (\$10 - 2)$, and $0 = 3 \times 0 \times (\$10 - 2)$
- In column 4: $60 = 4 \times 5 \times (\$5 - 2)$, $0 = 4 \times 0 \times (\$10 - 2)$, and $0 = 4 \times 0 \times (\$15 - 2)$

When we aggregate these values to get the row sums of $375, $440, and $260, the results suggest the $10 price point would lead to the greatest overall profitability.

With two-part tariffs, you price items separately even though you know customers will probably purchase both pieces. Price bundling is sort of the opposite. It aggregates prices of 2 or more complementary products for a single price.

9-8 CHANGES IN CHA-CHING

A smart company doesn't just set a brand's price and forget about it. There are a number of reasons to think about changing prices, including the product life cycle, coupons, and price discounts.

9-8a Pricing and the Product Life Cycle

Like any of the 4Ps, a firm needs to revisit the strategic questions about pricing from time to time. Two contrasting strategies are referred to as pricing for market penetration or skimming. If you want to disperse your brand quickly and widely throughout the marketplace, that is, penetrate the market, the brand would be priced low at the time of its introduction to stimulate sales and to encourage trial and word of mouth. This approach is intended to capture a large market share. It is a little risky because, if many customers immediately start buying your brand, you better be ready. The product better be good (no beta testing, thank you!), and your production capacity and your channels better be ready to serve. With time, the price is usually raised. As the brand reaches maturity and finds its segments, the product is adorned with more features that customers care about, etc.

In contrast, market skimming is a strategy where a high price is set because the company is seeking profit margin, not volume. The only customers who will buy this brand at a high price are the ones who really want it. Think of your digit-head friends who want the latest in software or hardware and who are willing to pay (a lot) for it. Think of the authors you like so much that you buy their new books in hardback, rather than waiting a few months for the lower-priced paperback or e-book to come out. Over time, the price is usually lowered to make the brand accessible to more customer segments.

Regardless of the starting point—whether high (skimming) or low (penetration)—modifications can occur as the product matures. For example, as segments develop, different product lines could be priced differently. As the brand matures, a drop in prices might restimulate sales, but, if a firm believes in the brand, sales would also be restimulated by maintaining (or raising) prices and by adding features and benefits. Finally, when the brand has one foot in the ground, prices often tumble because the firm wants to dump inventory.

9-8b Price Fluctuations

Another element of changing prices is a price promotion, through temporary price cuts or the issuance of coupons. These techniques are reliable in generating a modest short-term uptick in sales, but there are also equally predictable side effects that aren't as positive.

First, competitors can imitate price cuts immediately. So whatever market share increase in volume you were aiming for gets negated, and you (and your competitors) have shot yourself in the foot by squeezing your own margins. Second, price drops attract disloyal customers, and why not? Customers are savvy and often price sensitive, and they are quickly trained to buy when brands are on sale. Indeed, one motivation for your price drop was probably to widen the circle of customers who will purchase your brand and perhaps come back with future repeat purchasing. However, certainly some proportion of those newly attracted customers will be fickle and not return. You're betting on your brand and true product differentiation to retain customers. If your brand and product are similar to competitors, however, customers will switch back to cheaper substitutes when you raise your prices again.

Another dirty little secret is that price discounts are often not profitable. Yes, demand increases with deeper discounts, but only to a point. And even if the temporary price discount is profitable in the very short run, it may come at the expense of longer-run profitability. For example, for many consumer packaged goods, the uptick in sales due to a promotion is due to some households who accelerate their purchasing, stock up and inventory their goods, and wait to buy again only during the next sales promotions. Hence, sales may dip a bit after the promotion.

A final cause for concern of occasional price fluctuations is the deleterious effect on the image of the brand. From the company's point of view, price promotions are intended to increase sales. From the customer's perspective, the occasional savings are appreciated, but there is also some question as to why the brand would need a sale. Brands that are sufficiently high quality shouldn't need the gimmick of a promotion.

9-8c Coupons

Coupons are a slightly different pricing instrument. They're more temporary or ethereal because by definition they're relevant only to the segment of customers who are coupon clippers. It's likely that price is more important to these customers than brand image, so the concern of temporary price drops reflecting poorly on the brand is less of an issue for coupons.

Coupons are big business. By some estimates, 350 billion are available yearly in the United States alone, with an average value of about $1. Potential savings thus is $350 billion, so it's good for companies that the redemption rate is less than 1% (annually and across SKUs). Coupons are especially effective at encouraging new (current) customers to try current (new) products and brand extensions.

9-8d Competitive Strategy and Game Theory

In addition to concerns about the impact of price points or price changes on our own brand image, marketers must consider that the competition won't just sit idly by while we enjoy increased sales due to a price cut. Marketers frequently use game theory to try to estimate the likely results of various actions, most frequently price cuts and competitive response.

Say a competitor such as the market leader initiates action by dropping prices. We must then decide whether to cut prices also in order to convey to our customers our equitable value or to maintain prices and emphasize to customers that our brand is based on non-price features. Further, do we offer a line extension to diminish the brand confusion but risk cannibalization?

Game theory isn't about Nintendo; it's just a structured way to think about the behavior of interdependent players, like two (or more) firms. The point is to get players to think about the broader market, rather than only optimizing their own needs. While it may seem counterintuitive at first, and it is important to avoid collusion or even the appearance of it, the point is to find a solution to avoid price wars. Mutual cooperation can yield even better outcomes than both parties acting selfishly on their own accord. Go figure.

For example, Figure 9.18 illustrates a price cut game. Current prices are $5 per unit. Both firms are tempted to drop their prices to $4. Why? Currently, with us both at $5, we're selling 100 units each. That's fine. But if we drop prices and our competitor does not, more customers would flock to us. We'd sell 300 units, and our competitor would sell only 50. That's great! Well, unfortunately our competitor isn't stupid, so they're thinking the same thing: If they drop prices and we don't, they'd get 300 and we'd get 50. But if we're both so motivated, and we both therefore drop prices, we're back to splitting the pie, 50:50, but at worse margins. Brilliant.

Figure 9.18

Price Wars!

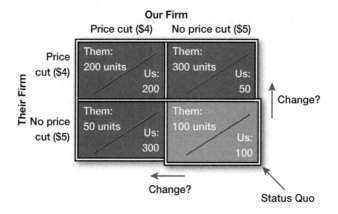

9-8e Auctions

As long as we're talking about changes, let's talk about dynamic pricing. The idea is that there isn't a fixed price; rather, the price is negotiated between the buyer and seller. In a sense, auctions have always been around, and they are interesting in part because they continue to grow in popularity online.

The factors discussed previously that increase or decrease demand are analogous to factors that give bargaining power to a buyer or a seller. Buyers have strength if they account for a significant portion of the seller's sales or if they have multiple options for meeting their procurement needs. Sellers have strengths when products are in short supply, in high demand, or differentiated, or simply when the economic times are good. Prices stay down when there is high supply relative to demand, intense brand competition, etc. Prices are boosted by controlled supply, high product value, product differentiation, high buyer dependency on suppliers, high switching costs, etc.

Auctions

Auctions have always been around as a mechanism of competition, pricing, and distribution. They have been a common means of sale for fruits and vegetables, tobacco, and timber. Contemporary auctions are numerous and financially voluminous, selling:

- Fish, Tokyo's Tsukiji market (founded 1923, $5.5B annual, Tsukiji-market.or.jp).
- Real estate, Williams Auction (founded 1957, $.75B, Williamsauction.com).
- Antiques, Tepper Galleries (founded 1937, Teppergalleries.com).
- Thoroughbreds, Keeneland (founded 1935, $1B, Keeneland.com).
- High-end artwork and other SKUs, Christie's (founded 1766, $5B, Christies.com) and Sotheby's (founded 1744; $5B, Sothebys.com).
- And, of course, anything on eBay (founded 1995; $8B).

Fun fact: In an old (1949!) issue of the *Journal of Marketing*, C. W. Kitchen described the challenges of auctions for perishables and the huge advantage of (then) new "*refrigerated-carriers*," known as "reefers."

The defining characteristic of an auction is that the price point isn't set or fixed, nor is it even negotiable between a seller and one buyer. Rather, buyers/bidders compete to obtain the item. As in any marketplace, sellers want to yield high prices, and buyers want low prices. There is a particularly odd sense of efficiency in that whoever bids the highest is very probably indeed the customer who values the item the most. Everyone else would have fallen out of the auction when the price exceeded their so-called reservation price—the point of indifference at which you say, "If you raise the price, forget it, I won't buy; if you drop the price, okay, I will." So, a reservation price is really a good estimate of the customer's willingness to pay. Naturally this price cap varies by segment and product category.

An auction can be comprised of very few bidding participants, as when B2B suppliers bid for projects (e.g., an architectural design for a new office building, territorial rights for energy and minerals, etc.). In consumer bidding, the numbers of potential buyers can be quite large.

Many nonprofits hold sealed auctions, during which attendees at the event offer to pay a certain sum for a desired item (sculpture, exotic travel, etc.), and there is no knowledge by any bidder what the other bidders' price offers are (to reveal such, oh très gauche).

In contrast, many large-scale consumer bidding systems (e.g., online) are open auctions in which all bids are transparent to all participants, and the bidding proceeds in a sequential manner. In so-called English auctions, bids increase among the players over time. As the price surpasses the value to a customer, that customer drops out of the auction, and, with time, whoever remains standing pays the last, highest bid, to obtain the item. In contrast, so-called Dutch auctions begin high and prices drop over time (though not below the seller's reservation price). When the price finally drops low enough that a buyer is willing to buy the item at that price, the item is sold and the auction is concluded.

Whether you are interested in auctions, or price changes, or price as a driver of image, if you can't remember the math of pricing, take away this: Competing on price is nearly always dumb. Find a benefit that your target segment values, and play that up and charge for it. Value is an assessment of what the customer gets (e.g., quality, psychological benefits) compared to what the customer gives up (e.g., cost, time, effort of driving to a store). Customers can be taught to value many benefits, and then the costs incurred seem "worth" the value. So be a smart marketer, and teach them what your brand's benefits are!

Mark-ups vs. Margins

- The difference between a mark-up and a margin is one's point of view. If you're a retailer, and you buy a sports watch for $100 and you sell it for $200, then your "mark-up" is ($200-$100)/$100 = 100%. The mark-up is the price you're adding going forward into the channel toward the customer.

- Now change perspectives. You're still the retailer, but you're looking at what proportion of the customer's price is profit coming back to you. That's the "margin" and it's ($200-$100)/$200 = 50%. We can add channel members and more price changes, and it will look more complicated, but the concept is the same:

  - From the manufacturer's point of view:

    $50 = cost of manufacturing (raw materials, labor, etc.)

    $150 = the manufacturer's price to the retailer

    →mark-up = (150-50)/50 = 200%

    →margin = (150-50)/150 = 66.67%

  - From the retailer's point of view:

    $30 = cost of retailing (rent, salespeople, ads, etc.)

    $40 = the retailer wants to build in a profit of $40

    $270 = the price to the customer

    →mark-up = (270-150)/150 = 80%

    →margin = (270-150)/270 = 44.44%

MANAGERIAL RECAP

Here are the key concepts of pricing for a marketer:

- Pricing strategies are basically: low, medium, or high:

  - The company and its costs dictate the lower-bound price, where price is a function of the costs and some markup (thus we calculate break-evens).

  - Customers' willingness-to-pay marks the upper bound, where price is a function of the customer's value of the item, minus some markdown (thus we learn techniques such as conjoint to try to obtain high-end price sensitivities).

  - In the middle, price is tweaked up or down relative to competitors' prices, depending on our firm's and brand's pricing strategies and goals.

- Pricing can be used to shape a brand's positioning, and can attract (repel) different target (non-target) segments, e.g., through tactics such as quantity discounting.

- There is a yin and yang in pricing between economic and psychological approaches to studying consumer behavior. Seemingly irrational behavior (so says an economist) may nevertheless be perfectly logical (so says a psychologist). Part of the reason marketing is interesting is because real life is not simple.

Chapter Outline in Key Terms and Concepts

1. Why is pricing so important?
2. Background: supply and demand
3. Low prices
   a. Breakeven for a good
   b. Breakeven for a service
4. High prices
   a. Using scanner data
   b. Using survey data
   c. Conjoint analysis
5. Units or revenue: volume or profits
6. Customers and the psychology of pricing
   a. Price discrimination, aka segmentation pricing
   b. Quantity discounts
   c. Yield or demand management
7. Nonlinear pricing
8. Changes in cha-ching
   a. Pricing and the product life cycle
   b. Price fluctuations
   c. Coupons
   d. Competitive strategy and game theory
   e. Auctions
9. Managerial recap

Chapter Discussion Questions

1. Lawyers are changing their pay structures. It used to be that they would bill hourly (top dollar for top lawyers, less experienced helpers had cheaper rates). Now they're beginning to price like consultants—per project. Thus they must begin assessing the value-added to the client firm of the legal expertise and assistance. What advice would you give a law firm to proceed fairly and profitably?

2. Why do you think the fashionista segment pays such high prices for designer clothing with the knowledge that it will be passé after the current season?

3. What are the kinds of purchases for which you'll "spare no expense"? What kinds of purchases do you want to buy spending as little as possible? What are the major differences between these two categories that drive your attitude regarding price?

Video Exercise: Washburn Guitar (7:02)

Washburn Guitar has been a maker of fine musical instruments since the company's founding in Chicago in 1883. The company promises that "each guitar [it produces] represents the finest quality at the best possible price." Washburn has four price points: (1) entry level at $349 and below; (2) intermediate level at $1,000 and below; (3) professional level at $1,000 to $3,000; and (4) collectors level at $3,000 and above. Amid the evolving perception that lower prices indicate lower quality, Washburn has taken steps to ensure the quality of its products at all price points. Interestingly, guitars made in the United States typically are of better quality and workmanship than are guitars made offshore. Consequently, U.S.-made guitars command higher prices. Indeed, most musical artists demand U.S.-made guitars. Washburn uses a manufacturer's suggested retail price (MSRP) as the pricing guideline for retailers selling its guitars. If discount and online retailers offer Washburn guitars for sale at below a minimum advertised price (MAP) that is set by Washburn, these distributors are warned to cease the practice. If the practice of violating the set MAP continues, the retailers lose their distribution rights for Washburn products.

Video Discussion Questions

1. How does the concept of segmentation pricing relate to Washburn Guitar's four different price points?

2. How does Washburn's four different price points reflect customer wants and needs?

3. Are Washburn's four price points an accurate indicator of differential quality? Why or why not?

MINI-CASE

Personal Brand Management

Impress4Less is a company founded by two b-school recent alumni. They both had taken advantage of their school's career placement services, and thought they could offer additional supplemental services and advice. They're constructing a website where anyone looking for help in positioning themselves for a new job might go to download templates of resumes, examples of personal brand brief 'elevator pitches,' videos of strong and weak interview answers, and the like. Their plan is to offer some of those basics for free, to get people onto the website. But what they're really interested in selling is their consultation time, consisting of feedback on resumes and help with practice interviews.

They're working with their former school's entrepreneurial club in proposing to launch their online premium service for $50. This past year served as a test market at the b-school. Given the friendly partnership, and as a learning opportunity for the students, Impress4Less shared some information on basic cost structures. Their fixed costs on this project were $3,000, and variables costs were $10 per user exchange.

Currently at the b-school, the situation is as it looks in the figure below (to the left); that is, 200 users purchased their services during the last academic year at the $50 price. But the club members get regular feedback (from classmates) that the $50 price tag seems steep, so they're asking Impress4Less for a price cut of 10%, essentially going to the figure at the right.

Case Discussion Questions

1. How many users would have to buy at $45 to at least meet last year's profits?

2. Should Impress4Less drop prices further? Could they raise prices above $50?

3. What assumptions are you making?

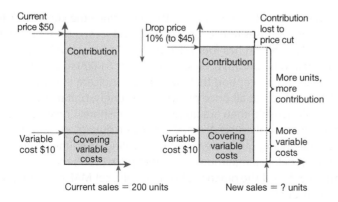

CHANNELS OF DISTRIBUTION 10

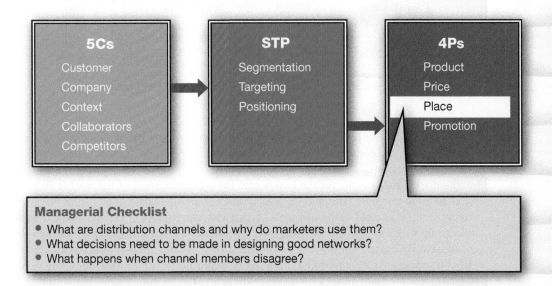

5Cs	STP	4Ps
Customer	Segmentation	Product
Company	Targeting	Price
Context	Positioning	**Place**
Collaborators		Promotion
Competitors		

Managerial Checklist
- What are distribution channels and why do marketers use them?
- What decisions need to be made in designing good networks?
- What happens when channel members disagree?

In just about Anytown, USA, on Saturday mornings during seasons when the weather is nice, the town holds a farmers' market (see Figure 10.1).[1] Local farmer Eli brings a portion of his week's corn haul, and local baker Emma brings her famous apple pies. Eliot's selling his asparagus and squash, and Eliza has flowers freshly cut from her garden. Emery's selling his chili, and Emily sells her oatmeal cookies. These providers register with the community center and pay a small fee to set up a booth to sell their wares.

The buyers are yuppie gentry who fill their SUVs with reusable bags of this very fresh, unbranded produce. During the week, these buyers shop at national chains, where the food is perfectly fine (it is fresh and there is a good variety). They also shop at upscale groceries (where the food might be fresher still and perhaps organic or exotic, and probably more expensive). Still, Saturdays harken back to the marketplace of old.

Providers have large quantities of their goods, e.g., Eli has more corn than his own family could possibly consume, so he'd like to sell some of it. Buyers wish to pick up only a few of any one particular item, e.g., several ears of corn (but not Eli's whole stash), a bunch of flowers (but not more than one vase full), etc. The different needs of the buyers and sellers can be met nicely in the market.

In marketing, we talk about realigning the discrepancies between the quantities and selections that the sellers and buyers offer and desire. Given that it is more efficient for any particular seller to produce a large quantity of a limited number of goods, and yet most buyers wish to purchase a smaller quantity of a wider variety of goods, the large supply of the sellers' goods must be made available to be sold in smaller batches (this process is known by the charming term *breaking bulk*). It might be a little hassle for the farmer to

Figure 10.1

Farmer's Market

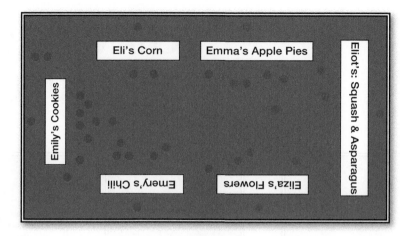

stand around all Saturday morning until all his corn gets sold in batches of 2 or 3 ears at a time (that is, some "costs" are involved), but he'd wait forever until someone was willing to buy his whole truckful.

The market has benefits for the buyers too. The central location of the market allows a buyer to go to purchase fruit and vegetables and homemade baked goods all in one convenient stop. (It's an old-fashioned mall!) Otherwise, the yupster in the SUV would track mileage up to Eli's farm for the corn, over to Emery's for the chili, back to Emily's for cookies, etc. Before you know it, the morning is shot (and car emissions have contributed to global warming). As a compromise, a consumer might hire a professional shopping agent to go to these locations to pick up these goods, saving the consumer time, but almost certainly incurring some service fee. Similarly, farmer Eli might hire a helper to meet him at his farm and haul away some corn to be delivered to consumers or grocers. Here too, the convenience of the helper relieves Eli of some hassle but will cost him for the assistance.

10-1   WHAT ARE DISTRIBUTION CHANNELS, SUPPLY CHAIN LOGISTICS, AND WHY DO WE USE THEM?

These scenarios are different forms of "channels of distribution," each of which is trying to solve the age-old problem, "How do I get my stuff to where consumers want to buy it?" A *distribution channel* is a network of firms that are interconnected in their quest to provide sellers a means of infusing the marketplace with their goods and buyers a means of purchasing those goods, doing all as efficiently and profitably as possible.

The actors in the distribution network include manufacturing firms, distributors or wholesalers, retailers, consumers, and other players with other names. In the end, the names aren't as important as the functions that the parties serve. These functions include customer-oriented activities, such as ordering and handling and shipping, product-oriented activities such as storage and display, marketing-centric activities such as promotion, financial activities such as, well, financing, etc. The links between these actors include the movement and ownership of physical products, the flow of payment and information, and assistance in promotions and other marketing activities. When managers speak of *logistics*, they're talking about coordinating the flow of all those goods and services and information throughout the channel, among the channel members.

In the spirit of the saying, "No one is an island," it's hard to do business without partners. But as soon as you start taking on partners and forming a network of distribution channel partners, not surprisingly, those partners want to make some money for the services they provide. So the tension in channels always takes a certain form: Does this channel member contribute value? Does the member provide more benefit than cost? This is the classic make-or-buy decision that firms constantly address: Should we do this (some function) ourselves (i.e., make it) or ask someone to do it for us (buy it, outsource it)?

One view of how channel members can make a marketplace more efficient and cost-effective is depicted in the contrast between Figures 10.2 and 10.3. In Figure 10.2, the manufacturers are delivering their goods to the consumers directly. In Figure 10.3, they go through an intermediary player, such as a common retail outlet. In the first scenario, the number of contacts in the network is the number of manufacturers *times* the number of consumers; in the second, the number of links is the number of manufacturers *plus* the number of consumers. Presumably some cost is associated with each link (e.g., managing that marketing relationship), and, as a result, if the costs are roughly the same, it follows that the marketplace with the fewest links, or costs, is more efficient. Thus, the system with an intermediary channel member (Figure 10.3), is more efficient than all firms going direct to consumers.

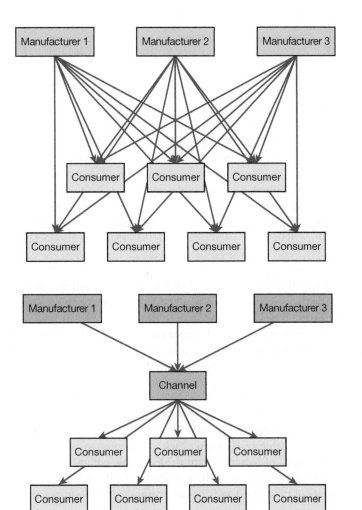

Figure 10.2

Manufacturers Direct to Consumers

Figure 10.3

Manufacturers through a Channel

The channel member in Figure 10.3 is not well defined, so Figure 10.4 shows explicitly the three general classes of distribution channels. For example, many laptop and cell phone companies make their products and sell them directly to consumers online (as well as through a channel), and these companies do so because they can make (or save) money doing both.

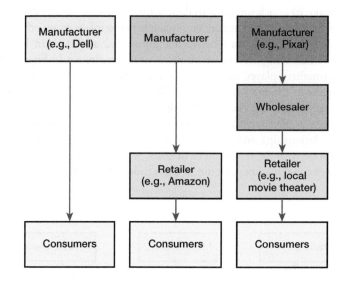

Figure 10.4

Forms of Distribution Channels

Next we see the template for companies that collect stuff from manufacturers in order to sell it and serve as a touch point to consumers. For example, book publishers (and zillions of other SKUs) can sell through Amazon.com, which provides a coordination service for consumers. It's handy for consumers, who can go directly to Amazon to obtain whatever they wish; it's handy for the book publisher who doesn't want to deal with that many consumers. And of course, it's handy for Amazon. Amazon is not capable or interested in producing all those SKUs. It is simply functioning as the electronic equivalent of the farmer's market—a place where buyers and sellers can meet to enact their desired exchanges.

Finally, in Figure 10.4 we see that companies can make something and hand it over to an agent who, in turn, hands it over to retail outlets to make the product available to consumers. For example, Pixar is in the business of making fun movies. The company may not be good at or interested in getting its movies to the audiences directly, and so it hires and expects to pay distribution partners. The distributors see to it that the movies are available in theaters, and the theater serves as the retail point of access for the consumer audience.

The three different channels systems have to deal with different issues. The PC or cell phone company doesn't have to deal with other companies, yield to their goals, split profits with them, or any of that. But they have to do everything themselves. Amazon has to have cooperation and reliability from its suppliers, and then it has to deal with customers. Pixar has to deal with its distributors and then is somewhat removed from its audiences.

Figure 10.5 illustrates these differences. Using the "vertical" lingo of marketers, when a company is dealing with partners that are upstream, it's called *supply chain management*. The partners that are downstream comprise the *channel members*; i.e., they provide the way to channel stuff to the customer. Referring back to the companies in Figure 10.4, a laptop company's suppliers (e.g., of batteries, hard drives, plastic computer casings) are invisible, but implied. Amazon's supply chain is the manufacturers. Pixar has suppliers (film, camera equipment, agencies of personnel) and channel members (distributors and theaters).

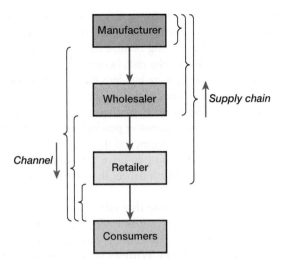

Figure 10.5

Channels and Supply Chains

So if the what of channels is a network of suppliers and providers, and the why of channels is efficiency, scales, and consistency in positioning, just how do we design effective marketing channels? To optimize delivery systems, we consider several factors: whether we want to distribute intensively or selectively, and how we will align the motives of all these partners to smooth over these large systems. Several kinds of partners are special (e.g., retailing, catalogs, e-commerce), so we will look at their concerns as well.

10-2 HOW TO DESIGN SMART DISTRIBUTION SYSTEMS: INTENSIVE OR SELECTIVE?

Although distributor partners add value, there is no question that some companies go it alone and are very successful. So how does a company decide to go direct or indirect, or, as most do, some combination of both? The first issue in designing a distribution system is that of *distribution intensity*: how many intermediaries will the manufacturer go through to distribute its goods to end user consumers?

Many consumer packaged goods (CPGs) are distributed *intensively*. For example, many brands of snack foods, personal care products, utility goods (pens, lighters, candles, newspapers and magazines), and so forth, are sold in many kinds of stores: drugstores, supermarkets, discount stores, convenience stores, etc. Why?

1. First, as a consumer, consider how far you'd drive for a pack of gum (not very far) because it's a low-cost item and often an impulse purchase. Accordingly, to stimulate sales, gum needs to be widely available to consumers.

2. Second, given that CPGs are inexpensive, companies require big volume sales to make big bucks, hence the extensive distribution.

3. These goods are relatively small, so it is easy for manufacturers to box up a lot of units into a fairly small box, put many boxes onto a truck, and get the goods all over the place to many various retail outlets.

4. Finally, these goods are simple: no sales force is required to explain to the consumer, "Okay, this is how M&M's work . . . ." So companies advertise directly to the consumer, who *pulls* the goods from the manufacturer.

In contrast, some goods and services are more complicated and expensive, both of which mean the purchases seem riskier to the consumer. So the consumer needs a salesperson to explain the purchase (e.g., choices among brands, features to select, etc.), and to reduce their feelings of anxiety associated with the risk, hence inducing a greater likelihood that they would buy. Salespeople can seem pushy, but, let's face it, they're useful. The guys at car dealerships, or those working at electronic stores, or the guys in department stores selling major household appliances probably know more than about these SKUs.

For the consumer's part, these more expensive purchases require information and deliberation. They aren't typically impulse purchases, and they aren't typically frequent purchases. As a result, the consumer is probably willing to drive 5 or 10 miles to a dealership or to a department store to buy some household appliance. Thus, the manufacturer doesn't need an extensive distribution system.

Every choice has pros and cons. It's true that sales forces are useful, but they are also expensive to maintain, so manufacturing companies can't afford to staff many retail outlets in a given geographic area. In addition, given that goods that require a sales force are expensive, customers don't buy a lot of them. Without frequent repurchasing, there is only a certain level of demand in any given area. Accordingly, such goods are usually available via *selective distribution channels* (i.e., not intensive distribution).

While companies like these advertise to consumers, they're really relying more on their distribution partners to help *push* the goods to the buying consumer (so they advertise and provide incentives to the sales force).

The intensity of distribution is a function of consumer convenience in access, information search, etc. If the goods are simple, inexpensive, easily transported, etc., it's typical that they're distributed widely and intensively. If the goods are complex (requiring assistance in purchasing) and relatively expensive (therefore feeling like a somewhat risky purchase), channels are often structured to be more selective.

Selectivity in channels offers additional benefits to the manufacturer. By definition, there are fewer relationships to manage, which means that the manufacturer has somewhat more control (e.g., over distributors engaging in price cutting), and costs of interactions are less (e.g., trade discount deals to push new products need to cover fewer parties). The extreme case of selectivity is the *exclusive channel*: e.g., a small city might have only a single Infiniti dealership. Exclusive channels can be a little tricky because they can tend toward being monopolistic (by definition, there is less competition), creating potential legal problems.

Bottom line: Channels are supposed to make access easier for customers, so think about the customer buying behavior for your product category. Channel design is an integral part of marketing, strategy, and positioning. If your SKUs are available everywhere, that says something about you: We're going to be there for you. If your SKUs are found only in select outlets, that says something else: We're special, and you're going to have to make the effort to find us.

The channel design needs to be consistent with all the other marketing elements. Recall that certain positioning elements tend to go together: Wide distribution usually goes with heavy promotion, lower prices, and average or lower-quality products, whereas more exclusive distribution accompanies exclusive promotional efforts, higher prices, and higher-quality merchandise. For example, high-end hair products choose to distribute exclusively through salons to reinforce their positioning and not show up in Walmart.

The extensiveness of distribution channels is also related to the brand's life cycle or to the company's maturity in the marketplace. The brand that comprises the sole offering of a new firm is typically sold through very few channels—probably a website primarily. Beyond that, it's hard to convince a retailer to support an unknown brand. As the company matures, it may go broader if doing so is consistent with the desired corporate and brand image.

10-2a **Push and Pull**

The terms "push" and "pull" refer to whether the manufacturer targets consumers or its channel partners with its marketing communications. Consumers are said to pull goods through the channel, whereas trading partners push the goods down the food chain. The manufacturer can use any marketing mix variables to push to partners or encourage pull from consumers, but you'll see there are some common trends.

We're very familiar with the many pull marketing strategies that assist marketers in encouraging consumer demand because we experience them as consumers (see Figure 10.6). A marketer can temporarily reduce pricing or enhance size or quantity. A marketer can offer trials (small sizes at low prices) or free samples (e.g., bundled onto a complementary product). A marketer can offer coupons (money redeemed at point of purchase), rebates (money redeemed post purchase), financing (e.g., buy now and don't pay for 6 months), and points toward rewards in loyalty programs. The marketer still must manage its relations with distributors and retailers, but pull strategies are targeted to the end user to engage the consumers' awareness and loyalty.

How to Push?
- Advertise to partners (and consumers)
- Distribute more selectively
- Employ sales force
- Usually selling more complicated, more expensive stuff
- Price discounts
- Quantity discounts
- Financing
- Incentives for sales force
- Allowances for marketing activities

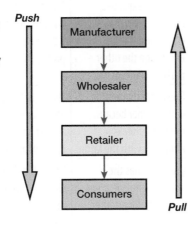

How to Pull?
- Advertise to consumers
- Distribute widely
- No sales force
- sell small simple stuff
- Price discount
- Quantity discount
- Larger package
- Inexpensive trial
- Free sample
- Bundled product sample
- Upgrades
- Coupons
- Rebates
- Financing
- Loyalty points

Figure 10.6

Push vs. Pull Strategies

Push marketing strategies involve manufacturers offering incentives to distributors (dealers, wholesalers, retailers) to sell product to end users. Although the manufacturer targets the channel member rather than the consumer, push marketing tools resemble those of pull. For example, a marketer can offer the distributor or retailer temporarily reduced pricing, an allowance to help cover marketing activities, a discount for purchasing larger quantities (e.g., a twofer or a bogo [buy one, get one free]), financing a payment for several months, spiffs (incentives for the sales force), etc.

The manufacturer may hope that the retailer will pass through to the end user some of these incentives (e.g., price discounts), and the retailer may or may not. The value of that retailer is still in what they do with the incentives; e.g., a price discount might not be passed along, but the retailer provides more shelf or floor space to the manufacturer's brands, and the manufacturer might be perfectly happy with that result. In the end, the manufacturer hopes that if they give the trade partners incentives, the partners will support the manufacturer's goods and services and push them on to the final customer.

Types of Power

When channels marketing people talk about a powerful retailer or a powerful supplier, here's what they mean:

Type of Power	Quick Image	Definition	Example
Coercive power	Bully	One party can make another do something by taking away benefits or inflicting punishment.	"We're Big-Retailer, and we won't stock your stuff until you give us a better trade margin."
Information (expert) power	Know-it-all	One party gets cooperation because they have information the other seeks.	"We're Big-Online-Retailer and we won't provide you with your SKUs sales data for your CRM database until you purchase more advertising in our space."
Legitimate power	Great Dane and a Chihuahua	By size or expertise, one party can make claims and threats which encourage the other party to conform.	"We're Big-Pharma-Supplier and we will not supply you with more of Drug X because it's running into testing problems."
Referent power	I want to be like you	One party cooperates with another because the former seeks affiliation with the latter.	"We're Little-Guy and we cooperate with Market-Leader because they have a great brand name. We're riding their coattails as we establish ourselves."
Reward power	I have goodies for you	One party has the ability to provide good outcomes for another.	"We're Big-Supplier and we do what we want, but when Big-Retailer asked us to make our package smaller, we did because they'll stock more and sell more for us."

10-3 POWER AND CONFLICT IN CHANNEL RELATIONSHIPS

Whether you're pushing or pulling, distributing intensively or selectively, you and your channel partners want to see happy customers and enjoy profitability, but there are many ways to achieve these goals. When channel partners differ in their opinions on how to do so, conflict can arise. The question is whether strategies and tactical incentives can be designed so that the goals of all parties are compatible. For example, a manufacturer usually desires that a retailer stock their entire line, but a retailer can see that certain SKUs don't sell well, so they don't want to waste shelf space or floor real estate with those unattractive items. Channel members also frequently bicker over (i.e., negotiate terms on) prices and margins. For example, suppliers will say that the retailers are charging the consumers too much; hence demand is not as strong as it could be. Retailers will counter that the suppliers' prices to them are also too high, and they must pass along high prices to make a decent margin.

A little bit of conflict can be healthy. Just as people working together can have divergent views, companies can also have diverse perspectives. The question is how conflict is handled when it gets to be too much. In handling conflict, the differences can be useful as motivation to find alternative solutions (e.g., system cost–cutting mechanisms) that are both mutually satisfying and superior in optimizing goals than either party had first considered.

Conflict can be quashed if one player is inherently more powerful than another. Perhaps it shouldn't be true that might makes right, but, indeed, power is usually defined by size and it is effective; e.g., if you produce a few lines of a niche product and Walmart doesn't like how you're doing something (your packaging, price points, delivery schedules, etc.), who do you think will blink first? Or if you're the big player and your partner is a little entrepreneur, you similarly expect your "Jump!" to elicit the appropriate response—"How high?" Power isn't a great way to resolve conflict in the long-term, however, since the less powerful player can feel resentful and look to leave the channel arrangement as soon as another opportunity becomes available. Or, worse, they could create a competing product, with the knowledge and technology learned from you! Similarly, sometimes conflict arises between two mighty companies, and then a show of strength will be ineffective; it will be a standoff that just generates a lot of hot air and noise.

Transaction cost analysis is a model that considers channel members' production costs and governance costs, both of which are ideally minimized. Costs of producing and bringing products to market are often reduced by having intermediaries because those channel partners operate with economies of scope and scale. Costs of governance are the relational issues incurred by trying to coordinate the enterprise and control one's partners.

A concern is that all players will act selfishly and opportunistically, but a more contemporary view is that of transaction *value* analysis, a perspective that emphasizes the benefits a company brings to its partners (beyond cost reductions). Marketers speak of all these plays and counterplays using human relationship terms: They speak of the communication between a supplier and distributor, the trust between a distributor and retailer, the satisfaction a retailer has with a supplier, etc.[2] Just as with people, when a conflict arises in channels, the best way through it is by talking to each other; communication enhances trust and satisfaction. It's also clearly important to deliver on one's promises (e.g., meet delivery dates, quantities, quality, etc.). Channel experts speak of trust as both the willingness and the ability to deliver on promises.

Other ways that channel members have used to strengthen relationships is to exchange some personnel for short stints to learn the perspectives and needs of the other party more intimately. All parties need to feel that they're being heard and that their needs are understood and being met. Sometimes it's helpful to remind all members of the channel network that they have the mutual goal of customer satisfaction. Hence, occasionally, multiple channel members may sponsor joint programs of marketing research in order to see just what the customer values, so that the channel members can determine together how best to respond to those requests.

Even when all these measures are insufficient, there are still other options, including mediation (negotiate through a third party who determines the two parties' utility functions) and arbitration (the third party makes a binding decision for the two). To preclude or abate conflict, part of the communication is negotiation. Just as differential power affects pricing, buyers and sellers rarely come to the table as equals when bargaining. Suppliers have more power when their inputs are important to the buyer, when their services are differentiated, and when there are no substitutes. Customers have more power when they're large, when they're relatively few in number, and when they purchase large quantities.

10-3a **Revenue Sharing**

Sometimes channel conflict can be about "r-e-s-p-e-c-t" and related issues, but it often comes down to money; e.g., the retailer complains, "I want a bigger piece of pie. Look at the great service my sales staff provides!" The manufacturer counters with, "But it's my brands that the customers are coming for, and while your service is nice and we appreciate it, it's not what they're buying, so we should get more than you." Let's look at some of the money issues.

First consider the scenario that a manufacturer sells directly to the customer. A consumer price is set, from which must be recovered the manufacturing costs (of producing the good or providing the service) and the retailing costs. For this scenario, the manufacturer incurs the various costs of interacting with the customer. So the manufacturer profit is a function of the customer price, the manufacturing and retailing costs, and, of course, demand.

When the manufacturer goes through an intermediary, not surprisingly that player wants to make some money too for the services they perform. There's a markup (a profit to be made) when the manufacturer yields product to the retailer, and there's a second markup (more to be made) when the retailer makes the product available to the consumer. If the channel is not managed well, we quickly run into a situation where, in order to recover these markup costs, we'd be tempted to set a rather high price to the end user consumer. In fact, the price may become so high that demand would start to drop off, and then both the manufacturer and retailer lose. This problem is called "double marginalization" because the manufacturer wants a profit (a margin) and so does the retailer (hence two margins). So what to do? You learned it in preschool: The channel partners must share.

Channel Profits

Channel profits: These terms summarize the discussion on "Revenue Sharing," a means of negotiating win-win channel relationships.

1. When the manufacturer sells directly to the customer:

   manufacturer profit $= (p - c_m - c_r) \times$ demand,

   where

   - $p =$ price to consumer
   - $c_m =$ costs to the manufacturer of producing the good or service
   - $c_r =$ costs of providing the retailer function, interacting with the customer, etc. (incurred by the manufacturer)
   - demand $=$ a function of price, quality, service, etc.

2. When the manufacturer goes through an intermediary:

   manufacturer profit $= (p_r - c_m) \times$ demand

   retailer profit $= (p - p_r - c_r) \times$ demand

   where

   - $p_r =$ price to retailer (i.e., wholesaler price)
   - $c_m =$ costs to the manufacturer of producing the good (assume same as above)
   - $c_r =$ costs to the retailer of providing the retailer function
   - demand $=$ a function of price, quality, service, etc. (assume same as above—just different channel member providing this function)

- If we've managed the channel properly, the customer shouldn't see any difference in price, and every player gets a piece of the pie. For example,

  manufacturer profit when going direct $=$

  manufacturer profit when going indirect $+$ retailer profit in indirect channel

  or:

  $$(p - c_m - c_r) \times \text{demand} = (p_r - c_m) \times \text{demand} + (p - p_r - c_r) \times \text{demand}$$
  $$= [p_r - c_m + p - p_r - c_r] \times \text{demand}$$
  $$= [p - c_m - c_r] \times \text{demand}$$

Suppose you take the D2C scenario, call the manufacturer profit instead "total channel profit," and divvy up the profits in some portion (equitably agreed to by the manufacturer and retailer). Then the consumer is not overcharged, the problem of double marginalization is solved, and demand is such that both the manufacturer and retailer can make some serious money. The money is simply reapportioned.

If that was a wee bit abstract, consider an example. Figure 10.7 shows a direct and indirect channel scenario on pricing to illustrate the impact of double marginalization. Say it costs a manufacturer $c_m = \$50$ to make a designer sweater, and the costs to set up retail are $c_r = \$50$ (for whoever incurs the cost). That is either the manufacturer if they sell direct or, in a moment, the retailer when they sell indirectly. Say the manufacturer marks up $100. If they sell it directly, the consumer would be charged $200.

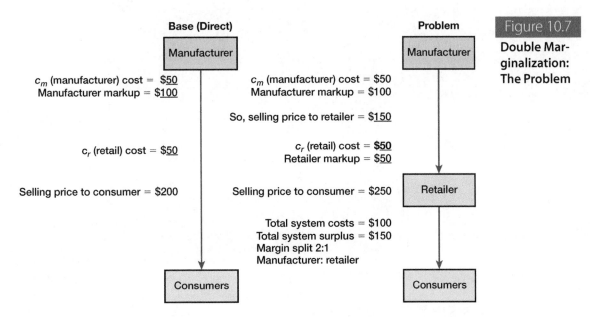

Figure 10.7

Double Marginalization: The Problem

If instead of selling the sweater directly, the manufacturer hands it over to a retailer to sell, pricing it at $p_r = \$150$ (which is $c_m = \$50$ and $100 manufacturer markup). Then the retailer wants some margin too, say $50, so they mark it up, and the price to the consumer is $p = \$250$ (which is $p_r = \$150$ and $c_r = \$50$ and $50 retailer markup). Costs total $100, and the surplus of $150 is split $100 for the manufacturer and $50 for the retailer. Say demand is "okay"; some 500 sweaters are bought. That gives the manufacturer $500 \times \$100 = \$50,000$, and the retailer $500 \times \$50 = \$25,000$.

Anatomy of Airbus' Channel Partners

1. Carson, California: Water engineering and plumbing
2. Irvine, California: Testing in-flight entertainment of 600 seat-back video monitors
3. Perth, Australia: Red clay with bauxite for aluminum to ▶
4. Texas: Smelted into aluminum chunks "the size of mattresses," then ▶
5. Davenport, Iowa: 1.2-mile aluminum mill to make wing pieces, which are ▶
6. Trucked to Baltimore, Maryland, and ▶
7. Shipped to a factory in Broughton, North Wales (Plant can fit 12 soccer fields.)
8. Put on ship, made in China
9. Rendezvous soon with fuselage, built in Germany
10. Shipped to Bordeaux and driven by tractor trailer to Toulouse overnight (French police close roads) for final assembly.

The final step in preparing the A380 is painting the aircraft for specific customers. Among the airlines purchasing the A380 are Emirates, Quantas, Singapore Airlines, Air France, Lufthansa, and Korean Air.

Several engines are available on the Airbus A380, from suppliers such as Rolls Royce and Engine Alliance, which consist of a General Electric engine and Pratt & Whitney fan.

To give you a sense of size, the big A380 is in the foreground, and the little toy in back is an A340, which is only slightly smaller than the huge 747! The A380 assembly requires • 18,000 suppliers in 30 countries, • 1,000,000 aluminum fasteners.

The plane: • houses 800 passengers, • has a 260-feet wingspan, • has a tail seven stories high.

For more, see Peter Pae's *LA Times* article, "Giant Passenger Plane Requires Giant Supply Chain." Thank you, Professor Mumin Kurtulus (Vanderbilt U) for this suggestion!

If the channel system could drop the price to the consumer to $200, demand would presumably pick up, according to the sales of other comparably positioned, but lower-priced sweaters. So lower the consumer's price to $p = \$200$, as depicted in Figure 10.8. The costs are still the same, that is, $c_m = \$50$ and $c_r = \$50$, so the question is what are p_r and the markups?

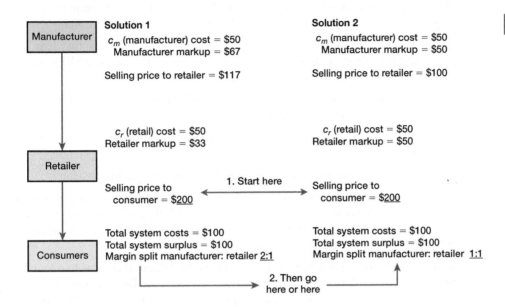

Figure 10.8

Double Marginalization: Solutions

Imagine the manufacturer proposes a 2:1 (or 67%:33%) split like before, then $p_r = 117$: the manufacturer makes $67, the retailer $33. These figures are less than before for both parties (the manufacturer had made $100 and the retailer $50). However, let's factor in the pickup on demand, say to 800, and now the manufacturer would make $67 × 800 = $53,600 and the retailer $33 × 800 = $26,400 (which is $3,600 more than before for the manufacturer and $1,400 more for the retailer). If the demand is even stronger—say 1,000 sweaters are sold—then the manufacturer makes $67,000 and the retailer $33,000 (an increase of $17,000 and $8,000, respectively).

If the manufacturer is feeling more generous and they propose a 50:50 split, and if the price to the consumer is $200, with total costs at $100, the manufacturer and retailer each would make $50. Then, with 500 sweaters sold, profits would be $25,000 (for both the manufacturer and retailer); with 800 sweaters sold, profits would be $40,000; and for 1,000 sweaters sold, the profits would be $50,000. This profit level was achieved by the manufacturer when the sweater was selling at $250, but, because fewer sweaters are sold and because the percentage shares favored the manufacturer, it's twice what the retailer had made. This move might "feel" generous on the part of the manufacturer, but in fact it can be used by the manufacturer to buy a lot of goodwill. So, later, the manufacturer might make requests of the retailer.

See? Spread the love around. Or at least the money.

10-3b **Integration**

Again, recall that channels aren't about the parties involved as much as about the functions they serve. So, if some channel relationship seems to be perennially bumpy, the make vs. buy decision can be revisited. A company can outsource something it currently makes, or it can bring back in-house something it had asked a partner to cover. For example, in the latter scenario, if revenue sharing annoys you, you're tired of channel conflicts, and you're a bit of a control freak, you can vertically integrate.

A manufacturer could engage in so-called forward integration by opening its own retail stores.

- For example, Sony and Apple computers used to be only in manufacturing; subsequently, they (partially) forward integrated, opening Sony and Apple stores.

- Ralph Lauren took its fashions forward in two retail channel formats; they have a few select flagship stores to carry their entire line (thus offering more SKUs than what they make available to department stores such as Bloomingdales).

- Perhaps the most popular means of forward integrating has been manufacturers' providing their wares online for direct purchasing.

A manufacturer can also engage in backward integration by controlling some of the raw material inputs.

- For example, Amazon no longer simply sells books—it also publishes them.

- Retailers backward integrate when they set up private labels (e.g., foods, fashions, toys). Private labels offer a number of advantages: (1) If they sell well, they give the retailer negotiating power with the manufacturers. (2) They can offer significant margins. (3) They can help the retailer differentiate itself.

These moves introduce additional forms of competition. Where there was horizontal competition between retailers of different types (e.g., pharmacy vs. discount house vs. department stores), there now can be vertical competition wherein the manufacturer finds itself competing with its partners. For example, a manufacturer's own branded retail store can compete with an independent channel retailer, and the manufacturer's brand may compete with a retailer's private label brand.

Sometimes it's hard to keep track of all the players in the channel. While the prototypical channel structures in Figure 10.4 look simple, the real world is, of course, messier. Companies that compete in one industry, even over one SKU, may collaborate in the production and selling of others. Today's network of companies and channel responsibilities are complex and amorphous, given our globally interconnected world (see Figure 10.9).

Figure 10.9

Global Channels

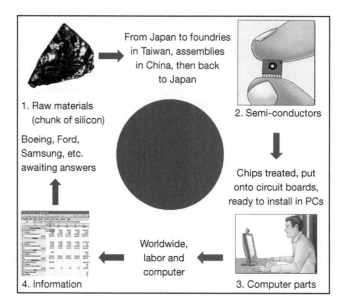

10-3c Retailing

A particular channel function that has generated a great deal of interest is retailing, in part because it is the most visible element to the end customer, and so it can have the most direct impact on image, positioning, and brand equity. Retailing has also been a topic of discussion as it has been gaining power and momentum over the past 10 to 20 years. Marketers reliably find that large, powerful retailers can make or break a new product.

Retail outlets are classified according to a number of criteria. They can be compared by the extent of the manager's ownership. Some are independent retailers (e.g., a local artist's gallery, the local florist, a village baker), and others are branded store chains (e.g., Clarks, Timberland) or franchises (e.g., Sonic, Midas). Alternatively, we can categorize retailers by their level of service, which tends to be positively related to their price points, from Costco and SuperValu to Neiman Marcus and Macy's.

Most frequently though, marketers and industry discussions classify stores by their product lines. *Specialty stores* carry depth but not breadth; e.g., a store may carry only men's athletic shoes, but they do not carry table linens or children's clothing. The product assortment is broader at *general merchandise retailers*, such as department stores, which carry shoes, linens, and kids' clothes, but perhaps not as many brands of men's athletic shoes as the specialty shoe store. Other general retailers include the monster-sized mass merchandisers (e.g., discount warehouse clubs like Costco or Sam's or hypermarkets), or smaller general stores, such as convenience stores and drugstores.

Top Food Retailers

The top food retailers are:

- In Europe: Schwarz (€69b), Tesco (€64b), Carrefour (€61b)
- In the U.K.: Tesco (£64b), Sainsbury's (£26b), Asda (£24b)
- In the U.S.: Wal-Mart ($121b), Kroger ($59b), Costco ($44b), Safeway ($34b)

Does the concentration in Europe surprise you? How about Walmart in the United States?

Marketers and smart CEOs have long recognized the importance of the frontline employees as the primary connection between them and their customers. Unfortunately, some backward CEOs think that their merchandise attracts customers, so retail staff should be paid minimum wage. Clearly the merchandise is important, but so are the employees; they are a salient representation of the brand to the customer.

A lot of research has demonstrated that there is a relationship between employee satisfaction and customer satisfaction. If a retailer isn't selective in hiring employees, and if the employees are not trained or paid well, then the service they provide will be suboptimal, and there are clear and immediate repercussions on customer dissatisfaction. Not surprisingly, this situation isn't particularly pleasing to employees either; they experience the stress of role conflict, that is, they may want to please the customer but not be able to do so. Sooner rather than later, they resign, and new workers are hired as replacements, and this churn exacerbates poor service, since newbies rarely know how to do something in an organization. If instead, the retailer has foresight, they'll select good people, train them, pay them and reward them well, and trust them enough to empower them to make on-the-spot decisions to make customers happy.

Markup? Markdown?

Imagine you're a retailer. You buy a piece of merchandise for $100. You sell it for $200. The markup is ($200 − $100)/$100 = 100%. The margin is ($200 − $100)/$100 = 50%. Just depends on the perspective.

Retailing falls under the general rubric of services, and just as the employees are more noticeable to customers, so are the operations elements, such as IT. A tool that marketers have found useful is to draw a flowchart depicting the front-stage, meaning all the elements that a customer sees, as well as the backstage elements of the service provision that the customer does not see but that also must run efficiently to support the front stage. Since services—such as a customer walking into a retail outlet, wandering around, picking up merchandise, putting some back, considering what to buy, finally checking out—all unfold in real time, the flowchart map can given the marketer a sense of the elements that need to be managed: What parts of the process flow smoothly? What parts bog down quickly during peak periods? What parts of the process might be streamlined or eliminated altogether?

One streamlining phenomenon that IT is facilitating is self-service. We take self-service for granted in a number of industries: retail banking, check-ins at airports, checkouts at hotels, etc. Internet retailing is also clearly a form of self-service; instead of flipping through a catalog and calling an 800-number to place an order with a customer rep, we go online and click, click, click. Beyond these forms, a number of retailers are experimenting with self-service in areas like checkout. There are personnel, e.g., at grocery or hardware stores, as backup in case the machines are too confusing and to discourage theft. IT has made the checkout staffing needs more efficient (e.g., one person supervising six self-checkouts instead of six checkers). It's a development to watch.

Finally, a classic concern in retailing is the old mantra you've heard, "location, location, location," that is, how to identify an ideal site location for one's store. Marketers are hired to study environmental data such as population densities, income and social class distributions, median ages, and household composition if that is relevant to a particular store (e.g., placement of a toy store vs. a dance club).

Site location models essentially predict the likelihood of a successful outlet as measured by predicted sales as a function of those density stats. If you're Starbucks, it's population density and urban, upscale, high foot traffic. If you're Walmart, it's rural for the store's footprint but well placed with respect to car traffic, and average or downscale socioeconomic ZIP codes.

Once they're succeeding, a retailer has multiple growth strategies available. First, a retailer can expand by providing *additional services* to serve their current customers better. For example, it's not unusual for companies known for a particular core service (e.g., a grocery store) to add peripheral services for the convenience of their shoppers (e.g., adding banking, a florist, a drycleaner, etc.). Alternatively, the retailer can maintain their focus on their current offerings but reach out to attract *additional segments* of customers.

Given the importance of location and channel access, another popular course of action is to go *multisite* and open additional stores. While this strategy seems easy—after all, you already know how to make one shop succeed—it can be a challenge to oversee quality control in multiple locations. Companies face special risks when they expand too quickly. *International* expansion is a form of multisite expansion, and it brings additional challenges in terms of tailoring one's brand (and entire marketing mix) to the local markets. International approaches include direct exporting, joint ventures, direct foreign investment, license agreements, etc.

In addition to setting up shop internationally, companies in other countries can serve as very useful channel partners. An important form of international channel support these days is global outsourcing. For example, outsourcing reliance on India is huge, for the technical training (engineers hired there are less expensive than comparable talent in the U.S., U.K., Germany, or Japan) and for skills in English, both verbal (call centers) and written (software code and medical records transcriptions). In addition, India's offerings are broadening to include the provision of auto parts, chemicals, and electronics.

China's role in outsourcing is also clearly huge because of the size and costs of its non-union labor force. Employees' roles are less versatile given the more recent heritage of English as a second language. Its capitalistic business environment is also less mature, and it needs to redress its stance on copyright violations before playing with the global companies. Finally, while its infrastructures are improving, they are still relatively weak.

Choices among outsource providers depend on the talent, costs, and size of the labor pool, the existence of relevant infrastructures (IT, transportation, e-power, telecom), a hospitable government stance on foreign investment (e.g., local taxation), costs of real estate and travel, and local ethics (e.g., the country's treatment of women). These less experienced companies and countries are also more amenable and motivated to tailor their services to the buyers.

Transportation, a.k.a. How to Move Stuff.

Transportation logistics are frequently estimated to be nearly 50% of distribution costs. The other large components are holding and storing inventory. With regard to transportation, the choices are really quite simple: Time is money.

Transportation	Comments
Air freight	Fast, reliable scheduling, expensive.
Trucking	Pretty fast, pretty reliable scheduling, wide availability, somewhat expensive.
Shipping	Really cheap. Really slow.
Pipelines	Cheap, but limited in applicability. Only liquids or gases (not furniture or automobiles), and only certain kinds of liquids at that (oil, not orange juice). Cable lines (urban and deep-sea) are important but also limited (electric, phone, data, computing).

Anatomy of Airbus' Channel Partners

1. Carson, California: Water engineering and plumbing
2. Irvine, California: Testing in-flight entertainment on 600 seat-back video monitors
3. Perth, Australia: Red clay with bauxite for aluminum to →
4. Texas: Smelted into aluminum chunks "the size of mattresses," then →
5. Davenport, Iowa: 1.2-mile aluminum mill to make wing pieces, which are →
6. Trucked to Baltimore, Maryland, and →
7. Shipped to a factory in Broughton, North Wales (Plant can fit 12 soccer fields.)
8. Put on a ship that was made in China

9. Rendezvous soon with fuselage, built in Germany
10. Shipped to Bordeaux and driven by tractor trailer to Toulouse overnight (French police close roads) for final assembly.

The final step in preparing the A380 is painting the aircraft for specific customers. Among the airlines purchasing the A380 are Emirates, Quantas, Singapore Airlines, Air France, Lufthansa, and Korean Air.

Several engines are available on the Airbus A380, from suppliers such as Rolls Royce and Engine Alliance, which consist of a General Electric engine and Pratt & Whitney fan.

To give you a sense of size, the big A380 is in the foreground, and the little toy in back is an A340, which is only slightly smaller than the huge 747! The A380 assembly requires: 18,000 suppliers in 30 countries and 1,000,000 aluminum fasteners.

The plane: houses 800 passengers, has a 260-feet wingspan, has a tail seven stories high.

10-3d Franchising

Franchising is a unique format of multisite expansion. It's a means for a company to quasi-integrate; the company can retain some control without complete ownership or capital expenditure. Franchising systems offer benefits to both the franchisor (the company) and the franchisee (the local frontline).

For the franchisors' part, they receive some capital, they enjoy some scales of economy, they know they have committed people in their franchisees, their expansion and investments are relatively reduced in risk, and, having put their franchises in good hands, they can focus on their core functions, such as their expertise in product development. For the franchisees, they immediately inherit a company with a well-known brand and some market awareness, supplier relationships are largely intact, there are templates for training the staffs they hire, and there is central firm support for many business concerns, including marketing.

The two major classes of franchising are product franchising and business format franchising. For product franchising, a supplier authorizes a distributor in some territory (a prescribed geographic area) to carry its products, use its brand name, enjoy the efforts of its advertising, etc. The biggest example of product franchising is the automobile dealership (e.g., Ford dealers are meant to sell Ford cars and trucks). Other product franchises include Coca-Cola bottlers, Dunkin' Donuts shops, Subway restaurants, etc. Business format franchising is an arrangement where the company offers a tried-and-true system in which to conduct business, along with the marketing support, brand name, advertising, etc. to the franchisee—i.e., the owner who will run the local arm of that business. Examples are fast food outlets, some hotels, and a variety of other businesses, such as 7-Eleven convenience stores, Supercuts hair salons, Senior Helpers, etc.

In either case, a franchisee pays an upfront fee to buy into the system and then continues to pay royalties to the franchisor. In exchange, the franchisee enjoys an established brand name, as well as corporate support on equipment, the training of personnel, and marketing and advertising. Franchises are a low-capital, low-risk means of being an entrepreneur with a safety net. Most owners have some business management experience, and they can see the advantages of the economies of scale; the profits earned by all the outlets help finance the operations of the entire system, e.g., marketing the brand name, advertising dollars, operations, capital (buildings, land, equipment), etc. While initial franchise fees can seem steep, these networks provide access and support at a level that an independent entrepreneur typically cannot reach.

The franchise system has appeal to customers also because the brand name implies a level of standardization and predictability in quality across the outlets; e.g., one Jiffy Lube is pretty much like another, or, if you're inside a McDonald's, you would be hard-pressed to identify which city you were in. Franchises are popular up and down the channel (for the manufacturer or franchisor, the retailer or franchisee, and the customer), and hence they continue to grow in many sectors, e.g., movie theaters, weight loss centers, ice cream shops, etc.

10-3e **E-Commerce**

An enormously important channel is the Internet, and, if you can believe it, its impact is still in its infancy. Retail sales online are about $180 billion, growing by about 10% a year, but that's still only about 11% of total retail sales (www.census.gov/retail).

Who's buying all these books, music, DVDs, and, well, just about SKU? First, in terms of demography, those online still tend to be younger and more affluent, but gaps are closing toward being representative of general markets. Second, the U.S. dominates, but not by much or perhaps not for long. The countries with the next largest Internet presences are Japan, Germany, the U.K., France, and Korea. China's population is around 1.3 b, with only 400 mm online. India's population is right behind (1.2 b), with fewer online users (fewer than 100 mm). Obviously, both China and India have a huge potential for growth. Figure 10.10 presents the largest Asian countries (by population) and their Internet percentage penetrations. With the exception of Japan, the largest countries have the least penetrations, signaling obvious opportunities.

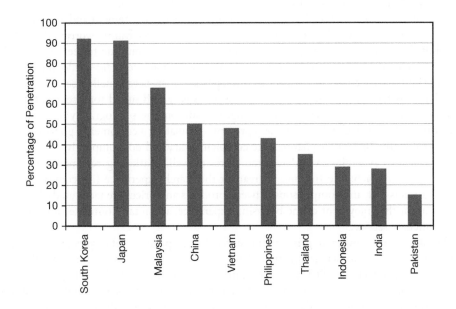

Figure 10.10

Asian Internet Penetration Percentages

The Internet is frequently characterized as a tool to empower customers. Figure 10.11 shows the increasing variety of channels through which a consumer might view entertainment programming. Price points and access durations vary, and the business models are still shaking out. As always, it's important to consider the target customer segment(s)

Figure 10.11

Channels Provide Convenience and Flexibility to Consumers

when designing or choosing channels: Different channels appeal to different individuals and customer segments. Increasing consumer choice is a central manifestation of empowerment.

In addition, e-commerce offers convenience and sometimes even smarter shopping. For example, the online services of "my lists" and order histories make reorders easier (e.g., Amazon's wish list, NetGrocer's last list, Netflix's ratings), etc. Web hosts' recommendation agents seem to enhance purchasing (but perhaps not lock in continued patronage).

10-3f Catalog Sales

The hard-copy predecessor to e-commerce was the direct-to-consumer catalog. The top 10 catalogers are B2B companies, including Dell, Thermo Fisher Scientific (lab supplies), IBM, Staples, and the like. The biggest B2C catalogers are Sears, JCPenney, Williams-Sonoma, L.L. Bean, Fingerhut, and Doctors Forster & Smith (pet supplies).

The advent of any new medium (e.g., the Internet) brings excitement and also naturally some concern that it will displace existing media (e.g., catalogs). But no worries: According to Multichannelmerchant.com, 80 of the top 100 catalogers continue to see sales growth. While conducting business via the Internet is dirt cheap, many costs for cataloging, such as color printing, have come down also (however, postage costs occasionally rise).

Marketers have shown that, while the Internet is very well suited for a search, catalogs still dominate when customers are browsing. In addition, the photography in catalogs is beautiful and sensual. Catalogs serve as a prompt, stimulating a customer to go to a website more frequently. Thus, these channels are complementary and not competitive.

The channel synergies extend to retail stores as well. Marketing researchers describe the strengths of each: The Internet is great for the search experience (it's convenient, the information is vast, and comparisons between products and prices are facilitated). Catalogs are great for the enjoyment of the browsing experience, and retail dominates for pre- and post-purchase service.

While a hard-copy catalog is, of course, fixed once printed, catalogers are also using technology and customer transaction databases to customize their printed offerings. The types of products and SKUs to include in one customer segment's catalog versus those that are sent to another can be modified, as can the frequency of the catalogs sent, the promotional incentives offered, etc. Catalogs can be used to yield sales directly and also to drive online or retail traffic. Increasingly, these promotional efforts are tracked, as when a catalog insert coupon is printed with an individual barcode, with the coupon redeemable at point-of-purchase. The redemption data further contribute to the database, not only to enhance subsequent personalization efforts, but also to continue to test the effectiveness of marketing offers.

10-3g **Sales Force**

We've talked about machines (the Internet, self-service IT systems) as a channel and about frontline employees at retail shops as channel representatives, but another human element of a channel is a company's sales force. For the companies high on push, such as many B2B channels, the sales force is an enormously important part of the corporate system and contributor to the bottom line. If we look at the performance of highly trained sales teams in industries such as shipping and metals, we see that the highest-educated and longest-tenured sales teams have growth rates in the mid-20% range. Particularly for more undifferentiated products, the quality of the sales force is often the single most significant means of differentiation. Stated another way, for these products, a company's sales force is its most important driver of performance.

The issues regarding sales forces are two: First, how many salespeople should we have (and where will they be deployed)? Second, how should salespeople be compensated for their efforts? The determination of the size of a sales force is usually done via some estimation of expected workload. We'd solve for the optimal number of salespeople by factoring in how many customers we must serve, how frequently we must call on a customer throughout the year, the average amount of time necessary to spend with each client, etc. For example, a particular SKU is sold to 100,000 drugstores and convenience stores, and the brand manager wants each salesperson to visit each account at least once a month, or 12 times a year. Say each visit lasts 30 minutes. The average number of hours worked a year would be 2,000 (50 weeks × 40 hours a week), but not all 2,000 will be face-to-face time with clients. Let's say that travel and administrative duties take away 500 hours. Then the minimum number of salespersons we'd require for this coverage would be

$$\frac{(100{,}000 \; accounts \times 12 \; visits \; per \; year \times 0.5 \; hour)}{1{,}500 \; hours} = 400 \; sales \; people$$

Naturally this number and the kind of salesperson most useful to the company will vary with the brand and corporate life cycle: Newer brands and companies might well take advantage of current selling partners. As the brand grows, the sizing issue is easier to clarify, and the salesperson's roles are beginning to be defined and specialized. As the brand matures, the salespeople need to be generalists in order to cover multiple products. And with the brand in decline, the sales force might be cut; indeed, the company might return to the use of selling partners.

Each company develops its policies to train and evaluate its salespeople. Sales managers are motivated by the criteria set for their performance reviews, to which their compensation is tied. Sales compensation is salary plus bonuses, but the question is a matter of proportion. The bonuses can be cash, trips, or chunks of wood (plaques).

Work performance criteria need to be clear from corporate so that the sales reps don't get frustrated that their work is for naught, and transparency is important for morale and feelings of fairness throughout the company. Numerous inputs can serve as components of performance evaluations, including sales data, perhaps by segment (e.g., client size) or by product line (e.g., pushing a new line), or improvement (e.g., sales compared to last year's or last quarter's sales). In addition to these outcome-based measures of conversion, there can be effort measures, such as time spent with clients, apparent expertise and product knowledge and training, the salesperson's attitude, or time-clock inputs such as number of days worked, number of calls placed, keeping selling expenses down, etc.

Just as the frontline in retailing is part of the brand image to the consumer, the sales force is part of the brand to the B2B customer. Here are the three biggest complaints by B2B buyers about salespeople: (1) "The sales person isn't following my company's buying process."

(2) "They didn't listen to my needs." (3) "They didn't bother to follow up." Avoid these problems, and the account is yours![3]

B2B ad: We can accommodate your company conferences and retreats.

10-3h Integrated Marketing Channels

As the number of channels proliferates, increasing care must be taken to coordinate and integrate efforts, data, customer touch points, etc. Companies are trying to understand customer behavior in order to see what channel attributes are important and what impacts customer choices. Companies are also trying to be strategic, considering how an additional channel would impact sales and profits and therefore how to allocate resources across channel options.

As always, when the decisions seem overwhelming, simplify and remember that the key to marketing is to think about the customer. From a customer focus, the marketer can design effectual distribution channels for the target segments to optimize the benefits they seek.

MANAGERIAL RECAP

Distribution channels are important to marketers because they're the link from the manufacturer to the customer.

- Numerous thoughtful decisions must be made in designing channel networks of partners, including the choices of intensive vs. selective channel partners.

- Channel entities are independent yet interdependent organizations; thus, from time to time, conflicts may arise. These are best addressed by employing good communication and trust, revenue sharing, or greater vertical integration.

Chapter Outline in Key Terms and Concepts

1. What are distribution channels and supply chain logistics, and why do we use them?

2. How to design smart distribution systems: intensive or selective?

   a. Push and pull

3. Power and conflict in channel relationships

   a. Revenue sharing

   b. Integration

   c. Retailing

   d. Franchising

   e. E-commerce

   f. Catalog sales

   g. Sales force

   h. Integrated marketing channels

4. Managerial recap

Chapter Discussion Questions

1. Go online and compare three franchises (e.g., franchise.org, americasbestfranchises.com, or whichfranchise.com). Choose two franchises in the same industry (e.g., fast food) and the third franchise from another industry (e.g., hair cutting). Make a table to report the fee structures (upfront, continued licensing), as well as benefits touted for franchisees of each franchise system. What would tempt you to pitch in with some friends and buy a franchise when you finish your degree?

2. If you were to take your company global, which 3 countries would be your first targets and why? What kinds of strategies and products fit with those countries' segments of customers?

▶ Video Exercise: Taza Chocolate (6:55)

Following the Mexican chocolate-making tradition, Taza Chocolate, based in Somerville, Massachusetts, manufactures a unique, stoneground chocolate with a very coarse texture and a very intense flavor. Making its chocolate from scratch (like, bean-to-bar), Taza produces chocolate bars, Mexican-style chocolate disks, and chocolate-covered nuts. Taza's products are carried in specialty and health food stores around the nation and on the company's website. Given the nature of the product, distribution is a critical element of Taza's marketing program. Taza markets its products through three distribution channels at different price points. As a manufacturer, Taza must produce a large volume of product in order to be cost-effective; the bulk of Taza's output is sold wholesale. The wholesale channel is an intermediate price point. A second channel occurs through distributors, and this pricing is below wholesale. A third channel is through direct retail, which has the highest price point; most of Taza's direct retailing occurs through the company's website, although it is working on opening a factory store.

Video Discussion Questions

1. What distribution channels does Taza Chocolate use, and what do they contribute to the company's overall marketing efforts?

2. Taza Chocolate prices its products differently based on the channel that is used for distributing them. Does this approach make good managerial sense? Explain your answer.

3. How does the concept of integrated marketing channels apply to Taza Chocolate's product distribution system?

MINI-CASE

Starbucks Fair Trade Line

Like a lot of massively successful consumer companies who want their customers to see they have big hearts, Starbucks offers a line of coffees for purchase made from small growers who meet certain economic and ethical standards. A challenge for Starbucks is that none of these such coffee growers are on a scale that offers any economy to the company for shipping, pickup, and processing. As a result, the costs to Starbucks are higher than for the mass suppliers of their standard coffees. Starbucks typically passes along some of those higher costs in higher prices to customers, reasoning that customers who care about such matters will happily pay for the extended benefits and feelings of goodwill.

Costs to growers continually rise, sometimes modestly, sometimes sharply. It's getting to the point where Starbucks wants to take a number of the pricier growers back to the table to negotiate better deals (for Starbucks), and of course, Starbucks holds the threat over their heads that the supplier will be dropped.

Case Discussion Questions

1. What kind(s) of power does Starbucks hold over their suppliers in this case?

2. Use the double marginalization problem and solution guides to structure two alternatives: one in which prices to consumers are maintained and profits are split 3:1 in favor of Starbucks, and one in which prices are raised 25% and profits are split 2:1 in favor of Starbucks. Assume the following: current price is $8.00 for a bag of this coffee, manufacturer costs have been $2.00, their mark-up has been $2.00 (and they're seeking more), retailing costs have been $1.00 and mark-up has been $3.00. What are the resulting mark-ups for the manufacturer and retailer (Starbucks) under each scenario? How will suppliers and consumers respond to either scenario?

ADVERTISING MESSAGES AND MARKETING COMMUNICATIONS

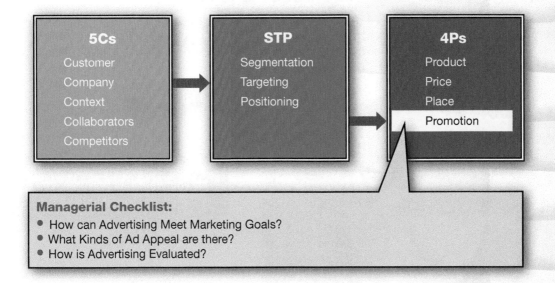

5Cs	STP	4Ps
Customer	Segmentation	Product
Company	Targeting	Price
Context	Positioning	Place
Collaborators		Promotion
Competitors		

Managerial Checklist:
- How can Advertising Meet Marketing Goals?
- What Kinds of Ad Appeal are there?
- How is Advertising Evaluated?

Many a CEO has wondered, "Has the money we've been spending on advertising been effective?" It's fair to raise the question of accountability, as long as the CEO does so thoughtfully. Let's see why such ROI questions are a little simplistic.

First of all: What is the advertising supposed to be effective at doing? What is the goal of the advertising campaign? Just as a fuller marketing plan must begin with a goal, so too should advertising begin with a clear understanding of what the campaign is supposed to achieve.[1] Typical goals include an increase in near future sales or a longer-term goal of an enhanced brand reputation. To be understood, an ad message needs to be simple, and so it is best focused on achieving a single goal. Most advertising cannot achieve multiple goals (any more than a single ops line, a single financial instrument, etc.).

In addition, advertising effectiveness can be very difficult to measure. That's okay; we marketers are held to a very high standard and CEOs want to know whether our marketing actions achieve their goals.

In particular, much of marketing is a long-term game; it is not intended to pay off immediately. If the goal is to strengthen a positive brand image, then a measure needs to be devised to capture whether that goal was attained. A marketing research project could easily measure the pre- and post-advertising attitudes in the relevant target segment to see whether they've improved. But, when the goal is to strengthen the brand image, the CEO cannot be flipping through this quarter's sales figures, hoping to see an increase. That is a mismatch between the goal and its assessment, and it would be unfair to whine that advertising wasn't working.

So what is advertising? Why do we need it? And how do we do it well?

Anatomy of Ad Content

Emotion/Image Appeal

Source: Calvin Klein
© Calvin Klein

Two beautiful people.

One pair of staring eyes, as if 'caught in the act'

Showing a lot of skin

Image-based message to women: "If you wear this perfume, you will be irresistible."

Image ads are very popular for perfumes (companies can't claim their flower-infused water is better than another's) and cars (when the vehicle is seen as a commodity, all the brand manager can do is point to the lifestyle it enables).

Lots of text to convey technical information.

Rational-based message: "You're smart if you choose our brand. Here are all the reasons why we're better than the competition."

Cognitive/Rational Appeal

Source: Bargainteers LLC

Cognitive ads are very popular for high-tech, such as laptops, tablets, and smartphones. These can be expensive purchases, and most consumers know they are not experts and wish to be assured that what they're buying is state-of-the-art.

11-1 WHAT IS ADVERTISING?

Advertising is the primary means by which a company communicates with its customers about its products, brands, and position in the marketplace. Product, price, and place also signal a brand's positioning, and certainly all these signals need to tell a coherent story. If ads claim that a brand is an exclusive, premium brand, the product needs to be of high quality, priced relatively high, and distributed relatively exclusively. But while the rest of the marketing mix is important, advertising is the most direct communication link.

For many people, the word "advertising" connotes television commercials, and certainly this is a fun form of advertising. TV commercials and print ads (in magazines, billboards, online banners) represent much of the typical advertising budget. But companies advertise their brands in everything they do, including event sponsorship, the packaging that encloses their products, the price points for those products, etc. Thus, many advertising gurus prefer the more general phrase "Integrated Marketing Communications" (IMC), which is broad enough to include other media (e.g., public relations, direct marketing). It reminds the marketer to be sure that the message has a holistic nature and that it is consistent and complementary across all media choices and executions. In this chapter, we focus on the content of the message being expressed in the ad, no matter where that ad is placed.

What Type of Ad Should We Run?

We can decide, "What type of ad should we run?" once we know:
→ "What's our advertising goal?" which requires that we know
→→ "What's our marketing goal?" for which we need to know
→ → → "What's our corporate goal?"

11-2 WHY IS ADVERTISING IMPORTANT?

First, advertising facilitates customers' awareness. The company has segmented the market and selected a set of target customers. The company now wishes to provide information to those target customers because the company thinks they will be intrigued by their brands.

Second, advertising attempts to persuade potential customers that the featured brand is superior to competitors' market offerings. A company expresses its brand positioning by emphasizing a feature or benefit that makes it seem better than any other options.

Advertising has both short-term and long-term effects. By "short-term," we mean not only that the effect occurs immediately or very shortly after the ad exposure but also that the effect is of short duration or short-lived. Several short-term effects can be shown. For example, customers' memory of ads and brands and attributes are easily measured. Attitudes are also easily surveyed and may be compared to prior attitudes (measured previously) to assess any change in valence.

Not unreasonably, advertising is expected to generate sales and profitability, but demonstrating this effect on the bottom line is rather complicated. Occasionally, increases in short-term sales can be observed during an advertising campaign. But marketers have learned that, if your goal is only to increase sales, nothing's quicker than a price promotion.

The financial impact is difficult to assess because advertising is complicated and thought to operate in a longer-term manner. By "long-term," we mean both that the effects of the ad might not appear immediately and also that the effects are sustained long after the ad exposure. Advertising effects might not appear immediately because they are cumulative and therefore difficult to attribute to a single ad campaign that was run five years ago. Ad results are sustained because, when used in this manner, the role of advertising is to strengthen brand awareness, positive attitudes, perceptions of brand equity, and so on. In turn, these enhanced attitudes become manifest in behaviors: more purchases, more expensive purchases, more frequent purchases, and word-of-mouth among the target customers. So, even though a CMO typically does not see an immediate sales bump from an ad campaign, everyone "knows" that advertising works and that the brand needs it. So we keep investing in advertising.

We next consider the content of the advertising message. Advertising has rich communication potential; ads can convey rational information as well as emotional imagery. To choose among the many types of ad formats, we have to know our marketing and advertising strategic goals. Again, we have to assess the ad's effectiveness, and we must measure effects against those goals. For example, if the goal is to increase awareness, we might run an ad chock-full of information and then measure customers' memory for the ad, brand, brand attributes, etc.

So, on to the "how" of advertising messages…

11-3   WHAT MARKETING GOALS ARE SOUGHT FROM ADVERTISING CAMPAIGNS?

Advertising can be used to address many goals. One popular model of goals is called **AIDA**: **A**ttention, **I**nterest, **D**esire, **A**ction. The flow goes like this: We first get the ad recipients' attention, then pique their interest, see if you can get them to be attracted to the brand, and then induce a purchase or intention to purchase.

Other advertisers have other models: Some describe the flow of the ad recipient from a level of awareness to greater knowledge, to more liking and preference, to a sense of brand conviction, and then to purchasing. Another variant goes from awareness to interest to brand evaluation, to trial and adoption. Another model describes the process as one going from an ad exposure to receiving the message to a cognitive response to a change in attitude to intention to buy and finally to the behavior of buying. It is currently fashionable to go still further and add levels such as brand affinity, attachment, connection, ambassador, zealot, etc.

Choose whatever model that suits you, but, as depicted in Figure 11.1, these goals largely fall into one of three camps:

1. *Cognition:* Increasing awareness and knowledge about our brand
2. *Affect:* Enhancing attitudes and positive associations about our brand
3. *Behavior:* Ultimately encouraging more buying of our brand

Figure 11.1

The Goal of an Ad Campaign: To Affect Consumer Decision Making

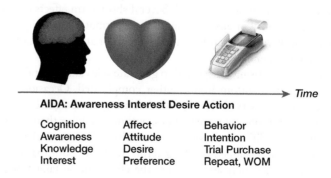

AIDA: Awareness Interest Desire Action

Cognition	Affect	Behavior
Awareness	Attitude	Intention
Knowledge	Desire	Trial Purchase
Interest	Preference	Repeat, WOM

In advertising, we wish to affect consumers' cognitions, emotions, or behaviors. We want to grab our customers' heads, hearts, and pocketbooks.

AIDA

A = Attention: Do customers know about us?
I = Interest: Would customers consider us?
D = Desire: Do customers want us and look for us?
A = Action: Do customers buy us, talk and post about us?

These goals are correlated with the product life cycle:

- Early in a brand's life, the job of an ad campaign is to get the word out and to inform the consumer of this new or improved market offering: "Here is the brand, here are its features, here are its points of differentiation from the competition."

- When the brand is growing, awareness is already strong, and ad campaigns are developed to enhance the positivity of the target segment's attitudes about the brand.

- At brand maturity, awareness has pretty well permeated the market, and customers have pretty set attitudes. Some people don't care for the brand, but hopefully many people in the target segment do. At this point, ads are intended to be reminders, "Hey, we're still here" or "We're offering a twofer." Advertising hasn't dropped off yet, but sales are strong; so a smaller ad budget (as measured by percentage of sales) is required to maintain a steady presence (sales, market share, etc.).

- Finally, when a product is in decline, ad spending is usually reduced greatly, and the poor brand slips into a coma and eventually is pulled from the market.

Of course, it's best if the elements of marketing are integrated. Thus, if a brand manager can keep the product fresh, the advertising would always have something new to say. For example, a laundry detergent might morph from powder to liquid to detergent with built-in fabric softeners. Then the ads follow the product changes and continue to inform consumers.

As you might imagine, these goals aren't equally easy to achieve. Increase awareness? No problem. Enhance attitudes? Can do. Encourage more buying? Uh, well . . . .

If you need convincing, here's a thought experiment. Say you're online and a banner ad pops up and it's about a new movie that's about to come out: "Star Wars 14!" You'd think, "Oh, I hadn't heard about that yet." With that one simple message, the communication has achieved the goal of informing you, of offering you awareness about a new product. You now know something you hadn't known just a moment before. Awareness? Check.

Let's say the banner ad continues with a picture and a few lines like, "Just as fun. Same Stormtroopers. Same awesome F/X. Saving the world again!" You might think, "That sounds pretty good." So the ad succeeded in making you think positively about the movie. Enhanced attitudes? Check.

Finally, say the banner ad closes with the tagline, "Click here to buy a ticket for this Friday, now!" Will you? Who knows? But you probably won't. Even if it sounds like a fun movie, maybe you're busy Friday, or maybe you prefer watching movies on your computer rather than at the theater. Your response doesn't mean the advertiser didn't succeed. You might add the movie to your mental must-see (eventually) list. That is advertising success, but it is pretty tough to measure.

In general, the goal of getting the consumer to purchase is not easily achieved or measured, but that doesn't necessarily render an ad ineffective. Even though a product may be simple (familiar, inexpensive, etc.), most purchases are complicated. A simple ad message cannot easily propel a customer to go buy. In addition, many product categories show buying inertia, and many of our purchases are so-called low involvement; that is, we just don't care about the product or the brand choice. We buy whatever we typically buy, and we don't even "see" ads for other brands, much less spend any cognitive effort in processing the messages. As this example illustrates, there are a zillion (well, at least several) factors that go into even the simplest purchase decision.

11-4 DESIGNING ADVERTISING MESSAGES TO MEET MARKETING AND CORPORATE GOALS

Advertising is a means of communication. A company says to its potential customers, "Buy our stuff!" "We have a new service!" "Look at our low, low prices!" "We're better than the competition!" As a result, marketers must understand the basic model of dyadic communication. In the classic model, there is a source (e.g., the firm), a message (e.g., the ad), and a receiver (e.g., customer). The source intends to send out certain information, which is encoded (i.e., expressed in a certain way) and then transmitted. The receiver then decodes the message. Hopefully, the receiver interprets the content of the message in a manner similar to what the sender had intended. But there can be errors along the way. Think of communicating with a friend. You might intend to say something, but it comes out wrong, or you say it right, but your friend takes it the wrong way. All of that can happen with advertising as well. That's why copy testing (marketing research examining the content of the ad) is important before launching the full ad campaign: to learn whether the intended target segment understands the message as the company intended.

M&M's

If marketing is said to be the 4Ps, here are the 6Ms of advertising:

1. What is the Market being addressed?
2. What is your Mission; the objectives of the advertising campaign?
3. What is your Message to be communicated?
4. How much Money will be spent?
5. What Media choices will be implemented?
6. How will the effectiveness of the campaign be Measured?

There are many kinds of ads, or ways to communicate, and most may be mapped pretty cleanly onto one of the first two goals of advertising; the message can be primarily cognitive (e.g., increasing awareness and knowledge) or emotional (e.g., enhancing attitudes and preference). Cognitive, or rational, appeals (or approaches) can be further distinguished into arguments (one-sided vs. two-sided, comparative vs. non-comparative ads), product demonstrations, and dramas. Emotional ads tend to use one of these elements humor, fear appeals, so-called subliminal ads, image appeals, and endorsements.

11-4a Cognitive Ads

A *cognitive,* or *rational, appeal* engages the consumer's brain. The ad gives the consumer a reason to buy the product that is practical or functional. It's a utilitarian (as opposed to hedonic) appeal. The ads tend to be informative, featuring the product's attributes and their benefits.

Nonprofits

Nonprofit marketing people talk explicitly about winning "hearts and minds." They know the pocketbooks will follow.

A *one-sided argument* means that the company focuses on expressing the benefits of its product to the consumer. This approach is a common one among advertisers; many examples exist, for example, a recent Brookstone features a "motorized grill brush with steam cleaning power!" as an ideal Father's Day gift with the pitch, "The ultimate power tool for your grill." One-sided ads are straightforward: they offer an explanation of the anticipated benefits.

In a *two-sided argument,* the company describes the pros and cons of its brand. Two-sided arguments are used when your target customers already know that your brand has some weakness. Thus, you might as well acknowledge it (and earn some points for honesty) and then go on to argue why your brand is nevertheless excellent. For example, direct-to-consumer ads by pharmaceuticals companies make claims for drugs that will help alleviate symptoms, but possible side effects must be acknowledged. (In contrast, if customers do not know the product's weaknesses, companies don't usually point them out via this kind of ad.) There are two benefits to two-sided arguments: (1) They stand out. Most ads are one-sided, with everyone claiming their brand is great. Two-sided arguments get attention because they are different. (2) Two-sided ads are seen as more objective or neutral because you're getting the pros and cons; hence they seem more credible.

In a *non-comparative ad,* a brand is mentioned, and its features, attributes, image portrayal, etc. are conveyed. The ad features a single brand (see Figure 11.2). The brand's benefits, imagery, and positioning are highlighted, and no competitors are featured or implied.

Figure 11.2

A Non-comparative Ad: one brand featured; very popular

jannoon028/Shutterstock.com

In a *comparative ad*, the featured brand name is mentioned, as is the brand name of a competitor (see Figure 11.3). This sounds a little insane: Why would you pay to advertise for the competition? Here are the rules of thumb: if you're the big player (i.e., the market leader), you treat your competitors as irritating little gnats that you wouldn't bother to acknowledge in an ad. However, if you're the little guy with a new brand, you might mention the big brand in your ad in order to gain an association with all the good qualities that consumers seek when they purchase the market leader's brand.

Figure 11.3

A Comparative Ad

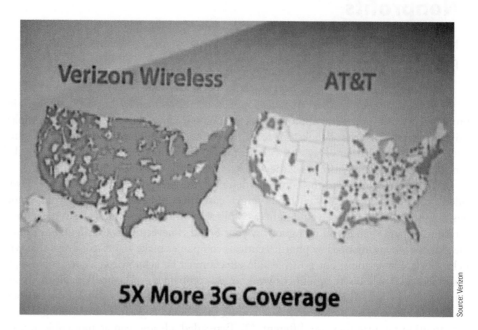

So, for example, the use of comparative ads is asymmetric in that Mercedes would never mention Acura, but Acura ads for their luxury car might liken the car to a Mercedes. However, Acura needs to be careful about actually mentioning Mercedes. It has been reliably shown that, if you're the small player and you use a comparative ad, your ad budget helps you, but it also helps the comparison brand. (To the victor go the spoils.)

Where would the advertising industry be without *product demonstrations*? Whether an ad shows a laundry detergent that can clean kids' mud-caked clothes or Dan Akroyd pulverizing a fish in a Bass-o-Matic on *SNL*, we love to see stuff in action. Demonstrations are vivid, and they make our expectations clear. We see precisely what we'd get for our money. All ads try to persuade us that the product is great, but demo ads show the product, and consumers can decide on the validity of the claim for themselves (see Figure 11.4).

A TV commercial is often a narrative *drama* or a slice-of-life vignette. Often a problem is depicted, and the brand is featured as the perfect solution. For example, a guy finds dandruff flakes on his shoulders, buys the right shampoo, and then all the women in his world think he's hot. A nice by-product of story-based ads is that they are easy to communicate from the advertiser to the viewer, as well as from the viewer to friends via word of mouth. Dramas are more memorable than sheer listings of product features and claims. The stories give the brand a context and show the viewer how the brand could be helpful in their lives.

Figure 11.4

A Product Demonstration Ad

11-4b **Emotional Ads**

Another type of ad that elicits emotions uses *humor*. Ad execs count on humorous ads to break through the noisy media clutter (see Figure 11.5). Humorous ads are popular because they're fun, and they win a lot of awards in the advertising industry because they're seen as clever.

Figure 11.5

A Humorous Ad

Unfortunately, humorous ads are not all that effective. Part of the problem is that people remember the joke, but they don't necessarily remember the brand being advertised. In addition, not everyone has the same sense of humor, and it is easy to insult some people with an ad that other people think is funny.

The final major problem of humorous ads is inherent in humor itself; humor is based on the element of surprise. Once you know the joke, the second time you see the ad, you already know the punch line. Pretty soon, you begin to ignore the ad and the message. Thus, humorous ads inevitably wear out quickly (the ad campaign can't last long because the audience becomes bored quickly). If you couple an ad's short life with the fact that ad creation and media placement is expensive, then it quickly adds up that funny ads just aren't cost-efficient.

Yet the life of a funny ad can be extended, if the ad execution varies, e.g., the GEICO insurance company's talking gecko appears in different scenarios. People also enjoy sharing humor. So the ad may generate buzz, be posted online, etc., thereby perpetuating free word-of-mouth communication.

Fear and *embarrassment* are negative emotions that have been used to sell both products and social marketing ideas: "Buy this deodorant (or mouthwash) so that you won't smell," "Stop smoking so that your lungs won't turn black." The problem with negative emotions, and with fear in particular, is that its effect is non-monotonic. That is, the ad might overdo it and be seen as so fear-inducing as to be creepy or horrifying. We cope with that kind of message by blocking it out, and therefore the ad has no effect on propelling the consumer to the desired behavior. For a fear appeal to be effective, the ad must provide a solution to reduce the consumer's fear, resolving both the problem and emotion by the end of the ad (see Figure 11.6).

A Fear-Appeal Ad

Source: Arena Communications

Subliminal ads have long been a curiosity. Long ago, a print ad for an alcoholic beverage featured the bottle and some of its contents poured over ice in a glass. The ad was claimed to contain the letters *s*, *e*, and *x* embedded in the ice cubes. The thought was that on some subconscious, precognitive level, people would be turned on and therefore favor this brand,

ethics

The American Marketing Association's Statement of Ethics speaks to several issues regarding advertising. Here are two professional standards:

1) Honesty: A company should honor its explicit and implicit commitments and promises to its customers.

2) Fairness: A company should represent its products in a clear manner, and avoid false, misleading, and deceptive promotions.

Here's a thought question—is it misleading to claim that a piece of clothing is "Made in the U.S.A."? What does it mean to say that—the garment was assembled here, but comprised of imported cloth; that the pieces were cut here but sent abroad for sewing; that the cotton was grown here or knitted here? It's a complicated, inter-connected world . . . .

and go buy it. About the same time, movie theater owners experimented with flashing ads at millisecond speeds on the screen during the movie with messages like "Go buy popcorn!" The messages appeared so fast that no viewer could detect the moment of having explicitly seen the message. Yet the message was thought to have an effect on the subconscious, propelling the audience member to mindlessly go to the lobby and buy a bucket of popcorn. (Most marketers believe this was an urban legend.)

These mind games were thought to be quite disturbing and unethical, and they are banned. The odd thing is that they were never shown to be effective. Indeed, more than one cynic in the advertising industry has remarked, "We don't use subliminal ads not because we're not supposed to. We don't use them because they don't work."

Yet it's a fine line. Many retailers play nondescript background music to set an ambience. It's known that music with a faster tempo seems to induce more energy and excitement, and people buy more. The music is audible so that it is not subliminal, but the effect is sort of sneaky. Some product placement in movies is rather overt; e.g., an actor drives a particular brand of car or uses a Samsung or Apple smartphone. But much product placement can be subtle. The question is whether the brand leaves an impression that can affect a viewer's subsequent purchasing. The brand is visible, not subliminal; so, strictly speaking, the practice is not forbidden.

11-4c Image Ads

When advertisers talk about "emotional appeals", they often mean that the ad conveys an image. The ad message is more abstract than a list of features and attributes (see Figure 11.7). Usually these are feel-good portrayals: "Use this brand, and you'll be more attractive" "Buy this, and you'll be able to emulate this cool person's lifestyle."

Many products in many purchase categories are seen as nearly commodity-like in the eyes of customers, and the category is so competitive that firms struggle to distinguish their brands from one other. Image is closely tied to branding; e.g., all soft drinks are sweet and bubbly, but this is the one for young people. Every restaurant has tasty food, but this one is family friendly. Every theater shows a variety of films, but this is the arts theater.

Image is about perceptions, and advertising imagery is extremely malleable among the marketing mix variables for creating perceptions regarding a product's positioning. Elements of the product itself, its price, and its distribution outlets all certainly contribute to perceptions of a brand's image. But advertising is the most amenable vehicle for convincing customers and potential customers of a brand's relative strengths.

Figure 11.7

An Image-Based Ad

Source: Gucci

11-4d **Endorsements**

Endorsements are ads that feature a spokesperson on behalf of the brand (see Figure 11.8). These ads can feature celebrities or experts or even seemingly regular people offering testimonials as satisfied past customers.

Figure 11.8

An Endorsement Ad

AP Images/Popchips/Rex Features

When a celebrity is used to endorse a product, the hope is that the positive associations attached to the celebrity would transfer to the brand. (This is literally known as "affect transfer" or "association transfer.") The star's endorsement basically says, "This brand is cool. Be like me!" The celebrity is typically attractive and successful, and the idea is that a regular consumer can achieve part of the celebrity's appeal and lifestyle by purchasing the item in the ad.

As with pretty much anything in life, there are risks associated with using a celebrity endorser. We've all seen when a celebrity goes a little wonky, and then the brand they've been endorsing can be affected by those new, bad associations. As an alternative, some brands have spokes-characters, like the Jolly Green Giant who looks over his vegetable garden, or Buzz, the Honey Nut Cheerios spokes-bee, and so on. These characters bring the brands to life, and you will never catch them doing bad things (at least not in public).

Experts who are not celebrities frequently serve as spokespeople for high-tech products, such as computer equipment or pharmaceuticals (e.g., doctors recommending drugs). Here, we don't expect mere transfer of positive affect, but rather a signal that the expert is offering credible information. So this otherwise possibly risky purchase for the consumer is made to seem less risky by the endorsement of some knowledgeable person.

Regular people sometimes provide testimonials. They're not celebrities, and they're not experts. They're just satisfied customers with the claim that, if the product worked well for them, it will for you too. These representatives tend to convey credibility too, due to their similarity to us, the target audience of regular people. In addition, we know celebrities are lending their names to products for cash. In fact, doing so can hurt their persona-brand (that they're money-grubbers), which explains why many celebrities are more likely to do endorsements abroad but not in their home markets. In contrast, even if "regular people" providing testimonials are paid, we can guess they're not paid as much as celebrities; plus, something about their being like us makes their voice sound more authentic and trustworthy.

There are several conceptual ideas about how endorsements (and a lot of other advertising tactics) work. One theory, called *ELM* (*elaboration likelihood model*), basically posits that there are two ways into your brain: a central path or a peripheral path.[2] An ad's central message is thought to be the content of the persuasion itself. The target segment processes the content because these customers are highly involved in the brand and product category, so they are motivated to process all the details of the information in the ad. In contrast, other information is classified as peripheral cues, including the celebrity endorser, their attractiveness, their credibility to be speaking on behalf of the featured brand, the style of the ad, etc. Peripheral clues can be pretty much anything that is not the central ad argument. Both sorts of information may be processed. If the central message is complicated, people who don't care that much about the brand may just look to the peripheral cues when judging the ad or brand.

Another theory is called *source credibility*, which means the consumer interprets the message as the most important piece of information but also processes the credibility of the source as a cue to the likely validity of the message. So a doctor touting pills sounds credible. They're a convincing source of information. (But note how often we've been fooled even with the disclaimer, "I'm not a doctor, but I play one on TV." We believe them anyway!) But a super model praising the technology in a new computer, well . . . .

One more theory (the last for now, I promise) describes the so-called *sleeper effect*, whereby a piece of information is conveyed by some source; it may be a celebrity, an expert, a friend, something you read in *The Wall Street Journal*, or even in the tabloids. Over time, we forget the source of the information. So, whether the original source was credible or not, it doesn't really matter. We encoded the information but disassociated it from the source. As a result, even if the cute actor or actress couldn't possibly know anything about the product they're touting, the consumer is affected by positive associations with the good-looking famous person.

There are many kinds of ads, and we've been discussing just the major classes. The one- or two-sided ads, comparative or non-comparative ads, product demonstrations, and dramas tend to be rational in content and are processed cognitively. In contrast, emotional responses are triggered by humorous ads, fear appeals, image ads, endorsements and even so-called subliminal ads (because they don't quite reach cognitive processing). Different combinations are possible; e.g., a humorous product demonstration. Different content (e.g., comparative or image) may also be mixed with different executional styles (e.g., drama or humor).

In most industries, different players try to attract their customers with different appeals that are consistent with their distinct position. However, in some industries, all the players use the same kind of appeal, e.g., product demonstrations show how fast or roomy a car is, and experts are used as spokespeople in ads for investments.

The choice among these options is facilitated when we return to the question: What is our advertising, marketing, corporate goal?

- For example, companies trying to increase awareness and create positive attitudes and buzz about a brand extension need to express the new features and benefits clearly in an ad. That goal might be less achievable in a humorous ad than in a straightforward, one-sided, non-comparative ad.

- Companies pulsing out reminder ads to reinforce its target customers' attitudes might wish to get their attention via an emotional appeal.

- When a competitor initiates a price war, instead of meeting the price cuts, a company would be better off to launch comparative ads to show the benefits of its (higher-priced) brands.

Finally, ads are likely to change throughout the product life cycle, with comparative ads used to launch a new product and mature brands advertised via image-based communications.

11-5 HOW IS ADVERTISING EVALUATED?

Whether the strategic goal of an ad campaign is cognitive (awareness, knowledge), affective (image, preference), or behavioral (trial, repurchase), there are methods for measuring the results. For cognitive tests, the primary consideration is memory. Advertising researchers call random samples of households and ask first a *recall* memory test ("Which brands do you remember seeing advertised last night on TV?"), and they note which ads are mentioned. In the advertising industry, this test is called *day-after recall* (*DAR*), and it is a stringent test: Did the ad make enough of an impression that the consumer remembers it, unprompted, a day later? DAR scores are a particularly big deal the day after the Super Bowl or any other huge event, during which air time is charged at high rates, as an assurance or test that the ads did as well as anticipated.

When the respondent can think of no more ads, the advertising researcher turns to memory tests of *recognition* ("Do you remember seeing an ad for Ford last night?"). Recall and recognition tests of memory can also be applied to assess the impact of online banner ads or magazine or billboard advertising ("Which brands have you seen advertised online during the past week?" or "What ads have you seen on the Metro recently?").

Traditionally, marketers and advertisers have believed that, while memory is not the same as persuasion, it's a necessary starting point. That is, the assumption is that an ad can't affect your attitude if you can't even remember having seen it. That assumption seems sensible, but recently it has been under question. The recent thinking does not negate the very likely effective path of memory to persuasion to buying, but now it is suggested that perhaps cognition and persuasion could also function implicitly. That is, even if consumers can't quite remember having seen an ad, it doesn't mean they didn't see it. And it doesn't mean that the ad won't impact their attitudes and possible subsequent buying patterns.

Conceptually, this implicit processing is thought to work along the lines of what's called *mere exposure*. The idea is that sheer familiarity due to repeated exposure to a brand name or logo or ad will in time enhance the viewer's favor of the ad and brand. Billboards are thought to operate in this manner. No one really wants you reading these signs while you're driving. But every day, to and from work or school, you see a picture, a brand name, maybe a brief message, and, with time, the sign is part of your life, and it gains some positivity. The same principle operates for the ads in the frames of websites; we don't even know they're having an effect.

While the cognitive goals (awareness, knowledge) are tested primarily via memory measures, testing whether affective goals (image, preference) have been achieved is done with numerous measures of attitudes and behavioral intentions. Tests of the persuasive powers of the ad are usually done prior to launching the ad campaign—to tweak the content or ad execution details. Creative types (in ad agencies) will say that you cannot tell a priori which ads will do well. That's nonsense; they just don't like having their work evaluated (in part because the feedback will involve at least a little tweaking to what the creative had considered "art" and also because creative types are more interested in the creative, not strategic, aspects of advertising). Ad copy testing is done in two stages: First, the overall concept is tested, and, second, the preliminary flow of the ad is tested.

Ad *concept testing* is usually conducted in a focus group setting. Focus group facilities recruit eight to 10 consumers who may be screened on criteria such as relevance to the target segment or usage in the product category but who are otherwise selected randomly. The ideas underlying the ad are explained, and illustrative props show the basic idea of the ad.

Rarely are completed ads shown and tested at this stage (they're too expensive, ~$500 k). Instead, the ad is somewhere in preliminary development ($10–20 k). It can be mocked up as a drawing like a cartoon strip—storyboard style—with each scene and possible dialog unfolding. Or the ad may consist of animated graphics shown on a computer.[3] Research has shown that an audience's reactions to the ads even in their rougher, proposal stage are correlated with real, completed ads. The consumers respond to the ad, to the brand, and to whatever else the company asks the focus group moderator to cover in one-and-a-half hours. After three or four focus groups concur that the ad agency is heading in a good direction, the ads are further developed and copy testing begins.

Copy testing is usually conducted via surveys. Larger random samples of consumers are recruited by advertising researchers to attend a "screening for possible new television programming." That's the typical cover story, and it's a load of hooey. The consumers travel to a relatively central location, such as a hotel near the city's airport. The supposed pilot TV series is shown, with several ads aired in natural TV show breaks. After 30 minutes, the attendees fill out dozens of pages of questionnaires asking about the TV show, the ads, their buying habits, and the like. Increasingly, copy testing is done online, with invites sent over email, requesting participants to go to a website to view the materials and answer the questions.

The survey items include measures of attitudes on stimulation (the ad made me curious or enthusiastic), information (gave me useful, credible info), negative emotion (the ad irritated me), transformation (the ad gave me enjoyment or gave me a pleasant, satisfied feeling), identification (I recognized myself in it, I felt involved with it). An ad's scores on these measures is compared to the ad agency's extensive database to determine how well the current set of ads might do, since the agency has other data indicating how well previous ads had done. Any ad must surpass certain basic scores: Does the ad evoke positive feelings? Is the ad remembered for the correct brand?

Anatomy of Ad Creation

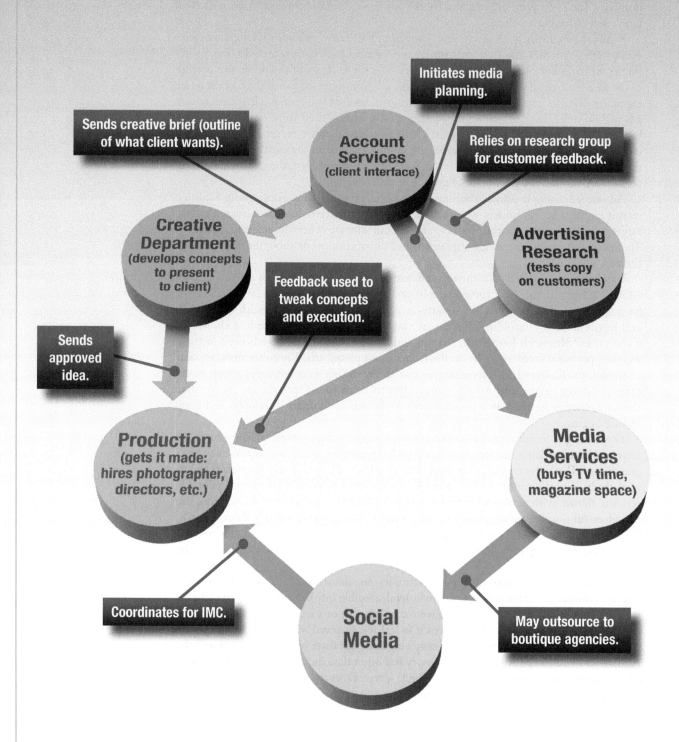

Initiates media planning.

Sends creative brief (outline of what client wants).

Relies on research group for customer feedback.

Account Services (client interface)

Creative Department (develops concepts to present to client)

Feedback used to tweak concepts and execution.

Advertising Research (tests copy on customers)

Sends approved idea.

Production (gets it made: hires photographer, directors, etc.)

Media Services (buys TV time, magazine space)

Coordinates for IMC.

Social Media

May outsource to boutique agencies.

11-5a A_{ad} and A_{brand}

In evaluating ads, marketers measure two basic attitudes: attitude-to-the-ad (A_{ad}) and attitude-to-the-brand (A_{brand}). A company and ad agency can pride itself on creating cool ads, ads that customers like, and ads whose scores on A_{ad} are strong and positive. But marketers care (and if the ad agency wants a long-term relationship with the marketing company, it should care too) that the ad is effective in making strong positive brand attitudes, the A_{brand}. And, of course, most marketers believe that the brand attitudes trigger sales, that is, ultimately $A_{ad} \rightarrow A_{brand} \rightarrow$ likelihood to purchase.

Another sort of measure of an ad's impact on a viewer is the dial procedures intended to capture moment-by-moment processing. In an ad copy test, a viewer is given a dial (or a mouse) to indicate response while continually viewing the ad. Turning it to the left means "I hate this," and turning to the right indicates "I think this is great." This idea is useful in editing ineffectual sections of an ad and in identifying which positive sections might be played up. Critics say that viewers' reactions to an ad have a natural lag, Therefore, measures taken after the ad or by accumulating and integrating all the moments over the course of the ad are better predictors of ad and brand liking than those taken at any particular moment. The technique is in its infancy, and, given its potential, perhaps the kinks will be worked out.

If advertising is intended to address the heads, hearts, and wallets, we can check diagnostics that measure these objectives. In Figure 11.9, the data for the bank indicate that there is a problem with awareness, at only 25%. But of the aware customers, a full 80% like the brand. Generating awareness is an easy problem to fix via advertising: Spend more money, and choose media that reach more broadly.

The hotel has a different story. Most people are aware (80%), but only 37.5% of them have positive attitudes toward the hotel brand. If the hotel itself is not great, then the attitude measure will be sticky. Otherwise, advertising can help the hotel by generating more favorable attitudes via more positive and more persuasive advertising.

Conditional probabilities of customers in the marketplace (e.g., 80% of customers who are aware of the bank brand have positive attitudes toward it).

	Awareness	Attitude	Trial	Repeat
Bank	25%	80.0%	100.0%	75.0%
Hotel	80%	37.5%	83.3%	80.0%
Car	90%	83.3%	26.7%	75.0%
Cruise	90%	83.3%	66.7%	50.0%

Time →

Figure 11.9

Marketing Diagnostics

The car scenario is different still. Awareness is strong. Attitudes are favorable. But the proportion of favorable attitude among those who have taken the car for a test drive is only $0.90 \times 0.83 \times 0.27 = 20\%$. This problem might not be one that advertising can resolve. The product might be priced out of reach (think Ferrari), or perhaps it's a channels issue (e.g., few dealerships).

The cruise scenario is one in which awareness is high, and attitudes are positive. There is good trial, but people aren't coming back. This profile might suggest a problem with the product itself. If that's the case, we can advertise till we're blue in the face, but we have to deliver on our promises. There are limits to what advertising can do. On the other hand, for cruises, customers may simply wish to try something different for their next holiday. In such a scenario, the company would need to extend its product line.

MANAGERIAL RECAP

The key concepts of advertising communications messages are these:

- Goals must be set before ads can be evaluated.
- There are several classes of advertising communications messages.
  - Rational or cognitive ads include one- and two-side arguments, comparative and non-comparative ads, product demonstrations, and dramas
  - Emotional ads include humorous and fear-inducing appeals, image, and endorsements
- Advertising is tested via concept testing and copy testing. The content of what is measured depends on the corporate strategic goals of the ad campaign, and those assessments can include:
- Memory tests (recall and recognition)
- Attitudinal tests (enhancement of the favorability of the product and brand)
- Behavioral measures (likely to purchase the brand or generate positive word of mouth)

Chapter Outline in Key Terms and Concepts

1. What is advertising, why is it important, how can it be used to achieve marketing goals?

2. Ads can be cognitive, emotional, image-based, celebrity endorsement

3. Advertising is evaluated via memory and A_{ad} and A_{brand}

4. Managerial recap

Chapter Discussion Questions

1. Rip up your favorite magazine, and classify any 5 ads according to whether you think they're aiming to achieve a cognitive, emotional, or behavioral goal. Which ad do you like the most? Did any stimulate you to learn more about the brand?

2. Imagine you were designing an ad for a (choose one): car, laptop, health clinic. What would your ad look like if you were targeting: a) old people, b) kids, c) super rich people, d) What celebrity would you have endorse your brand? Why?

3. If you had to reach a customer segment of "tweens" (kids between 8 and 13), which medium would you choose? What about for men in their 30s? Men in their 60s? In which medium would you advertise if you ran one of your city's performing arts centers?

Video Exercise: Ogden Publications (7:48)

Ogden Publications, a publisher of a variety of magazines, uses integrated marketing communications to coordinate and achieve consistency across all aspects of its marketing efforts. Ogden's marketing department—consisting of a circulation team, a creative services team, a merchandise and events team, and a public relations team—searches for ways to collaborate more effectively with each editorial team so that there is consistency of key brand imagery and marketing messages across the company's various magazines, websites, and marketing materials. The circulation team is responsible for managing overall readership by using touch points such as direct mail, magazine insert cards, email campaigns, and newsstands. The merchandise and events team is charged with developing new products and identifying new events to attend. The creative services team provides creative development for marketing as well as for the rest of the company. The PR team is responsible for gaining media exposure for Ogden. The overall message across Ogden's various magazines is that Ogden provides "cool information that is relevant."

Video Discussion Questions

1. What are some of the key customer touch points for Ogden Publications?

2. How does Ogden Publications use integrated marketing communications to provide a consistent message across these customer touch points?

3. How does Ogden Publications benefit from using integrated marketing communications?

MINI-CASE

Celeb-Relief

John Russell, who goes by Jack, is a busy executive by day, but he likes to volunteer at a local, no-kill animal shelter at least one weekend a month. He helps by walking dogs and feeding them, and, given his business acumen, the shelter calls on him to do more administrative tasks as well, anything from animal intake to giving the shelter advice about their website. At the shelter's board meeting six months ago, Jack was asked to propose a low (very low) budget advertising campaign. He's supposed to present his proposal next week.

Jack's been thinking about how to pull off an ad campaign on a shoestring budget. It helps that animal shelters tend to be local businesses (and every locality having one or more of its own). So far, his proposal includes two billboards: one to be located on a highway downtown that runs north-south, the other on one that runs east-west. He hopes they can afford two or three radio spots of advertising. But if the shelter can't pop for the radio ads, he might at least be able to use one or two of their upcoming events as an opportunity to get PR announcements on the radio. The main part of the campaign would be the development and dissemination of brochures about the shelter's good works that would be sent to homes as direct marketing and posted in local grocery stores and other high-traffic venues, as their respective managers permit.

In terms of the content of the campaign, Jack was flipping through a recent issue of *Newsweek* and noticed an article on how many stars lend their names to causes, from George Clooney shedding light on genocide in Dafur, to Sean Penn helping to rebuild Haiti, and, of course, Bono's perennial fight against world poverty. Jack thinks the same principle could hold here. Next week, Jack Russell will propose to the shelter's NPO (a nonprofit organization) board that a celebrity become their spokesperson. One question is which celebrity would make sense? He has several slides, listing several options.

Case Discussion Questions

Which option(s) make sense?

1. Jack wants to reach out to a star of Clooney's or Penn's or Bono's status. It would be cool.

2. Another option might be the shelter's manager-in-chief.

3. A third option is the town's mayor.

4. A fourth option is one of the state's representatives.

5. A fifth option is a guy named Alex Green, who graduated from a local high school and went on to be really successful and who has given money to local charities since making it big.

INTEGRATED MARKETING COMMUNICATIONS AND MEDIA CHOICES 12

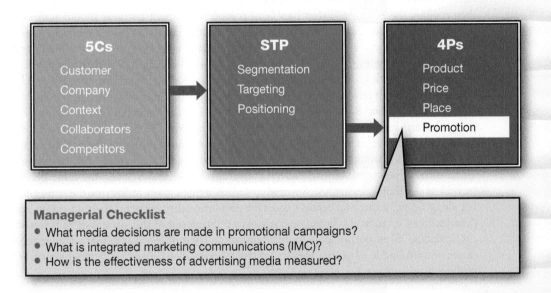

5Cs
Customer
Company
Context
Collaborators
Competitors

STP
Segmentation
Targeting
Positioning

4Ps
Product
Price
Place
Promotion

Managerial Checklist
- What media decisions are made in promotional campaigns?
- What is integrated marketing communications (IMC)?
- How is the effectiveness of advertising media measured?

Advertising is about shaping a message and getting the message to the target audience via some optimal combination of media.[1] This chapter focuses on the media decisions. Many media choices are available to the marketing manager, and each can optimize the achievement of different kinds of goals. Ad budgets are usually fixed, so choices must be made, and the resource allocation across media can be complicated. With the proliferation of media came the notion of IMC, integrated marketing communications: the idea that marketing planning should ensure that a company's various advertising efforts send a coherent story across the different customer touch points.

12-1 WHAT MEDIA DECISIONS ARE MADE IN ADVERTISING PROMOTIONAL CAMPAIGNS?

There are several media questions to answer: (1) How much do we spend? (2) What's the schedule of expenditure? (3) Which media do we use as channels of our communications?

Take the first question: How big should the ad budget be? The amount of most companies' entire communications package (i.e., advertising in all its various forms, including the purchase of the necessary media) is determined by one of three methods:

1. The advertising budget as a percentage of last year's sales
2. Approximately what the company believes is parity with competitors
3. Working backward from the company's strategic advertising goal (e.g., enhance awareness or positive attitudes) to calculate the necessary expenditures.

The first method is easy. The only challenge is arriving at the actual percentage value: 7%, 10%, 15%? Most companies would begin with their past numbers or an estimate of the industry norm and then adjust: If the marketing goal is merely to maintain brand share, then roughly the percentage that they (and competitors) spent last year should suffice. If the company has done something newsworthy with the brand, an increase in advertising monies is necessary to get the word out. If the company is seeking to milk the brand and redirect funds to their other brands, the percentage would be adjusted slightly downward.

The second method is also relatively easy. There are service providers (e.g., Schonfeld, Saibooks) who keep tabs on how much companies in various industries tend to spend (e.g., beer companies spend 8–10%). If every competitor spent approximately the same percentage on advertising, then their market shares would be proportional to their ad spending shares; indeed, the ratio for each company of the proportion of ad spending to their market share proportions would be approximately 1. As you can see in Figure 12.1, the market leader usually spends the most on advertising and has the greatest sales; the other brands spend less and their sales are less. Somewhat surprisingly, in many industries, the companies fall along a line, indicating a fairly constant proportionality between their spending and their incomes. A particular brand or company can break out of this pack if there is reason, e.g., spending disproportionately more ad dollars to try to move up the market share food chain, or spending less because they're a niche brand with a cult-like following, rendering traditional advertising less necessary, etc.[2]

Figure 12.1

Proportion of Ad Spending to Sales

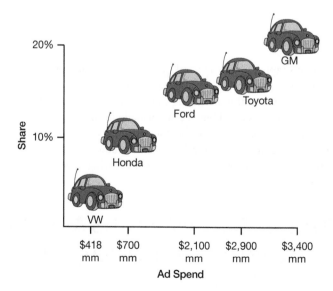

Although these methods are easy, they are a bit simplistic. When sales decline (for reasons of a soft economy or a decrease in the brand's popularity), each approach would suggest cutting the ad budget. Smaller ad budgets would mean less presence in the marketplace, thus perpetuating a cycle of decreased sales.

A third approach is to be more strategic and treat advertising expenditures as an investment (in the brand and company), with the expectation that an investment should return sales and profits. This approach can be somewhat challenging because advertising effects are difficult to measure, and often they are intended to produce long-term effects such as brand building. To set an ad budget, we need to understand how advertising exposures are measured. Then we set our exposure goal, and then we can estimate how much to spend to achieve that goal.

12-1a Reach and Frequency and GRPs

First, let's get the jargon down. Advertising agencies work with a unit called *GRP* (*gross rating points*). Whether we're talking about placing an ad on TV or in a magazine or on the side of a bus, a GRP is a simple function of reach and frequency:

- *Reach* is defined as the share (percentage) of your target audience that has seen your ad at least once.

- *Frequency* is the average number of times your target audience saw the ad (within some set duration, say the three month period during which the ads were in circulation, or a three-month testing period within a longer ad showing).

- GRPs, then, are defined as the simple product:

$$GRP = Reach \times Frequency$$

For example, if your ad reached 25% of your target audience, on average 3 times, the ad is said to have delivered 75 GRPs. If your ad reached 75% of your target, on average once, the ad would have delivered 75 GRPs also, but the results look different. For the first, the frequency is greater, so we'd expect the small portion of the target who saw the ad to be really familiar with the brand. For the second, the reach portion was bigger, and, while we might have hit a basic level of awareness, one ad exposure probably was not hugely effective in changing attitudes, if that was a goal.[3]

So, if the marketing goal is (at least minimal) awareness among a larger segment (i.e., greater reach than frequency, as in the second scenario), the ad would have to be run during a highly viewed TV show (for example), which would likely be quite expensive. If the goal is deeper knowledge and more favorable attitudes in the smaller segment (i.e., greater frequency than reach), the ad could be run three times during a specialized TV show with a smaller viewer audience (which would also likely be less expensive).

For reach, the goal is to expose as many of the target customers as possible to the ad. The challenge is to find the media that are most cost-efficient for finding as many of those customers and primarily only those customers.

Big Ad $penders

Who spends the most on ads? Cars ($2 b), movies ($1 b), pharma ($500 mm), and big banks (on credit cards, $350 mm).

For frequency, the rule of thumb used to be that an ad needed to be seen and processed three times for it to be persuasive. This notion that three repetitions is a magic number is now recognized as simplistic. The good news is that sometimes seeing an ad once or twice can be sufficient, and the bad news is that sometimes a customer needs even more exposures than three. The fundamental question comes down to the usual one: What's the goal? Awareness and memory can probably be attained with fewer ads. Persuasion might take longer, particularly if the product is complicated or the viewer is unfamiliar with it. In addition, sometimes more is not better. If the product and ad are pretty readily understood, then subsequent exposures to the ad can lead to so-called wear-out and reduced effectiveness. People start disassociating from the ad, thinking random thoughts, and attitudes toward the advertised brand start to drop.

In general, regardless of the budgeting method, it is important to acknowledge that, although working on ads can be great fun, they can be very expensive. The cost to produce a finished (and fairly simple) 30-second television commercial is at least $500,000. Companies spend this money because they believe in advertising and know its value as a communications tool. Research has shown a positive relationship of the levels of advertising and promotional spending to the market value of the firm. However, of course, the direction of causality is unclear: Do the heavy levels of ad spending by these companies ensure their continued success? Or are these companies the only ones with pockets deep enough to advertise a great deal?

Different Media

Marketers have lots of fun media choices:

1. Celebrities: whenever it's announced that another celebrity has struck a deal to be paid megabucks to endorse some brand, it raises eyebrows—can the celebrity possibly be worth it? Research suggests yes, at least for sports stars. When the athlete signs on, there is a boost in sales in an absolute sense and relative to competitor brands. Furthermore, there are lifts in sales and stock returns every time the athlete meets some major achievement. The effects on stock enhancements seem long lasting, but sales bumps begin to decline over time. (See Elberse and Verleun, "The Economic Value of Celebrity Endorsements" in the *Journal of Advertising Research*.)

2. Sponsorship: speaking of athletes, let's consider the prices of the real estate of soccer jerseys. The cost of renting these human billboards ranged from $40.9 mm for FC Barcelona and $35.7 mm for FC Bayern Munich to $3.5 mm for LA Galaxy and, well, $0 so far for Colorado Rapids. Is it worth it? Brand exposure in the presence of such adrenaline and excitement, you bet. (See the *Bloomberg Businessweek* article "Full Frontal Sponsorship" by Roger Bennett.)

3. Product placement: The product types that use TV and movie placement the most are cars (especially Mercedes, Chevy, BMW, Cadillac), beer (Miller), and soft drinks (Coke, Pepsi); placements for liquor have declined. In video games, Pepsi, Siemens, and Burger King rule. When the content of the TV, movie, or video game programming is coded as being positive, neutral, or negative in tone, product placement is split almost perfectly at 33% across the board. Strange—wouldn't you expect that the product placement dollar would specify a positive context? When the product presentation is coded as full-frontal vs. partial product displays, the full-on dominates, but only 2:1. (See Galician's, *Handbook of Product Placement in the Mass Media*.)

12-1b Media Planning and Scheduling

Marketers have long tried to answer questions regarding ROI or ROMI (return on marketing investments), essentially estimating a breakeven for an advertising expenditure. Again, with the caveat that no measure is perfect, here's how to approach this estimation.

In Figure 12.2 we see a number of television shows, plotted by their ratings or their popularity with the viewing audiences and by the costs for 30 seconds of airtime during the shows. There is naturally a positive correlation between these two indicators; you pay more to get more. But the relationship is not perfect. Some TV shows are bargains, delivering more audience exposure than they charge, and others are a little costly, charging a bit more than they'll deliver in terms of audience viewership.

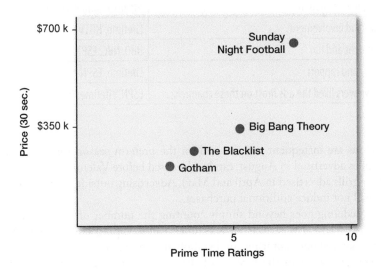

Figure 12.2

Advertising Time Costs More During Popular TV Shows

Let's say you advertise during the show *Big Bang Theory*. That show's rating is 5.6, which translates to 6.3 million TVs tuned in to the show in the marketplace households. (One rating point is 1% of all households with TVs. Currently the number of U.S. households measured is approximately 112,000,000, so 1%, or 1 rating point, is 1,120,000.) The show charges $328,000 per 30 seconds. If you're McDonald's and you're trying to encourage people to go pick up breakfast tomorrow on their way to work, how many meals would you have to sell to make the advertising charge worth it? If a meal contribution is $0.50, then you'd need $328,000 ÷ 0.50 = 656,000 purchases (tomorrow, this week, whatever your timeline). That number is only 10.4% of the viewers who had been exposed to the ad (656,000 ÷ 6.3 million). It seems achievable.[4]

In terms of timing, or media planning, there are basically three kinds of media schedules: continuous, occasional, or seasonal. For *continuous* schedules, the ad exposure is regular; it doesn't have to be a perfectly predictable schedule (e.g., every Friday, a half-page in *The New York Times*) or even all that frequent, but the idea is that you're fairly constantly reminding the consumer that you exist. The periodicity depends on the length of the buying cycle (advertise frequently for soft drinks, less frequently for tires). You want to advertise a little more frequently than the object is purchased, to keep it in consumers' minds, but not so much as to risk overexposure and boring your customers (not to mention overspending on advertising).

In *occasional* media scheduling (sometimes called *flighting* or *pulsing*), you are not omnipresent, but you pop up from time to time. Given that you're advertising less frequently, this approach will be less expensive and therefore possibly more cost-effective. Obviously, one should advertise in synch with purchase cycles. During times when ads aren't aired, competition can swoop in, but you're probably doing the same to them during their downtimes. Furthermore, if you're building brand image, you'll be less vulnerable to competitors' poaching.

Types of TV Shows

ESPN Research identified four personalities of TV channels:

TV Channel Personality	TV Channel Exemplars
Integrity and information	History Channel, Discovery
Relevance and involvement	Lifetime, HGTV
Entertainment and fun	HBO, NBC, ESPN
Personality and rapport	Lifetime, ESPN
And P.S., viewers liked the ads most on these channels:	ESPN, Lifetime, HGTV

Seasonal ads are infrequent and focused on the preterm season for the product (e.g., school supplies advertised in August, candy advertised before Valentine's Day and Halloween, outdoor grills advertised in April and May). Advertising outside the season is not done because it will not induce additional purchases.

Media scheduling goes beyond simply counting the number of times an ad was aired in a household whose TV set was on and tuned to the appropriate channel. Advertising agencies are savvy about capturing the psychological processes of advertising effects. For example, agencies factor in the recency of the ad exposure when examining subsequent purchase behavior (reasoning that ads viewed last week will have less of an impact on the contents of grocery cart than an ad you saw last night).

12-2 INTEGRATED MARKETING COMMUNICATIONS ACROSS MEDIA

With a sense of how much to spend and when to schedule the advertising, we face next the choice of communication outlets. This choice used to be among TV, radio, newspaper, magazine, and billboard. Now, the choice is even more complicated with so many more media (e.g., more TV stations, radio stations on XM, the Web), and audiences are fragmented across those many media and using technology to zip past ads.

To try to capture these splintered audiences across the varied media that engage them, marketing gurus have encouraged the strategy of *integrated marketing communications* (IMC). To make informed choices and select the appropriate media outlets, the marketing manager needs to understand the strengths of the various individual media available. It is ultra important that the marketing messages are seamlessly integrated across the media selections.

The philosophy underlying IMC is totally logical: Keep in mind the company's overarching strategy, and ensure that all marketing activities send a consistent message, beginning with the communications (i.e., consumer and trade advertising and promotions, product placements, personal selling, direct and database marketing, etc.) and including other marketing mix elements (e.g., product design and packaging, pricing, channel availability).

Research suggests a positive relationship between IMC practices and good brand outcomes: high levels of awareness, brand loyalty, and sales. Yet, even if the IMC goal sounds great, it's not that easy to execute in practice, in part because traditional advertising agencies aren't that good at PR, direct marketing, or certainly nontraditional advertising tactics, such as when they are using social media. To resemble full-line service providers, some ad agencies acquire smaller, specialized agencies, and others outsource part of their overall IMC plan. Ultimately, regardless of how it is achieved, the integration across media is the responsibility of the marketer and brand manager.

Creative Communications

- International football sponsors:
    - Qatar Foundation pays $41 mm to have its name on the FC Barcelona jerseys.
    - Aon spends $33 mm to decorate the chests of the Manchester United players.
- Flashmobs took off with T-Mobile's train station events, choreographed to look spontaneous, with the tagline, "Life is for Sharing."
- Whirlpool donated appliances for houses built by Habitat for Humanity.
- To get in better touch with Hispanic consumers, Kleenex sponsored a contest for amateur artists to submit ideas for package designs. Winners received cash prizes, and the top three designs were in distribution during National Hispanic Heritage Month.

Early suggestions were that, to effect a common strategy, all the IMC messages across all the media should be the same. More recently, marketers recognize that while some elements should be consistent (e.g., the brand name, logo, general flavor, and positioning), the varied media have varied strengths, and the message should play to the medium's strengths. For example, a TV ad is vivid and dramatic, but the message needs to be kept simple, whereas complicated products can be explained better in print (magazines, online, direct marketing). The goal is consistency in the general positioning, but the different media offer supplemental information.

Media Synergies

Research suggests there are indeed synergies across media in IMC advertising campaigns. For example, websites haven't made catalogs obsolete; instead, their roles are changing.

Online shopping is:

- Easy for purchasing.
- Efficient for search.
- Suited toward goal-oriented purchasing.

Direct mail catalogs:

- Are colorful and vivid.
- Facilitate browsing.
- Drive consumers to the website!

IMC gurus say that 1 + 1 can equal 3. Advertising in a consistent yet complementary manner across two or more media can have the impact of having spent even more in a traditional single-medium budget.

12-2a Media Comparisons

Figure 12.3 indicates the relative strengths of popular media—TV, radio, newspapers, magazines, billboards, the Web, and direct mail—on business criteria. TV ad spots are by far the most expensive (e.g., $5–100 k for 30 seconds during prime time). Yet even with today's TV channel fragmentation, this medium still yields the largest reach numbers (sheer audience size). While reach is strong, frequency can be challenging to achieve because of the expense. In addition, reach via the mass media is relatively broad, not targeted.

Figure 12.3

Media Choices: Relative Strengths on Business Measures

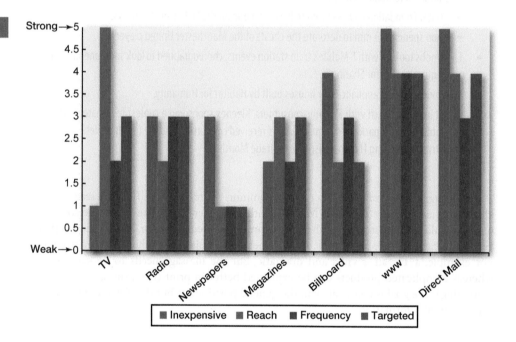

Traditional TV is considered a mass medium, but special TV and cable channels serve more focused audiences. Similarly, some magazines have broad appeal, but others can hit a target segment quite efficiently (i.e., with little excess expenditure). Radio spots and newspapers are often planned and purchased nationally, but, alternatively, each can also certainly be planned and purchased for local markets. These media can capture known segments, such as radio by genre or in-flight magazines for the flying audience. Billboards and other urban methods (e.g., subway ads, ads on buses, ads before previews in movie theaters) are relatively inexpensive but are effective in achieving good local numbers.

Radio, newspapers, and magazines are certainly less expensive than TV (e.g., $250 for one minute of radio, $5 k for one page and one day in a decent paper, $5–15 k for one page in one issue of a magazine), but, of course, they also deliver smaller audiences. Bigger magazines (where bigger implies greater reach) naturally cost more; for instance, a full-page color ad in *BusinessWeek* is roughly $100 k and $200 k in *Newsweek*. Back pages cost still more. Particular costs and GRP delivery depends on whether the radio station is local or the newspaper a national.

TV Tidbits

- Even in households that receive more than 100 channels, on average, consumers watch only about 14 channels.
- When we sit down to watch, we (1) first go to one among our 14 favorite channels, (2) next we check listings, (3) next, we zone out, channel surf, and select nearly randomly.
- TV segments of customer media choices are as follows (based on research by ESPN Research and Quirks.com):

Segment	Watch their TV shows primarily:	Because:
1	On-demand	It's convenient. Viewers can control the experience (e.g., pause, rewind). They can watch any episode, and the shows don't take up space on their DVRs.
2	Live	They're ardent fans, and they schedule their lives around their shows. They want to be cool and talk about the show at work the next day.
3	Via DVR	It's convenient, and they're busy. They like high-def, and they can keep episodes they like.

Each medium has its own personality. For example, newspapers have the advantage of extreme timeliness. Magazines require longer lead times for production, but they have nice reproduction quality. So-called "beauty shots" of products in magazine photos are as high-quality as those on TV. Newspapers and magazines also have the advantage of being nonintrusive because readers choose to pick up the magazine at a time of their convenience and can flip past a print ad quickly if they wish to do so. Each medium has drawbacks as well, like the flipping past the ad.

The media with the best customization options are online advertising and direct mail. The varieties of ads on the Internet are still very inexpensive, and data-based profiling enhances the technology's ability to target. Still, online penetration isn't yet 100%, and users have to actively find the brand and company; hence reach is not yet a strength of this medium.

Direct mail is relatively inexpensive, but it is not terribly efficient. That is, recipients will receive some of the direct mail appeals as "junk" mail. With better database programs, the reach of the particular target audience can be quite focused.

Figure 12.4 displays the relative strengths of these media in terms of the content they can deliver. TV messages need to be simple and straightforward, and radio messages even more so, given that fewer sensory modalities are engaged in receiving the message. TV allows for vivid, dramatic portrayals, including humorous and emotional appeals, much of which gets lost in the more impoverished media. On the other hand, print vehicles (magazines, papers, direct mail, online, etc.) are the perfect outlets for conveying detailed product information.

Figure 12.4

Media Choices: Relative Strengths on Ad Content

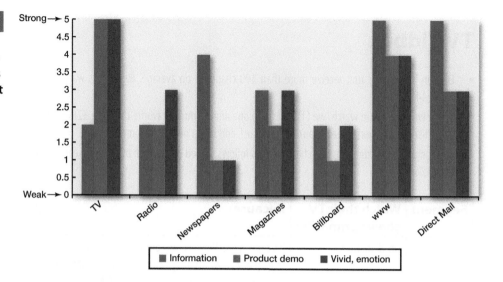

12-2b **Beyond Advertising**

IMC is about integrating a brand message across any media, not just traditional advertising outlets. In addition to advertising, whatever personal selling staff a company has at its disposal, the firm's sales promotions, public relations, and all related departments should be expressing a consistent, complementary message. All of these media (broadly defined) are supposed to work as a team on behalf of the brand.

The key advertising concepts are still applicable. For example, the AIDA process (attention, interest, desire, action) works in selling too: A salesperson must first get the attention of the potential customer (by prospecting a database, qualifying the potential customers, and approaching them). Then come the customer's interest (through a sales presentation), the desire (e.g., through a product demonstration, being ready to handle the customer's objections), and the action (closing the deal and following up with service).

Personal selling and a company's *sales force* are essential communication vehicles for many companies and industries. Personal selling is huge; the Department of Labor estimates some 14 million jobs (over 10% of the workforce) are in selling. These sales-related positions include the guy doing road trips to sell machine parts or insurance, as well as the counterperson at Nordstrom's, as well as the order takers at 1-800-cataloger.

Although we've said that direct marketing and Internet are tailorable media, nothing beats a face-to-face conversation to try to figure out what a customer wants and how a company can deliver. Sales forces are clearly high-cost due to labor (salary, training, etc.), but they're nevertheless important, especially for the sale of complicated, expensive goods and services. So, while sales forces exist for consumer products (e.g., Avon, Amway, Dell, life insurance companies, etc.), they're enormous in B2B and pharma (e.g., Eli Lilly, Novartis). It's thought that an expensive piece of medical equipment, a high-volume photocopier, a new eco-friendly chemical, or a new cholesterol-reducing medication are all too complicated to s ell online or via a catalog. A salesperson is needed to explain all the product features, as well as other details such as service and leasing agreements. As Figure 12.5 indicates, different media have different strengths.

Marketers face three primary questions in designing a sales force:

- How many salespeople do I need?
- Where do I deploy them?
- How do I compensate them?

Advertising	Personal Selling
• Customers can be anywhere	• Need geographic concentration
• Product is simple to understand	• Product is often technical, complicated
• Product is fairly standard	• Product can be customized
• Relatively inexpensive, less risky	• High priced, B2B items
• Advertising can be expensive	• Sales force can be expensive
• Results can be difficult to establish	• Quick feedback, measurable results

Figure 12.5

Choice between Advertising and a Sales Force

Sale forces are larger when a company wants an aggressive product launch and when a company wants to protect its territories from encroaching competition. Sales territories are determined by existing sales and competition but also from strategic assessments of the desired markets. Compensation is always some proportion of salary and commissions; the proportions tend to have more to do with tradition and competition than with any psychological assessment of the motivating factors.

Sell!

Inc., Money.CNN, and others track the largest sales forces in the world:

- *Top in computers:* Microsoft, Xerox, Cisco
- *Top consumables:* PepsiCo, Sysco, Interstate Bakeries, Coca-Cola, Anheuser-Busch
- *Top medical:* Schering Plough, J&J, Pfizer

These days, most sales forces are facilitated by CRM databases. Customers' purchases and preferences are stored, so the salesperson can refresh his or her memory of the buyer and company before a sales meeting, updating the database immediately after each contact (also vendors: SAP, Oracle, and the unavoidable Salesforce.com).

12-2c Choice Between Advertising and a Sales Force

The costs of sales forces include more than compensation. Salespeople are partners, members of your distribution channel, and, just like your end users, they want deals. So while consumers might think they're bombarded with advertising, as Figure 12.6 indicates, companies' expenditures on advertising and sales promotions directed to consumers is only a small piece of the pie. The largest portion of their marketing communications budgets is directed to trade: their channel partners.[5]

Recall the concepts of push and pull in channels of distribution. Push is a top-down effort, selling to customers through a sales force and retail partners. Pull is a bottom-up drive from customers

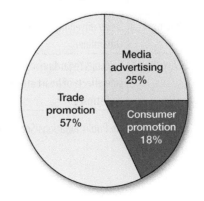

Figure 12.6

Allocation of Communication and Promotion Budget

Media advertising 25%

Trade promotion 57%

Consumer promotion 18%

seeking their products. Pull (advertising to consumers) is important to a brand manager when the company's intermediaries stock a large number of competing products, and the partners don't care about supporting any of them in particular. Then, advertising and sales promotions are necessary vehicles. Direct-to-consumer (DTC) pharma ads are a very popular and effective example of pull.

Push relies more on personal selling, and a brand manager needs to direct promotional efforts more to members of the channel than to the final user. Channel members don't care about ads per se as much as money, and so trade allowances are frequently used. These are price reductions that the manufacturer offers to the intermediary (wholesaler or retailer) in exchange for their doing something such as allocating space to a new product (so-called slotting allowances) or buying more product during special periods. Sometimes these trade bonuses are passed along to the retailer's salespeople in the form of cash or training and product demonstrations, free merchandise, or conventions and trade shows.

Public relations (*PR*) is another means of providing information and building brand attributes. PR lines of communications are the attempt of an organization to reach its customers, suppliers, stockholders, government officials, employees, or the general community. PR can be conducted from within the company, run by its advertising agency, or (most often) outsourced to PR specialists.

Whenever anything "newsworthy" is happening, PR people issue *press kits*—news releases. These used to be in print; now they take the form of video clips. The information features a blurb on whatever's going on (e.g., a new product launch), as well as background propaganda about the company, bios, history, whatever is needed to round out the edges. That background information is also available on a website that is maintained for year-round inquiries. PR people arrange events such as speaking engagements (e.g., CEO Joe to speak at this year's new bank opening), sponsorships (e.g., a poster and coffee at a professional conference or trade show), or community philanthropy (the bank puts its name on Little League uniforms or sponsors a walk for charity).

PR

Part of the utility of PR is its versatility. It has been exercised in the wake of oil spills, brake failures, package tampering, and political and sports figure misbehavior. Newsweek identified several cases:

Company	Problem	PR Spin
Johnson & Johnson	Recalls	Customers can trust them. The company is transparent in owning up to problems and addressing quality control issues.
Boeing	Delay unveiling the 787 Dreamliner	It's Boeing, for heaven's sake. They're strong in many businesses. We need to sit tight.
Glaxo	Lawsuits regarding a drug's side effects of heart attacks and strokes	They are settling cases quickly, and proceeding with business as usual—developing vaccines to grow in emerging markets.

For more, see the Public Relations Society of America (prsa.org) or Council of Public Relations Firms (prfirms.org).

Most companies use PR in recovery mode, in an attempt to smooth over some complicated or embarrassing event, such as when a product is reviewed critically or when customers boycott a brand. Company reps communicate to the customers, shareholders, and press to counter argue the criticisms and to enhance and strengthen positive images and brand and corporate equity.

It's even smarter to practice continual (albeit pulsing) proactive PR, which can be both for brand building and for inoculating the firm against possible future criticism. Positive PR can be large-scale, such as ingredient menus for restaurant chains, or local, such as sponsoring fund-raising events or local teams.

The intent of PR is to convey a positive image and to educate a constituency about the company's objectives, such as recent innovations. In general, the job of a PR firm is to generate goodwill on behalf of the company.

Publicity is another tool of communication; it's not paid for by the brand's company. So it can carry the appearance of objectivity, e.g., some new brand feature praised by a third party, such as a newspaper or Website that provides news coverage. Press releases are, of course, constantly prepared by a company, but there is no guarantee that any influential media will bother to pick up on what a company deems newsworthy.

Sometimes the publicity indeed comes from a third party, such as when a popular press business magazine like *Fortune* publishes its annual "100 Best Companies to Work For" issue. Companies included in these listings are celebrated, and you just can't buy that kind of attention. On the other hand, the company has no control over the spin on the story, and publicity can be negative, requiring some recovery on the part of the company's own PR group.

Product placement is more subtle than most advertising. It's been around awhile but has become increasingly popular (over $1 b annually) as brand managers struggle to find creative means of getting in front of viewers who are increasingly zapping ads. In movies (e.g., James Bond's cars), on TV (*Survivor*), and in video games, products and brands are being integrated into the show. The product is integral to the scene, so the viewer can't zap past it, and the inclusion of the product carries an implicit endorsement by the actors onscreen.[6]

While ads are more useful than product placements in providing information, both can result in the transfer of positive associations.[7] Both ads and product placement are also met with some viewer skepticism, since it's known that both are paid for. A somewhat related phenomenon is the placement, or plant, of a brand advocate in chat rooms. When a brand is talked up and the chat is thought to be authentic, it is very powerful and persuasive, but if the rest of the chat room attendees smell a plant, the tactic can backfire.

Event sponsorship, usually of sports but sometimes of other cultural or artistic endeavors, has a long tradition. The event is exciting, and the brand draws from its positive valence and energy.

Walter G Arce/Shutterstock.com

NASCAR: the champion of sponsorship.

NASCAR racing is a popular vehicle for sponsorship (17 of the 20 biggest spectator sports are NASCAR races). Big crowds attend (the average attendance per race is 100,000; the average ticket price is $90), TV audience sizes and ratings are soaring (Fox, NBC, and TNT have a multibillion-dollar deal for coverage), merchandise exceeds another $2 b, and corporate money is pouring in through sponsorship (already over $1.5 b according to Fortune).

Working for a company whose brand helps sponsor an event is exciting, but it's not entirely clear that sponsorship is cost-effective in apportioning advertising budgets. For example, when companies like Coca-Cola, GE, Kodak, Omega, Panasonic, and VISA sponsor events like the Olympics or the World Cup, do they need the exposure? When companies like Atos Origin or Manulife sponsor these events, does the exposure help them (e.g., achieve heightened brand name awareness)? Yet so-called ambush marketing is frowned upon because companies that associate themselves with such prominent events don't have to obtain and pay for sponsorship rights.

If you want to find the tough demographic audience of 35- to 40-year-old white-collar men with bachelor's degrees making almost $100 k, sponsor Fantasy Football. These guys are into Fantasy Football big time, and (oops!) they're checking their teams' performance while at work.

Sales promotion is still another tool in the IMC mix. The best known form of sales promo is the coupon: a newspaper or magazine cutout to take shopping for a small discount on a future purchase.

Coupons are very popular, so there are many forms: FSIs (freestanding inserts in newspapers, magazines, and direct mail), printouts at the checkout, point-of-purchase coupon pop-outs (on the shelves where the products are featured), Internet printout coupons to take to retail shops, etc. In addition to coupons, sales promos include rebates, promo prices, trade-ins, deals for loyalty programs, free trial-sized (i.e., small) products, contests and sweepstakes, etc.

Sales promotions activate purchase interest, thus effecting short-term sales boosts. Sales promotions are also thought to be effective devices for enticing customers to switch brands.

12-2d The IMC Choices Depend on the Marketing Goals

There are many media, any of which could be useful and all of which should be coordinated. Advertising can be carried via print TV, radio, the product's packaging, movie product placement, sales promotion (coupons and rebates, loyalty cards), the sponsorship of events and experiences, public relations and publicity, personal selling, direct marketing, etc. For each element, the brand manager and CMO need to answer two questions:

1. Who is the target audience?
2. What is our goal: awareness, provision of information about features and benefits, enhancement of brand attitudes, the strengthening of preferences, the stimulation of purchase trial, the encouragement of repeat purchasing, the attraction of brand switchers?

The effect of the ad campaign on that target segment with respect to the select goal can be and should be measured. Other effects might also result, but one should not expect that all the goals could be met with a single blip of advertising and IMC.

If you sell something that is seasonal, you'll advertise just prior to that season. Otherwise you have a choice of advertising continuously or occasionally. Big companies with big ad budgets can advertise continuously, but little brands can advertise continuously if the less expensive media are used. So the choice between continuous and occasional is not just budget.

Further, if the marketing goal is brand awareness, occasional ads won't cut it. The advertising needs to be fairly frequent until the basic knowledge has nearly saturated the target market. Note that the target needs to be well-defined to be able to send media to it and to test it later. In addition, the level of so-called saturation needs to be defined: Do you want 90% awareness? 60%? To be profitable, the saturation percentage can be smaller if the target market is large.

Once there is awareness, to prompt continued purchasing, correlate the frequency of advertising with the customers' purchase cycle. If the item is purchased frequently, then advertise frequently.

Modify all these actions depending on your marketing strategy. If, for example, the brand in question is a cash cow at the end of its product life cycle, you're likely to be advertising less frequently. If the brand in question is one the company wishes to grow aggressively, ramp up above previous years' budgets and above competitors' spending.

Regarding media choices, there are two questions: What can you afford? What fits best for your target segment? If yours is a little brand with a meager budget, you're precluded from national TV or the sponsorship of big sports event. That's okay; there are plenty of other options. Even local TV or local sports events are fine alternatives. Be creative with buying (or, better, with creating and maintaining) databases to target your audience. Find out what magazines they read and what websites they visit, and advertise there.

Regarding the IMC across the message pieces, draw up a pie-in-the-sky message—all that you want to convey to your customers—from the facts of the features to the benefits and images. Then put the images in the visual media and the facts in the written media. Use a common tagline, and design the appearance to tie the messages together. Doing so will ensure a sense of consistency and complementarity, both of which reinforce brand equity.

Ad Ethics

Is it okay when Miller produces and advertises Plank Road beer as if it's from a small brewer? Is it okay when squeaky clean Disney produces R-rated movies under the name Miramax? Isn't it impossible to tell customers everything about products and how they're made? (For more, see Davidson's *Moral Dimension of Marketing*.)

Figure 12.7 is an example IMC schedule that encompasses timing, media selection, and the message for integration. Many companies make the most of their money during the Christmas holiday season. Thus this example company hypes up for December. The ads in the winter (March) and spring (May) feature the brand and the company (to maintain its reputation). The messages are reminders in content: "We're here, and we're good quality, and here are some reasons you should like us." Media selections are targeted (magazine ads or specialized cable TV ads), as well as broad (online) and price promotions (coupons), are used along with the advertising.

Figure 12.7

Figure 12.7

An IMC Schedule

Jan	Feb	March
		Brand promotions, magazines ads, online coupons
April	May	June
	Company ads, target segment cable TV ad	
July	Aug	Sept
	Brand; back-to-school online deals, local paper inserts	Attitude brand ads via local radio sports, refer-a-friend
Oct	Nov	Dec
Top-of-mind ad; 3 TV ads say go online for more information	Spur purchase; events: parade float, 3 ads during college football games	Pre-Christmas: 3 local TV ads & paper inserts. Post-holiday deep discount

At the end of August, a slight shift in message occurs. Kids are going back to school, and this event prompts another coupon and a referral program.

Things get really heated right around Halloween and November. Messages that had simply been nice reminders are getting more focused, keeping the attitude-enhancing aspects but encouraging a salient top-of-mind readiness in recall and, of course, encouraging purchases. Advertising expenditures are growing, as the ads are placed in more numerous and more expensive media outlets (e.g., large metropolitan radio spots, national TV ads, etc.).

Thanksgiving kicks in some novelty, with the sponsorship of two highly televised events: a float in a popular Thanksgiving Day parade and three announcer mentions during a big college football game. In the second week of December, local TV ads are aired in three large markets, and on the weekend, between the second and third weeks of December, city newspaper insert ads are bought for those three markets, plus the next 20 in size. Prices are also cut 15%.

Whatever product is left after the big Christmas rush is sold at a 50–75% discount (depending on the retailer relationship). The company sits back to recover from the activities of the last few weeks of the year and to regain energy to start the game all over again in March.

The company is thoughtful about varying media choices, scheduling and planning, and the overall content of the communication pieces that fit together. This is IMC as an integral whole—across message and media.

12-3 HOW IS THE EFFECTIVENESS OF ADVERTISING MEDIA MEASURED?

Depending on the goal sought, advertising effectiveness can be assessed in a number of ways. In the previous chapter, we discussed measures of memory (recall and recognition), attitudes, propensity to purchase, and so forth. Coupling that ad content with this chapter's concerns over media, it should be clear that things get both more complicated, and yet there are some synergies.

For example, if the marketing goal is to enhance awareness and memory, then reach is the more likely media goal than frequency, and this can be measured by viewership, readership and circulation numbers, traffic indices, and many measures of exposures. If brand awareness is already pervasive in the target segment, and if the goal of the ad campaign is an attitude adjustment, then surveys (even quick three-item smartphone surveys) will be necessary.

Advertising researchers (on memory or attitudes) ask respondents whether they can remember the source of the ad: Did they see something on TV? Hear something on the radio? Receive a piece in the mail? And so on. Consumers aren't typically accurate in their identification of the media sources, which further underlines the importance of exposing consumers to your messages via multiple media. The marketing concern is primarily that the message reaches the consumer via any medium. But the fact that consumers can't tell you where they saw the message means it's more difficult to assess, for example, a ROMI on the radio portion of the ad budget vs. the direct mailing piece.

The ways to test advertising are many. The same scanner data that allow marketers to run experiments in stores on price points are also used to assess ads in the marketplace. For all households in a ZIP Code, advertising researchers can find out what national or local ads have been running on TV, radio, newspapers, etc. For the households in certain research companies' panels (e.g., such as those run by A.C. Nielsen or Information Resources, Inc.), finer measures of advertising exposure are possible, e.g., was the household TV on during the ad showing, etc.?

Many studies have been conducted with such data. For example, to address the question of whether spending more on advertising results in more sales, a huge real-world marketing research study was conducted. Researchers found that increasing ad budgets, relative to the competition, doesn't increase sales in general. Think about it. Sometimes an ad might not seem to predict something like sales or share because there is little variance in the system. That is, if everyone in the industry tends to advertise a lot, then the relative market share positions wouldn't shift much. On the other hand, if everyone advertises less, they'd all be more profitable because advertising is costly). Again, presumably market shares wouldn't change much, but cutting advertising is not a good idea for the long term. Companies are supposed to be advertising to communicate with customers, but sometimes it almost appears as though they advertise because competitors are doing so.

While varying ad weights (budget expenditures) may have limits in affecting sales and shares, research has found that qualitative differences, such as better ad copy or strategies to reach current non-category users, etc,. can increase the likelihood that TV advertising will positively affect sales. As another indicator that content matters, researchers have also found that an increase in media weight (i.e., advertising budgets) is related to sales for ads that both evoked positive feelings and failed to evoke negative feelings. Finally, some marketers would say, why bother spending ad dollars on retaining customers who already have a strong positive preference for the featured product. Instead, eliminate these wasted (or redundant) dollars, and spend on consumers who are more ambivalent to prevent their switching to the competition.

Online advertising is still new enough that advertising researchers are trying to determine just what should be measured. Click-thru rates (from banner ads) are a simple no-brainer, but they also track downloads, inquiries, purchases, returns, etc. Then costs can be assessed against these measures: cost per click, cost per download, cost per acquisition, etc. Costs of online advertising are low, but click-through conversion rates are also low, so online costs-per aren't terribly impressive. That is, cost effectiveness of online advertising may not be great, but cost per se is so extraordinarily low that the inefficiencies are ones that most advertising managers are willing to live with.

Finally, just as advertising media need to be integrated, by way of IMC, messages and media themselves may be optimally integrated. Consider the following example. A national electronics firm that produces hearing aids was interested in learning how to get its message to people who have various forms of hearing loss, as well as what they should say. Hearing aids are a tricky product because, while young people can have suboptimal hearing, for many people, hearing loss first occurs as they age. So wearing a hearing aid is an admission of aging and it's seen as somewhat embarrassing. So what to do?

In this example, a test market was run in which public media were tested against private media. An example of the public media was a videotape of what a TV ad would look like. An example of the private media was a direct marketing piece, sent to the home, which could be read in the privacy of one's own home. In addition, different messages were created. One was a supposedly humorous ad (making fun of the confusions that hearing losses can create), and one was an ad that essentially promised that the hearing aid would help the wearer interact better with his or her family, friends, and coworkers. The funny ad worked better on the video, and the promise ad worked better in the direct marketing materials, and the direct marketing worked better than the video. The bottom line is that it's not that one message was better than another or that one medium was better than another; it's that there are synergies, and some messages are conveyed more effectively via certain media. The challenge is to find the fit that works for your brand and product. The integration "I" in IMC needs to be across media and messages.

MANAGERIAL RECAP

Media decisions about both expenditure and timing are integral in running advertising promotional campaigns.

- Marketing managers must oversee the media choices to integrate the marketing communications so that customers hear the company's message in one clear voice.

- The effectiveness of advertising is measured using long-term and short-term measures.

Chapter Outline in Key Terms and Concepts

1. What media decisions are made in advertising promotional campaigns?

   a. Reach and frequency and GRPs

   b. Media planning and scheduling

2. Integrated marketing communications across media

   a. Media comparisons

   b. Beyond advertising

   c. Choice between advertising and a sales force

3. The IMC choices depend on the marketing goals

4. How is the effectiveness of advertising media measured?

5. Managerial recap

Chapter Discussion Questions

1. What did we learn from the cost assessment manager?

2. Which of the first two managers' directions (direct mail or email) would you support?

3. What is the strategy? If the company wants to emphasize customer acquisition, what would you recommend? If the company wants to emphasize customer retention, what would you recommend?

4. What else would you like to know for a more thorough assessment?

MINI-CASE

Where Should We Place Our Ad?

A software company that is fairly well regarded for two large product lines has TurboTax in its sights. They've developed a tax package that they think their current customers will like, and they think this software will give them a chance to bring new customers to their products.

The company has developed an informative, yet succinct, and even somewhat humorous ad. One of the top managers is saying the company ought to ship out the ad in brochure form, along with a DVD with a demo file on it, as a form of direct mail. Another guy is saying that, because the product is high-tech, they should reach out to customers through an email campaign. The brochure should be a PDF file with an embedded link to the same demo file that the direct mail recipients would receive.

The boss is indifferent (doesn't know much about marketing, history, biology, or what a slide rule is for), but he cares about costs. So a third manager called up some media providers and compiled the following prices.

| | New Customers | | Current Customers | |
	direct mail (list rental)	e-mail (list rental)	direct mail (list in CRM system)	e-mail (list in CRM system)
Cost per 1000 (CPM)	$1750	$500	$750	$50
Click-thru rate	—	10%	—	20%
Rate of purchase	2%	3%	4%	5%
Cost per sale	$88	$167	$19	$5

13 SOCIAL MEDIA

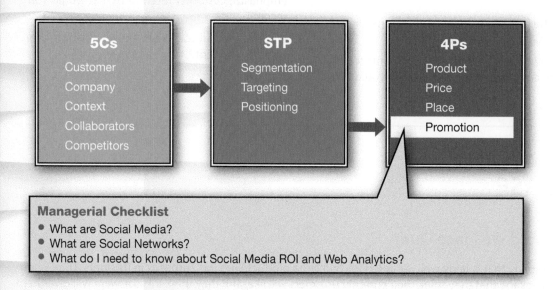

5Cs
Customer
Company
Context
Collaborators
Competitors

STP
Segmentation
Targeting
Positioning

4Ps
Product
Price
Place
Promotion

Managerial Checklist
- What are Social Media?
- What are Social Networks?
- What do I need to know about Social Media ROI and Web Analytics?

13-1 WHAT ARE SOCIAL MEDIA?

Once upon a time, there were ABC, CBS, and NBC. No HBO. No Fox. You had to be near a wall to talk on the phone. Amazon was a river, google was a number, and byte was a typo. How primitive!

The enormity of today's media choices—the Internet alone—makes it a wonderful time to be alive. The media are obviously part of the social media story. Computer technology continues to get smaller, more powerful, and less expensive. And it seems omnipresent.

Mobile marketing is growing because our cell phones are so convenient: They contain our identities and those of the people we talk to frequently. They are our portals to email and Facebook, our primary means of sharing information and entertainment. We engage in simple social conversation, forward funny emails, and share videos, links, and music. We are both voyeurs and exhibitionists in sharing photos and evidence of recent behavior. The GPS units embedded in our phones help us find destinations and help marketers find us.

Tweet

From comedian Steve Martin: Did you know it's possible to Tweet a concise, grammatical, correctly punctuated sentence that is exactly one hundred forty characters long?

Brands on Facebook

Some companies are already pretty sophisticated about buzz marketing. The brands with the most Friends/Fans on Facebook are: Facebook, Coca-Cola, YouTube, McDonald's, MTV, Red Bull, Nike Football, Samsung Mobile, Oreo, FIFA World Cup, KFC, Converse, PlayStation, and Starbucks.

At the same time that electronic and information technologies are becoming more accessible and pervasive, traditional media are experiencing their own changes:

- Newspaper circulations are declining. While optimists continue to launch new magazines every year, magazines' overall sales and circulations are down as well.

- The number of radio stations has grown, boosted by satellite servers such as XM or Sirius. But listeners are tuned in for less time each day than just a few years ago.

- Television channels also continue to grow. The bad news about this fragmentation is that, with more TV channels, the audience for any given show is typically smaller (consumers are spread thin across the multitude of options). The good news is that targeting is facilitated when the segments of viewers are somewhat more homogeneous.

The other part of the social media story is, of course, its social or human element. People enjoy connecting with each other. Belonging to different communities and interacting with all kinds of people in our social roles is part of our self-identity.

The most fundamental means of interaction is a dialogue. In social media, customers have become participants in a dialogue with marketers or brands. Traditionally customers had been mere recipients of one-way messages shot out by marketers, but now they have means of talking back. Customers post positive endorsements about brands, and they also use the Web to vent. Marketers are realizing that they're losing control, and they are scrambling to reinsert themselves into the conversation and steer it in fruitful directions.

13-1a Types of Social Media

The phrase "social media" is usually applied to people interacting and connecting with others via online software or with alternative electronic access technologies (e.g., their smartphones). There are so many variations that it is more useful to consider their properties rather than their particulars. First, some social media offer very rich, vivid sensory experiences, such as virtual worlds or video games, with their dynamic sights and sounds that compel the user to interact and engage. By comparison, other social media seem relatively simple, even impoverished, such as blogs and forums, which tend to resemble little more than protracted strings of emails.

Second, social media differ from one another in that some are primarily social in nature, such as social network sites, which serve as places to asynchronously hang out with friends. On spaces like Facebook, friends chat and share photos, music, and videos. Sharing slices of life with friends is the goal. Other media have more industrious goals, such as collaborating on wiki content, seeking jobs via professional sites like LinkedIn, or reading technical blogs to extract advice from experts.

Third, social media vary with regard to whether the interactions are pointedly commercial. On this dimension, there are not many pure forms: For example, Facebook may seem to host noncommercial gatherings, and yet there are ads floating about, and retail links have begun to sprout. Online brand communities for Kraft, Starbucks, or Lego, hosted by their respective companies, obviously have purchase as their ultimate goals, but their brand communities—Kraft Recipes, My Starbucks Idea, and Lugnet—are built by user groups who are more interested in simply celebrating the brand experience.

13-1b Word-of-mouth

A particularly important phenomenon for business is that social media facilitates word-of-mouth (WOM). Long before social media technology, marketers have known that customer word-of-mouth is very powerful. Consumers view ads with some skepticism, knowing that the point of the message is persuasion. By comparison, if a customer hears the endorsement of a brand from a friend, that message is seen as more objective because the friend presumably has nothing to gain from making such assertions. As Figure 13.1 illustrates, you might tell several friends about a new brand, and they in turn tell several friends of theirs.

Who Gets WOM?

Harris Interactive polls regularly show:

- The most WOM occurs for:
    - *Restaurants and Movies.* WOM helps because consumers seek novelty and variety.
    - *Computers.* WOM helps reduce perceptions of risk, due to the products' expense, and most consumers lacking technical expertise.
- WOM occurs much less for:
    - *Medicines and Financial Products.* They're personal.
    - *Simple or Inconspicuous Goods.* WOM isn't necessary or exciting.

Figure 13.1

Word-of-Mouth Networks

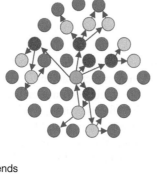

◯ You
● Your friends
◯ Your friends' friends (and so on, and so on...)

A number of metaphors describe this phenomenon of people talking about a brand, e.g., people might say that a YouTube video about a brand has gone viral, or a new Groupon issuance is generating a lot of buzz. What makes a product or event newsworthy? What makes opinion leaders tell their friends about the latest products they've found? How does word-of-mouth work?

Word-of-mouth works on naturally exciting products, where the notion of buzz makes sense. Yet creative brand managers have launched clever ad campaigns that get talked about even for pretty mundane products too. The key is that the product and the message are meaningful to the customer. The hook can be humor, a give-away, or support of social causes. For example, insurance is a little dry, but the Geico Gecko has many friends on Facebook—probably more than you! Mash-ups of real brand material with nostalgic TV commercials and irreverent content are another way to pique some interest and heighten buzzability. Distinct from whether the product category seems WOM-worthy, some extroverted consumers generate more word-of-mouth (positive and negative) than others. Word-of-mouth travels via communication in social networks, so let's understand those structures.

13-2 WHAT ARE SOCIAL NETWORKS?

Networks have been studied in many realms—epidemiology (e.g., contagion), transportation (e.g., hub and spoke), and now business (e.g., word-of-mouth). The key is a focus on connections. A *network* is defined as the set of actors (or nodes) and the relational ties that link them. *Actors* may be customers, firms, brands, concepts, countries, etc. The connections between the actors are *relational ties* (or *links*). Ties can be symmetric ("X and Y are coworkers") or directional ("X likes Y"), and they can be binary or vary in strength.

Networks are often depicted in graphical form (called a *sociogram*), but their analysis requires tabular representation (called a *sociomatrix*). Figure 13.2 shows a network for 6 actors and its corresponding matrix data. Actors B and E have a strong mutual link, and there is a weak unidirectional link from C to B. F is isolated, and actors B, C, and E form a group. While the graphical depictions can be impressive for large networks, the information is converted to matrices for analysis.

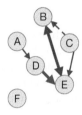

	A	B	C	D	E	F
A	—	0	0	2	0	0
B	0	—	0	0	4	0
C	0	1	—	0	2	0
D	0	0	0	—	4	0
E	0	4	0	0	—	0
F	0	0	0	0	0	—

Row → Column
E.g., D → E represented in $X_{D,E}$

Figure 13.2

A Sociogram and a Sociomatrix

13-2a Identifying Influentials

Many kinds of network analyses may be conducted on a sociomatrix. Our current agenda is to identify likely WOM generators. There is a natural intuition that, in social networking sites as in any social circle, some members are more connected and influential than others. Marketers would like to leverage these interpersonal group dynamics, ideally locating the highly connected influential members, to induce their trial of products and in turn to initiate and propel the diffusion process.

To do so, network marketers study how actors are embedded in their network to locate those who are relatively central—in the thick of things. Centrality indices are computed for each actor in the network to describe his or her position relative to the others.

The easiest and most common way to characterize centrality is to count the number of connections each actor has with the others in the network (see Figure 13.3). An index of degree centrality is derived for each actor. Those with many links are said to be relatively central, and those with fewer links are more peripheral.

Thus, the identification of potential WOM generators is fairly easy for two reasons: (1) You can see how easy these indices are calculate. (2) Distributions of links

Finding opinion leaders in networks is easy.

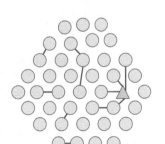

Figure 13.3

Degree Centrality

Triangle actor has the most ties, or the highest degree.

in most networks follow an 80/20 rule, in that most of the links are connected to a small number of actors.[1] Thus, when you're staring at a network graph, or when you're having a computer analyze its sociomatrix, you have to be kind of dense to miss them.

Opinion Leaders

- Art critics, book critics, and wine connoisseurs are trusted because they are objective and not beholden to their respective industry. You might believe that the likelihood with which you would see a movie is not affected by a movie critic's opinion, but in general, a movie does better that receive a critic's blessing.
- Fashion Week in New York in February and in Paris in March celebrate and influence retailers' fashion buyers for the season. More directly influencing the consumer is *Vogue's* September issue; the issue is fatter than most of its models.

Before leaving network analyses, two more ideas are worth sharing: cliques and structural equivalence. Network marketers looking for cliques are talking about exactly the same thing you did when you were in high school: Cliques are groups of people in the network. Cliques are common in delineating brand communities, cell phone friend networks, affinity groups, and more, and they can be a nice way to find homogeneous segments of like-minded people.

What about structural equivalence?

13-2b Recommendation Systems

Structural equivalence is the other pattern sought when analyzing networks. Two actors are said to be structurally equivalent if their links to others are the same (see Figure 13.4). Structural equivalence is the logic underlying recommendation agents employed by big SKU-offering sites like Amazon. Two customers are essentially equivalent if their purchase patterns are similar; whatever one buys, the other might also find appealing. Thus, a recommendation is made based on similarities between the SKUs bought by one customer compared with those bought by others. These systems are still far from perfect, but they'll clearly be around (and better articulated) in the future.[2]

Figure 13.4

Structural Equivalence in Networks

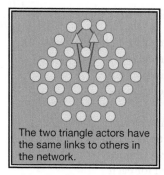

The two triangle actors have the same links to others in the network.

SKUs are columns in XL

Customers are rows

A popular application is to identify customers who have similar links in their online purchases.

Recommendation systems are an odd manifestation of social media. They are social in that the data of purchase patterns or ratings are aggregated over many people, but ultimately these endorsements come from strangers. Yet, indeed, consumers trust online recommendations:

- When consumers read an endorsement in a chat room dedicated to a sport they follow or a health condition they are monitoring, they usually make the assumption that others who visit the Website, read it, and post to it are similar to themselves and hence bring credibility and relevance.

- When consumers read a rating of a book or piece of music online, they usually make the assumption that the majority of people can't be too far from wrong.

Recommendation Agents

Recommendation agents are another form of CRM. Companies keep track of your purchases and then they match you with other customers whose purchases have had some overlap with yours. The implication is that you and these other customers are probably in the same segment and have similar preferences. Thus, things they've bought and you haven't form the system's recommendations to you, and things you've bought but they have not are recommended to them.

Geek squad: How's it done? Imagine a huge spreadsheet with millions of customers as rows and with hundreds of thousands of SKUs in columns. There's a 1 in a cell if that customer-row purchased that SKU-column. Otherwise the database is mostly full of zeros. Cluster analyses are conducted in an iterative fashion. First the rows (customers) are clustered, then the columns (SKUs). Wherever the clustering converges are segments of customers and purchase groups of products. Every customer in each segment can be sent a prompt recommending every SKU in the product grouping. Easy!

These scenarios share the fact that, while the word-of-mouth originates with strangers, it nevertheless seems spontaneous and not paid for, and therefore it seems authentic in a manner not easily achieved in advertising. As you can see, social media seem to have exciting potential for marketing, social networks are fairly easy to track, and recommendation agents are a boon as a systematic means of cross-selling.

What's the resistance? Many CEOs are conservative in spending money on something they can't understand, and many CEOs are old enough that they can't understand the at-

Social Media.

Andresr/Shutterstock.com

traction of social media. As a result, CEOs want to know the ROI for social media. Never mind that marketers hadn't completely cracked the nut of being able to measure ROI for traditional media. It's a fair question to ask. So let's see if there's an answer.

13-2c Social Media ROI, KPIs, and Web Analytics

"What's the ROI if we do this social media thing?" The question sounds eerily similar to the one posed some 20 years ago when companies asked, "Should we have a Website? What can it do for us? How can we make money from it?" We know how that turned out, and for social media also, companies will figure out what makes the best sense for them.

> *The costs of social media are primarily labor.*

As with traditional media, we can begin to answer ROI questions only if we know the goal that the marketing action was intended to achieve. Once we know the goals, selecting the media and measures is rather straightforward. We'll assess whether resources have been well spent by comparing costs to the measures intended to track the effectiveness of the investment.

Early on, social media held the allure that they looked to be nearly free. The approach is certainly less expensive than advertising via many kinds of traditional media. Every day, something seems to go viral, yielding vast reach essentially for free, fueling the hopes that future marketing efforts will be extremely cost-effective. But managers know now that marketing via social media is not free. At the least, their 24/7 maintenance requires thought and labor. Thus, when estimating ROI, the primary expenditures might not be so much media buys or explicit budgetary contributions as salary equivalents of people's time allocations. In this sense, time is indeed money.

If the costs are mostly labor, what are the measures of effectiveness or the key performance indicators (KPIs)? KPIs for social media are analogous to traditional measures for advertising effectiveness. Specifically, marketers are always interested in quantifying reach, frequency, monetary value of customers, customers' behaviors, attitudes, memory (recall, recognition), and so on. In social media, measures for these marketing goals simply take on slightly different forms.

13-2d Pre-purchase: Awareness

Let's begin with popular marketing goals. In the pre-purchase phase, marketers want customers to be aware of their brand and consider it for purchase. Reach is a classic measure of the size of the audience that has been exposed to some brand information and who might therefore have some familiarity with the brand. Reach can be achieved via traditional media and measured via online capture, e.g., as in a magazine ad that tempts the reader to learn more by going online and landing at a particular page associated with the magazine source. Reach can also be achieved wholly online, as a function of ads on popular sites, purchased status on search engines, even via click-throughs on annoying banner ads.

If we wish to enhance awareness, we seek media that optimize reach—media that, ideally, fit our target audience, if possible. Tweets, Facebook postings, and contests to submit videos of user-proposed jingles on YouTube would all work. They're all brief and intended to be a bit more fun than informative. In contrast, lengthy expert blogs, Webinars, podcasts, and such would remain untapped; the customer isn't ready for that detail.

If there is an existing customer base (i.e., for anything other than a brand new product), marketers can reward current customers with incentives to generate word-of-mouth. WOM in customer networks is very rewarding to firms because they are usually bringing in new acquisitions. Completely new customers are the most difficult for a company to find.

Online purchase.

JMiks/Shutterstock.com

13-2e Pre-purchase: Brand Consideration

Next, still in the pre-purchase phase but getting customers to consider our brand, marketers want to offer more information to build customers' knowledge of the brand, as well as more persuasion to make their opinions as favorable as possible. To do so, marketers need to use media that convey more content. Marketers pay for search engine ad placement, post some information teasers in related brand communities, and provide podcasts containing product information and customer testimonials. By comparison, brand consideration goals aren't achieved as readily by providing information on social networks. People use Facebook to socialize or to be entertained, not to engage in product research.

Many of the measures in this phase fall under the broad category of *search engine optimization (SEO)*. When customers have a preferred brand, they can go directly to purchase sites. When they don't, they'll do a search. The keywords depend on where they are along the knowledge continuum. If they have heard of the brand, they will search the brand name to learn more about it. If they are vague about the brand name they will search the product category to see the scope of competitors. And if they're even less familiar, they will search the general benefits they are seeking to see which products and specific brand names pop.

To narrow the search for consumers, search engines can be used to measure the relevance of a Website or an information page by counting the number of times the searched words appeared on that Web page or document. Unfortunately, this criterion of relevance was easily (and frequently) manipulated. The innovation of Google's PageRank algorithm was to count the number of incoming links, weighted by the importance of the sending site. SEO gurus say there are two important paths to enhancing the likelihood that a brand pops to the top of the search results:

What are Companies Doing?

- Adidas encourages its employees to post on social media sites, but asks that when they post on Adidas-hosted sites, that they identify themselves as employees.
- Doritos solicited ideas for new flavors via videos.
- Los Angeles Times asks that its employees use the same criteria for posting in social media as in their traditional outlet—authenticity, professionalism, and verify sources.
- Mercedes-Benz challenges its customers to post photos of all the stuff in their cargo area to show its roominess.
- Oreo posts, and encourages customers to post, pictures and novel recipes.
- Starbucks uses its Facebook page to inform customers about differences among their teas.
- Taco Bell got permission from the Unicode Consortium, which regulates emojis (oh, brother), to use a taco emoji.

1. Put the most meaningful keywords in the Webpage title. Page titles are very important to SEO.
2. The order of those words also matters, so lead off with the most relevant ones.

At the stage of brand consideration, several measures are prime Web analytics: frequencies, durations, and rates. *Frequencies* are the sheer number of visits and estimates of the number of unique visitors; that is, the second number is an attempt to remove the duplications from the first number. Even the second number has its limitations, however; e.g., imagine a couple trying to choose which car to buy next. Both parties may visit several Websites, from their home computers and from those at work (only during lunch, of course). That's at least four computers, even though the search is one.

Durations are usually measures of times spent per page and the overall time spent on the site. *Rates* include bounce rates, i.e., the percentage of sessions for which a visitor lands on the Website and needs only one page viewing to decide, "I'm so out of here!" Then they click off the Website altogether. Rates also include conversion rates, i.e., capturing when a visitor transitions from a looker to a doer, and we'll discuss those next.

13-2f Purchase or Behavioral Engagement

Ideally, customers are moving toward purchasing. However, just as any salesperson knows, a number of steps serve as precursors that nevertheless are hopeful signals of the ultimate purchase. Thus marketers speak of inducing any kind of action that begins to engage the prospective customer. For example, once customers visit a Webpage:

- What do they open? What do they download?
- Do they watch demos that may be available?
- How much time are they spending on which purchase-related pages?
- Do they register to subscribe to newsletters?
- Do they sign up for RSS or other timely sources of news?

YouTube

Customers simply love videos. Videos can be used to:

- Inform (and sell!)
- Educate (and sell!)
- Entertain (and sell!)

(For more, see *YouTube for Business*, by Miller.)

Web analytics experts disdain the Contact Us buttons, instead recommending that a Web visitor fill out a form so that the company can capture at least basic information on this customer and sales opportunity.

Companies can provide exclusivity to Web visitors, e.g., preordering a product not yet available to others. Brand fans may be asked to post opinions and reviews. Sales promos may be made available from site visits or tweeted out to followers. Customer service can unfold in real time, e.g., announcing flight cancellations as a courtesy or sending a map to a customer's phone who has clicked on a product online (or scanned a bar code in a store) to find the nearest retailer (who doesn't have a stock-out).

KPIs are pretty clean when measuring behaviors. Either they happen or they don't; it's not a gradual or subjective thing like, "How positive is a customer's attitude toward my brand?" Thus metrics include numbers of posts regarding the brand on blogs or social networks or audience build as measured by incoming links and the speed of that growth. Conversion rates are straightforward to compute. They consist of frequencies of Web visitors to engage in the focal behavior (purchase, sign up for email distribution, etc.) relative to the number of visitors who come to the Website. That is, the rates compare the desired outcomes to the number of visits or to the number of unique visitors.

It should be clearer to see how easy ROI will be to compute. Costs of the actions depend on the marketing goals: estimates of acquisition costs, payment for placement in search engines or banner ads, sending emails from a rented address database, etc. On the KPIs side, the effectiveness of those actions can be assessed by these frequencies, rates, and durations. Web analysts track the number of visitors coming via different routes, and they follow the customers' traversal to the particular engagement behavior of interest.

13-2g Post-purchase

The wise companies care about their customers long after the purchase. The online environment offers more direct data about what happens post-purchase than we've had thus far IRL. If customers are satisfied, they may post positive reviews. If they're ecstatic, they may post extremely happy endorsements. The company may wish to reward these so-called brand evangelists (or brand ambassadors or brand advocates).

If the customers are unhappy, the company can at least read the nature of the complaint and work to address it. Companies can intervene to try for service recovery, bringing the customer back on board. Even grumbling customers respond to incentives; company apologies, problem solutions, and restorative benefits can help in retention, prevent customer defections, and turn a bad situation around.

In the same way that the marketing media activity differs slightly from pre- to post-purchase, they will also vary over a product's life cycle. It is not unusual for blogs, wikis, and lead user communities to be essential during product development and when generating enthusiasm in the marketplace prior to launch. Webinars might then pick up the product introduction. Networks might capture troubleshooting issues that the company's customer support can readily handle.

Twitter

Twitter is popular because, with it, people never feel:

- Out of touch
- Lonely
- Bored

Popular sites are those that are:

- Informative
- Interesting
- Funny

(For more, see *Twitter Revolution*, by Micek and Whitlock.)

What's especially fun about this day and age is the enormity of the data to play with—all of which are captured easily and tracked in some form of dashboard. Then the analytics are up to you: Do you want your data compared geographically (e.g., state by state) or by time zone? Do you want to watch performance over time—e.g., the number of brand share mentions today compared to yesterday, this quarter vs. last, this week vs. prior to the ad banner launch, etc. What can be done is limited only by your strategic creativity.

13-2h How to Proceed?

Anything that is new and anything that is growing as quickly as social media tend to throw managers for a loop. Where do we begin? There are many social media, and the choice of an initial medium can be difficult. Social media can be so exciting that managers believe they must engage via all possible channels. This goal is obviously impossible and also not desirable. As we have seen, some media fit some marketing goals better than others. In addition, some media fit the target market better than others; tweeting about twofer drinks at a popular bar works for 20-year-olds, but not for 60-year-olds. In addition, being selective of the social medium is important because they do require maintenance and constant activity; otherwise followers lose interest. Trying to keep current on many media would keep the marketer spinning.

Although the explosion of media is great for consumers, it is very challenging for marketers. Even prior to the arrival of social media, marketing decisions about how to allocate advertising budgets were complicated, as marketers tried to find attractive viewer profiles. Resource allocation decisions have become more complex than ever.

How to Do it?

- Marketing researchers were trying to determine which brands played well on Facebook and why. They found that:

  - Facebook users often profiled hedonic activities, those that are fun or adventurous, or their participation in volunteerism. The particular activities tended to be: golf, tennis, wine class, cooking class, shopping, fundraisers, and mission trips. The brands that tended to be featured were: Callaway golf clubs, William-Sonoma, Polo, Brooks Brothers, Saks Fifth Avenue, Chanel, Chateau Margaux, Red Cross, and the American Cancer Society.

  - Users also profiled their personal interests and goals, such as eating right, exercising, going to the movies, socializing with friends, and traveling. The brands they found in these categories of mentions included brands like: Nabisco 100 Calorie Snacks, Nike, Star Wars, Starbucks, Whoopsie Daisy Designs, and Hampton Inn.

  - See "Consumers' Use of Brands to Reflect Their Actual and Ideal Selves on Facebook," by Hollenbeck and Kaikati in the *International Journal of Research in Marketing*.

  Finally, everyone advises: be authentic, i.e., don't sound like a script. (See Kerpen's *Likeable Social Media*.)

Yet, with the right attitude, marketers can embrace social media as heartily as many of their customers have, once they see the potential in doing so. Word-of-mouth conversations or other customer-to-customer information flows have become a rich new source of consumer insights. Marketing researchers learn a lot from lurking or Web crawling and scraping:

- Tweets, blogs, and discussion forums are monitored to make more accurate predictions about new product launches. A great deal of data results from categories with many releases, such as music, books, or movies.

- Marketers use text analyses on Facebook to get a read on customer opinions about their brands. These comments may be on the brand's own Facebook page or gotten from an easy search of the brand name through other, seemingly unrelated postings.

- Beyond the brand itself, content analysis has been useful in detecting developing consumer trends. Posted musings give insights into what people consider important: What are people talking about? What do people care about?

- Brand managers check Websites for misinformation, to try to nip bad grassroots PR in the bud.

In addition to passive listening, marketers can actively create interventions:

- Marketers enter online communities and ask for (paid) volunteers to be user groups to test beta products and offer feedback. Online lead users are easy to find.

- Marketers conduct experiments. In the so-called A/B split tests, one group is exposed to one ad or new product description or whatever element of the marketing mix the marketer is testing. The other group is either a control group, or they see a different version of an ad, new product description, etc. The marketer then compares brand attitudes or subsequent sales in test markets to detect some lift due to the marketing intervention.

- More complex experiments are also obviously possible. A company may wish to measure comparative click-through rates, member sign-up rates, or purchase valuation, as a function of whether the ad appeal is more rational or emotional, whether video or script endorsements are featured, which price is posted and whether a discount is available, etc.

- GPS data function much like live cookies, storing information for your convenience upon return (and still protecting your privacy). The purpose of GPS units in phones was originally consumer service for mapping; e.g., "How do I get where I want to go from here," or "Where is my 15-year-old daughter?" GPS units are becoming geo-retailing units, and they will soon offer extremely timely (intrusive) opportunities for marketers. A motivated company will know where its customers are at all times. The company's claim will be, "When you walk near my product, I can send you a promo."

Finally, if it still seems overwhelming, many companies are willing to help. They can help collect data, store it, provide simple but quick—indeed nearly instantaneous—analyses, help you figure out what to measure, etc. Two big brand providers in the marketspace are Google and Omniture (with Adobe), but many other software providers purport to do the same; e.g., see the software tab at Toptenreviews.com.

Marketers can embrace social media as heartily as their customers.

In general, social media pundits advise that any corporate postings or representations have to start by being interesting; otherwise, they won't even by read. The content needs to be honest, not defensive, and not too corporate. There needs to be transparency for customers, employees, and stakeholders, where transparency usually means being honest, building trust, and presenting the opportunity for two-way dialog. Social media have sufficient variety and prevalence that they can be a tremendous marketing tool—if the company can offer something that provides value to those customers and reaches them in a way that matters to them.

MANAGERIAL RECAP

Social media are an abundant opportunity for marketers. Word-of-mouth feels objective or authentic to consumers, compared to advertising. That makes social networks an important and provocative channel.

- Social media are Web-based means of interacting with friends and strangers by posting opinions, pictures, and videos.

- Social networks are the structures of interconnections among customers that propagate word-of-mouth. Networks can be drawn and analyzed, and the actors measured on indices of centrality to assist the marketer in finding opinion leaders and influential consumers.[3]

- Social media ROI and KPIs can be computed with the help of online analytics, as for any marketing effort, once the marketing goals are understood.

Chapter Outline in Key Terms and Concepts

1. What are social media
   a. Types of social media
   b. Word-of-mouth
2. What are social networks?

   a. Identifying Influentials
   b. Recommendation Agents
   c. Social Media, ROI, KPIs, and Web Analytics
3. Managerial recap

Chapter Discussion Questions

1. How would you describe this algorithm in network terms? Would you use the same network principles if you were to design a competing algorithm?

2. Critics say this method doesn't account for the fact that many Websites are not managed well; they might not be updated, links might not work, etc. How would you improve on this algorithm to address these concerns?

3. What would you do to enhance the chances that a video you post will go viral?

4. What would you do if you found out that a colleague had posted your slides to a recent presentation on a public slide-sharing platform? How do you define intellectual property rights; when is something yours?

5. Do you ever read product recommendations before buying? You don't know these people—how do you discern which ones to believe? What cues do you use to figure out who knows what they're talking about?

MINI-CASE

Google's PageRank

Google's PageRank is an algorithm that attempts to inform you where people are coming from when they land on your Website and which sources are the most frequent. Note that, as its name suggests, a page rank is an index estimated page by page; it's not an overall Website assessment.

Nevertheless, say you're trying to determine the rank of your home page. You figure that's a good start, and customers can navigate more precisely once they're in your domain. The ranking model begins by checking all the incoming links to the home page over some given duration (say, the last 24 hours or the last week, depending on the site traffic and how current the information must be). Customers can land on the home page starting from many links, and the links generating traffic to you differ in their importance. In particular, the influence of the incoming pages varies, as weighted by two factors:

1. The page rank of the source link (higher is better)

2. How many outbound links that source page contains (A lower number is better, in that the link to your home page is therefore more selective.)

Thus, if page A contains a link to your home page, and it has a high page rank of its own and relatively few outreaching links, it carries more weight than page B with its lower page rank and more outreach links.

This algorithm is obviously iterative because we need to estimate the ranks of pages A and B before we can bring them into the estimation of the rank for your home page. In theory, the iterations could continue *ad infinitum*. In the actual algorithm, there are starting values, and about 100 iterations bring most estimates to the convergent approximation. Finally, Google then exercises the universal modeling prerogative of including a term for wiggle room or a fudge factor.

CUSTOMER SATISFACTION AND CUSTOMER RELATIONSHIPS 14

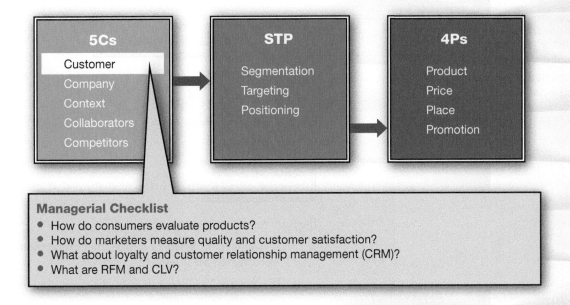

5Cs	STP	4Ps
Customer	Segmentation	Product
Company	Targeting	Price
Context	Positioning	Place
Collaborators		Promotion
Competitors		

Managerial Checklist
- How do consumers evaluate products?
- How do marketers measure quality and customer satisfaction?
- What about loyalty and customer relationship management (CRM)?
- What are RFM and CLV?

14-1 WHAT ARE CUSTOMER EVALUATIONS, AND WHY DO WE CARE?

Marketers are interested in their customers' assessments of how their company is doing. Customer evaluations come in many forms: customer satisfaction, perceptions of quality, customers' intentions to repurchase the same brand or from the same provider, the likelihood that a customer will generate word-of-mouth (speaking favorably to friends and family and coworkers), etc.

Marketers don't track customer evaluations just because they're interesting. Marketers know that satisfied customers contribute to the bottom line. Given the hierarchy of customer behavior, from awareness to trial to repeat and loyalty, the hope is to satisfy new customers so that they become loyal. Truly loyal customers love the brand, purchase frequently, are zealous in telling others about it, and are even willing to pay more for the brand and all it means to them. In this chapter, we'll look at customer evaluations and see how they translate to customer relationship management (CRM) and customer lifetime value (CLV).

14-2 HOW DO CONSUMERS EVALUATE PRODUCTS?

When you buy something—whether it's toothpaste or athletic shoes, a travel package or dental services—marketers think that you evaluate the goodness of the purchase against some sort of expectations.[1] This comparative evaluation process is depicted in Figure 14.1.

Figure 14.1

Customer Evaluations = Experience – Expectations

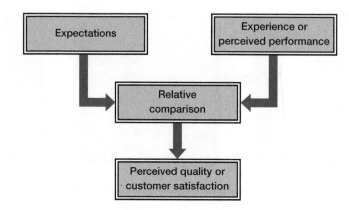

> "The brave company listens to its customers. The foolish company does not."

There are three possible outcomes:

- If customers' experiences surpass their expectations → customers are delighted!

- If customers' experiences meet their expectations → customers are satisfied.

- If customers' experiences fall short of their expectations → customers are dissatisfied.

This comparative model is intuitively appealing, and it has captured the minds of marketers, as evidenced by the many ads that state, "We wish to exceed our customers' expectations."

The comparative evaluation process is thought to operate whether the purchase is low or high involvement. For the *low-involvement* purchase, such as a routine repurchase of your habitual brand of toothpaste, the process may be nearly instantaneous and equally quickly forgotten. Even so, when you got the toothpaste home, if it was somehow different (e.g., it cost more (or less), or the packaging looked different, or the taste seemed extra minty), it would prompt you to think about your toothpaste more than you normally do. Your expectations for toothpaste are usually latent (i.e., you don't obsess over your toothpaste attributes normally), but those expectations would now become more explicit as you think about whether you like the toothpaste that you just used and that seems different. Your expectations, while normally tucked away, come to the forefront and serve as the basis for the comparison.

For *higher-involvement* purchases, the comparison process is typically quite deliberative and conscious. These are purchases that someone cares a lot about or that are more expensive or complicated. For example, brands of athletic shoes have some very loyal segments of customers because, in our society, shoes aren't just shoes; they're a means of self-expression. Athletes purchase the shoes because they want high performance, whereas fashionistas seek attractive styles. Each segment thinks about the purchase and holds certain expectations, and the shoes need to live up to those expectations.

The comparison of a purchase to expectations is also thought to occur whether the item purchased is comprised primarily of search, experience, or credence characteristics. As discussed briefly in Chapter 6, for *search* goods, such as the athletic shoes, more of the qualities sought are obvious from visual examination, objective, and concrete (e.g., the color, size, style, price), and the evaluation process is thought to be straightforward (e.g., a holistic, or attribute-by-attribute comparison to expectations, perhaps weighted by attribute importance).

For *experiential* purchases, such as the purchase of a travel package, where the evaluation cannot be completed until there is some trial or consumption, marketers acknowledge that, prior to purchase, expectations might not be fully formed. The experience itself simultaneously shapes the evaluation as well as the expectations. For example, a customer might hold rather generic expectations of hotels when they're checking in, but when they check out, they might muse, "Gee, the hotel with the pool could have been nicer." This process is referred to as constructing counterfactuals (on the spot, you think of how things might be different). Many purchases have these kinds of experiential elements.

Finally, expectations also form a basis for comparison in *credence* purchases, such as dental services or many professional services. Most consumers don't have the expertise to evaluate their dentist's abilities, so we instead evaluate what we can, e.g., the ability to book a timely appointment, courtesy of the frontline staff, friendliness of dentist, appearance of dental offices, price if we are paying, etc.

14-2a Sources of Expectations

If purchase experiences are judged relative to expectations, it is important to understand expectations. The source of expectations that consumers trust most is their own experience. The experience can be direct, as in the last time they shopped at a particular retail outlet, visited a particular coffee shop, saw their dentist, etc. Or the experience can be indirect, and then the experiences we draw from range along a continuum of similarity. For example, the beauty of franchises is that all the outlets in the chain are supposed to resemble each other. So, when visiting a coffee shop in another city that shares the brand of your favorite coffee shop near home, you project that the experience should be roughly the same. The overarching brand is supposed to lend consistent expectations, and we benchmark the performance accordingly.

Sources of Expectations

- Personal experience
- Friends' advice
- Marketing info
- Third party, such as online ratings

Sometimes the indirect experiences seem even less related, or the purchase happens infrequently so we don't have a lot of direct experiences to draw upon. Nevertheless, in trying to function as quasi-rational beings, we draw from what we can. For example, in a first-time visit to a realtor, most new home buyers don't know what to expect. But we might think, "It'll probably be something like dealing with a bank account manager and a salesperson," and so our expectations are extrapolated from a general category of past experiences with professional service providers.

If we have little personal expertise in making brand choices, our next favorite and trusted source of information is our friends. We seek people whose judgments we trust. Our friends usually have somewhat similar value systems and often similar preference structures, and they have no commercial gain in expressing an opinion for one brand over another. Sometimes we seek opinions from people who are experts, perhaps coworkers, who are not as close to us as friends, but they are people we acknowledge as having more information than we do about the category we're about to enter. And, as we saw in Chapter 13, social media is exerting a good deal of influence on customers' behaviors.

The third class of information that contributes to our expectations is any *marketing mix* element originating from the company, including:

- Positioning claims made in advertising.

- Suggestions of quality inferred from the price point or the frequency of sales and coupons.

- Inferences we draw from the exclusivity (or non-exclusivity) of the distribution outlets in which the merchandise is available.

- Product performance descriptions from retail salespeople, and so on.

This class of information is tricky: It is usually very detailed and in many ways quite objective (compared to our own subjective personal experiences or those of our friends). Yet consumers trust this source of information the least because they expect the company to be biased; i.e., of course, it will say good things about its products.

Finally, third-party communications can help consumers form expectations. Customers can get ideas from movies, television, books, the Internet, *Consumer Reports*, and other third-party objective rating services about quality, value, and service experiences. The bad news for the marketer is that these sources of information are usually beyond their control. However, that neutrality is also why this information seems especially valid and objective to customers.

Glimpses like this raise our expectations.

Zorandim/Shutterstock.com

14-2b **Expectation and Experience**

Next, let's examine the nature of experiences. In particular, marketers have found that customers routinely evaluate the *core* of the purchase itself (e.g., reliable performance, tangible cues to quality including the appearances of the facilities, the employees, the firm's communications materials) and, when applicable, the interpersonal aspects of *service* that may surround the purchase (e.g., a front line that is responsive and able to offer personalized attention to a customer's unique needs, employees who seem competent in their knowledge of the organization, and employees who express empathy and who are courteous).

What's interesting is that both the core components (e.g., dinner at a nice restaurant) and the peripheral, value-added supplemental components (e.g., the service or the wait time at the restaurant) contribute to customer satisfaction and dissatisfaction, but in slightly different ways. Specifically, if the core is good, it doesn't enhance satisfaction much because it was anticipated to be good; it should be good, and the customer expects any provider to be able to meet this commodity-like requirement. But if the core is bad, it can affect dissatisfaction. So, if the dinner (the core) was not good, the customer can be dissatisfied, but the company doesn't get any points if the dinner was good. By comparison, the supplemental services can affect satisfaction or dissatisfaction. If the dinner is fine but the service is great or bad, even though the service is not as "important," it affects the customer's judgment.

Just FYI, this distinction is analogous to that between so-called hygiene and motivating factors. The *hygiene* attributes of goods or services are the must-have features (so if they're missing, customers are dissatisfied). For example, a hotel room should be clean; if it's not, the customer would be dissatisfied. At the same time, if it is clean, the hotel chain doesn't get brownie points toward customer satisfaction because it didn't do anything unusually good. *Motivating* factors show that the company is going above and beyond customer expectations, thereby enhancing customer satisfaction. For example, a mint on the pillow before retiring is not expected, so that extra touch contributes to satisfaction. Note that if the mint had been missing, it wouldn't contribute to dissatisfaction.

It is also important to know that customers evaluate companies and brands based on every data point they see, every so-called moment of truth or point of interaction between the company and the customer: the search effort (online or trying to find a retailer's address while driving); the shopping experience; the apparent quality of the purchase, its price, the checkout process, etc. To gain a better understanding of all that entails the customer experience, marketers have suggested mapping the shopping experience as a flowchart. Doing so forces them to be explicit in depicting, from beginning to end, the myriad interactions

Jell-O

When quality initiatives first entered the world of hospital management and concerns for patient/customer opinions increased, many hospital administrators lamented, "We pay tons of money for the best physicians and the best medical equipment, and we find that our patients complain about the Jell-O!" It may not seem fair, but it makes perfect sense: The patient/customer cannot evaluate the physician or the equipment and instead makes the (fair or unfair) assumption that they're excellent and even comparable across hospitals. The patient/customer can, however, reflect on how frequently a physician visited, how nice the nurses were, how warm the hospital setting seemed, and what the hospital food was like. As a result: "Yes, you are your Jell-O!"

between the customer and company. A flowchart allows marketers to understand the company from the eyes of the consumer, and it makes us understand what corporate elements must be in place to support the front line in their attempts to provide superior service. Flowcharts have been used to generate quality measures at each stage (e.g., "We answer 95% our calls within two rings"), identify pressure points of likely repeat problems (e.g., queues, inefficiencies), and suggest redesigns to streamline and make systems more efficient for both customers and employees.

As difficult as it seems to some companies to satisfy customers, the good news is that most customers' expectations aren't unrealistic. Marketers talk of three kinds of expectations: *ideal* levels of quality, *predicted* or expected levels of quality, and merely *adequate* levels of quality. Some customer segments are demanding, but, for most purchases, most segments have an average predicted level of quality as their expectation marker. The wiggle room between the low, adequate level of expectations and some point slightly exceeding the middle, predicted level of expectations is referred to as a *zone of tolerance*, a range of performance that would be acceptable in the eyes of the customer.

What Most Customers Look For

- Quality in the core purchase
  - Reliability
  - Tangible cues (e.g., retail appearance, price)
- Quality in the attendant service
  - Responsiveness, customization
  - Competence
  - Empathy

Expectations depend on price or, more generally, any cost incurred to the buyer (e.g., having to drive farther for a sale, engage in a more protracted search online, etc.). As a result, some marketers would say that firms should seek to enhance not customer satisfaction but rather customers' perceptions of value. *Value* is defined as the trade-off of the quality of the purchase received compared to the price paid and other costs incurred. For example, we all would agree that a consumer has a right to have higher expectations when buying a brand-new Ferrari compared to parents who are buying a beater for their 15-year-old kid to learn to drive.

Expectations are dynamic, and the purchase experience that pleased a customer last year may no longer suffice this year. Marketers lament this what-have-you-done-for-me-lately attitude among customers, but it's a phenomenon in every industry.

Expectations also vary cross-culturally, as when defining good value or beautiful design. Marketers have also found that individualistic cultures, in which personal success and achievement are valued (e.g., the United States or Europe), are more likely to be satisfied when the quality of reliability and of service provider responsiveness is strong. Customers in collectivistic cultures, in which social ties are highly valued (e.g., Asian or Latin American countries,), appreciate the relational aspects of frontline employees (e.g., assurance and empathy). Different cultures even expect different things from Websites; their appearance and what information is provided. As a result, rolling out products to new customers in new markets should be done thoughtfully (e.g., beginning with conducting local marketing research).

14-3   HOW DO MARKETERS MEASURE QUALITY AND CUSTOMER SATISFACTION?

Manufacturers have gone through the total quality era, with programs such as 6σ (i.e., only three or four errorful parts per million produced) or ISO9000 compliance, and now marketers are facing an even tougher challenge. How can we measure customers' perceptions of quality and satisfaction and expect such precision? The answer is simple: We can't.

There are occasionally objective measures of quality, such as the risk a passenger incurs by flying a particular airline carrier, based on ratios of accidents to numbers of passengers safely served. However, rarely can we set precise measures of quality standards and expect to conform. For example, a cereal manufacturer can decide, "I want 10.2 ounces of cornflakes in each box—no more and no less. I don't want more flakes to go into the box because in the end we'd lose money. I don't want less because I want my customers to be happy." Barring a glitch in the machine, each box will have 10.2 oz of cornflakes. Now imagine creating a comparable standard for much of marketing: "I want my ad to be seen by 10.2 million viewers; I want my revenue sharing offer to incentivize cooperation from 75% of my suppliers." It's not clear how we could measure these achievements, and it's not clear that human beings are capable of such standardized and perfectly consistent behavior.

Surveys are ideal instruments to obtain customers' perceptions. Critics may wish we had 10.2-ounces-of-cornflakes standards, and they may complain that we seek softer numbers, like "90% of our customers check the 'top two' boxes" (satisfied and very satisfied)." Yet consider what we'll do with the numbers. Our ratings data would be no more subjective than those of our competitors or than our numbers from a comparable survey conducted last quarter, etc. So while these may be imperfect measures, the numbers nevertheless allow us to gauge our performance relative to benchmarks (past or competitive performance).

Is Anybody Listening?

- Best Buy has become very active in reading its customers' reviews, and sharing feedback with its vendors when appropriate.

- Hershey Company knows that listening to its customers can provide guidance and leads to brand loyalty. They also use their customer feedback data to fine-tune forecasts and choose test market and product launch cities.

- Marriott reads its guests' feedback and grades the issues according to customers' satisfaction or levels of problems and tries to address the problems.

- When Netflix did not listen to its customers and proceeded to split its DVD and streaming businesses, resulting in price increases of around 40%, they lost almost one million subscribers and half their stock value and they popped up on lists of "most hated" companies in America.

Anatomy of a Customer Satisfaction Survey

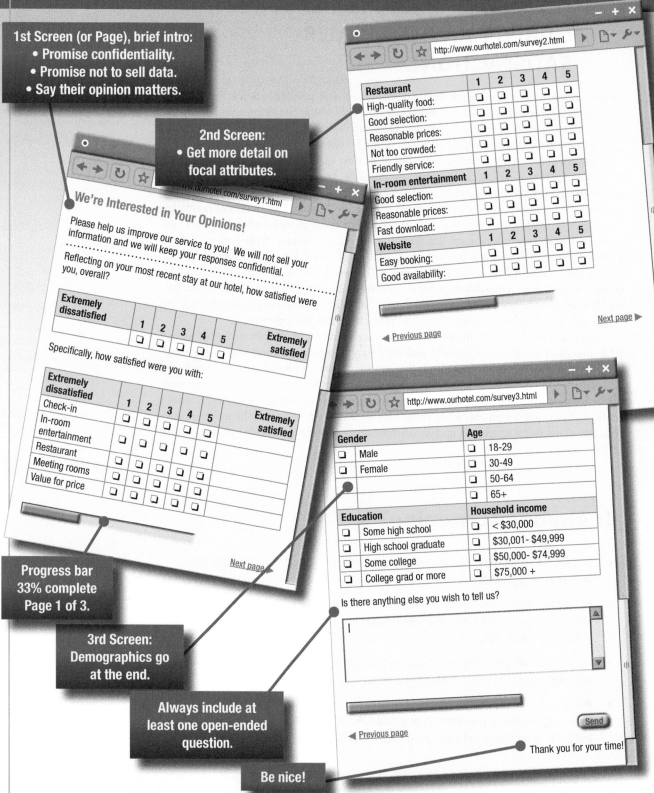

1st Screen (or Page), brief intro:
- Promise confidentiality.
- Promise not to sell data.
- Say their opinion matters.

2nd Screen:
- Get more detail on focal attributes.

We're Interested in Your Opinions!

Please help us improve our service to you! We will not sell your information and we will keep your responses confidential.

Reflecting on your most recent stay at our hotel, how satisfied were you, overall?

Extremely dissatisfied	1	2	3	4	5	Extremely satisfied
	☐	☐	☐	☐	☐	

Specifically, how satisfied were you with:

Extremely dissatisfied	1	2	3	4	5	Extremely satisfied
Check-in	☐	☐	☐	☐	☐	
In-room entertainment	☐	☐	☐	☐	☐	
Restaurant	☐	☐	☐	☐	☐	
Meeting rooms	☐	☐	☐	☐	☐	
Value for price	☐	☐	☐	☐	☐	

Next page

http://www.ourhotel.com/survey2.html

	1	2	3	4	5
Restaurant					
High-quality food:	☐	☐	☐	☐	☐
Good selection:	☐	☐	☐	☐	☐
Reasonable prices:	☐	☐	☐	☐	☐
Not too crowded:	☐	☐	☐	☐	☐
Friendly service:	☐	☐	☐	☐	☐
In-room entertainment	1	2	3	4	5
Good selection:	☐	☐	☐	☐	☐
Reasonable prices:	☐	☐	☐	☐	☐
Fast download:	☐	☐	☐	☐	☐
Website	1	2	3	4	5
Easy booking:	☐	☐	☐	☐	☐
Good availability:	☐	☐	☐	☐	☐

◀ Previous page   Next page ▶

Progress bar 33% complete Page 1 of 3.

3rd Screen: Demographics go at the end.

http://www.ourhotel.com/survey3.html

Gender		Age	
☐	Male	☐	18-29
☐	Female	☐	30-49
		☐	50-64
		☐	65+
Education		**Household income**	
☐	Some high school	☐	< $30,000
☐	High school graduate	☐	$30,001- $49,999
☐	Some college	☐	$50,000- $74,999
☐	College grad or more	☐	$75,000 +

Is there anything else you wish to tell us?

```
|
```

Send

◀ Previous page

Thank you for your time!

Always include at least one open-ended question.

Be nice!

Dissatisfaction

- What bugs customers most?
    - Frontline people who are incompetent or rude.
    - An initial complaint that wasn't handled well.
    - Heaping insult upon injury.
    - A purchase that was too expensive.
- When they're dissatisfied, what do customers do?
    - Switch brands.
    - Complain to friends.
- Few dissatisfied customers complain directly to the company because:
    - They figure it won't make any difference.
    - It's not worth their time or effort.
    - They couldn't figure out where to go to complain.

It's a drag to hear negative feedback, but, if the company doesn't facilitate hearing it, then see above: Customers will switch brands!

Marketers have made peace with the fact that the numbers represent customers' perceptions; that is no longer the issue. But there's a popular management adage, "If you can't measure it, you can't manage it." So marketers want some customer data.

Some marketing gurus claim that just one or two indices can reflect the overall health of an organization. However, survey results are more actionable if they measure multiple facets of the customers' thoughts about the firm. Look at it this way: If everything is going well, you can have one or many indices—who cares? But if things aren't going well, and marketing managers are trying to assess and improve performance, they need more information.

For example, say a department store just received its annual "Happy Stats" but found, to its dismay, that the customer satisfaction score dropped from last year. The store was able to glean more diagnostic information from the survey because it had been structured to cover several contributing factors. The scores on the questions about the store's prices and the quality of the staff were stable from last year, but there were drops in kitchenware and children's clothing regarding their assortment selections. The store could make a decision to pull out of one of these lines of businesses, but customers would be happier if these areas were more fully stocked. That is, there is still a managerial decision to be made, but at least the data are clear and helpful.

In terms of customer dissatisfaction, when things go wrong, research suggests that the primary means to regaining the customer is through an empowered frontline employee. That employee needs to be capable of immediately redressing the problem, empathizing with the customer, and offering a perk for the customer's troubles.[2] We worry about recovery because, if customers are dissatisfied, they can go to the competition or drop out of the category altogether. Instead, as we consider in the next section, marketers seek customer retention and long-term relationships with customers, at least the ones we find to be valuable.

Quality

Quality and satisfaction are not the same thing. For example, experts may create excellent technology, but the customer who doesn't "get it" will be dissatisfied. Conversely, some electronic toy may be lacking bells and whistles, yet customers may be perfectly happy with it (perhaps due to its simplicity).

14-4 LOYALTY AND CUSTOMER RELATIONSHIP MANAGEMENT (CRM)

Customer satisfaction isn't a goal in itself. Companies are in business to make money.[3] You could perhaps be a monopoly and make money even with unhappy customers, but most industries attract competition, so your sole provider status won't last for long. Plus, who really wants to be in business with unhappy customers? Companies and employees, from CEO to frontline workers, take pride in providing good products to customers. They enjoy having customers who appreciate them and want to return, customers who are enthusiastic about their brands and who tell their friends about their good experiences with the company and its products.

In addition, we need to push beyond customer satisfaction. Many measures capture customer evaluations from opinions, such as preference or satisfaction or purchase intentions. We want to see positive reinforcing behaviors, such as repeat purchasing and customers generating word of mouth. In addition, for true loyalty, we want to see customers who have positive attitudes toward the company or brand, not just repeat purchases.

Mantra

Contrary to the age-old mantra, the customer is not always right!
Unfortunately, right or wrong, they often have big mouths, e.g., posting on Facebook.
Remedy? First step: Check to be sure that your brand has found the right segment.

If marketers want to be taken seriously and have input at the executive C-level, they need to translate these marketing metrics into money metrics to impress the finance guys.[4] A popular means of attaching a financial value to a customer is via the assessment of customer lifetime value, per customer or at least per segment.

Success Paradox

Marketers believe that customer satisfaction should result in more sales. With success, the segment of buyers gets larger and, by definition, more heterogeneous. It is difficult to please all customers with a single market offering, which is why marketers segment in the first place. A larger market share, with more customer differences in expectations and experiences, can then result in customer dissatisfaction. What to do? Re-segment, launch another product line, repeat. (See research on ACSI: American Consumer Satisfaction Index by Professors Claes Fornell and Michael Johnson, University of Michigan.)

It's nice when our customers are happy!

Customer satisfaction is thought to be the first step in a longer-term relationship. Early, primitive efforts at customer relationship marketing (CRM) were frequently driven by price discounts, reasoning that a company could buy a little loyalty by locking in their customers (e.g., "Buy nine coffees, get the 10th free"). There are certainly debates: Is it true loyalty. Or is it merely inertia or ingrained purchasing habits? Or how do we keep the members of loyalty programs separated from the non-loyal segment of customers? But the bottom line is that loyalty programs can keep customers from defecting, as well as induce some additional purchasing.

Recently, the loyalty pendulum has swung in the opposite direction, with companies charging their loyal customers more, figuring that the loyals like the brand so much that they're price insensitive. It's not unusual, for example, for companies to entice new customers with special deals, while not rewarding current customers with comparable promotions. These extremes are just another indicator of how frequently price is used as a knee-jerk lever. But just because price is easy to change doesn't mean it's the best element in the marketing mix to change. And whether the loyals pay more or are rewarded with lower costs or more benefits, plenty of research supports the clear tie between satisfied returning customers and bottom-line corporate financials.

14-4a   Recency, Frequency, and Monetary Value (RFM)

Whereas a loyalty program invites customers to become members to enjoy certain benefits for frequent or heavy purchasing, a CRM (customer relationship management) program is a tool in the company that tracks spending, regardless of whether customers are segmented into loyals or disloyals and rewarded or not. Early forms of CRM system began with primitive information: customer identification and contact information, and some form of RFM, that is, information on the recency, frequency, and monetary values of the customers' purchase history.

Figure 14.2 represents these three dimensions as a cube, and the most desirable customers—e.g., those we might wish to send premium offerings via emailed direct marketing efforts—are those in the "recent/frequent/high value" area of the cube. Traditionally, these three factors comprise the key ingredients to so-called scoring models. To find the most desirable customers, the RFM behaviors are recorded, coded, and weighted using expert system judgments of the importance of each component.

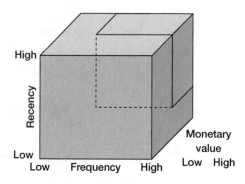

Figure 14.2

Recency-Frequency-Monetary Value

Regarding the first step, codes might be assigned like these: "If the most recent order was placed within the past three months, then $R = 3$ points. If the most recent order was between three and six months, $R = 2$. If the most recent order was between six and 12 months, $R = 1$. Any customer who hadn't purchased within the past year receives a code of $R = 0$. Frequency and monetary values are coded similarly.

In the next step, R, F, and M are multiplied by weights judged to reflect their importance, such as 5 for M, 2 for R, and 1 for F. A single score is obtained for each customer, as the simple function $[(5 \times M) + (2 \times R) + (1 \times F)]$. Customers with the highest scores are deemed most worthy of special attention. RFM models are still used and still useful, but they emphasize past customer behaviors (purchasing, Web surfing, etc.), whereas more sophisticated models allow us to extrapolate into future earnings of customer segments, as we'll see in a moment.

In addition, the best CRM programs begin with the RFM behaviors, but they go beyond these data to learn more about their customers. With better customer knowledge, companies can provide specially tailored offerings through cross-selling efforts; i.e., the product assortment itself is modified, or the channels through which the goods and services may be accessed are made more flexible, etc. Specifically, CRM databases typically contain:

1. *Contact information:* Name, address, phone, email, permission status.

2. *Demographics:* Economic worth, age, marital status, partner's name and age, children (names and ages), region of country.

3. *Lifestyle and psychographic data:* Homeowner or renter, car ownership (type and year), media preferences, payment preferences, relevant product ownership, recreational preferences.

4. *Internet info:* Time spent on Websites, number of visits to site.

5. *Transaction data:* Source and date of first transaction, R, F, M, what was purchased, form of order (Web, phone, etc.), mode of payment.

6. *Rate of response to marketing offers:* Promos and other incentives redeemed.

7. *Complaints.*

And so forth—pretty much anything the company can get its paws on to compile. Finally, expenditures are cross-tabbed with everything to try to find patterns.

Good CRM programs take planning and money, and they require ongoing monitoring of customers. Even just the coordination and maintenance of the database is nontrivial. Companies are still struggling with how to design an information system that integrates inputs from all relevant touch points (call centers, order placements, Websites, etc.) and that may be accessed in useful formats for managerial usage (system recommendation agents, useful profiles for call center recipients, predictions about responses to promotions, etc.).

14-4b Customer Lifetime Value (CLV)

Just as customers assess the value of their purchases—what quality do I get compared with the price I paid?—companies can assess customers in terms of their worth to the company. Some customers are costly to acquire, and others are more costly to retain. How can we segment our customer base to maximize our profitability and know which segments to serve? To answer these questions, companies are getting smart about estimating *customer lifetime value* (CLV).[5] We'll look at a process for thinking about and estimating CLV, to see how all the pieces come together in a reasonably good and yet fairly simple model.

Figure 14.3 shows conceptually how CLV unfolds. Models of CLV involve three kinds of components: (1) numbers about money, (2) numbers about time, and (3) a financing finesse. The money inputs we need are: (a) estimates of acquisition costs, (b) estimates of retention costs, (c) average contributions (for the segments under consideration). The time inputs are (a) a decent guesstimate at the likely retention rate from year to year and (b) a sense of the average lifespan duration for the particular product or brand. Finally, if the estimates are to be useful in forecasting and budgeting, a simple financial adjustment of a discount rate is important.

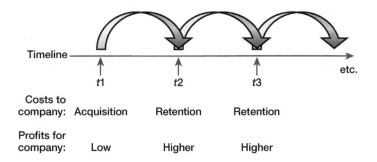

Figure 14.3

Customer Lifetime Value (CLV) Conceptually

To see the model, let's consider an example: Mobi-Med is a mobile provider of healthcare consultation and services for all but the most complicated conditions, e.g., screening and physicals, annual vision and hearing tests, immunizations (e.g., kids going back to school, travelers going to exotic locations), diagnostics via portable X-ray, ultrasound, cardio EKGs, even some basic lab work. Business is booming for several reasons: (1) Healthcare costs are disturbingly high, and, while people pay cash for many of MobiMed's services, customers don't have to wait for appointments, and the retail exchange is very pleasant. (2) Some technology is portable. (3) Most health complaints that motivate customers to seek advice are fairly simple and can be handled by a variety of healthcare staff.

The MobiMed founder, an MD/MBA, attracts new customers via advertising and coupon promotions. Once a month, the company takes out an ad in the local paper, alternating between a weekend flyer at $50 each and a half-page ad at $200 each. The acquisition costs thus are ($50 × 6) + ($200 × 6) = $1,500 per year. Both kinds of ads contain a nominal coupon embedded in them, which helps MobiMed track how the customer came to hear of their services and which helps them measure the effectiveness of the ad money expenditures. Approximately 60 customers redeem coupons in a year, or just over 1 patient a week. Thus, acquisition is $1,500/60, or $25 a head.

In addition, MobiMed has a sales manager who works part-time (20 hours), with no benefits (other than health!) but who is loyal because he's paid $45,000. When he's on duty, he's supposed to spend 10% of his time, or two hours a week, logging sales calls. Thus, note that the sales call budget is essentially 10% of $45,000, or $4,500. In any given week, while many calls are placed, the yield is approximately one customer a week, or about 50 a year. Personal selling is almost always more expensive, but the belief is that customers contacted via a salesperson is already beginning to develop a relationship and therefore is more likely to convert to being a loyal customer. In this scenario, the cost is $4,500 ÷ 50 = $90 per capita.

We can track these groups separately to test the comparative effectiveness of the two acquisition approaches, but our goal at the moment is simply to compute CLV. Thus, we'll take the average acquisition cost to be (60 × 25 + 50 ×90) ÷ (60 + 50) = $54.55. This $55 is the first number entered into the spreadsheet in Figure 14.4.

Figure 14.4

Crunching Customer Lifetime Value (CLV)

		Time 1	Time 2	Time 3	Time 4...
a.	New customer acquisition cost	$55			
b.	Retention costs		$20	$20	$20
c.	Retention rate	100%	75%	70%	65%
d.	Cumulative retention (multiply adjacent rates)		75%	52%	34%
e.	Avg customer contributions	$100	$150	$200	$250
f.	Net contrib. = (Contribution e – Acquisition a or – Retention b)	$45	$130	$180	$230
g.	Expected avg contribution (f × d)	$45	$97.50	$93.60	$85.00
h.	Financing finessing, e.g., for discount rate of .07, divide each g by [1.07^(t – 1)]	1.0	1.07	1.145	1.225
	today's value	$45	$91.12	$81.75	$69.39
					Final sum: $287.26

Next, MobiMed estimates retention costs. Each customer who has ever been treated is issued $100 worth of coupons throughout the year, and, on average, $20 are redeemed. The retention figure is represented in row b in the spreadsheet.

Retention rates begin at 0.75 and decline slowly thereafter. Row c in the spreadsheet lists the loyalty rates per segment, and row d shows how those numbers multiply and accumulate.

Average contributions begin at about $100 a year and grow. These values form row e in the CLV computation.

You might think the lifespan for customer lifetime value is 80 years or something like that, but obviously that's not likely to be true for any brand. For example, people are mobile, moving about every seven years. Once MobiMed goes national, customers could take their membership with them, and loyalty to the chain could be sustained throughout the patient's life. In any event, for the ease of computation, we're going to pretend the lifespan is a mere four years.

We now have all the components to crunch the CLV numbers. (We'll tweak the financial discount at the end.) In Figure 14.4, the net contributions begin with the averages in row e; subtract the acquisition costs of time 1 or the retention costs of subsequent times, as noted in row f. Row g figures the expected contributions, based on the net contribution in f and the cumulative retention rate in d. Row h takes the time horizon out on the discount rate. At the bottom right is the sum, the CLV for a customer (over four years).

The basic CLV calculation is very simple. Once the basic template is in a spreadsheet, you can extend it to other scenarios and make it more sophisticated. For example, costs and revenues, even retention rates, usually vary across segments, so at the least there could be multiple versions and different resulting estimates per segment. There is obviously a lot of flexibility in capturing CLV. The important thing is to get the assumptions as right as possible and to use the numbers as guides regarding which segments to continue to target, which customers to try to please, and which customers to let defect.

Let's broaden the view to include CRM, not just models of computing CLV. Marketers can think of CRM as a holistic strategic approach in managing customer relationships to create shareholder value. From this view, CRM is core business, and the firm is customer-centric. The strategy is to win and retain profitable customers. Alternatively, marketing can be more analytical about CRM as plans are enacted to route and analyze data and to store information appropriately. Finally, marketing can get quite operational when implementing plans to capture and create those databases. Customer information must be collected, automated, and integrated to be useful to the firm, such as in turning around and sending out messages or products to customers.

What's important is to keep an eye on the goal. It's fun to calculate CLV, but we do it because it fits a strategic initiative to serve certain segments of customers better, as well as our corporate goals for growth and profitability.

Firms frequently demonstrate their implicit knowledge of CLV. For example, a Honda product line begins by appealing to young customers with limited budgets and who Honda hopes will grow into customers whose lifestyles and wallets might appreciate fancier, more expensive models as they can afford to do so. The product line is a classic means of a company trying to extend the duration of its customers' lifetime, as well as contribution margins, in CLV.

A newer development in loyalty programs is the transference from physical cards to mobile technology. Customers are rarely without their smartphones; hence, they might use their loyalty programs more frequently, hiking up the contributions as well, if they are as accessible as their phones.

MANAGERIAL RECAP

Customers are thought to evaluate goods and services by making comparisons to their expectations. Their expectations can come from previous experience, word-of-mouth, or marketing efforts such as advertising.

- Quality and customer satisfaction can be precisely measured in the production of goods, but not as easily for services. Surveys can be used to ask customers for their evaluations of any kind of purchase.

- Beyond customer satisfaction, marketers care about long-term criteria such as loyalty and customer relationship management.

- Customer lifetime value is a means of translating marketing efforts into financial results. CLV allows firms to match customer benefits to revenues to ensure that each customer relationship remains profitable.

Chapter Outline in Key Terms and Concepts

1. How do consumers evaluate products?
2. How do marketers measure quality and customer satisfaction?
3. Loyalty and customer relationship management (CRM)

   a. Recency, frequency, and monetary value (RFM)
   b. Customer lifetime value (CLV)
4. Managerial recap

Chapter Discussion Questions

1. How would you interpret the data? Where *is* the hotel chain doing a good job?

2. How could you tease out the effects of customer satisfaction vs. cultural biases?

MINI-CASE

Happy Global Customers?

Joe Pike is a CMO in a consulting firm out of Miami that specializes in creating loyalty programs for its clients. As a first step, he gathers customer satisfaction data, and the results for an international hotel chain follow.

Brazil:

	Strongly disagree									Strongly agree
Overall, I was satisfied with the hotel.	1	2	3	4	5	6	7	8	9	(10)
The hotel prices were good value.	1	(2)	3	4	5	6	7	8	9	10
The hotel exceeded my expectations.	1	2	3	4	(5)	6	7	8	9	10
I will recommend this hotel to others.	1	2	3	4	5	6	7	8	(9)	10

Japan:

	Strongly disagree									Strongly agree
Overall, I was satisfied with the hotel.	1	2	3	4	5	6	7	8	9	(10)
The hotel prices were good value.	1	2	3	4	5	6	7	(8)	9	10
The hotel exceeded my expectations.	1	2	3	4	5	6	7	8	9	
I will recommend this hotel to others.	1	2	3	4	5	6	7	(8)	9	10

England:

	Strongly disagree									Strongly agree
Overall, I was satisfied with the hotel.	1	2	3	4	5	6	(7)	8	9	10
The hotel prices were good value.	1	2	3	(4)	5	6	7	8	9	10
The hotel exceeded my expectations.	1	2	3	4		6	7	8	9	10
I will recommend this hotel to others.	1	2	3		5	6	7	8	9	10

These data draw from three samples: Brazil, Japan, and England.

Here is the hotelier's response to seeing these data: "Wow, we're doing great in Japan, and pretty good in Brazil except for their perception of value. Maybe the English don't care that much about hotels."

Marketing managers of global multinationals frequently gather customer satisfaction data from their customers all over the world. The question is how to make sense of the data. When the Japanese customer satisfaction ratings look higher than those in England, does that mean the Japanese customers are truly more satisfied, or is something else going on?

Joe has a lot of experience with international data and knows the cross-cultural literature. There are known response tendencies found in different countries. These are stereotypes, of course, but here are the generalities typical in such data:

- Some cultures are said to be "enthusiastic," meaning that the ratings display high variance. Thus, customers in the U.S., Brazil (and many other South American countries), France, Italy, and Australia produce data indicating that, when customers are happy, they're really happy and when they're not, they're really most sincerely not.

- Other countries, such as England and Germany, are more "reserved." The numbers on surveys show less variability. Ratings tend to be near the midpoint, which means customers won't indicate liking or disliking anything all that strongly.

- Some countries (e.g., Japan and some other Asian countries) have an "acquiescence" or courteousness bias, saying things look favorable when maybe deep down that's not quite what they think. Thus, when the Japanese ratings appear more positive, giving the impression they're happier, it's more likely that they're just being polite on the survey.

15 MARKETING RESEARCH TOOLS

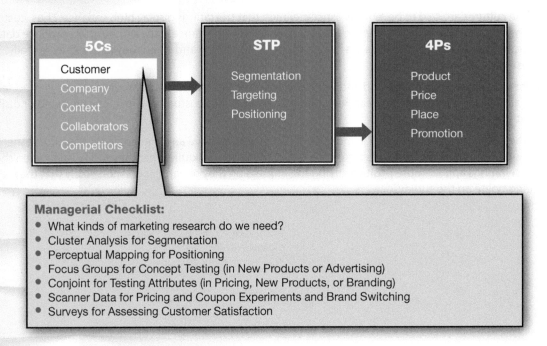

5Cs	STP	4Ps
Customer	Segmentation	Product
Company	Targeting	Price
Context	Positioning	Place
Collaborators		Promotion
Competitors		

Managerial Checklist:
- What kinds of marketing research do we need?
- Cluster Analysis for Segmentation
- Perceptual Mapping for Positioning
- Focus Groups for Concept Testing (in New Products or Advertising)
- Conjoint for Testing Attributes (in Pricing, New Products, or Branding)
- Scanner Data for Pricing and Coupon Experiments and Brand Switching
- Surveys for Assessing Customer Satisfaction

15-1 WHY IS MARKETING RESEARCH SO IMPORTANT?

Every marketing decision should be based on facts. Marketing research is about gathering those facts.

The smartest marketers are always monitoring their customers, the environmental context, their competitors' actions, their relationships with their collaborators, their own company strengths—the 5Cs. And the smartest marketers make decisions about their products, place, promotion, and price—the 4Ps—based on marketing intelligence. As Figure 15.1 indicates, marketing research methods can be used to obtain many insights about marketing and customers.

Marketing information should be gathered constantly, so that the company can be knowledgeable and poised for action. Customer relationship management databases are an important example of ongoing data collection and management systems. In addition, occasions frequently arise that require periodically pulsing the market with specific marketing research projects. Whether the assessments are continuous or periodic, they require knowledge of marketing research techniques.

- STP
  - cluster analysis for segmentation
  - multidimensional scaling for perceptual mapping, targeting and positioning
- 4Ps
  - conjoint for new products
  - scanner data for pricing
  - surveys to assess customer satisfaction with Internet as a distribution option
  - experiments to verify ad testing
- 5Cs
  - secondary data to understand context
  - observational data to check on competitors
  - networks to study collaborators
  - interviews to study company's employees
  - surveys for customer satisfaction

Figure 15.1

Examples of Relevant Marketing Research

Figure 15.2 depicts the typical flow in the research process, from formulating the marketing and marketing research problem, to data collection and analysis, to reporting the results. Data collection can take quite a number of forms, as Figure 15.3 suggests.

- Define marketing, and marketing research problem
- Try to answer questions with secondary data
- Design primary data collection
  - Sample (e.g., random sample, stratified sample by segment)
  - Technique
    - Qualitative: interviews, focus groups, observations and ethnographies
    - Quantitative: surveys, experiments, scanner data analysis
  - Instruments (e.g., questionnaire, focus group moderator guide)
  - Mode of Administration (e.g., web survey, mail, personal interview)
- Data collection
- Data analysis
- Communicate results (white paper, presentation, recommendations)

Figure 15.2

Marketing Research Process

Figure 15.3

Kinds of Data

Kind of Data?	Definition?	Examples?	Advantages?
Secondary	Already exist	Library, online	Quick & cheap to get
Primary	Design, collect, analyze	Focus group, surveys	Can be quite precise

Kind of Study?	Used for?	Examples?
Exploratory	Formulate marketing questions	Focus groups, interviews
Descriptive	Obtain large scale stats	Surveys, scanner data
Causal	Study effects of manipulating 4Ps	Experiments

Marketing research is tremendously flexible; it can be used to address just about any business question, and there are many ways to do so. This chapter focuses on six popular techniques:[1]

1. Cluster analysis for segmentation

2. Perceptual mapping for positioning

3. Focus groups for concept testing (in new products or advertising)

4. Conjoint for testing attributes (in pricing, new products, or branding)

5. Scanner data for pricing and coupon experiments and brand switching

6. Surveys for assessing customer satisfaction

15-2 CLUSTER ANALYSIS FOR SEGMENTATION

A couple of MBAs who are feeling a little broke are thinking they could start an NPO to fund young people to go to college. There are many such nonprofits, but not many (or no particular branded ones) seem to support the goal of offsetting these costs. The team wishes to first verify or test its assumptions by looking at people's perceptions on these issues. They figure there must be a segment of customers who will be sympathetic.

The results of their study are presented in Figure 15.4; it's a typical executive summary of a segmentation study. The segment names are catchy titles that the marketer creates to label the segments and to summarize the qualities that the customers have in common, e.g., people who give charitably to medical associations, the arts, environment societies, etc. The size column reflects the proportion of customers in the database who belong to each segment. The beneficiaries column contains the questions from the survey that each group resonated with the most.

Figure 15.4		
Segmentation of NPO Supporters		

Segment Name	Size	Beneficiaries
Health and Medical	30%	American Cancer Society
The Arts	20%	Ballests, Museums, Operas
Greenies	15%	Nature Conservancy, World Wildlife Fund
Children	10%	Make-a-Wish, St. Jude's Charity, Unicef
Other	25%	Religious, Local (e.g., Animal Shelter, Food Bank)

Let's see what's behind the segmentation summary and how the marketers got these results. Figure 15.5 shows the survey that gave rise to the data. The marketers asked customers about their charitable giving behavior, as well as their opinions about higher education—its importance in society and its cost.

Figure 15.6 contains part of the data set. For example, the first customer tends to give money to environmental and medical causes, but not to a lot to kids' causes, and is not overly concerned with the price tag on colleges.

Next the marketer imputes the data into a cluster analysis. Clustering methods form smaller groups of customers, where, within a group, customers are seeking similar attributes.[2]

How important is it to support these nonprofit causes for a better society?

	Not very important						Very important
Medical causes like American Heart Assn.	1 2 3 4 5 6 7						
	1 2 3 4 5 6 7						
The arts, like ballet or museums	1 2 3 4 5 6 7						
Environmental concerns, like WWF	1 2 3 4 5 6 7						
Children's charities, like Make-a-Wish	1 2 3 4 5 6 7						

To what extent would you say that you agree with these statements?

	strongly disagree						strongly agree
Higher education is very important.	1 2 3 4 5 6 7						
More college educated people make for a better society.	1 2 3 4 5 6 7						
My success in life was largely due to my going to college.	1 2 3 4 5 6 7						
People don't really need to go to college.	1 2 3 4 5 6 7						
Only the very privileged can go to university these days.	1 2 3 4 5 6 7						
Higher education is too expensive.	1 2 3 4 5 6 7						
I would help sponsor a kid (not my own) to go to college.	1 2 3 4 5 6 7						

Figure 15.5

Survey Used to Interview Customers

Customer ID#	Med	Art	Envir	Kids	Imp	More	Suc	No Need	Priv	Too Exp	Spons
1	5	4	7	1	4	2	4	2	1	1	1
2	3	7	3	5	4	7	3	4	1	1	3
3	3	5	2	4	5	4	2	4	7	7	4
4	5	5	1	3	7	2	2	2	4	2	7
5	6	5	3	3	4	3	4	3	3	1	3

Figure 15.6

NPO DataSet

Different groups look for different attributes. In these data, there are 11 variables, and, although clustering techniques have no problem with processing even more variables, it is difficult for us to imagine what 11-dimensional scatterplots look like. So in Figure 15.7, the problem is simplified a bit.

In the left plot, we can see the pretty clear patterns of the first and third clusters, people who support environmental concerns and people who are concerned that higher ed is so expensive that only the privileged can attend. Customers near the origin don't care as much about either issue. In the next plot, we see the second cluster identified as those who support the arts and believe that education enhances society. Finally, in the plot at the right, there seems to be a customer segment that is willing to sponsor a child through college Altogether, the intuitions of the MBA team seem to be valid; they may be on to something in creating an NPO to support scholarships, and there seems to be at least one segment of people who would be willing to help.

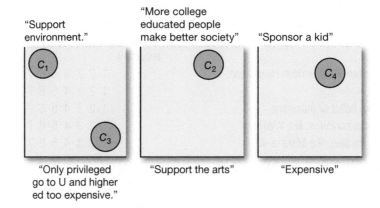

Figure 15.7

That's all there is to it. Get data from your customers and process it through a cluster analysis. There are many clustering techniques, so you will have to hire a marketing researcher for the fine points. But this example shows you the essence of how to find segments. Note, of course, that a cluster analysis helps you identify segments (and their sizes), but it does not tell you which segment to target—that's dealt with in Chapters 4, 14, and 16.

15-3 PERCEPTUAL MAPPING FOR POSITIONING

Positioning studies are used to understand customer perceptions of brands in the marketplace. Marketers and executives find perceptual maps extremely appealing. They are pictures of competing brands as well as attributes, which together offer a sense of competitive strengths and weaknesses. There are two approaches to creating a perceptual map: an attribute-based approach and multidimensional scaling (MDS).

15-3a Attribute-Based

To create a map based on attributes, customers complete a survey that looks like the one in Figure 15.8. The customer makes two kinds of ratings: (1) How does our brand rate on a number of attributes? (2) How important is each of these attributes? A local gym called BeFit Gym had aspirations for growth, including expansion to multiple locations, and their hopes and plans motivated this particular study. They solicited a positioning study of their gym and some national chain competitors. They asked customers about their perceptions regarding how well each gym fared on the bases of variety of equipment, variety of classes, helpfulness of staff, value, and the extent to which the gym brand "reflected their personalities."

The analysis begins by merely simply averaging over these questions. Doing so results in a pair of means for each attribute; e.g., there is a mean on whether the gym is good value and a mean for how important value is to this customer.

These pairs of means are used to plot the attributes in a 2-dimensional chart, as in Figure 15.9. The higher the mean performance on an attribute (in the first 5 ratings) determines how far to the right the attribute will be plotted. The importance of the attribute (in the second five ratings) is the coordinate on the vertical axis of the chart.

How does {*our brand*} rate?

	Not as good as others						Better than others
Variety of equipment	1	2	3	4	5	6	7
Variety of classes	1	2	3	4	5	6	7
Helpful staff	1	2	3	4	5	6	7
Value	1	2	3	4	5	6	7
Reflects my personality	1	2	3	4	5	6	7

How important are these qualities to you?

	Not very important						Extremely important
Variety of equipment	1	2	3	4	5	6	7
Variety of classes	1	2	3	4	5	6	7
Helpful staff	1	2	3	4	5	6	7
Value	1	2	3	4	5	6	7
Reflects my personality	1	2	3	4	5	6	7

Figure 15.8

Perceptual Mapping (Attribute-Based): BeFit Gym

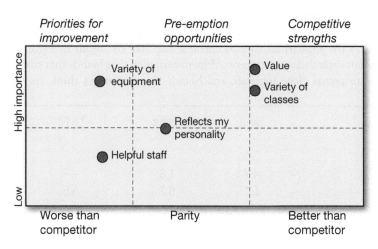

Figure 15.9

Perceptual Map (Attribute-Based) for Competitive Analysis

Along the horizontal axis, these data indicate that the BeFit Gym is perceived to be a good value and offers a good variety of classes, relative to the other gyms tested, but it is not as strong on the other attributes. Along the vertical axis, these data indicate that value, equipment, and classes are the most important features of the gyms, whereas a gym having a helpful staff is less so.

This very simple construction (simple survey, simple data analysis, simple plotting) of an attributed-based perceptual map yields pretty helpful insights. The gym has strengths, including some in areas that are important to customers. Unfortunately, the gym is seen as weaker in some areas that are also important (e.g., variety of equipment). Attributes on which a brand is doing poorly and yet that are important to the customers would be priority number one for fixing.

Multidimensional scaling (MDS) takes a slightly different approach. Rather than asking customers, "What's important?" MDS simply starts by asking, "How similar are these two brands" for every pair in the set. So in Figure 15.10, the first ratings are the similarities judgments for all pairs of the four gyms. The next ratings cycle through each gym, and ask how each brand rates on each of a number of attributes.

Figure 15.10

Perceptual Mapping (Multidimensional Scaling)

How similar are these cars?

	Very similar						Very different
BeFit Gym & Gold's Gym	1	2	3	4	5	6	7
YMCA & LA Fitness	1	2	3	4	5	6	7
LA Fitness & BeFit Gym	1	2	3	4	5	6	7
Gold's Gym & YMCA	1	2	3	4	5	6	7
BeFit Gym & YMCA	1	2	3	4	5	6	7
Gold's Gym & LA Fitness	1	2	3	4	5	6	7

How does BeFit Gym rate on these qualities?

	Not great						Really great
Good value	1	2	3	4	5	6	7
Comfortable	1	2	3	4	5	6	7
Fun to drive and own	1	2	3	4	5	6	7
Attractive design	1	2	3	4	5	6	7
Reflects my personality	1	2	3	4	5	6	7

(Then the other brands are rated on the same qualities.)

Figure 15.11 shows what the similarities data look like. LA Fitness and Gold's Gym are seen as the most similar, and Gold's Gym and YMCA are the most different.

MDS takes the similarities data to create a map like the result in Figure 15.12. This figure represents brands as points in two dimensions, such that brands that customers think are similar are points close together, and brands that customers think are different are

Figure 15.11

Average Ratings over n = 75 Respondents 1 = "Very similar" to 7 = "Very different"

	BeFit	Gold's	LA Fit	YMCA
BeFit	—			
Gold's	5.0	—		
LA Fit	4.7	1.8	—	
YMCA	5.1	6.2	5.5	—

Figure 15.12

MDS Representation

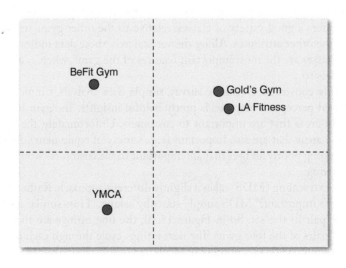

points that are farther apart. Hence, recall, LA Fitness and Gold's Gym were similar, and here they are close in space.

Next, the marketer must interpret the North-South/East-West of the map. To do so, we overlay the basic perceptual map with the attribute ratings to obtain Figure 15.13.[3] Now the interpretation is a little clearer. LA Fitness and Gold's Gym are similar, and what they have in common is that they offer a good variety of equipment, they seem to fit the users' personalities, and they have reasonably helpful staffs. (These two gyms project high onto those vectors.) BeFit Gym does well on classes and value, as we had seen in the raw data, and it does not fare as well on staff or the personality measure.

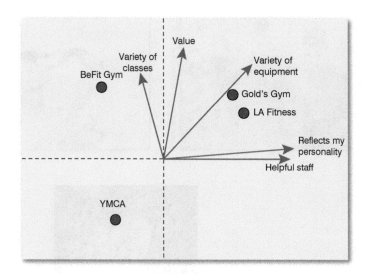

Figure 15.13

MDS Representation with Attribute Vectors

B2B

U.S. marketing research providers were surveyed and 56% said they were doing some B2B research. B2B marketing research also seems robust to economic fluctuations, at least compared to B2C marketing research.

- Some industries are bigger users of B2B marketing research (e.g., health care products and services, financial (banking, insurance, credit cards), and technology industries. Other industries use B2B research less, e.g., in consumer packaged goods and retailing, manufacturers tend to overlook their partners and instead go directly to the consumer.

- What kind of B2B marketing research is conducted? Clients ask for "attitude and usage" studies, and customer satisfaction surveys (66% of marketing research companies have conducted these studies within the last calendar year). They commission studies of brand tracking throughout their products' life cycles, from concept testing to later stages of new product development (50%). The next most popular kinds of marketing research projects examine ad copy testing and brand equity and market structure estimations (30%).

- How is the B2B marketing research conducted? Most respondents are contacted via phone and online reaches (42% together, 37% online only, 13% phone only). In person reaches are rare (4%) and good old-fashioned mail surveys, rarer still (1%).

These perceptual maps offer a great deal of descriptive information about current positions among competitors. It is a strategic question to consider possible repositioning efforts. Thus, for example, Figure 15.14 shows one of the directions BeFit is considering. If it can create more superficial personalization, it hopes to be seen as more personal and more fun as well.

Figure 15.14

BeFit Gym Re-Positioning as Personality Plus

15-4 FOCUS GROUPS FOR CONCEPT TESTING

There's something amazingly compelling about focus groups—watching a group of 8 to 10 consumers discuss your products and your competitors' products in the contexts of their lives. All the while, you're munching M&M's behind a one-way mirror and schmoozing with your colleagues. Focus groups are usually used as exploratory techniques, meaning, you don't quite know yet what questions you'd put on a survey. The sample sizes are smaller (running maybe 3 to 4 groups of 8 to 10 customers), so, really, predicting how the market-place will respond as a function of these focus groups is not a great idea. It's best to follow up the focus group leads with a larger-scale survey. But there's just something remarkable about watching a live person say something good, or bad, about your brand.

An exploratory technique is used in the early stages of a marketing inquiry. Most often, focus groups are used as a vehicle for concept testing in the early stages of new product development or when working toward the development of an ad campaign.

A person is hired to be a moderator, or someone who keeps the discussion going. The moderator tries to address all the items on the client's wish list, to bring out the quieter group members, to control the overbearing group members, etc. If the topic is a sensitive one (e.g., dealing with some health issues), it can help if the moderator is similar to the focus group participants (e.g., in age, gender, ethnicity) to put them at ease and establish rapport.

The moderator kicks off the group discussion with some warm-up exercise, e.g., going around the room with brief introductions and an easy question, e.g., "How do you use this product in your lives?" Then questions from the client are introduced, e.g., "Here are two different ads my client is working up. Which one speaks to you more, and why?" Then the discussion is off and running. "I like the sexier one" or "I disagree, I think the wholesome one makes better sense for this product," etc. When the discussion starts dwindling on this topic, the next topic is introduced. After one-and-a-half hours, the group is thanked, dismissed, and paid.

If you've been an observer, you should jot down notes about your impressions before your work team starts talking about what they think the conclusions are. If you weren't an observer, these sessions are usually taped, and, often as not, transcriptions made as well. Moderators are also usually paid to interpret the session because they have more experience than you in watching focus groups interact; they are in a better position to tell you whether to really worry about that one disgruntled member or that one overeager member, and so forth. On the other hand, you know more about your company and brand than any moderator, so the path to truth lies somewhere between the two extremes.

Other qualitative techniques are available, and they ebb and flow in their popularity among marketers. One is a set of observational techniques, ranging from having so-called secret shoppers act as customers purchasing your brand and competitors' to make comparisons, to having auditors watch consumers make choices in grocery store aisles or among clothing racks at the Gap. The strategy of brands and retail outlets, if done well, should be easily discernible; e.g., different stores' positioning should reflect themselves in different merchandise, different ambience, different frontline personnel, and, of course, different shoppers. Ethnographies are a mix of observation and interviews with other participants. While surveys can deliver large sample sizes and some certitude about numbers, qualitative methods offer rich, deep understandings of customers' motivations.

15-5 CONJOINT FOR TESTING ATTRIBUTES

Conjoint studies are very popular for questions of pricing, new products, and branding. The studies are run to understand how consumers make trade-offs. For example, in the design of a new product, engineers and R&D departments are always keen to add as many bells and whistles as possible, but then, of course, doing so drives up the price. So the question is: What do customers really want, if they can't have everything (all the features and a cheap price)? Conjoint analyses help uncover the attributes that are most valued by consumers and provide guidance as to the attribute values to combine for optimal product design.

Figure 15.15 presents all possible combinations of a new service that an airline is thinking of designing. The airline wonders what features its frequent fliers would like included in their loyalty program: Should there be access to an elite club at the large airports (yes or no)? Do the customers value being high priority for upgrades (yes or no)? Should the loyalty program and these benefits be free or available at a fee (e.g., $50 annually)? These three features are easily provided by the airline, so the question is: What do the customers want?

Anatomy of a Market Segment

Focus groups are used to elicit qualitative feedback on brand perceptions, testing new product concepts, reacting to "storyboards" depicting a potential ad campaign, etc.

Why are focus groups so popular?

- There is something compelling about watching customers talk about your brand.
- Also, they're flexible, they can probe to see whether something interesting comes up, the resulting data are rich and deep, they get at the why of customer behavior, they help generate some business ideas and clarify others, and the group dynamics can be synergistic and creative.
- On business specs, they're relatively inexpensive, and there is a ready industry of providers.

Focus group rooms can be set up for a variety of uses, such as showcasing products, like shampoo …

… Or technology like high-definition screens to show websites or new designs for a restaurant, retailer, hotel.

Matej Kastelic/Shutterstock.com

Focus groups can also be used to obtain quantitative ratings, but then the focus groups should be followed up on with more extensive surveying on larger, representative samples.

© Spencer Grant/PhotoEdit Inc.

A focus group room as seen from behind one-way mirror. The viewing room is where management gathers to watch the group discussions without interfering with the free flow of ideas and commentary.

© Jon Feingersh/Blend Images/Jupiterimages

Focus groups of the "future" are already here! There are participants in our town (in the room) and participants on the screen are in another city.

FAQs:

- How many in the focus group? Eight to ten.
- How many groups? ~Three (per segment).
- Moderator should be similar to participants if discussing "personal" (e.g., health) issues.
- Hire a company to do the focus group. If your team or your company runs the focus group, it will be biased.
- Ask focus group facilitating company for both video files and transcripts.

Figure 15.15

Conjoint
Design

Monthly 1 day $30/mo	Scheduled 1 day $30/mo	Monthly 2 hour $30/mo	Scheduled 2 hour $30/mo
Monthly 1 day $60/mo	Scheduled 1 day $60/mo	Monthly 2 hour $60/mo	Scheduled 2 hour $60/mo

The two (club) by two (upgrade) by two (pricing) design results in eight combinations (as in the eight boxes in Figure 15.15). Consumers are asked to rate or rank these eight combos in terms of their most to least preferred.

Figure 15.16 shows one flyer's data. The first five columns are data that are constant for every flyer; they comprise the design of the new service offerings. The consumer's judgments are the ratings in the last column. Perhaps not surprisingly, this customer would most prefer to have club access and upgrades for free. The very next question would be, okay, "If you can't have all that, what are you willing to give up?" If you give up the club access, that tells us you don't value that feature as much as upgrades and a free program. If you say you're willing to pay, then that tells us you want the perks (club access and upgrades) and are not price sensitive. Thus, even going from first preferences to second preferences, customers already begin to tell us about the attributes that are important to them and the trade-offs they're willing to make.

Figure 15.16

Conjoint Data
for 1 Customer

Row	Column	Schedule?	Window?	Fee?	Rating*
1	1	0	0	0	5
1	2	1	0	0	6
1	3	0	1	0	7
1	4	1	1	0	8
2	1	0	0	1	1
2	2	1	0	1	2
2	3	0	1	1	3
2	4	1	1	1	4

*Like the least 1 2 3 4 5 6 7 8 like the most predictor variables coded: 0 = no, 1 = yes

In a conjoint, we run a regression on these data: The variables "club," "upgrade" and "fee" are the predictors, and the consumer's judgments are the dependent variable, as in this model:

$$\text{Rating} = b_0 + b_1 \text{Club} + b_2 \text{Upgrade} + b_3 \text{Fee} + error$$

Running the numbers in Figure 15.15, the regression yields the following (b) weights:[4]

$$\text{Predicted rating} = 5 + 1 \text{Club} + 2 \text{Upgrade} - 4 \text{Fee}$$

The interpretation is this: We start in the middle of the scale (i.e., the five). Then, as the club variable goes from code of zero (no) to one (yes), preference ratings go up (by one unit).

As the upgrade variable goes from code of zero (no) to one (yes), ratings go up (upgrades are desirable, by two units). Finally, as the fee variable goes from code of zero (free) to one ($50), ratings go down (free is preferred to fee, by four units). The sizes of the weights are interpretable (as are the signs). Thus, we've learned that fees are the most important feature of this service offering, and club membership the least important.

It should be pretty clear how helpful this information would be in designing a new product or brand extension. What's also great, as you've seen, is that a basic conjoint is quite simple: both the data collection and the data analyses.

15-6 SCANNER DATA FOR PRICING AND COUPON EXPERIMENTS AND BRAND SWITCHING

Scanner data have reshaped marketing and business. Scanners began in grocery stores to help inventory management, but it quickly became obvious that the information obtained was far more valuable. Whenever you go to a grocery store, your purchases are scanned, and in that simple gesture, the company knows what you bought, how much of everything you bought, what brands you bought, and how much you paid for everything. If you offer your loyalty card for discounts and coupons, the company uses your buyer identification number to tie your current purchases to your past buying history.

In addition, these companies hire store and area auditors to integrate into the database what the prices were for competing brands, whether any brands were on sale or specially featured (e.g., in end-of-aisle displays), which brands were advertised in local weekend newspaper inserts, etc. Finally, beyond your grocery scanner swipes and

Big Data

Scanner data, CRM databases, or any huge data set requires "data mining."

- The databases contain millions of customers and SKUs.

- The analytical techniques aren't that different from those used on smaller data sets.

- The challenges of working with a large data set include IT (memory for storage) and time (for the number crunching to be completed).

- The largest practical concern for businesses is simply the coordination of disparate data. Data come from many sources:

  - Customer behaviors (e.g., purchase transactions, customer service and call center transactions, web site visitations, warranties registrations),

  - Attitudes (e.g., post-purchase satisfaction survey data, sales contacts follow-ups),

  - Demographic data (e.g., ZIP Codes from purchase data yield geographic and income estimates).

- The sources must be organized to have any value, before the data miners begin their dig.

the auditors supplementing the data, panels of consumers, hired by marketing research firms, agree to participate (usually for ridiculously nominal gain), have their media tracked (e.g., electronic hookups to TVs and the Web), and provide the companies with household information (income, ZIP Code, number and ages of children, etc.). Companies can use these single-source data to tie purchase patterns to demographics and media.

bleakstar/Shutterstock.com

Most companies need help to understand the onslaught of their big data.

These data can be used to forecast demand or to watch consumer responses as a function of all kinds of marketing mix activities. For example, if you want to know the answer to the question, "If we raise our prices by x amount, what happens?" These questions are answered via so-called causal, or experimental, methods. The idea is that, if you manipulate something (like price) and all else remains constant (which can be a big assumption in the real world), then any change in sales for your brand would be attributable to your intervention. Price or packaging can be tweaked in one market, in one store, or in one town, and subsequent sales can be compared to those in the other markets or stores that serve as the control group. This kind of study provides the cleanest test possible of the ROMI (return on marketing investment) of any marketing mix lever: Tweak the marketing, and watch the sales move.

Also, many things happen in the marketplace that you can't control. Maybe you don't raise prices, but your competitor does. Then what happens? This scenario is referred to as *naturalistic observation*: You're not tweaking the environment, but you're constantly monitoring it. You can still run regressions to try to forecast and understand what happens under different scenarios; it's just that it's likely that many factors are moving simultaneously, so it's more difficult to attribute sales differences to one localized action, such as a competitor's raising prices.

Experiments have the advantage of internal validity. This means that, when we tweak something and all else is held constant, we can be rather confident in our causal statements: "We did X, so the changes are attributable to X." Natural observation has the advantage of external validity, meaning that it's a little easier to believe that our findings will generalize to the real world because indeed it is unfolding in the real-world setting. These strengths are somewhat at odds. For example, field studies are conducted in the real world, so they are strong in external validity, but they tend not to be as clean in terms of internal validity. Often numerous alternative explanations must be eliminated before we can be certain about the reasons for the results we've seen. We may wish to attribute our sales increase over recent weeks to, say, our added promotional efforts, but we'd need to eliminate

Field Experiment

A brand manager was studying the effect on pharmaceutical sales of three classes of factors:

1. *Product characteristics*: Some drugs may sell better due to qualities inherent in the drug and its intended actions. For example, drugs taken to address chronic conditions (e.g., statins to lower cholesterol) or lifestyle choices (e.g., birth control pills) may well sell more than periodic pills for acute symptoms.

2. *Competitive strategies*: Some drugs may sell better because they come from certain firms, with a certain approach to business, as measured by its drug's FDA ratings, how long the drug has been in the market, the firm's order of entry (e.g., the so-called pioneer effect).

3. *Marketing and the promotional mix*: Some drugs may sell better because they have good marketing teams working on them. For example, they have a budget for detailing—i.e., having the sales force visit hospitals and doctors' offices to explain new drugs, to build relationships, and to provide samples.

What worked? Product characteristics helped sales (i.e., whether the product itself was good or not), and marketing helped sales. Not surprisingly, there was a synergistic boost between the two; i.e., good product supporting good marketing is the best of all worlds. Wondering about the company's business philosophy? It didn't make a dent. (For more info, see Latta's "What's Having the Most Impact?" at Quirks.com.)

the possibility that sales were going to increase naturally, due to reasons such as the seasonality of the product being sold. The good news is that the strengths of these two kinds of studies are complementary, so smart companies engage in both.

15-7 SURVEYS FOR ASSESSING CUSTOMER SATISFACTION

Many companies are interested in getting feedback from their customers. As a result, a little industry within marketing research has sprung up to offer their services at creating and evaluating customer satisfaction surveys. Surveys involve a bit of an "art," and so relying on someone with experience is a good idea. The basic idea is not complicated. You write survey questions, pretest them, and then put the survey out to a sample of your customers.

Questions about customer satisfaction can be as straightforward as, "How would you rate the service you just received at our car dealership: 0 = very dissatisfactory to 100 = very satisfactory." It's also common to ask customers how the purchase rates compared to their expectations; e.g., "How did your visit at our hotel seem to you? 1 = Fell short of my expectations, to 4 = Met my expectations, to 7 = Greatly exceeded my expectations."

Beyond customer satisfaction, many surveys ask about repurchase intentions and intentions to generate word of mouth; e.g., "How likely is it you would fly with our airline again, for your next trip? 1 = Very unlikely to 9 = Very likely." And, "I am going to tell my friends to come to this restaurant: 1 = Strongly disagree to 5 = Strongly agree."

It is important to include survey questions that will be actionable. If customer satisfaction is high, that's great. If it's low, some diagnostic questions must be asked that point to the measures a company should take to enhance customers' perception of quality (recall Chapter 14).

Surveys are supposed to be short, so the respondent doesn't have to endure much pain or boredom, and shorter surveys enhance response rates. Responses are kept confidential, for research purposes only, not for subsequent sales opportunities. Marketing researchers are supposed to attend to strict ethics (for AMA's standards, go to ama.org). Respondents can be consumers or B2B customers. Surveys can be administered in person (e.g., the people who intercept you at shopping malls with clipboards), over the phone, via fax, and increasingly on the Web.

What's cool about surveys is that you can ask customers about anything. Even more impressive is that they'll answer you on just about anything. Recall the NPO segmentation study earlier in this chapter. We had 11 survey items, rather a lot of variables. A first step to simplify the analysis would be to reduce that number. That reduction is done by means of factor analysis.

Factor analysis is a technique that begins with a correlation matrix, like that in Figure 15.17. (This set of variables is a subset of the NPO study, to keep things simple.) Factor analysis examines the strong and weak correlations to identify underlying factors common to the responses. Some of these correlations are larger than others, indicating that perhaps they're measuring the same underlying concept or factor. If two items are highly correlated, then we could take advantage of the fact that they're somewhat redundant by maybe just taking an average of the two items as we proceed to other models, such as regressions and forecasting.[5]

	Q5	Q11	Q9	Q10
Q5 = Higher education is very important	1.00			
Q11 = I would help sponsor a kid . . .	0.93	1.00		
Q9 = Only the very privileged . . .	0.48	0.52	1.00	
Q10 = Higher ed is too expensive	0.25	0.25	0.91	1.00

Figure 15.17

Correlations Among Some NPO Survey Items

Figure 15.18 provides the factor analysis solution. Within each factor, we're looking at the large numbers because those items "define" the factor. Thus, these results indicate that a perception of education being important and a willingness to help out hang together; i.e., many of the customers who rated education as important (or unimportant) also rated a higher (lower) willingness to sponsor. All this is to say that the items were correlated and perhaps form a single factor. The second factor reflects the apparently overlapping opinions that only privileged people can go to college and that college is too expensive.

	Factor 1	Factor 2
Q5 education important	0.94	−0.01
Q11 help sponsor	0.96	0.01
Q9 only privileged	0.18	0.89
Q10 too expensive	0.12	0.99

Figure 15.18

Factor Analysis on NPO Data

The computer produces a matrix that looks just like this figure, and it's up to the marketer to interpret what each of the factors "means." The meaning is driven by whatever the variables with high coefficients seem to have in common. For example, for factor two, we have to decide what "privilege" and "too expensive" have in common—something about money, obviously.[6]

Helpful Data

Here are some helpful data sources:

Stats on people and economies

- *U.S.*: census.gov, usa.gov/statistics, ita.doc.gov
- *Global*: worldbank.org, un.org, country-data.com, greenbook.org, euromonitor.com

Big, full-service marketing research providers

- Nielsen.com, iriworldwide.com, quirks.com, npd.com

Special interests

- *Small biz*: sba.gov
- *Europe*: esomar.org
- *Asia*: apec.org
- *Latin America*: latin-focus.com
- *Health care industry*: dssresearch.com
- *Media*: www.arbitronratings.com
- *Customer satisfaction*: jdpower.com

Factor analysis and cluster analysis are nicely complementary techniques. A factor analysis can be used first to group variables into factors. Then a cluster analysis can be used, using the smaller set of factors (rather than the larger set of raw variables) to group customers into segments.

MANAGERIAL RECAP

There are many marketing research techniques, and just about any can be used to *address marketing* questions related to the 5Cs, STP, and the 4Ps. In particular, some methods nicely match some market*ing* responsibilities:

- Cluster analysis identifies groups of similar customers and ideal for segmentation studies.
- Surveys and MDS are used to create perceptual maps, which are useful in assessing current competitive positions.
- Focus groups offer a natural vehicle for investigating customers' early reactions to corporate ideas, e.g., new product concepts, new advertising approaches.
- Conjoint methods ask respondents for preference trade-offs, which allows marketers to infer the attributes that customers value most.
- Scanner data allow the investigation of brand switching and loyalty and price sensitivity and the conducting of marketing experiments.
- Surveys are very flexible, and these days are common instruments for assessing customer satisfaction. Survey results can be cleaned up and simplified using factor analyses.

Chapter Outline in Key Terms and Concepts

1. Why is marketing research so important?

2. Cluster analysis for segmentation

3. Perceptual mapping for positioning

   a. Attribute based

4. Focus groups for concept testing

5. Conjoint for testing attributes

6. Scanner data for pricing and coupon experiments and brand switching

7. Surveys for assessing customer satisfaction

8. Managerial recap

Chapter Discussion Questions

1. It's common for a top-level manager (i.e., your boss) to watch a single focus group and get excited about something a customer says, and prepare a marketing plan around it. Why do you know this is premature? How would you handle your boss?

2. Imagine designing a conjoint for your b-school's café. In particular, you're in charge of the daily pizza orders. Pizzas are tricky—while they're a simple food, they can be created in a zillion combinations. What factors should you test in terms of your fellow students' likely preferences? Wheat crust vs. white, thick vs. thin, plain cheese vs. sausage vs. sausage and green pepper vs. vegetarian (you get the picture). Design a conjoint that would result in identifying 2 or 3 popular slices that your café managers could order every morning. The student body knows you're responsible—how do you make most of them happy?

Video Exercise: Research Design at LSPMA (14:25)

Lake-Snell-Perry-Mermin Associates (LSPMA) is a decision research firm that works on behalf of clients to determine what different segments of the population believe and feel about issues of interest to the clients. A third of LSPMA's work is for political candidates, another third is work for progressive issues organizations, and the remaining third is work for foundations and major institutions. LSPMA uses telephone polls, online polls, and in-person and online focus groups to collect data and to identify population (or audience) segments. Audience segmentation enables an LSPMA client to identify groups of people who are supportive of its issue(s) or cause(s), groups who can be converted to being supportive, and groups who will never be supportive. A client can then target its resources toward connecting with and persuading those segments that are likely to be the most receptive to the client's message. The research enables the dividing of the audience into segments; once segments are identified, they are tracked in future decision research. Although audience segmentation can be useful, it can make the population seem more divided than it actually is.

Video Discussion Questions

1. Why do political organizations need marketing research conducted by LSPMA?

2. What is the relationship between marketing research conducted by LSPMA and identifying the needs and wants of specific market segments?

3. Why would a business rely on a marketing research firm that is heavily into political polling?

MINI-CASE

How to Design an Attractive Wearable Redux

Recall from Chapter 1, an electronics firm was contemplating what attributes would appeal to its customers if it were to issue a new wearable. The features that the brand team focused on, and the dummy variable codes, were these:

- Design appearance: small smartphone (1)   wristwatch (0)
- Apps activated by: touch (1)   voice (0)
- Annual Fee: $0 (1) $20 (0)
- Co-branding with teams: yes (1)   no (0)

They ran a conjoint study on every 10th customer who came into one of their retailer partner's stores until they had a sample of 100. The 4 factors listed above result in 16 combinations ($2 \times 2 \times 2 \times 2 = 16$). Each person rated the 16 possibilities from 1 (would not consider buying such a wearable) to 100 (would definitely purchase such a unit). The regression results follow:

Wearable attractiveness = 0.6 design + 0.2 activation + 0.9 fee + 0.1 co-branding.

Case Discussion Questions

1. What features matter to customers, and which do not?

2. What would the optimal wearable look like? If you were to cluster the customers first, and then run a separate conjoint on each cluster, do you think the results would vary? Could the company create different wearables to satisfy multiple segments?

3. Are you worried at all about the sample—are customers who visit the retailer representative of those who might purchase online?

4. What features do you wish the company had included that might appeal to customers more?

MARKETING STRATEGY 16

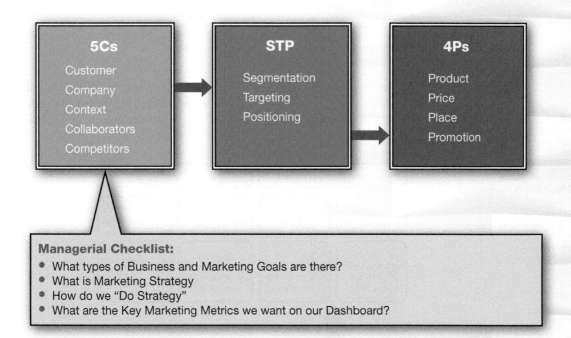

5Cs	STP	4Ps
Customer	Segmentation	Product
Company	Targeting	Price
Context	Positioning	Place
Collaborators		Promotion
Competitors		

Managerial Checklist:
- What types of Business and Marketing Goals are there?
- What is Marketing Strategy
- How do we "Do Strategy"
- What are the Key Marketing Metrics we want on our Dashboard?

Strategy can mean a lot of things, so we'll begin by discussing business and marketing goals, and then we will look at several approaches to thinking about marketing strategy. We'll assess our company's current standing and what it will take to achieve our goals. Then we'll consider measures to evaluate the extent to which we've been successful at doing so.

16-1 TYPES OF BUSINESS AND MARKETING GOALS

Let's begin by thinking about business very simply. Then we'll see more clearly what marketing goals should be set to achieve the broader business goals.

No company is in business merely to break even year after year. Even nonprofits want more money to be able to support their socially responsible missions. So let's agree that growing profit is the ultimate goal. Even that simple statement can be achieved via multiple paths. We know that:

(1) Profit = Sales Revenue − Costs

Breaking the right-hand side down into its components:

(2) Sales revenue = Sales volume (in units) × Price
(3) Costs = Variable costs + Fixed costs

If we plug equations (2) and (3) into equation (1), we obtain:

(4) Profit = (Sales volume × Price) − (Variable costs + Fixed costs)

Further,

(5) Variable costs = Variable unit costs × Sales volume (in units).

Thus, substituting (5) into equation (4), we see:

(6) Profit = (Sales volume × Price) − [(Variable unit costs × Sales volume)
        + Fixed costs].

Every year, a zillion new popular-press business books are published, each promising the secret to riches and fame. Equation (6) shows that there is no secret. The answer to riches is very simple (which is not to say easy). As Figure 16.1 also depicts, to increase profitability, we need to increase sales volume, change prices, or decrease variable or fixed costs.

Figure 16.1

$Cha-Ching

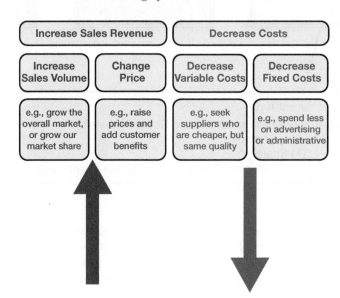

We can *grow sales volume* by:

1. Growing the market or the size of the overall pie.
2. Growing our market share or our slice of the pie. Either of these can be achieved by
3. Receiving more revenues from our current customers if we can up-sell to them our more expensive offerings, or
4. Getting our current customers to buy more frequently, or
5. Stealing customers from our competitors, or
6. Finding another segment whose needs might not be far from those of our currently satisfied customer base. We can
7. Create new products to satisfy our current customers or attract new ones. We can
8. Reduce brand switching of our customers out to other competitors by enhancing our brand equity,
9. Achieving lesser switching by means such as by raising our customer satisfaction, or
10. Adding value through a loyalty program, or
11. Otherwise raising switching costs so that leaving our brand is not attractive.

Strategies 1–11 give us 11 means of increasing sales already! We can also:

12. *Change prices.* Unfortunately, most companies think this option—cutting prices—as deceptively easy to do. A drop in prices may bring additional volume in the short term, per any economic prediction. But a marketer cares about the likely ensuing damage to the long-term brand image and brand equity. Operationally, low prices and low margins also necessitate the hassle of having to deal in large volume. Furthermore, when we were looking at pricing, we saw that striving to be the low-price provider often initiates price wars and worse future margins. A far more profitable option is to:

13. Raise prices, which yields greater margins. A terrific side effect of this simple attempt to bring in more revenue is that customers usually believe that high prices are a cue to higher quality—that is, higher prices are also beneficial to higher-end brand positioning. Such an enhancement of perceived benefits to the customer also leaves the customer

14. Less price sensitive. If our customer information indicates that, unfortunately for us, they are price sensitive, we can

15. Shift our target segment to more upscale buyers.

In our business delivery, we can tighten up our system to *decrease variable costs.* We can

16. Try to find less expensive but requisite quality suppliers, or

17. Outsource the parts of our business that appear to be expensive for us but might be scalable and less expensive for a business partner, or

18. Choose to become a niche provider, to keep units down and price higher for our special customers.

Definitions from Dictionary.com

- *Goal*: The purpose toward which an endeavor is directed; an objective
- *Objective*: Something that one's efforts or actions are intended to attain or accomplish; purpose; goal; target
- *Strategy*: A plan, method, or series of maneuvers for obtaining a specific goal or result

In general, we need to become a leaner provider.

The other cost-related lever is to *decrease fixed costs.* We can:

19. Spend less on R&D, unless our company prides itself on being innovative, or

20. Spend less on advertising. It's probably not a good idea to cut out advertising per se, so that our brand associations won't suffer in the future. But we can certainly cut advertising spending by being more creative with our current advertising dollar, e.g., fewer TV spots, more social media. We can

21. "Milk the brand," an expression that will make more sense in a moment, but briefly the idea is to just let our strong brands speak for themselves and not spend much on their continued development or maintenance.

There—just beginning, we've already listed 21 approaches! Next, we'll see these ideas and more in other contexts.

Strategy Snippets:

- P&G owns the high-end diaper market in the U.S. but had to figure out how to translate that in China. They thought they'd have diapers made there locally (to reduce costs and keep prices lower), but those failed. P&G is having much better success selling high-end diapers, with the new claim, "Made in Japan!"
- India may have variable infrastructure, but a company can get around that. PepsiCo will start selling Doritos, Tostitos, Pepsis and Mountain Dews to Indian customers directly, online.

16-2 MARKETING STRATEGY

There are numerous strategy gurus, each with a favorite approach to framing business and marketing situations. We'll look at the most popular frameworks. Marketers take responsibility more for increasing sales revenues and tend to pass much of the responsibility for decreasing costs to the operational side of the business. So it will come as no surprise that these strategic perspectives follow suit, emphasizing increased sales more than decreased costs.

16-2a Ansoff's Product-Market Growth Matrix

One very popular strategic tool makes no bones about it: It's all about sales growth. The question is what will be the source of that growth? Will we stick with our current product portfolio and simply try to get more purchases from our current customers or attract new customers? Can we create new products that might appeal to our current customers or use them to attract new customers? In other words: new stuff or new peeps?

Figure 16.2 shows all four possible product and market combinations. In the upper left of the matrix, we see the strategy of *market penetration*. In this scenario, we have no plans of expanding our product lines, nor do we seek new customers. We will simply encourage our current customers to purchase from us more frequently. This strategy is low risk, but obviously it also might max out quickly.

Figure 16.2

The Ansoff Product-Market Growth Matrix

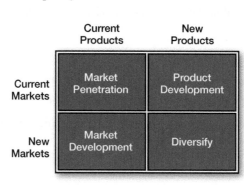

In the lower left, we still have no new products, but we're reaching out to new customers. We're hoping to construct *market development*. Perhaps we have found a new use for our product that naturally suits a new customer segment, or perhaps we plan to advertise through new outlets (e.g., social media) to reach different demographics (e.g., younger customers).

In the upper right, we are introducing new products to our current customers. This *product development* strategy might fit well for a company that prides itself on being innovative, but it might be more of a stretch for relatively conservative companies. Entertainment and high-tech industries are masters of creating new products; they have the template (e.g., a DVD), and they just tweak the content. This approach is also thought to be a great way to really delight one's customers and strengthen their loyalty to us—by giving them even more value.

Finally, in the lower right, we have *diversification*, the most difficult and therefore riskiest strategy in this framework. We are trying to introduce new products to new customers, and obviously we're out of our depth in both. It is smarter to achieve diversification after first going through product development or market development; i.e., get to know either a new product line or a new customer base before trying to do both simultaneously.

16-2b The BCG Matrix

Figure 16.3 shows the BCG matrix, another strategic framework that has been useful to marketing managers for portfolio analysis. It is also all about growth—the industry's growth and the company's relative growth compared to competitors within the industry. The company does a self-assessment of its overall business and an assessment of the industries in which it competes. All of a company's products (or brands) are classified according to whether each has a strong or weak market share and whether that market share occurs in the context of a slow or growing market.

Relative Market Share

	High	Low
High	Star	?
Low	Cash cow	Dog

Market Growth Rate

Figure 16.3

The BCG Matrix: Portfolio Analysis

The classes have memorable labels. A brand with a relatively large share in a growing market is called a *star*. Conversely, a brand with small share in a market that's not growing is called a *dog*. The other classifications are *cash cows*, describing brands that are doing well (strong market share), in a non-growth industry, and *question marks*, which are brands that aren't doing well in an industry that is.

A company wants to optimize the number of its stars. It will also fiercely protect its stars. Thus, if company A's strategy is to enter into the market space near company B's star, company B will typically move swiftly to do whatever necessary to hold onto its star.

> *To grow: make new stuff or find new peeps.*

Cash cows are also desirable. These brands are literally milked; that is, usually advice is given that not much marketing attention (or budget) should be paid to these brands. It's not clear that that's great advice because, in the spirit of a product's life cycle, withdrawing marketing support can propel a brand into faster decline. But the overall point is that the brand is very strong (awareness, trial, repeat purchasing, loyalty, etc.), and it is being leveraged for the greater good of the company by not devoting resources to it.

The future of question marks is somewhat unknown and also somewhat under the company's control. The industry shows potential, so the company might wish to support the brand with richer marketing (quality improvements, promotional campaigns, temporary price cuts to attract more trial) in an attempt to transform the question mark into a star

Many places try to appeal to the growing customer interest in medical tourism.

with an enhanced market share. These question mark products may be in development via new technologies, entering different markets, etc., and they may need time and additional supporting resources to pay off for the company.

Finally, the dog brands should be minimized. The company could just let them be, and reap whatever profits they bring in, however meager. Alternatively, if these brands have any residual value, they're also candidates for divestment. Note that moving a dog "west" to become a cash cow is not easy and moving it "north" to be a question mark doesn't give us clear closure. (What will that question mark become?) So, who let the dogs out? Probably the brand manager.

16-2c **The General Electric Model**

The so-called General Electric model is a strategic tool that forces the marketing manager to make explicit some judgments about the brand's (or the company's) performance, as well as the assumptions that the company operates under with respect to expected performance.

As shown in Figure 16.4, two dimensions are measured: market attractiveness and business strength. These dimensions are analogous to the external and internal pieces of SWOT analyses. For the external element (market attractiveness), the particular ratings might vary, but in this example, the strategist is asked to fill in two sets of numbers:

1. *The figures in the column labeled "Weights":* How important is sales volume, market growth rate, and competitive intensity to the firm? Constrain these weights to sum to 1.0.

2. *The perceptions about how well the brand (or company) is doing in each of those areas:* The ratings are made on a 1–5 scale, where 1 = awful and 5 = outstanding.

For the internal element called business strength, a number of sub-dimensions are also rated, both for importance (the weights) and the achievement level (the performance ratings).

Next, we multiply the weights and ratings to obtain the numbers in the "Value" column. Those values are summed, and the sums are plotted in Figure 16.5.

Figure 16.4

**The General
Electric Model**

Market Attractiveness		Weight	Rating (1–5)	Value
	Sales volume	0.2	4	0.8
	Market growth rate	0.4	3	1.2
	Competitive intensity	0.3	4	1.2
				3.2

Business Strength		Weight	Rating (1–5)	Value
	Market share	0.2	3	0.6
	Brand strength	0.2	3	0.6
	Unit costs	0.6	2	1.2
				2.4

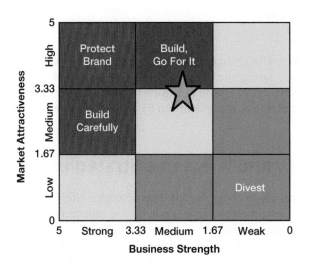

Figure 16.5

**The General
Electric Model**

This brand or this line of business is in a moderately attractive market, but the brand or firm is not doing as well as it might. Obviously, controlling the attractiveness of the market is difficult, but we need to find a way to get our business strength score up. Ideally, we'd be in one of the green (go-go-go) cells. We want to avoid the red disaster cells.

When we look at our business strength scores (Figure 16.4), we can diagnose that we are apparently an expensive shop; we need to control our costs better. These scores are important (the largest weight by far), and we get our lowest performance scores here. We're not doing remarkably well on market share or brand strength either, but neither of those facets are as important (at least according to our own previously stated judgment).

16-2d Porter and Strategies

Porter offers another approach to classifying strategies.[1] He says, generally speaking, a company can dominate its market in one of three ways. First, it can strive for *cost leadership*, producing goods and services more efficiently than the competition. To deliver that, the company might have such resources as easy access to plentiful, good raw materials, cheaper labor sources, better information, or other technologies, etc. The cost savings might be passed along to customers in the form of low prices, or they might be retained as higher margins than those of the competition, thereby fueling other actions, e.g., R&D, more advertising, etc.

Second, a company might take the approach of *differentiation*. This strategy is an attempt to distinguish one's products as unique in the industry. Differentiation may be fostered through excellent quality in products and customer service, distinctive design, exclusivity, value-addeds bundled into the core purchase, etc.

Porter Examples

- Cost leadership: "We're efficient!"
  - Costco, Dollar General, jetBlue, Priceline, Walmart
- Differentiation: "We're unique!"
  - BMW, Build-a-Bear, Nordstrom, Volvo
- Focus: "We do one thing very well!"
  - Jeep, Lego, Redbox

Porter calls the final approach *focused*. Whereas the cost leadership and differentiation approaches are said to be broad, the focused strategy is narrow. The mantra of these companies is typically, "We do one thing very well." Such players often serve niche markets, and customers in that segment can be very satisfied, very loyal, and rather price insensitive.

16-2e Treacy and Wiersema Strategies[2]

Another major approach to classifying business strategies offers a slightly different set of three philosophies. Companies can seek to achieve and maintain *operational excellence*, *product leadership*, or *customer intimacy*.

Operational excellence is the ability to deliver products or services smoothly and reliably. In some industries, it is a necessity; e.g., a package delivery company or a cell phone company wouldn't go far if they could not provide excellent operations.

Product leadership is achieved by providing predictably excellent quality in products and services or by being a market leader in terms of innovations in those products and services. The churn of new products in high-tech and electronics is a show of competing for product leadership. Just watch who's producing the newest, coolest toy.

Treacy and Wiersema Examples

- Operational excellence: "We're smooth and reliable!"
  - Dell, FedEx, IKEA, McDonald's, Southwest Airlines, TurboTax
- Product leadership: "We're excellent and special!"
  - Apple, BMW, Johnson & Johnson, Mont Blanc, Sony
- Customer intimacy: "We know our customers very well!"
  - Amazon, Home Depot, Fidelity Investments, IBM, Lexus, Verizon

Customer intimacy involves the knowledge of customers' fuller set of needs, and trying to offer them a full package of benefits, highly tailored to their unique desires. While there are non-tech versions of intimacy (e.g., a customer's relationship with a good hairstylist, realtor, banker, etc.), it's no surprise that this approach is huge—and hugely effective—online. On the Web, customer relationship management hits new highs because of the data storage and access capabilities. Hence, all the recommendation engines for books, music, movies, and such demonstrate a strong advance toward customer intimacy.

In sum thus far, there are probably as many ways to think about strategy as there are strategy theorists. We will describe a few more as the chapter unfolds, but these—Ansoff, BCG, GE, Porter, and Treacey and Wiersema—are the biggest.

16-3 HOW TO "DO" STRATEGY

While the word "strategy" sounds abstract, in truth it is usually grounded in practicality. A company must know itself, its environmental context, its competitors, its collaborators, and, of course, its customers (yes, the 5Cs) before knowing where it wants to go next or deciding there is a problem to solve or an opportunity to exploit.

Strategic planning involves a reflection on our corporate identity. We pose the questions: Who are we? Who do we want to become? Stated differently, recall the $2 \times 2 \times 2 \times 2$ positioning matrix in Chapter 5. The questions are: Are we positioned where we want to be? Do we wish to be high quality, high price, selective promotion, and exclusive distribution? Or do we wish to be basic quality, lower price, broader-band promotion, and mass distribution? If we wish to vary from either of these extremes, why do we think that makes sense for us? How do we proceed?

Strategic planning questions may be revisited for a number of reasons:

- A company may simply be a thoughtful, reflective one that revisits its assumptions from time to time.

- The company may be considering launching a new product, or a line extension, or a new partnership, or something new, and it wants to be smart about it, either by being consistent with its current business or in using the new action to move purposely through the positioning matrix.

- Contextual issues may arise, such as the economy's tightening up, or a competitor's getting acquired by an international company.

- A company or industry might be experiencing changes in profitability or in its component drivers (equation 6).

Note that these scenarios are easily discoverable via periodic SWOT analyses. That's terrific, since SWOTs are so easy to do and to communicate.

Corporate Ethics

- If a company screws up, how should it be punished? A firm can't go to jail. Picking some executives as scapegoats doesn't capture the complexities of decision making in large organizations. So, a company pays fines. But who really pays the fines—the company can increase their prices to recapture its finances! Plus, the fines are tax-deductible!

- Is it okay when consumers don't know certain facts? For example, Miller markets "Plank Road" beer as if it's from a small brewery and Disney produces R-rated films under the name, Miramax. Some might argue that it's impossible to tell customers everything about their products and how they're made.

- What about pricing—what constitutes a "fair" price? Economics tells us that the right price is where the supply and demand curves cross, but does that mean it's fair? When buyers and sellers agree on price in their negotiations, does that mean the price is fair? Customers often complain about prices being too high, but they rarely understand the complexities of a company's costs (e.g., for wireless phone service, health care provision, etc.). If we also believe in the economic premise of utility maximization, and so believe that buyers and sellers are both looking out for their own interests, how often or how easily could they arrive at a price they both consider fair? As a final twist, consider that economists might say that the market determines the price, but marketers want more than a single transaction with their customers.

- In their Sustainability Survey, PricewaterhouseCoopers reported the top reasons that companies try to be socially responsible. The reasons aren't exactly altruistic. Companies hope their responsible actions will provide them an enhanced reputation, a competitive advantage, cost savings, and a way to meet industry trends. A survey of MBA students said they thought that the benefits to companies would be a better public image or reputation, greater customer loyalty, a more satisfied and productive workforce, and fewer regulatory or legal problems.

- Some nice corporate practices:
  - Xerox employees who are selected for its Social Service Leave Program can take a year off with full pay to work for a community nonprofit of their choice.
  - Green Mountain Coffee Roasters pioneered in helping struggling coffee growers by paying "fair trade" prices (which exceed regular market prices), and offering microloans to coffee-growing families.
  - Chick-fil-A supports foster homes, summer camps, and charity golf tournaments.
  - Home Depot no longer stocks lumber or wood products from endangered forests.

- For more, see Davidson's *Moral Dimension of Marketing* and the *Sage Brief Guide to Marketing Ethics*, LA, CA: Sage.

16-3a SWOT's S&W

An important assessment in strategic thinking is to know your company's strengths and weaknesses, and its corporate identity with regard to the company's typical philosophy toward the marketplace (see Figure 16.6). For example, some companies pride themselves on being innovative and want to invest in R&D so that they can enter the marketplace with cool new things frequently and regularly. Other companies have a more conservative, careful culture, so they will rarely lead temporally (although they may lead in market share). Similarly, some companies are more inclined to take offensive initiatives (initiating price wars or launching competitive advertising claims), while others are more likely to respond defensively.

Whether a company shows tendencies toward offensive or defensive actions isn't correlated with size; a company with a large market share may have the resources to take the initiative and lead the other players in a new direction, but small entrepreneurial companies frequently create something new in the marketplace that may elicit responses from other (bigger, older) competitors. In addition, the role that a firm plays in the marketplace can change over time—it is not unusual for a company to be more aggressive (risk seeking) in its youth and to age toward conservatism (risk aversion) when it has market share, sales, and customers to protect.

	Favorable	Unfavorable
Internal (Corporate)	Strengths	Weaknesses
External (Environment)	Opportunities	Threats

Figure 16.6

SWOT: Strengths, Weaknesses, Opportunities, and Threats

Companies can be referred to as leaders for various reasons. They may have the largest market share. They may have been first to market. They may be known for being innovative, quick to improve another company's ideas, a company known to please its customers, etc., showing leadership in any of a number of ways. And, of course, life is rarely black and white, so there aren't just leader and follower companies. There are leaders, quick followers, followers, also-rans, barely-in-the-games, etc.

Furthermore, while many companies think of themselves as innovative, it's not clear that being first to market is always a good thing. For example, launching really new products can be risky, adoption can be slow, and the pioneering company can take quite a hit. In comparison, the so-called quick-follower companies can learn from the leader's mistakes and benefit from customers' learning how the new offering might be valuable in their lives. Yet few companies want to think of themselves as quick-followers.

Finally, it's completely rational to have a slightly split personality in that a company can be a leader for some of its brands in their respective industries and more of a follower for its other brands. For example, the company's orientation to offense or defense may vary across its brand portfolio. Mature, cash cow brands are treated carefully, whereas more risk is taken with newer ventures. This distinction depends on the products' life cycles and the stage of maturity of their industries. Lastly, dynamics naturally coincide with the 5Cs, such as the economic context. If innovativeness is central to a company's identity and economic times are good, then venturing into a large-scale offensive action can be sensible. If the corporate culture is more conservative or if the economic context is weaker, then more moderate actions make better sense, such as mere line or brand extensions in the case of new product launches.

16-3b SWOT's O&T

A reexamination of strategic goals can also be brought on by changes in the external elements of SWOT or when observing the effects of the 5Cs on perceived opportunities and threats (see Figure 16.6). If market shares are being eaten away by new competitors or if our prices are no longer attractive to our customers, how shall we respond? These motivating questions would bring us to the strategy table.

When considering any variation of goals, keep in mind that, when all is said and done, there are really three strategies. The first two are a little lame, but they're done all the time. The third is more exciting, but naturally it's more complicated.

The first strategy is to *do nothing*. We'd let a brand sink or swim on its own with no infusion of marketing budget (and we'll probably watch the brand decline). This passive strategy might be used on a cash cow brand, to funnel funds to another brand that needs resource support.

The second strategy is to *do nothing differently* from the status quo. We may have a mature brand in a stable market, so we maintain business as usual—same price, same marketing support, etc. This strategy is somewhat non-thinking. If business is good, keeping on track seems sensible enough (i.e., "Don't fix what's not broken"), but when business drops or competitors step it up, a status quo strategy won't yield good results.

The third strategy is to *do something different.* Then the question is: What do we wish to change? Very common, very popular, and very timely goals follow.

- *Let's Make More Money!* Most organizations have monetary goals: A company can set sales objectives in terms of some currency or relative to other providers (i.e., market share goals). We can aim for profitability objectives, such as routing some cash cow monies toward some question mark brands. Sales goals can be stated in terms of units or of change from last year or quarter. Goals can be stated per region, e.g., minimal or typical growth in the company's standard markets but more aggressive growth in the company's newer markets. Sales goals can be formulated against investments made toward the current sales, per the philosophy underlying the ROI or ROM (return on marketing) or ROQ (return on quality initiatives), etc.

- *Let's Delight Our Customers!* A company can try to enhance customer satisfaction, create an attractive loyalty program to lock in customers, reward customers for being influential and spreading good word-of-mouth, etc. If marketing research indicates customization is valued, the firm might investigate whether it can offer such personalization profitably. Perhaps CRM systems could be used to tailor messages to the target segment better and, in turn, reducing acquisition costs and enriching customer lifetime value.

- *Let's Reposition Our Brand!* Strategic goals must integrate all 4Ps, but sometimes it seems like the focus is more on one P than the others. For example, goals regarding better promotional communications can include spending our advertising dollars more wisely, figuring out which media make most sense to our segments and for which part of the message. Place or distribution goals involve identifying what channels the target customers find most desirable. Perhaps multichannel touch points are no longer needed; e.g., some industries are successfully moving their value-sensitive segments to self-service or lower-cost channel interactions.

- *Goals About Broader Social Concerns.* Different goals arise when a company broadens its scope and sets goals beyond marketing and sales per se. The goals may reflect the health of the broader organization such as human resource and internal marketing (e.g., employee wages and benefits, career development, reduction of turnover, etc.) or societal concerns—giving back to "context" C (e.g., charitable or community contributions, boosting the stability of local employment, demonstrating leadership in environmentally friendly business practices, etc.).

The core of marketing is 5Cs, STP, 4Ps. Typically, we don't have control over all the 5Cs, but the other elements have some malleability. So, shall we seek new target segments? Change one of the 4Ps? If we change one P and we're truly practicing integrated marketing and wish to build consistency for brand equity, we need to be sure to examine how the other Ps are affected. For example, if the boss says, "We should raise prices," think through what the other Ps should look like to ensure that a consistent message is sent to the customer.

Corporate vision goals, not unlike personal goals, can be complex, numerous, interconnected, and at times overwhelming. And, like individuals making progress by focusing, companies usually make faster progress by choosing the goals that, at the moment, for the times (see the 5Cs) and for the company's philosophy seem the most important. After these goals are achieved or modified, the company can stake more territory and achieve more goals.

Nomad_Soul/Shutterstock

There are lots of ways to proceed. Marketing strategy helps define your choice.

16-4 KEY MARKETING METRICS TO FACILITATE MARKETING STRATEGY

How do we see our strengths and weaknesses through the eyes of customers? How do we know what our competitors are doing? We monitor marketing metrics.

An old management adage goes, "You can't manage what you don't measure." More recently, it's morphed into, "You measure what matters." The clear implication is that, if something is important to a company or its CEO, they're going to want to know how the company is doing. So it needs to be measured.

Measures are important both in the assessment phase (how we are doing) and in the strategic planning phase (what measures we will raise or lower). So let's consider some of the measures on goals that a company might pursue.

Measure what matters and make your measures matter.

First, we'll surely keep an eye on a company's profitability. It was the beginning of this chapter, and it is the motivating basis of a company's actions.

But let's look beyond just finance. We can also measure indicators such as customer or employee satisfaction, a company's stewardship of the environment, etc. In terms of marketing, we can look at sales, share, average prices, levels of awareness, and penetration in trial. Some of these measures should be correlated with a company's financial health. Some indeed will be leading indicators.

Much has been made lately of a company's so-called dashboard. The idea is that there are many indicators of a company's success, like the indicators on your car's dash representing fuel, speed, engine temp, and so forth. Alternatively, take the sporting analogy of a scorecard: How are we doing on RBIs, errors, scoring, etc.? Choose your analogy, but the point is that companies also have multiple dimensions in which they can be measured. Some measures will confirm the ways the company is great and has advantages over competitors. Other measures can serve as a diagnostic in identifying problems that the company can strive to perfect. Anyway, whether we're keeping score or we're monitoring the dash, what are we looking for?

Figure 16.7

Dashboard

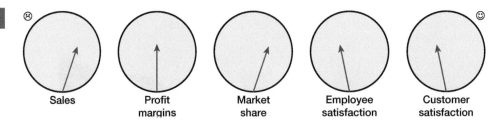

Figure 16.7 shows what a simple dashboard might look like for a company (or brand) whose sales are good, market share is good, profit margins are so-so, and employee and customer satisfaction aren't so great. What story does this profile of indicators tell? This particular brand operates in monopoly-like conditions; thus sales and share are indeed strong because the customers don't have many alternatives. The lack of options might contribute to the relative poor status of customer satisfaction. The company's weak profit margins suggest that it's not managing cost efficiently, which does not portend well for the poor employee satisfaction. Why are they dissatisfied? Are employees not paid well? Are they working with old equipment? The solutions to either of these problems would cause the profit margins gauge to tilt farther to the left.

Dashboard Measures

- *Financial:* Sales, profits
- *Marketing:* Share, customer satisfaction, average prices charged
- *HR:* Employee Satisfaction, low turnover
- *Operations:* Lean, mean, green, customer-pleasing machine

Dashboard indicators represent information analogous to what our car is trying to convey: Are we driving on empty? Are we going too fast? Is our engine overheating? What's the temperature in the car? And so on. When the gauges head to the center or to the left, there's not necessarily reason for panic, but the levers give us a heads-up: Is it time to ease off the pedal (stop pushing our employees), go get fuel (invest in new plant equipment), turn the A/C down (conduct some marketing research to find out what bells and whistles would make our customers happier), etc.?

Dashboards can take any shape. Figure 16.8 collects a number of diagrams in different formats that together express the attributes that this company cares about: revenue per customers over time and loyalty per segment, market share against the two primary competitors, quarterly customer satisfaction confidence intervals, and employee turnover per department. Use whatever format works for you. What's important is that you're overseeing multiple measures to optimally manage the company.

There are parts of marketing strategy that may sound overwhelming, but you can do it, and you can do it well! Remember: if you *think about* your customers, try to *think like* your customers, and simply *try to please* your customers, you will beat the competition. It is that easy. Really!

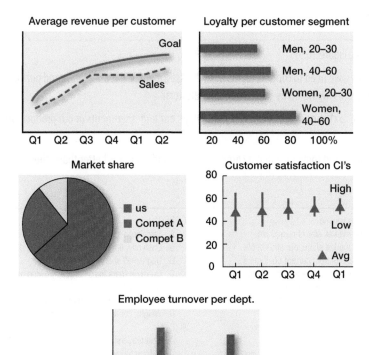

Figure 16.8
**Marketing
Metrics
Visualization**

Ag→Manufacturing→Services

- A recent report by McKinsey's Global Institute describes how manufacturing is important for developing and advanced countries. In developing countries, it is commonly acknowledged that manufacturing helps take a country's citizens from an agricultural subsistence to circumstances with greater incomes and living standards. By comparison, in already developed countries, manufacturing is still where a great deal of innovation and competitiveness occurs, R&D grows and contributes, exports are created, and indices of productivity grow.

- Globally, manufacturing typically creates some 16% GDP and 14% of employment. As manufacturing grows toward 20-35% of GDP, its relative contribution declines, not because manufacturing itself is in decline, but because as wages have risen and consumers have money to spend, they begin to spend more money on services, so it appears that service sectors grow and accelerate. Governments and educational systems are considered important conduits to the growth of either manufacturing or services, and to the transition from the one to an emphasis on the other. The results of manufacturing continue to dominate international trade—70% compared to 30% services, which are more likely to be created and consumed locally.

MANAGERIAL RECAP

Many marketing strategies can be successful (see Figure 16.9):

- Before even thinking about making changes, we need to conduct an honest self-assessment. What does our brand portfolio look like and what are our strengths and weaknesses, as measured by our dashboard indicators?

- Then we're ready to consider what we'd like to change and how we'd like to change: our target segments or our product, price, place, promotion.

- There are many ways to increase profitability, and some may fit our corporate culture and strengths better than other ways. There are also goals beyond profitability.

Figure 16.9
 	
Strategies, Strategies, and More Strategies to Increase Profits
	I. Growing sales volume
	  A. Grow the market, size of overall pie
	  B. Grow our market share, our slice of pie
	  C. More revenues from current customers
	    1. Up sell them our expensive offerings
	    2. Get them to buy more frequently
	  D. Steal customers from competitors
	  E. Find new customer segment(s)
	  F. Create new products for current/new customers
	  G. Reduce our customers' brand switching
	    1. Raise customer satisfaction & brand equity
	    2. Add value through loyalty program
	    3. Raise switching costs
	II. Changing price
	  A. Cut price, but worse margins and rely on volume
	  B. Raise prices
	    1. Cue to quality, customers price insensitive
	    2. Seek upscale buyers
	III. Decrease costs
	  A. Decrease variable costs
	    1. Find less expensive suppliers
	    2. Outsource
	    3. Be niche provider
	  B. Decrease fixed costs
	    1. Cut back R&D (if we're not "innovative")
	    2. Spend less (or smarter) on advertising
	    3. Milk cash cow brands
	IV. Ansoff Product-Market Growth Matrix
	  A. Market penetration
	  B. Market development
	  C. Product development
	  D. Diversification
		V. BCG
		  A. Star (large share, growing industry)
		  B. Cash cow (large share, non-growth industry)
		  C. Dog (small share, slow market)
		  D. Question mark (small share, growing market)
		VI. The GE model
		  A. Market attractive, business strength
		  B. Weight, combine, matrix insertion
		VII. Porter
		  A. Cost leadership
		  B. Differentiation
		  C. Focused strategy
		VIII. Treacy and Wiersema
		  A. Operational excellence
		  B. Product leadership
		  C. Customer intimacy
		IX. Positioning matrix
		  A. High quality, high price, selective promotion, exclusive distribution
		  B. Basic quality, low price, broad promotion, mass distribution
		  C. If veer from either, have a good reason
		X. Company & Portfolio Strengths
		  A. Offense or defense?
		  B. Aggressive (risk-seek), conservative (risk averse)
		  C. Leader or (quick) follower?
		XI. Currently popular goals
		  A. Make more money
		  B. Delight our customers
		  C. Reposition our brand
		  D. Broader societal concern
		XII. Ultimate strategy choices
		  A. Do nothing
		  B. Do nothing different
		  C. Do something: What? See above.

Chapter Outline in Key Terms and Concepts

1. Classic Marketing Strategy Models and Frameworks
   a. Ansoff's product-market growth matrix
   b. The BCG matrix
   c. The General Electric model
   d. Porter and strategies
   e. Treacy and Wiersema strategies
   f. SWOT
2. Types of business and marketing goals
3. Key marketing metrics to facilitate marketing strategy
4. Managerial recap

Chapter Discussion Questions

1. Consider the Treacy and Wiersema strategies for market dominance. Which of them (operational excellence, product leadership, customer intimacy) do you think guides these companies: Calvin Klein, Harley, Hermes, Lego, Microsoft, Nokia, Starbucks, Virgin.

2. What strategies would you say dominate corporate philosophies in these countries: the U.S., China, Japan, Germany, Brazil? Are their "brand managers" watching the right indicators?

3. Think of a company you'd like to interview with, and list 1-2 specific factors for each of Porter's five forces.

Video Exercise: Blu Dot (6:00)

Blu Dot cofounders Maurice and John discovered they did not like the furniture they could afford after graduating college and could not afford the furniture they wanted. Blu Dot was conceived as a business venture to address what was perceived as a void in the U.S. furniture market. The furniture market can be segmented into several levels, ranging from the promotional level of inexpensive furniture on up to expensive, high-end furniture that is custom designed and accessible only through interior designers. The challenge for Blu Dot was to merge the affordability of the low-end furniture market with the craftsmanship and quality of the high end. Each Blu Dot product is expected to rely on a smart design composed of two components, be simple to put together, use straightforward materials and manufacturing processes, pack flat, ship efficiently, and be attractive and interesting. Blu Dot's pricing is determined on the basis of cost plus the specified profit margin needed.

Video Discussion Questions

1. What would a SWOT analysis of Blu Dot reveal to a marketing professional?

2. What are Blu Dot's strategic goals?

3. Is Blu Dot's strategy one of cost leadership, differentiation, or focus? Explain your answer.

MINI-CASE

How to Watch Movies

Consumers looking for entertainment have many options. Each content provider has business strengths and weaknesses. For example, Netflix has a recommendation engine and a relatively vast library for streaming. Hulu can be freely accessed because of advertising sponsorship, but has limited selections, movies in particular, and in availability durations. Cable services' "on demand" features are not free, but some customers like the convenience of one-stop shop for cable and phone, etc., and selections are limited (in numbers and duration). Redbox has altogether different model, with vending for DVDs located in popular places (e.g., near McDonald's, in airports), interchangeable pick-ups and returns locations, and of course limited selections.

Case Discussion Questions

1. How would you advise any of these companies with regard to their strategy, positioning, and tactical execution? Take one (Netflix, Hulu, cable, or Redbox), and draw a scenario in which strengths might be retained, weaknesses strengthened or eliminated, and future directions pursued to make the business model more solid, more profitable, and less prone to competitive matching or attack.

2. Could a Blockbuster type of shop re-enter this arena; i.e., a storefront where consumers go to pick up and drop off DVDs, or is that customer model now defunct? If you could imagine it, what would you recommend they do? If not, imagine you were to design an entertainment provider from scratch (movies and video games, mostly), what would it look like—STP and 4Ps? What elements in the 5Cs are likely to be most relevant to address in the near future?

3. If these companies start looking even more similar and commodity-like in the next 3-5 years, how would you advise one of them to break out of the pack and distinguish itself by offering . . . what?

4. How can any of these providers take greater advantage of a CRM philosophy? Most of them have little by way of retention programs, e.g., customers can cancel or rejoin anytime. Are there any benefits for staying?

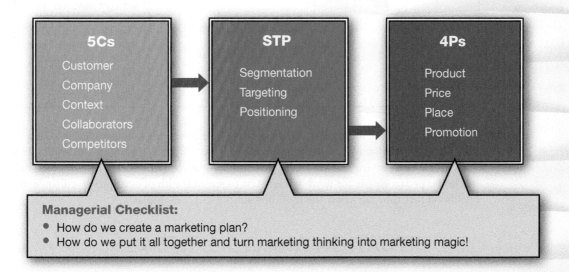

Managerial Checklist:
- How do we create a marketing plan?
- How do we put it all together and turn marketing thinking into marketing magic!

17-1 HOW DO WE PUT IT ALL TOGETHER?

You've been reading and reading about marketing. Now, as Nike would say, we need to just do it.

As Figure 17.1 indicates, the marketing plan begins with an executive summary. It provides a brief overview of the content of the larger planning document that follows. The marketing plan retraces the marketing framework. Figures 17.2 through 17.5 collect the main themes and call out questions from each of the previous chapters. Compiling these provides a good review, and seeing all the questions posed together gives perspective on how the pieces fit together.

A marketing plan begins with an assessment of where things currently stand. This situation analysis is documented by the 5Cs. We draw on those Cs to develop segments and choose segment(s) to target, per the strategizing that is STP. The STP section usually involves summaries of marketing research, e.g., a segmentation study. Marketing and financial goals then stipulate the objectives the company wishes to achieve and how success and ROI will be measured. The next big section is an action plan for positioning by implementing the marketing mix 4Ps. Typically, this section is long and detailed because it contains both the big picture on strategy and also the nitty-gritty details on tactics.

There are many workbooks designed to assist in writing a marketing plan.[1] They function like an interviewer, asking multitudes of questions about your brand. We'll proceed similarly.

The questions and logic in Figures 17.2 through 17.4 offer a static approach, but we have also created an interactive module, available online to guide you in creating a marketing plan.

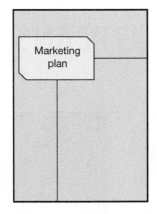

Figure 17.1

The Sections of a Marketing Plan Follow the Marketing Framework

Marketing plan

Table of Contents

1. Executive summary
2. Situation analysis (5Cs)
3. Market analysis and strategies (STP)
4. Tactical plans (4Ps)
5. Appendices

Executive Summary
A good executive summary is no longer than 1 page. It is a minireport, stating highlights and recommendations. It is self-contained and not a teaser. Details are provided in as many appendices as necessary. This summary is usually written in prose (full sentences), not bullet points.

In this chapter, we'll illustrate all three parts of a marketing plan, applying it to one of three different marketing scenarios: marketing a nonprofit, getting into social media, and launching a new service. Alternatively, we could look at the plan for a single product, but it is better pedagogically for newbie marketers to see a breadth of examples to enhance the likelihood that they can apply the tools beyond the single exemplar.

17-2 SITUATION ANALYSIS: THE 5CS

We'll begin by addressing the 5Cs with the scenario of being a marketing consultant for a nonprofit. The 5Cs of the marketing framework are blown up in Figure 17.2, with the managerial checklist questions posed from their respective chapters to remind us of the basic issues. Table A17.1 in the appendix to this chapter provides the marketing questions in the interactive marketing plan builder.

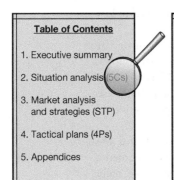

Table of Contents

1. Executive summary
2. Situation analysis (5Cs)
3. Market analysis and strategies (STP)
4. Tactical plans (4Ps)
5. Appendices

Situation Analysis

2.1. Customer
2.2. Company
2.3. Context
2.4. Collaborators
2.5. Competitors

2.1 Customer
- Describe segments' demo psychographics, buying behavior), level of satisfaction (measured?).
- Loyalty and CRM program useful? Get RFM, CLV.
- Price sensitive?
- Channels used?
- Changes now, future?
- Compare current and potential customers. Nonbuyers—why not?

2.2 Company
- Who are we (known for, good at)? Do a SWOT.
- What do we want to become? Formulate strategy

2.3 Context
- Political and legal (stable partners, new laws)
- Economy (growth, consumer mood)
- Society (demographic, attitudes)
- Technology (IT, other machines); threats or opportunities?

2.4 Collaborators
- Good supply chain relations?
- Good relations with downstream channel members?

2.5 Competitors
- Who are our major competitors, broadly defined?
- Their strengths?
- How might they respond to our actions?

Figure 17.2

Situation Analysis: 5Cs

Company. In a marketing plan, we'll start with a corporate self-examination. Much of the company C is knowing our own strengths, such as in a SWOT analysis, and knowing our goals, which we've delineated in the strategy chapter.

Recall the discussion in Chapter 15 about clustering types of NPOs. There seems to be an opportunity to create an NPO that provides scholarships to offset university students' expenses, especially if it is to achieve strong brand recognition (like so many successful medical or children's charities). Thus, an NPO was registered last year, called "Brain Trust." Some progress has begun, thus far only locally, but several good lessons have been learned that will facilitate rolling out nationally next year. So far, the answers to the company C questions on the marketing plan would be:

Company Questions	Proposed Answers
• What are we known for? Do a SWOT!	• A central point to coordinate the receipt and dispersal of scholarships, to enhance college attendance and graduation rates.
• Who do we want to become?	• A brand as well-known as Unicef or World Wildlife Fund so that we would be the first NPO that donors would think of when wishing to demonstrate their largesse.

Customer. If we don't start with a good understanding of our customers, we're toast. The only way to know our customers is to get data on them. We can begin by studying secondary data to know the background trends, but at some point, we're going to have to roll up our sleeves and get in touch with our customers. We need to get fresh data on our current customers, past customers, potential customers, our competitors' customers—everyone.

Consider writing a marketing plan for any product or brand.

Many NPOs have reasonably good data on their donors. Last year, Brain Trust began by renting lists of 50 universities' alumni and 10 cities' voter registration lists. Each person on the lists was sent two solicitations: One was a hardcopy mailing in mid-December (to cash in on the holiday spirit or in anticipation of annual taxes). The other was via email for some people (and hardcopy for others), and the months were varied (in an experiment to see when and how responses might be most favorable).

Donors were allowed to specify how their dollars are to be spent in terms of (1) the kind of students to support and (2) the particular universities they'd attend (as noted by the alumni lists). However, what was obviously the most appealing was the choice to support students by the topics they were interested in studying. For example, some employees from DuPont and 3M (at least according to their addresses) sponsored chemical engineering students, whereas several alumni of a liberal arts college near Los Angeles earmarked their provisions for drama students, etc.

The target age of donors from the alumni lists were between 30 and 60 years old. The voting lists' targets ran a little older, between 45 to 65.

Most donors enclosed checks of $20 or $50. Brain Trust doesn't yet have a loyalty program, but it is being scrupulous about putting any new information into its CRM database (which was first populated by the alumni and voting lists). For donations of $100 or more, the CRM database triggers the NPO to send out a nice calendar (each month has a picture of some well-known brainiac).

Brain Trust ran a couple of focus groups to explore various elements of their programs. One of the themes they heard was that people thought they had to donate large amounts of money, and they'd be embarrassed to give $5 or $10. In truth, obviously the NPO could use even small donations. With that description of the NPO's donors, we fill in their customer answers.

Customer Questions	Proposed Answers
• Demographics	• 30–60 or 45–65 years
• Psychographics	• Care about higher education
• Buying behavior	• Give $20 or $50 once a year
• Customer satisfaction?	• Never measured, assumed okay if repeated
• Do we have a loyalty program?	• No, but give a calendar for $100+ donation
• Why don't non-donors donate?	• They think they have to give large amounts.
• Channel for donors?	• Send check by mail
• Are our buyers price sensitive?	• Let donors know that giving only a little is okay and to give more frequently.
• Changes to expect?	• Should grow as awareness grows

Context. Regarding context, assess the macro-environmental issues you must attend to, e.g., legal, technological, social changes, and trends. If you're working in the industry, you'll be familiar with these factors. If you're new to the industry or job, start reading in-house white papers and go online and study up. Here are the basic questions to pose for an understanding of the business context:

Context Questions	Proposed Answers
• Economy	• Concerned with economy
• Politics	• Unknown; never tried a different appeal to Democrats and Republicans
• Legal	• N/A
• Technology	• Move more giving online, perhaps online videos of students' testimonials.
• Societal	• Emphasize the many benefits of an educated populace.

The NPO hopes giving will increase as the economy recovers; people probably don't want to give away money that they think they might need. The examination of the context factors pointed the Brain Trust people to something they hadn't considered before: the possibility that the Democratic and Republican donors might seek different things (e.g., education vs. fiduciary responsibility). So now they're thinking about how to explore that idea. No real legal issues have popped up, so they count themselves lucky (and we'll leave it alone). In terms of technology, it obviously would be easier for the NPO and more cost-effective if more donors would give directly online. In terms of broader societal concerns, the NPO mission seems to be already fairly enlightened.

Sometimes marketers gloss over these contextual factors, and sometimes that's okay. After all, many of these factors are relatively stable; we revisit the questions only as we see changes in the environments or as we change our company or brand or target segments. In addition, early in one's career, strategic decisions like, "Should we go into Indonesia or Brazil next year?" are few and far between. But, as you advance up the corporate ladder, increasingly your job responsibilities will become more global (literally), and you need to do a quick check to convince yourself that the factors aren't relevant in the new (to you) marketplace or, when they are, how they affect your goals and plans.

Collaborators. Networks of support functions can be complex. Even good relationships between providers in the supply chain and the firm or with the channel members downstream from the firm can be in flux, such as when new products are offered, with implications of shared shelf space or shared ad space, etc. We've discussed various means of trying to maintain good relations, so we'll begin by documenting the nature of those network ties.

The NPO admitted that they hadn't thought about collaborators per se before trying to do this marketing plan exercise. But doing so prompted them to consider who its suppliers and distribution partners were. One sense of the term "supplier" is the route through which the NPO obtained its list of potential donors. While that seemed to work, it also seems limiting going forward. In terms of the downstream channel, the NPO began to think about where they might place ads to reach a broader base.

Collaborator Questions	Proposed Answers
• Good relations with supply chain?	• Fine so far, perhaps try to partner with some professional associations?
• Good relations with distribution channel members?	• Perhaps post ads on professional sites, LinkedIn, etc., to broaden appeal

Competitors. In the spirit of a SWOT analysis, our strengths are defined somewhat relative to other providers in the marketplace. The discussion at the NPO was grim when the marketing plan turned to the question of competitors. While there may be few or no direct competitors (focused on higher ed), there are many competitors in the sense of an NPO to whom a person or household might give their donor dollar. Furthermore, many competitors dominated due to their very strong brand names. (It had to be pointed out to the NPO that, in fact, there are even zillions more NPOs, albeit relatively less known.)

Competitor Questions	Proposed Answers
• Who are they?	• Any donation behavior: medical and health, museums and the arts, etc.
• Competitors' strengths?	• Some have very good brand names.

At this point, we compile our NPO answers and have the basis for part one of the marketing plan: the situation analysis.

Situation Analysis for the NPO

Our current customers are: 30–65 years old and care about higher education. Their satisfaction is assumed okay if they donate repeatedly. We're beginning a CRM program and issue a calendar if they give $100 or more. This is what our customers do: They give $20 or $50 once a year, they send a check by mail, and they are price sensitive.

We need to tell them that giving only a little is okay and get them to give more frequently. Here are possible customer issues to consider: Giving is not strong yet, perhaps due to the economy or lack of awareness, so could we develop a loyalty program and convince them that giving only small amounts is still helpful.

Currently, as a company, our position is our uniqueness in the NPO world to support higher ed. This marketing plan is to further strengthen brand recognition.

Our current business environment reflects people's concerns with the economy. The NPO has never tried different appeals to Democratic and Republican donors; it is possible they seek different things. No legal issues are looming. We would like to move more of our donors' giving online, and perhaps there we could post small video clips of our students.

We might be able to leverage more donations if we partnered with some professional societies. We might consider a greater ad presence online, e.g., via LinkedIn.

Our competitors are many—whoever receives donations. In particular, certain competitors may be a threat, given the strengths of their big brand names.

17-3 **STP**

With the 5Cs nailed down, we should have a good background for understanding and interpreting our customer segments, which in turn offers a clearer basis for choosing the segments to target. Figure 17.3 blows up the STP portion of the marketing management framework for our planning purposes, and Table A17.2 in the appendix emulates the interactive module on the STP strategic questions and choices. We'll start with segmentation, and recall from Chapter 3 that numerous variables could be relevant: demographic, geographic, psychological, behavioral, and more.

Table of Contents	**3.1 Segmentation**	**3.2 Targeting**	**3.3 Positioning**
1. Executive summary 2. Situation analysis (5Cs) 3. Market analysis and strategies (STP) 4. Tactical plans (4Ps) 5. Appendices	• What kinds of customer knowledge do we need to form segments? (Do we have demographic, geo, psych data? Shall we run surveys?) • Use cluster analysis to identify segments, and descriptive data to validate the "marketing segmentation" scheme.	• Choose segments to target: • "Size" the market, estimate its profitability (lifetime customer value). • Consider fit with corporate goals, and actionability (can we find target).	• Positioning via perceptual maps. • Where are we in the positioning matrix? • Write position statement.

Figure 17.3

Market Analysis and Strategies (STP)

We're changing examples now, leaving the NPO behind, to look at STP in the context of a social media host company. This new scenario arose because some recent alumni have asked us to give some marketing consulting advice to them, to be passed along to a friend named J.J., who runs a social media and social networking site. The purpose of the site is to host friendship communications like any other social network service, but J.J. wants to sell travel vacation packages through testimonials and word of mouth. (We'd have to think through whether we believe this is a viable business concept, but for now, we're simply trying to create the heart of the STP part of a marketing plan.)

Naturally, to date, J.J.'s site isn't the size of Facebook, but he's got about 800,000 users who sign on at least once a month. When people sign up (for free), they are asked some basic demographic questions, which, of course, J.J. can tie to their online behavior. He can see that most of his frequent users are young (mid- to late-20s), most of whom are online to stay connected to friends. A very small proportion (less than 10%) click through and actually buy trips. He has almost no users 40 years old or older. He's okay with a younger profile, as long as they have some money to spend. He realizes that attracting people in their 30s and even 40s is likely to bring in more people with greater discretionary income. Compiling that description, we can characterize J.J.'s users, nonusers, and his aspirant users:

Segmentation Questions	Proposed Answers
• Current customers	• Mid- to late-20s, some stay connected to friends, some click through and buy trips
• Nonusers	• 40s and older
• Ideal customers	• Late-20s+ with good disposable income

In targeting, we need to choose segments that are big enough to pursue. Specifically, we'll consider whether the segments (1) have potential to be profitable enough, (2) have enough growth potential to pursue, (3) fit in with our corporate goals, and (4) are actionable, which often means finding an easily identifiable characteristic to serve as a proxy for the more central quality we're seeking.

For the online social network service, we helped J.J. crunch some numbers. He's a geek and loved seeing what we could do. It was already obvious to him that he wasn't making money off the people who went online to network but not to buy, but he hadn't previously had the concept (or the value) of his acquisition costs pointed out before. Thus, not only were these people not bringing in money, they were costing him real money. The people who eventually traveled took about a trip once every other year (the site is only about five years old, so these data, while better than nothing, are probably a little "soft"). The average trip purchased was $1,350, so, on average, this segment brought in about $625 a year. The stark monetary picture startled J.J. who had tried for a young, hip Website. His alumni friends are encouraging him to not worry so much about being hip and instead worry more about money, and therefore probably bringing in a slightly older, way richer crowd. They also helped him begin to prioritize his segments for potential outreach.

Targeting Questions	Proposed Answers
• Estimate size and profitability	• Friendship connectors bring in no direct $ and only minimal from WOM; buyers are worth $625 a year (they take one trip every other year, approx. $1,350).
• Corporate fit	• Maybe aim a little older; maybe we should stop trying so hard to be hip (we may be turning off older crowd).
• Rank desirability of segments	• 25–35—better disposable income than younger, and more time than 35–50 crowd

The P of STP is positioning. Positioning is executed via the 4Ps, and we'll turn to them shortly. We also recall from Chapter 5 other principles of positioning including perceptual mapping and writing a positioning statement.

The social media network site is obviously not the only game in town. There are also plenty of travel channels. J.J. wants to offer high-end travel, and the notion of the referrals was originally to help ensure that only similarly high-end others would be traveling companions on the trip. J.J. was thinking about instituting an invitation-only threshold to sign on and become members, thinking that this exclusivity would be a good signal and would distinguish his site from many others (in social networks or travel). The problem then becomes how to seed the invites. As with any service that is fundamentally network based, this service would succeed better with some scale, but his numbers seemed acceptable already in this regard.

Positioning Questions	Proposed Answers
• High quality and high price? Or low quality and low price?	• High quality: Prices are high but we say they're good value.
• Compare to competitors?	• No one is exclusive.
• Distribution: mass/exclusive? Promo: heavy/light?	• To succeed, need some scale, which suggests wide availability/presence and mass promo if cheap (e-referral program).

Now we compile our social media answers and have the basis for part two of the marketing plan: strategic development.

Strategic Development for Social Media Network Host
Based on our marketing research, customer segments may be described by age, online activity, and purchase activity of the trips. We currently serve the segment of young 20s. Some stay connected to friends; some click through and buy trips. We are considering moving toward (or also) serving mid-20s+ with good disposable income. And for now, we are not interested in serving customers in their 40s or older.

To serve a customer base of sufficient size and profitability, we should pursue: Friendship connectors bring in no direct money and only minimal from WOM; buyers are worth $625 a year (they take one trip every other year, approx. $1,350). We believe that a focus on this customer base fits with our strategic corporate goals: Maybe aim a little older, maybe we should stop trying so hard to be hip (we may be turning off older crowd). We considered other segments, and their relative attractiveness is as follows: 25–35; they have better disposable income than younger visitors, and more time than 35–50 crowd.

In terms of positioning, overall, we will seek a strategic market position of: high quality. Prices are high, but we say they're good value. This market space should compare favorably to our competitors' positions: No one else is exclusive. The marketing mix variables are described shortly. As an overview: To succeed, we need some scale, which suggests wide availability/presence and mass promo if very cheap (e.g., e-referral program).

17-4 THE 4PS

After segmentation and targeting, we will begin to craft the tactical decisions to achieve our desired product positioning, using all 4Ps: product, price, promotion, and place. In Figure 17.4, we see the key questions for each P as we had elaborated on in each of their respective chapters.

Regarding the *product* P, there are numerous questions to address in marketing planning:

- Do we seek a high-end quality position in the market place, or one of offering value to our customers?

- What is the assortment of product features we wish to offer to satisfy our customers and attract new customers? And what customer service plans supplement our core business?

- Is this a new product? Are we taking our product to a new segment?

Figure 17.4

Tactical Plans: 4Ps

To do so, we switch once again to offer a breadth of examples and trigger different thoughts. To illustrate the 4Ps, we're going to focus on an engineering colleague's innovation. It's a hovercraft in a seated chair form. This fellow had been playing around with the still relatively new models of hoverboards that look like skateboards. But even as he tried to create improved models, he found that people would be totally excited about the concept but when they tried it, they'd inevitably lose their balance and fall off the first several tries. For some people, depending on how badly they got dinged up, the first fall was enough to kill their interest. For others, after several falls, most people could stay on the hoverboard for 30 seconds. He figured that amount of time would increase with practice. Still, he didn't want to be responsible for creating a product that nearly universally resulted in initial falls, figuring he, or the company he was hoping to create, would get sued left and right.

So he fooled with the model a bit, attaching the hover mechanics to a plastic molded chair (he knew he could make the chairs look nicer before launching the product). He was focused on working out the hovering ability of the machine and the maneuverability. The resulting machine was operated with a pen-sized joystick on the right arm of the chair (a little like a motorized wheelchair but of course without the wheels). With this model, balance was not an issue. If there was an issue at all, it was that users who tested his beta-machine wanted to see how high they could make the chair go. Altogether, it seemed that this new hovercraft had potential.

The tricky thing about new products, of course, is that they're so new. We can recommend a company to him that would conduct some interviews (and later surveys).

In terms of the basic product parameters, the thought was to position the hoverchair as highly innovative, with a rather high-end price point. The features were mostly about fun, and product was early in a life cycle. At the moment (prelaunch), there are no brand associations yet, and he would need to build awareness in a new space.

Product Questions	Proposed Answers
• Are we high-end or basic?	• High-end, innovative
• What are our primary features?	• Convenient, trusted, good product
• What are our brand associations?	• Few due to minimal awareness as yet
• Where are we in the product life cycle?	• Brand new

Regarding price, the classic questions are:

- Do we want a high price to be consistent with high-quality positioning or for skimming purposes early in a product's life cycle, or low price to be consistent with a value offering or for penetration early in the life cycle?

- What supplement pricing components will we entertain: couponing, occasional discounting or consistent pricing (e.g., EDLP), warranties, loyalty programs and rewards in some currency (price rewards or points)?

Your engineering colleague is leaning toward going to market, and you can almost see the dollar signs in his eyes. In any event, given the novelty and sheer fun appeal of this hovercraft, he very likely could demand a rather high price. Price discounts probably don't make sense yet, and as competitors enter the market (because if he's successful, they surely will), he will need to decide whether to keep his price high or drop it as competitors undercut his product.

Price Questions	Proposed Answers
• What are our customers' price sensitivities?	• Minimal: Price will be too high for many customers, but the desire for the product may well make those who can afford it relatively insensitive; i.e., willing to pay a high price.
• Offer occasional price discounts?	• No reason: Benefits outweigh the high price, no competition yet.
• Beneficial to price differently from competitors?	• No competitors yet, but keep price high to gain margin and return on R&D.

For promotional campaigns, the questions from the marketing framework start us off:

- Do we want to promote a lot for mass exposure or minimally for a more exclusive appeal?

- What is the goal of the integrated marketing campaign?

- What is the message of the advertising communications?

- What media fit our position, and have we attained true integration in the IMC?

This fellow hasn't thought very far ahead yet and was somewhat aghast to hear how much it costs to promote through various media. To help him keep costs down, and reasoning that online promotion might be a sensible place for his target segments, we can help him think about search engine optimization (SEO). He also has an uncle high up in Brookstone, so he's hoping to place postcards or some literature in their retail stores and catalogs. If search engines are all he can advertise on (due to little front money), and posting some video demos on a Facebook page, then click-thrus would be a natural measure of ad effectiveness. He wants to be able to afford a one-page print ad soon in *PC Magazine* and another maybe in *Road and Track*, thinking these readers are like his target customers

Promotional Questions	Proposed Answers
• Our marketing communications (advertising) goals?	• Search engines, get into Brookstone, videos onto Facebook.
• How to measure ad effectiveness?	• Click-thrus.
• How to budget across IMC?	• Aim for *PC Magazine, Road and Track*.

For place:

- Will customers be able to find us, e.g., online? For those who do go to the Website, does it look good, and is it consistent with our intended positioning (e.g., exclusive vs. mass)?

- Is our online arm of the business truly integrated, or are we running an incidental Website?

Place/Distribution Questions	Proposed Answers
• Will we be extensive or selective?	• Selective currently.
• Use more pull or push?	• Pull.
• Any conflicts to resolve?	• No, still forging relationships.

Lastly in developing a marketing plan, we'll check to see whether plans for the 4Ps are internally consistent, or are we sending confusing messages—say, signaling exclusivity (via channel choices) while at the same time screaming "mass" (via low price points or poor quality)? Are we confident that our proposed Ps are those that our targeted segment desires? If we're not confident, let's go out and retest the mix. Yes, that's a hassle. Yes, it means a delay and spending more research money. (Or don't do it—go ahead and launch something, watch it fail, and then comfort yourself that, "Gee, at least we saved that research money!" Ha!)

bikeriderlondon/Shutterstock.com

Marketing will continue to make consumers' lives better!

We now compile our final data to create part three of the marketing plan: the 4Ps section.

Market Positioning via 4Ps

Our service is in the initial phase of the product life cycle. The quality should be considered by customers to be high end and innovative. Our customers primarily seek novelty and fun. When they think of our brand, they still have minimal awareness or associations because we're so new.

Regarding price, our customer price sensitivity is likely to be minimal among customers who can afford the product. Price discounts are probably not relevant, at least yet. We are also not worried about segmentation pricing per se yet. We have no competitors, though some are likely to follow. We'll keep prices high to enjoy high margins and an ability to reinvest in more R&D.

Our marketing communications (advertising) goals are search engines and getting into Brookstone and similar catalogs and stores. We will measure the effectiveness of our promotions by click-thrus.

Our ideal distribution system may become more extensive, but currently it is very selective. We expect to see consumer involvement and pull. We don't have partner conflicts yet because we're still developing retail relationships.

In sum, this marketing plan offers a strategic vision to attain long-term customer satisfaction, their loyalty, and our firm's profitability.

17-5 SPENDING TIME AND MONEY

Finally, to make sure that the marketing plan isn't pie-in-the-sky, we'll include estimates on scheduling and expenditures. These logistics and monetary details help keep the marketers and extended team on track, and it's the language of the C-suite.

Let's revisit our friends at the Brain Trust NPO. Their immediate goals are to encourage more giving online, to give support to more students, and to strengthen brand equity. Their time line and budget estimates follow.

Time Line	Marketing Activities	Budget
September	Create donor appeal materials	$15,000
September–October	Create marketing literature for reach beyond lists	$17,000
November	Refresh video and other content online	$3,000
December	Direct mailing of donation requests	$15,000
January–March	Measure response of December push	$2,000
April	Email version of donor requests	$3,000
Eight-month program	Total = $55,000	

Obviously these time and monetary elements are rough, thumbnail sketches. They should be included in the plan, along with other appendices as shown in Figure 17.5. When the elements are elaborated in greater detail, then the estimates of durations and expenses can also be made more precise. Doing both—more refined detail and more precise estimates—would make the marketing plan much improved. The better the marketing plan is, the closer it is to being actionable and the more accurately the implementation can be forecast. When the components of the timeline and budget are more detailed, it enables even better planning, audits of costs, tighter ops delivery, etc. Finally, more precision can shed light on weaknesses in the plan, presumably before executing the plan.

Figure 17.5

Typical Marketing Plan Appendices

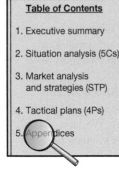

Table of Contents

1. Executive summary

2. Situation analysis (5Cs)

3. Market analysis and strategies (STP)

4. Tactical plans (4Ps)

5. Appendices

Appendix A: Marketing Research

- Secondary data findings to support 5Cs

- Focus groups current brand associations

- Summaries of industry reports and trends analyses

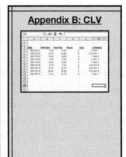

Appendix B: CLV

Appendix C: Pilot Tests on 4P Recommendations

- Survey feedback

- Ad copy testing

- Conjoint on line-extension

Go Online

To help you, the online exercise is interactive—a simple spreadsheet—so it's easy to do what-if scenarios and tweak the input data and assumptions to see varying results.

- Go to www.cengagebrain.com and download the spreadsheet for the marketing plan.
- In the first three tabs, input your answers to the questions about the 5Cs, STP, and 4Ps.
- Then click on the fourth tab to reveal your marketing plan.

MANAGERIAL RECAP

We've pored over these questions about the 5Cs, STP, and 4Ps throughout the book. Few of the questions are trivial to answer. But in answering the prompted questions, you'll have compiled the heart of the marketing plan. You now have the data of the document, and the rest is just elaborating and editing. The marketing plan comes together as a document to remind you and your colleagues of the goals and to serve as a guide in achieving those goals.

It's important to know that all of marketing (strategy and planning) is iterative. In particular, something to look for is whether there is internal consistency throughout the plan; it's critical for good branding and good marketing that the whole of the plan be synchronous. For example, after working through the 5Cs and STP, you might be well into the 4Ps when you might realize, "Oh shoot! This plan makes no sense, considering what we said about our target [or whatever]." Thus, return to targeting, tweak, and move forward again.

In a sense, marketing plans are always works in progress. While they're intended to keep everyone on track, they're also not carved in stone. Thus, as situations change, so must we modify the marketing plan. For example, we occasionally encounter challenges that bounce us back up to earlier considerations that we thought we had nailed down. Perhaps we had ignored economic factors in the context because, in our country, the economy is stable. Yet if one of our strategic goals is to go into underserved markets in places with poor infrastructures, then our working assumptions have changed because now we must address new questions: how to set up shop locally with issues we hadn't encountered before. Thus, we have to go back and elaborate on the economic conditions under context in the 5Cs. That's okay. That's what cut-and-paste is for. Revise!

Admittedly, our marketing planning exercise is just the beginning. There may be time to talk at just the big-picture level, but not so when creating marketing plans. Be detailed, listing absolutely every factor even remotely relevant, to cover various contingencies.

Think like an entrepreneur. If this brand is your baby and you have responsibility for it, and if you and you alone will bring it to market, consider the myriad decisions you need to make. Every one of those zillions of decisions, questions, factors should go into your marketing plan. Offer all the details, and let your colleagues, partners, or boss shoot holes in it now. Better that than you waving your hands saying, "Oh don't worry—it'll be fine," going to market, and dealing with disaster. Plan every grueling detail!

Lastly, massage the document to be readable. Use the 5Cs, STP, and 4Ps labels as headers throughout the document. Writing is a lot like marketing—be sure your document speaks to its intended audience. Writing a plan for your boss will look different from the version you'd show investors, for example. In other words, market your marketing plan!

That's All Folks

You've seen a zillion marketing issues throughout this book. It's time to take the concepts and put them into practice. Marketing planning is the road map or blueprint for the implementation of all the collective marketing decisions.

Having a good understanding of marketing will be extremely useful in your career, whether you're going to be a marketer or not. Don't forget: Put the customer above all else. If you do, you'll conquer the competition. Yes, it's that easy. ☺

Chapter Outline in Key Terms and Concepts

1. We put it all together via a "situation analysis": the 5Cs
2. STP
3. The 4Ps
4. Spending time and money
5. Managerial recap

Chapter Discussion Questions

1. Pick your favorite brand and look at the 5Cs for that company. What is the brand's "situation analysis"? Based on that assessment and what you know of the brand, what recommendations would you make to the company regarding that brand or its business?

2. With talk of elections all over the place, look at voters through an STP lens. How should a politician of your favorite party proceed?

3. Imagine a young person, recently graduated from college, who is trying to launch their career as a <pick one: comedian, singer, sports agent>. Sketch out the best set of 4Ps you could suggest to them to help them get their ideal jobs and make career progress toward their goal.

Video Exercise: White Rock (5:02)

White Rock Beverage, a producer of soft drinks and sparkling waters, was founded in 1871. In 1900, White Rock was the upscale beverage of choice, ranked number one in the market; a century later, White Rock ranked number 100. When the company's current president, Larry, who is the great-great-grandson of the founder, took over the business it was struggling mightily. One customer controlled half of White Rock's distribution, and that customer dropped the White Rock brand. To keep the business afloat, White Rock adopted a hybrid distribution system and acquired a new brand. Growth has been fueled by the acquisition of the Old Brooklyn brand of beverages. White Rock revamped Old Brooklyn's production process to make it a tastier, healthier product—a move that is consistent with White Rock's positioning as a brand that is healthy and unique. The Old Brooklyn brand gives White Rock the opportunity to gain entry into premium outlets like Trader Joe's and Whole Foods, as well as into supermarkets with premium beverage sections. After getting the White Rock brand back on track, the company has enjoyed continued growth, but it is nonetheless a mature brand. The more substantial growth opportunity is in the Old Brooklyn brand.

Video Discussion Questions

1. What does a SWOT analysis reveal about White Rock?

2. How has White Rock used market segmentation, targeting, and positioning in developing and executing a plan to ensure the survival and success of the company?

3. How has White Rock used the 4Ps of marketing—product, price, place, and promotion—to develop and execute a plan for ensuring the survival and success of the company?

MINI-CASE

Jeeves

When people feel like they have more money than time, certain services flourish. Imagine setting up a butler service called Jeeves. Jeeves would see to all the logistics details in your life that consume more time than you wish to grant them. Jeeves will take care of your information needs, from making doctors' appointments or play dates for the kids, to stylist appointments for you, to helping you banking, paying bills and even coordinating and evaluating your investments, if you wish. If you were stinkin' rich, you'd also have a chef and a driver. While strictly speaking, these domains fall outside the usual butler responsibilities, in the Jeeves service, the butlers fill in with whatever household and related duties the customer wishes to be done, and a payment package is chosen accordingly. Thus, your Jeeves can drive your kids to school, and pick up groceries to have a 7 p.m. dinner ready for the family, if those are add-ons you desire (and for which you're willing to pay).

Case Discussion Questions

1. Create a marketing plan to introduce Jeeves to your local community. Gather the secondary data that you can, to help substantiate the business case. Make clear notes throughout the plan where you would seek additional primary marketing research to provide guidance about those components of the plan. Etch the market and its segments, and characterize the segment(s) you would target.

2. Create a storyboard for an external Website and an internal one. The external Website would be the positioning you want customers to see, thus create pages for that Website that is a composition of the 4Ps for Jeeves. The internal Website is for your sales force to give them parameters about different price packages and the like.

APPENDIX

On the book's website at www.cengagebrain.com, you can download an Excel® spreadsheet that contains all of these Chapter 17 tables.

The Online Marketing Planning Builder will expect the following inputs:

TABLE A17-1

5Cs

Customer:	Fill in descriptions here:
Demographics (e.g., age, income, household composition, ZIP Code):	Customer 1
Psychographics (e.g., attitude to product, to competition, to ads):	Customer 2
Buying behavior (e.g., frequency, only on sale, etc.):	Customer 3
Current levels/measures of customer satisfaction:	Customer 4
Do we have a loyalty program, efforts at CRM?	Customer 5
Why don't non-buyers buy?	Customer 6
When our buyers buy, what channel do they prefer?	Customer 7
When our buyers buy, do they seem to be price sensitive?	Customer 8
What changes have we seen over buyers? Expect any in future?	Customer 9
Company:	
What are we good at? Known for? Do a SWOT!	Company 1
What do we want to become? Future strategy.	Company 2
Context:	
Is the economy a factor? Is it stable? Growing? What's the consumer mood?	Context 1
Are politics a factor? Are our partners stable?	Context 2
Is legal a factor? Are any consumer laws looming?	Context 3
Is technology a threat/opportunity? Machines? IT?	Context 4
Any societal concerns? Demographic shifts? Attitude shifts?	Context 5
Collaborators:	
Good relations with supply chain providers?	Collaborators 1
Good relations with distribution channel members?	Collaborators 2
Want any modifications?	Collaborators 3
Competitors:	
Who are our major competitors (define this broadly)?	Competitor 1
What are our competitors' strengths?	Competitor 2

Segmentation:	Fill in descriptions here:
Base segments on data; gather marketing research to conduct cluster analyses; describe marketplace in terms of demographics, psychographics, buyer behaviors: First, describe current customers: Next, describe nonusers: Finally, describe ideal customers:	Segment 1 Segment 2 Segment 3
Targeting:	
Estimate size and profitability (lifetime customer value) of segments: Characterize fit with corporate and marketing strategy of each segment: Using financial and strategic info jointly, rank desirability of segments:	Target 1 Target 2 Target 3
Positioning:	
Strategically choose high-quality/high-price or basic-product/low-price position: Show how strategic position compares to competitors' positions: Sketch distribution (wide or exclusive) and promotion plans (mass, light):	Position 1 Position 2 Position 3

TABLE A17-2

STP

Product:	Fill in descriptions here:
Choose high-end quality or basic-quality level:	Product 1
Use conjoint on target segments to determine primary attributes/features:	Product 2
What are our brand associations, and what do want to trade in/out:	Product 3
Where are we in the product life cycle; is it time to jump-start:	Product 4
Price:	
Given strategic positioning, shall we price high (skim) or low (penetrate): If price low, conduct internal audit to assure exceed breakeven. If price high, conduct marketing research to assess. Customers' price sensitivities: Shall we consider occasional price discounts: How might we benefit from pricing differentially to our segments:	Price 1 Price 2 Price 3
Place/Distribution:	
Design distribution system to be extensive or selective:	Place 1
Integrate with promotions as push or pull:	Place 2
Do any conflicts need to be resolved? Communication, contract, profit-share:	Place 3
Promotion:	
What are our marketing communications (advertising) goals?	Promo 1
How to measure the effectiveness of the ads, whether goals were achieved:	Promo 2
How to apportion advertising budget across media for true IMC:	Promo 3

TABLE A17-3

4PS

TABLE A17-4	**Marketing Plan**
Compiling the Answers to Yield a Marketing Plan	*Executive Summary:* This marketing plan begins with a situation analysis: a description of our current state of affairs and possible changes to that status quo. We present strategic choices in selections of customer segments to pursue and the market position that we seek to achieve to best serve them.

Situation Analysis:

Customers:

These are our current customers: Customer 1, Customer 2, Customer 4, Customer 5.

This is what they buy: Customer 3, Customer 7, Customer 8.

Here are possible customer issues to consider: Customer 9, Customer 5, Customer 6.

Company:

Currently, we are: Company 1.

This marketing plan is to facilitate our achieving the goal of becoming: Company 2.

Context:

Our current business environment is economically: Context 1.

Politics and legal factors may include: Context 2, Context 3.

Technology enters in, in that: Context 4.

Overall societal factors may be: Context 5.

Collaborators:

Our business partnerships with our supply chain providers are: Collaborators 1.

Our channel members: Collaborators 2.

Overall, our partner network: Collaborators 3.

Competitors:

Certain competitors (Competitor 1) may be a threat, given their strengths (Competitor 2).

Strategic Development:

Segmentation:

Based on our marketing research, customer segments may be described as follows.

We currently serve: Segment 1. We are considering moving toward (or also) serving Segment 3.

For now, we are not interested in serving Segment 2.

Targeting:

To serve a customer base of sufficient size and profitability, we should pursue: Target 1.

We believe that a focus on this customer base fits with our strategic corporate goals: Target 2.

We considered other segments, and their relative attractiveness is as follows: Target 3.

Positioning:

Overall, we will seek a strategical market position of: Position 1.

This market space should compare favorably to our competitors' positions: Position 2.

The marketing mix variables are described shortly. As an overview: Position 3.

(continued)

Market Positioning, Strategies and Tactics:

Product:

Our product is at this phase in the product life cycle: <u>Product 4.</u>

The quality of our product should be considered by customers to be: <u>Product 1</u>.

Our customers primarily seek these benefits: <u>Product 2</u>.

When they think of our brand, they think of these associations: <u>Product 3</u>.

Price:

Given our strategic positioning, here are our pricing considerations.

Our customer price sensitivities seem to be: <u>Price 1</u>.

Our suggestions on occasional price discounts are these: <u>Price 2</u>.

We recommend segmentation pricing as follows: <u>Price 3</u>.

Place/Distribution:

Our ideal distribution system would be: <u>Place 1</u>.

We will use promotions to spur trade partners and consumer involvement per: <u>Place 2</u>.

We will address potential partner conflicts via: <u>Place 3</u>.

Promotion:

Our marketing communications (advertising) goals are: <u>Promo 1</u>.

We will measure the effectiveness of our promotions by: <u>Promo 2</u>.

We will apportion our advertising budget across media as per this IMC plan: <u>Promo 3</u>.

In sum, this marketing plan offers a strategic vision to attain long-term customer satisfaction, their loyalty, and our firm's profitability.

ENDNOTES

Chapter 1

1   Thank you to Professors Andrea Dixon (University of Cincinnati), Inder Khera (Wright State University), Constantine Polychroniou (University of Cincinnati), and Larry Robinson (The Ohio State University) for the insightful focus group that launched this project.

2   This last P also often goes by the term "distribution" or even "channels of distribution," implying the paths through which goods are made available from the manufacturer to the consumer. The term "distribution" is used more often than "place," but "4Ps" sounds better than "3Ps and 1D." (It's better marketing!)

Chapter 2

1   Of course, a customer can choose to delay a purchase, and that is an action too. Delays allow buyers time to gather more information, form clearer opinions about brand choices, etc. Or they might choose to not purchase altogether. See research by Professors Ravi Dhar (Yale University), Mary Frances Luce (Duke University), Stephen Nowlis (Washington University in St. Louis).

2   Buyers' goals naturally affect their shopping; see research by Professors Margaret Campbell (University of Colorado), Paul Herr (Virginia Tech), Arie Kruglanski (University of Maryland), Suresh Ramanathan (Texas A&M University), Nader Tavassoli (London Business School), and Stijn Van Osselaer (Erasmus University Rotterdam).

3   For more on consumer behavior, see books by Professors Wayne Hoyer (University of Texas), Deborah MacInnis (University of Southern California), and Michael Solomon (Auburn University). In B2B, read the *HBR*s on value propositions by Professors James C. Anderson (Northwestern University) and James Narus (Wake Forest University).

Chapter 3

1   Thanks to Professors Darren Boas (Hood College), Richard Brown (Freed-Hardeman University), Renee Foster (Delta State University), Harry Harmon (University of Central Missouri), Gary Karns (Seattle Pacific University), Ann Little (High Point University), Chris McCale (Regis College), Chip Miller (Drake University), James Oakley (Lewis University), Antony Peloso (Arizona State University), Charles Schwepker (University of Central Missouri), Donald Shifter (Fontbonne University), Deborah Spake (University of South Alabama), Keith Starcher (Geneva College), and Clay Voorhees (Michigan State University) for their helpful feedback.

2   So, like Goldilocks, we must find segments that are not too big and not too small, but just right.

3   Research by Professors Claes Fornell (University of Michigan), Eugene Anderson (University of Miami), and Michael Johnson (University of Michigan) suggests that success can bring its own problems. Success usually means more sales from more customers. Yet, as a segment size grows, the group becomes more heterogeneous (by definition, given human nature). It then becomes increasingly difficult to serve such a large diverse segment well. At that point, it is worth investing in a new segmentation study to refine further the current known segment structures and to consider additional product lines.

Chapter 4

1   Thanks to Professors Desislava Budeva (Florida Atlantic University), Robin Coulter (University of Connecticut), Gavan Fitzsimons (Duke University), Harry Harmon (University of Central Missouri), Devon Johnson (Northeastern University), Ann Little (High Point University), Chip Miller (Drake University), Nicolas Papadopoulos (Carleton University), Anthony Peloso (Arizona State University), Donald Shifter (Fontbonne University), Tillmann Wagner (Texas Tech University), and Bruce Weinberg (Bentley University) for their helpful feedback.

Chapter 5

1   Thanks to Professors Robert Fisher (University of Alberta), Mary Gilly (University of California, Irvine), Kent Grayson (Kellogg School of Management at Northwestern University), Harry Harmon (University of Central Missouri), Ann Little (High Point University), Chip Miller (Drake University), Anthony Peloso (Arizona State University), Joe Priester (University of Southern California), and Donald Shifter (Fontbonne University), for helpful feedback.

2 See Chapter 15 for details on how the graphs are created.

3 This map conveys perceptions, not geography, so the cities are not aligned north-south/east-west as they are IRL.

4 For two fabulous profiles of these extremes, see Fishman's book, *The Wal-Mart Effect*, and Michelli's, *The Starbucks Experience*.

5 J. D. Power compares cars' reliability (life spans and maintenance) and shows that quality is not perfectly correlated with price. Some "overvalued" car brands have been Land Rover, Volkswagen, Volvo, Mercedes. Yah, but they're cool! Some "undervalued" car brands have been Mercury, Infinity, Buick, Lincoln, Chrysler.

6 A counter-argument may be made for high-end goods where exclusivity is part of the mystique, e.g., for years, Tiffany & Co. advertised nationally even though it only had three stores. Yes, the positioning matrix is a simplification, but also note that we are interested in sustainable strategies. For example, Tiffany bling is now available online, making them less exclusive in terms of retail presence. Still, the goods are exclusive in that their price point makes them unavailable to many consumers.

Chapter 6

1 Thanks to Professors Melissa Bishop (University of Texas at Arlington), Adam Duhachek (Indiana University), Mary Gilly (University of California, Irvine), Charles Hofacker (Florida State University), Tracy Meyer (University of North Carolina at Wilmington), and Donald Shifter (Fontbonne University) for their helpful comments.

2 Pricing is simply one of the easiest of the 4Ps that marketers use to control yield management.

3 The real world is more gray, of course. For example, while services tend to be more perishable than goods, there are certainly some goods that are more perishable than others (e.g., bananas vs. jet skis). Further, marketers can make goods more perishable when striving for other desired ends; e.g., just-in-time delivery systems comprise very little (if any) inventory, toward the goal of being responsive to customers' needs.

4 See research by Professors Gian Marzocchi and Alexandra Zammit (University of Bologna), Neeli Bendapudi (University of Kansas), Roland Rust (University of Maryland), Mary Jo Bitner and Amy Ostrom (Arizona State University), and Paul Bloom (University of North Carolina).

5 Thank you to Professor Kevin Cotter at Saint Mary's College of California.

Chapter 7

1 Thanks to Professors Harry Harmon (University Central Missouri) and C.W. Park (University of Southern California) for their helpful feedback.

2 Hey, it's a compliment. Dorks rule the world!

3 Businessweek.com identified Helvetica as the font common to several companies' logos: American Airlines, BMW, Jeep, Lufthansa, Microsoft, Panasonic, Sears, Staples, and 3M.

4 Think of the original "branding" on cattle to discourage poaching from herds.

5 See research by Professor Jennifer Aaker (Stanford University), Kevin Keller (Dartmouth University), Stephen Ball (Sheffield Hallam University), Karen Becker-Olsen (College of New Jersey), Susan Broniarczyk (University of Texas), Ronald Paul Hill (Villanova University), Sanjay Sood (UCLA), Isabelle Szmigin and Peter Turnbull (University of Birmingham).

6 See research by Professors Joško Brakus (University of Rochester), Bernd Schmitt (Columbia University), and Lia Zarantonello (Bocconi University).

7 See research by Professors Albert Muniz (DePaul University), Thomas O'Guinn (University of Illinois), Ann Morales Olazábal (University of Miami), Hope Jensen Schau (University of Arizona), and John Schouten (University of Portland).

8 A corporate brand (or an umbrella brand) has been shown to enhance consumers' likelihood of purchase and adoption. (See research by Professors David Corkindale, University of South Australia.) Umbrella marketing also goes by the names franchise branding, family branding, or mono-branding.

9 The company has subsequently sold off some of these brands, not because they weren't good brands, but for strategic purposes, that is, to focus their business lines. Indeed, because the brands had strong equity, they were profitable transactions.

10 See research by Professors Kusum Ailawadi (Dartmouth University), Paul Berger (Boston University), Pierre Chandon (INSEAD), Chris Dubelaar (University of Utah), Morris George (University of Connecticut), Robert Jacobson (University of Washington), Anita Luo (University of Connecticut), Neil Morgan (Indiana University), Scott Neslin (Dartmouth University), Lopo Leotte do Rego (University of Iowa), Gary Russell (University of Iowa), and Roland Rust (University of Maryland).

Chapter 8

1 Thanks to Professors Rick Briesch (Southern Methodist University), Erin Cavusgil and Serdar Durmusoglu (Michigan State University), Stefan Michel (Thunderbird School of Global Management), Rebecca Slotegraaf (Indiana University), and Bruce Weinberg (Bentley University) for their helpful comments. A very handy website is pdma.org (Product Development Management Association).

2 Sorry to say, little critters.

3 For a meta-analysis on the diffusion model, see research by Professors Fareena Sultan (Northeastern University), John Farley (Dartmouth University), and Donald Lehmann (Columbia University) in the *Journal of Marketing Research*. They found that p tends to range from 0.02 to 0.06, and q from 0.3 to 0.6 and that, for whatever product category and for whatever market (e.g., U.S. vs. Europe), $p{:}q$ was on the order of just about 1:10.

4   Internetworldstats.com.
5   Businessweek.com.

Chapter 9

1   Yes, another BE for practice. It's important to be facile with BEs. As straightforward as it seems, pricing is hard to do well. The main purpose of some companies is to help others select prices (e.g., IBM's DemandTec services or SAP's Khimetrics). Mostly all they do is break-evens.

2   Price elasticity is also referred to as the "% change in quantity sold, given a 1% change in price." This equation is simple in being linear (the effect of changing a price from low to medium would be predicted to be the same as moving price from medium to high), whereas the effects in real life might be more subtle. (e.g., the effect of changing a price from high to higher might result in a huge drop-off. So the "line" in Figure 9.1 may be curved at the end.) With luxury goods, customers might want what is more expensive, as an exclusive, more unique purchase. That curve would rise from the lower-left and increase toward the upper-right.

3   Okay, so pricing is never simple. In this example, the same profit is also obtained at $1.75 (350 − 200) as at $1.50 (450 − 300). Apparently there's a flat spot in the demand curve. Thus we could price at 1.50 or 1.75, so the
    final decision is one of strategy: Go high for an upscale image, or go low for customer reviews as good value.

Chapter 10

1   Thanks to Professors Jan Heide (University of Wisconsin) and Phil Zerrillo (Singapore Management University) for helpful feedback.

2   See research by Professors James Anderson (Northwestern University), Sundar Bharadwaj (Emory University), Gary Frazier (University of Southern California), George John (University of Minnesota), Das Narayandas (Harvard Business School), James Narus (Wake Forest University), Robert Palmatier (University of Cincinnati), Alberto Sa Vinhas (Washington State University Vancouver), and Kenneth Wathne (Norwegian School of Management).

3   See research on sales forces by Professors Kevin Bradford (Notre Dame), Kent Grayson (Northwestern University), David Lichtenthal (Baruch College), Vincent Onyemah (Babson College), Dominique Rouzies (HEC, Hautes Etudes Commerciales de Paris), and Frederick Hong-kit Yim (Hong Kong Baptist University).

Chapter 11

1   Thanks to Professors Adriana Bóveda-Lambie (University of Rhode Island), Robin Coulter (University of Connecticut), Robert Fisher (University of Alberta), Kent Grayson (Northwestern), Gary Karns (Seattle Pacific University), Chris McCale (Regis College), Charles Schwepker (University of Central Missouri), and Keith Starcher (Geneva College) for their helpful comments.

2   For more information, see the vast literature by Professors Richard Petty (Ohio State University) and Joseph Priester (University of Southern California).

3   Finished commercials cost $100,000s, but animatics cost only about a tenth of that, and the cost is even less for storyboards. While these draft forms can seem rough, research indicates that the correlation between customer reactions to animatics and a finished commercial are very high (marketingpower.com).

Chapter 12

1   Thanks to Professors Melissa Bishop (University of Texas, Arlington), Robert Fisher (University of Alberta), and Kent Grayson (Northwestern University).

2   We're not claiming causation with this correlation plot: Marketers hope that larger ad budgets enhance sales (ad budget→sales), but big companies have more money to spend (sales→ad budget), and for that matter, big companies have more dealerships or retail outlets (distribution→sales), etc.

3   It's the business of firms like Arbitron and Nielsen to collect these data, so you can imagine they're continually working to improve these measures. For example, marketers care that measures of reach and frequency are "unduplicated," i.e., not capturing the same eyeballs twice.

4   There's also a difference between ratings and advertising measures of share. Share is the % of TV sets that are turned in to the desired show. Together, measures are usually reported as ratings points/share. For example, Nielsen ratings may indicate that a TV show received a 10/15 during its broadcast, meaning 10% (or 11,200,000) households were watching TV, and 15% of them were tuned in to this program.

5   According to a recent A. C. Nielsen study, "Annual Survey on Trade Promotion Practices."

6   Product placement in shows is largely tolerated by U.S. viewers, but showing products on TV for money is illegal in most of Europe, though the EU is considering alterations in law structures to facilitate commercial funding (Economist.com, Promomagazine.com).

7   Negative emotions can transfer too, so many brands (e.g., Coke, Pepsi) don't advertise during news broadcasts. The viewing experience is usually a bummer, and the brand managers don't want to inherit the negative baggage.

Chapter 13

1   Networkers call this a "power law."
2   For information on recommendation agents, see research by Professors Anand Bodapati (UCLA) and Muhammad Aljukhadar (HEC Montreal). Also see research by Professors Wendy Moe and Michael Trusov (University of Maryland); they've shown the social effect of user ratings on subsequent user ratings, and their collective significant effect on sales (albeit more modest than the influence of unbiased and independent product ratings).
3   Fun introductions to networks include Malcolm Gladwell's *The Tipping Point* and Duncan Watts's *Six Degrees*.

Chapter 14

1   See research by Professors Leonard Berry (Texas A&M University), Claes Fornell (University of Michigan), Richard Oliver (Vanderbilt University), A. Parasuraman (University of Miami), Roland Rust (University of Maryland), and Valarie Zeithaml (University of North Carolina).
2   For more on customer dissatisfaction recovery, see research by Professors Michael Brady and Joseph Cronin (Florida State University).
3   Nonprofits want to make money too. It's just that their surpluses go to their social benefits and causes.
4   See research by Professor Robert Leone (Texas Christian University), Katherine Lemon (Boston College), John Roberts (Australian Graduate School of Management), and Frederick Hong-kit Yim (Hong Kong Baptist University).
5   See research by Professors Douglas Bowman (Emory University), Bruce Hardie (London Business School), Vikas Mittal (University of Pittsburgh), and Michael Haenlein and Andreas Kaplan (ESCP Europe, Paris).

Chapter 15

1   If you want more, have we got a recommendation for you! Dawn Iacobucci and Gilbert Churchill, *Marketing Research: Methodological Foundations*, 11th ed., on Amazon.
2   Cluster analysts say: customers should be homogeneous within a cluster, and heterogeneous across clusters.
3   This overlay is known as attribute-vector-fitting. Imagine a little data set with 4 rows, 1 for each brand, then 2 columns, 1 for each coordinate (on dimensions 1 and 2). Add a column for the means for each brand on how good it is on the first attribute, e.g., value (and then add more columns for the means of all the remaining attributes). Then run a regression using the 2 dimensions' variables to predict the attribute variable (and run another regression for each additional attribute). The resulting beta weights give you the coordinates to put in these vectors. Cool, huh? Then, the final step is to overlay respondents onto these maps, in what are called "ideal points." That is, if a brand could have just the right set of features to make the customer perfectly happy, what combination of features would those be? Perceptual maps with ideal points, one point per customer, are frequently used to identify market opportunities.
4   In standardized regression (β) weights, the model is: Preference = 0.22 Club + 0.44 Upgrade – 0.87 Fee.
5   For research on survey construction, see work by Professors Charlotte Mason and J. B. Steenkamp (University of North Carolina) and by Geeta Menon and Vicki Morwitz (New York University).
6   The regressions and forecasting examples weren't exactly random or off the cuff. Let's say you have a dependent variable like "intent to purchase" that you're trying to model as a function of 5 predictors. If 2 of those predictors are themselves pretty highly correlated, keeping all 5 variables distinct will likely blow up the regressions due to multicollinearity. If an average of the 2 highly correlated variables is created, so that now there are 4 predictors (3 of the previous variables, plus an average score that replaces the 2 correlated variables), the results are almost always clearer. Magic!
7   Take a look back now at the cluster analysis on these data. Note the x-axis in the left plot of Figure 15.7 and the y-axis of the middle plot. They were formed using the factors, combining two items each. Cool, right?

Chapter 16

1   Michael Porter, *Competitive Strategy: Techniques for Analyzing Industries and Competitors*.
2   Michael Tracey and Fred Wiersema, *The Discipline of Market Leaders: Choose Your Customers, Narrow Your Focus, Dominate Your Market*.

Chapter 17

1   A great reference is the American Marketing Association at ama.org.

INDEX